Cases on Applying Knowledge Economy Principles for Economic Growth in Developing Nations

Danilo Piaggesi
Knowledge for Development (K4D), USA

Helena Landazuri
Knowledge for Development (K4D), USA

Bo Jia
Tsinghua University, China

IGI Global
PUBLISHER of TIMELY KNOWLEDGE

A volume in the Advances in Finance, Accounting, and Economics (AFAE) Book Series

Published in the United States of America by
IGI Global
Business Science Reference (an imprint of IGI Global)
701 E. Chocolate Avenue
Hershey PA, USA 17033
Tel: 717-533-8845
Fax: 717-533-8661
E-mail: cust@igi-global.com
Web site: http://www.igi-global.com

Library of Congress Cataloging-in-Publication Data

Names: Piaggesi, Danilo, 1956- editor. | Landázuri, Helena, editor. | Jia, Bo, 1996- editor.
Title: Cases on applying knowledge economy principles for economic growth in developing nations / Danilo Piaggesi, Helena Landazuri, and Bo Jia, editors.
Description: Hershey, PA : Business Science Reference, 2021. | Includes bibliographical references and index. | Summary: "The goal of the book is a variety of perspectives on the conditions under which the Knowledge Economy concept -and the triple helix approach-- are of value for developing countries, and which adaptations are being applied to adjust to local circumstances"-- Provided by publisher.
Identifiers: LCCN 2021022566 (print) | LCCN 2021022567 (ebook) | ISBN 9781799884170 (hardcover) | ISBN 9781799884187 (paperback) | ISBN 9781799884194 (ebook)
Subjects: LCSH: Knowledge economy--Developing countries. | Economic development--Technological innovations--Developing countries. | Information technology--Developing countries--Management.
Classification: LCC HD30.2 .C3786 2021 (print) | LCC HD30.2 (ebook) | DDC 338.9009172/4--dc23
LC record available at https://lccn.loc.gov/2021022566
LC ebook record available at https://lccn.loc.gov/2021022567

This book is published in the IGI Global book series Advances in Finance, Accounting, and Economics (AFAE) (ISSN: 2327-5677; eISSN: 2327-5685)

British Cataloguing in Publication Data
A Cataloguing in Publication record for this book is available from the British Library.

For electronic access to this publication, please contact: eresources@igi-global.com.

Advances in Finance, Accounting, and Economics (AFAE) Book Series

Ahmed Driouchi
Al Akhawayn University, Morocco

ISSN:2327-5677
EISSN:2327-5685

Mission

In our changing economic and business environment, it is important to consider the financial changes occurring internationally as well as within individual organizations and business environments. Understanding these changes as well as the factors that influence them is crucial in preparing for our financial future and ensuring economic sustainability and growth.

The **Advances in Finance, Accounting, and Economics (AFAE)** book series aims to publish comprehensive and informative titles in all areas of economics and economic theory, finance, and accounting to assist in advancing the available knowledge and providing for further research development in these dynamic fields.

Coverage

- Auditing
- Economics of Innovation and Knowledge
- Economics of Risks, Uncertainty, Ambiguity, and Insurance
- Finance and Accounting in SMEs
- Economics Geography
- Accounting Standards
- Applied Accounting
- Investments and Derivatives
- Taxes
- Economic Theory

IGI Global is currently accepting manuscripts for publication within this series. To submit a proposal for a volume in this series, please contact our Acquisition Editors at Acquisitions@igi-global.com or visit: http://www.igi-global.com/publish/.

The Advances in Finance, Accounting, and Economics (AFAE) Book Series (ISSN 2327-5677) is published by IGI Global, 701 E. Chocolate Avenue, Hershey, PA 17033-1240, USA, www.igi-global.com. This series is composed of titles available for purchase individually; each title is edited to be contextually exclusive from any other title within the series. For pricing and ordering information please visit http://www.igi-global.com/book-series/advances-finance-accounting-economics/73685. Postmaster: Send all address changes to above address.

Titles in this Series

For a list of additional titles in this series, please visit: http://www.igi-global.com/book-series/advances-finance-accounting-economics/73685

Transitioning From Globalized to Localized and Self-Reliant Economies
Ruchika Gupta (Amity University, India) Priyank Srivastava (Amity University, India) Shiv Ranjan (Amity University, India) and M. Affan Badar (Indiana State University, USA)
Business Science Reference • © 2022 • 256pp • H/C (ISBN: 9781799887058) • US $195.00

COVID-19 Pandemic Impact on New Economy Development and Societal Change
Cristina Raluca Gh. Popescu (University of Bucharest, Romania & The Bucharest University of Economic Studies, Romania & The National Institute for Research and Development in Environmental Protection (INCDPM), Romania & National Research and Development Institute for Gas Turbines (COMOTI), Romania)
Business Science Reference • © 2022 • 425pp • H/C (ISBN: 9781668433744) • US $195.00

Microfinance and Sustainable Development in Africa
Yahaya Alhassan (University of Sunderland in London, UK) and Uzoechi Nwagbara (University of the West of Scotland, UK & Cardiff Metropolitan University, UK)
Business Science Reference • © 2022 • 368pp • H/C (ISBN: 9781799874997) • US $195.00

Redefining Global Economic Thinking for the Welfare of Society
Md Mashiur Rahman (Bank Asia Ltd., Bangladesh) Richa Goel (Amity University, Noida, India) Anthony P. Gomes (TeamPeople, USA) and Md Almas Uzzaman (Independent Researcher, Australia)
Business Science Reference • © 2022 • 268pp • H/C (ISBN: 9781799882589) • US $225.00

FinTech Development for Financial Inclusiveness
Muhammad Anshari (Universiti Brunei Darussalam, Brunei) Mohamad Nabil Almunawar (Universiti Brunei Darussalam, Brunei) and Masairol Masri (Universiti Brunei Darussalam, Brunei)
Business Science Reference • © 2022 • 269pp • H/C (ISBN: 9781799884477) • US $225.00

Evaluating Trade and Economic Relations Between India and Southeast Asia
Anita Medhekar (Central Queensland University, Australia) and Harpreet Kaur (Central Queensland University, Australia)
Business Science Reference • © 2022 • 347pp • H/C (ISBN: 9781799857747) • US $195.00

Handbook of Research on Global Aspects of Sustainable Finance in Times of Crises
Ibrahim Yasar Gok (Süleyman Demirel University, Turkey & Freie Universität Berlin, Germany)
Business Science Reference • © 2022 • 442pp • H/C (ISBN: 9781799885016) • US $285.00

IGI Global
PUBLISHER of TIMELY KNOWLEDGE

701 East Chocolate Avenue, Hershey, PA 17033, USA
Tel: 717-533-8845 x100 • Fax: 717-533-8661
E-Mail: cust@igi-global.com • www.igi-global.com

This book is dedicated IN MEMORIAM to Pablo Valenti.

Pablo was a pioneer in the field of ICT for development and Knowledge Economy, and he greatly contributed to the economic development of Latin America and the Caribbean.

Table of Contents

Detailed Table of Contents

The results of the Brazilian Census 2010 show that of a total population of 193 million people, approximately 46 million people of Brazil's total population have some kind of disability. Brazil is one of the world's leading IT markets and the largest IT market in Latin America. This chapter presents a program started by the Government of the State of Sao Paulo through its Secretariat for the Rights of Persons with Disabilities (SEDPcD) in 2013 that aims to promote the rehabilitation and social inclusion of persons with disabilities. Adopting the application of the concept and instruments of the knowledge economy as core strategy and through the application of ICT-based assistive technologies, the program develops solutions to a level where they can be applied massively in a cost-effective way.

For generations, humanity has experienced socioeconomic disparities that are yet unresolved. Although education and training have transformed some individuals in society, they have not addressed the broader issues of sustainable employment for many underserved communities. Governments, corporations, policymakers, and numerous stakeholders have continued to address the problem, yielding disappointing results. Growing inequality in society continues to be a major concern. Vertical inequalities between the poor and the rich and horizontal inequalities between various groups of society have remained high for centuries. This chapter focuses on a variety of individual elements that outline the current challenges to humanity in an unequal society that certain communities continue to face, citing an unsustainable

With the acceleration of the digital transformation and technological upgradation of various industries, in the wake of application of new technologies such as 5G, artificial intelligence, and the internet of things, the demand for data storage, computing, transmission, and applications has greatly increased. Remote working, remote education, and e-commerce on account of the pandemic have led to a drastic increase in data consumption as well. The processing and analysis of massive data requires the construction of an information infrastructure—Internet Data Center (IDC). In the past few years, China's government has been dedicating itself to the task of constructing IDCs in some underdeveloped areas and establishing more detailed regulations. This chapter introduces some basic policies and implications behind this and a mathematical way to quantitatively analyse the investment efficiency of R&D resources in China's different regions. Several recommendations for the government and the society at large have also been outlined in this chapter for improvement in the whole ecosystem for IDCs in China.

Colombia's economy is the fourth largest in Latin America. Though there has been significant growth in modern industries, most industries are still driven by agriculture and commodities. The main challenges Colombian industries face include becoming more energy-efficient, modernizing processes and organizational structures, and reducing their environmental impact. In the meantime, the Republic of Korea has made significant efforts to fuel its economy through innovation, and there is also a similarity in terms of both countries' interest and commitment to use ICT as a basis for their growth. This chapter presents a project that is a pilot test of adaptive transfer of "green" ICT technology innovation developed by specialized agencies/private sector in the Republic of Korea, to be applied to a host of Colombian industrial sectors volunteering to participate with the purpose of improving production through environmentally friendly technology.

Faced with the objective of carrying out environmental education campaigns and arousing the attention of Sao Bernardo do Campo´s residents to the correct disposal of used cooking oil, in 2019 a cooperation agreement between the Municipality of Sao Bernardo do Campo and the Triangulo Institute aiming at recycling used cooking oil was signed. The collection execution began with the installation of the used cooking oil voluntary delivery points. Before the installation, the awareness and training of the team involved in the receiving activity was carried out; in addition, it is important after the collection to pack, transport, and dispose of the oil.

Section 6
Urbanization and Transportation

Building confidence for zero emission buses has been the strategy to create demand in Latin America. A few cities have more e-buses than any other region in the world outside of China. It all started by testing hybrid and electric buses, sharing data, building innovative economic models, making site visits, and sharing results in workshops. It all occurred during the last 10 years. Institutions including development banks are now committed to assisting with the transition towards zero emission public transport in cities. A number of bus suppliers offer their technologies, most of them from China as Europe is still behind in the Latam e-bus market. Most barriers have already been broken, and confidence in the technology and the market has brought investors to the region. E-buses are key to reducing greenhouse emissions in the region, and the accelerated transition is helping cities with this challenge.

The protective actions of restoration, especially when they affect urban spaces formally declared as areas of restoration, must have an urban reflection and be projected and reflected in the corresponding planning and management techniques. Planning legislation provides the instruments (plans) and the proper techniques to make urban planning adjusted to the parameters of the restoration performing actions that seek to promote the rational use of the natural and cultural resources, in particular the territory, the soil, and the urban and architectural heritage that are the support, the object, and the scene of the quality of life.

Foreword

As a child, around the age of ten, I started to develop a great interest in looking at works of art. The focus of my interest, at the time, was linked to a specific spot in one of the shelves in our living room. A few artbooks, which my father wholeheartedly collected and cherished, mainly carrying general titles such as *Old Masters of Art*, or *The History of Art*, or *Renaissance paintings*, were piled horizontally on this shelf. I used to spend much time looking at the different colorful images while slowly turning the pages in these books. My favorite image was the one depicting the *Adoration of the Magi* of the Italian artist Gentile da Fabriano (1370-1427). The celebratory atmosphere of the whole gathering in the small city of Bethlehem aimed at paying homage and wonder at the newly born Christ was a source of joy for my eyes. I loved the many colors, the abundance of gold, and the various textures of the precious textiles worn by the three magi. Yet, most of all, I was amazed by the great sense of depth in this painting: the exhaustive details in the background, where tiny images of huge caravans made their way to Bethlehem from far lands at the horizon, added to the pristine and spotless depictions of the images adoring in silence the newly born Christ and created a magical sense of depth in time and space. Like in each birthday today, presents were received. These came in precious containers filled with exotic and foreign substances, which were brought by each of the magi from their homelands. Two women standing behind Mary were looking with astonishment at the half-opened cylindrical containers, most probably wondering at their unfamiliar exotic contents.

Years later, while revisiting da Fabriano's Adoration of the Magi, I realized how each of these imported (ultramarine) presents was in fact an ambassador of a specific geography, an agent of other foreign knowledge, unknown to the people and place where they landed. In fact, each substance, tooled object, or each masterfully executed work of art, was a transmitter of knowledge. Moreover, by evoking a sense of amazement, the unknown object of wonder would activate the beholder's curiosity and raise questions such as: what is it? how was it made? how does it function? These questions about the **what** and the **how** of objects clearly demonstrate how natural substances and especially artifacts are directly linked to the processes of the production of knowledge.

And yet, our modern notion of creating a clear division between science and humanities in general and art and technology in particular sets the stage for our common perception that art and technology are divorced. Whereas art has been, and to some extent still is, explained in terms of creativity and the outstanding ability of the genius artist, technologies are usually associated with scientists and people involved in the restoration and preservation of art rather than in the creative act of its making.

In this short foreword I propose to rethink the overlapping zones between art and science/technology. Moreover, like the social anthropologist Alfred Gell in his *Art and Agency*, I would like to consider art as a component of technology and to advocate, like the philosopher of science Thomas Kuhn in his famous book *The Structure of Scientific Revolution* as well as like the sociologist Bruno Latour's recent voice in his *Down to Earth*, that the production of scientific knowledge and of art are both social practices.

Intersection between art and science have long histories. Their origins can be discerned in specific scholarly figures like the Roman encyclopedist Pliny the Elder who writes in his *Naturalis Historia* on science, zoology botany and art, or the Renaissance genius Leonardo da Vinci, who was a scientist, inventor, and artist. In fact, any drawing and painting is the visual product of human thinking, and, as Julia Voss claims in her Book *Darwin's Pictures: Views of Evolutionary Theory 1837-1874*, Darwin's notebook sketches illustrate his mode of thinking. In several cases, as Voss argues, his sketches were in fact *Bildakt*, namely images that act as a tool **for** further thinking rather than illustration **of** thinking. What I want to emphasize here is that thinking, even if scientifically, is an aesthetic act. Paintings and any visual representation are products of translations, in which cognitive ideas find forms and shapes and are organized in compositions. But, at the same time any visual product made by a scientist or an artisan operates within, and is connected to, cultural-aesthetic notions. Painting, drawing, and sketching are tools for activating our creative thinking; and thoughts can thus produce theories.

In addition, artifacts and any other objects, being them of artistic or simply utility value, are the outcome of technical process. Perhaps the main distinction we make between objects of art and **simply** objects, is the fact that we tend to assign to the former a certain high level of technical achievement. We tend to call this high level of artistic production **excellence** and celebrate our amazement in front of these objects. But we should avoid associating this excellence with the aesthetic only and keep in mind that these are all human products of the application of technique. This is exactly why Alfred Gell calls material visual products "technologies of enchantment". Perhaps the best example of artifacts that embody this ambiguity of artistic aesthetic and high technology are arms and armor. These objects, like swords, spears, shields, helmets, which clearly belong to the technologies of war, manifest to us their (acidic) beauty, while we look at them as displayed behind vitrines in art museums.

Technologies that are the outcome of scientific research are, like art, socially produced. Science and art are disciplines of social make-up; by looking at them this way scientific facts might appear to us less objective and unassailable than we would wish them to be. Like art, they are the products of social networking. In fact, recently art-historians are starting to discuss and study artifacts beyond the moment of their creation as to delve into their creators' personal histories. In doing that, art-historians are making the after-life of artifacts come to the fore. This, in turn, is encouraging the field to search for histories of restorations and preservations, all of which are strongly bound to technology and scientific inventions (Lynn Meskell's *A Future in Ruins*, Caroline Fowler's *Technical Art History as Method*). And thus knowledge, art, science, and technology are again inextricably bound.

This IGI book, *Cases on Applying Knowledge Economy Principles for Economic Growth in Developing Nations*, undertakes the ambitious task of examining the global production of knowledge and the transformation of technology as a means to generate new social benefits. In tackling this task, this book is a further contribution to the long history of human aesthetic desire, the "will for art" as a substantial element of our social fabric – a struggle between human aspirations and the limitations imposed by materials/supplies and technical capacities.

Avinoam Shalem
Columbia University, USA

Preface

OVERVIEW OF THE SUBJECT MATTER

The rapid advances and pervasive diffusion of information and communication technology (ICT), combined with the growth of the Internet has led to deep transformations in the world's economic, social and institutional structures. ICT applications affect the performance of businesses and the efficiency of markets, foster the empowerment of citizens and communities as well as their access to knowledge, and contribute to strengthening and redefining governance processes at all institutional levels.

Nevertheless, as all major and wide-ranging technological advances, the ICT revolution is at the same time creating enormous opportunities and posing daunting challenges. On one hand, it has the potential to increase productivity and wealth, generate new activities, products, and services, and improve the well being of the population, notably in regards to education and health levels. On the other hand, the uneven distribution of such opportunities can lead to further alienation of marginalized communities and an exacerbation of existing socioeconomic inequalities. Thereby, a balanced access and effective use of ICT tools and networks in the new global economy, along with an integrated process of technological innovation are critical for reducing poverty, increasing social inclusion, and improving living conditions for all.

Numerous studies have focused on the direct contribution of ICT and technology innovation in general to socioeconomic development; while their findings and conclusions vary according to the context and application, there is an overall agreement that access to information can transform production processes, increase income potential, and improve the living conditions of the poor. ICT is an effective tool that, when supplemented by investments in connectivity, innovation, education, health and a solid infrastructure, increases competitiveness and contributes to economic growth, social development and poverty reduction.

In order to provide a balanced framework to make the most efficient but also equitable use of these technology advances, the concept and architecture of the Knowledge Economy (KE) can be particularly useful. Investments needed to create a KE and enabling policies that would make it viable and durable converge in a "virtuous" circle to transform the intangible nature of Knowledge into an asset with market value able to contribute substantially to economic growth.

This publication examines these subjects and discusses how the applications of KE principles have played out for countries in Europe, Latin America, Africa and Asia; it also discusses options and opportunities for developing countries, as well as the role of governments, International Financial Institutions (IFI) and other sectors of society in support of their efforts.

THE KNOWLEDGE ECONOMY CONCEPT: ORIGINALLY AND TODAY

In 1966, the concept of knowledge as an economic value was first introduced by Peter Drucker in his book "The Effective Executive" (1966), initially focusing on its application at the level of the firm speaking of a "knowledge-based organization". In 1969, Drucker used the term "knowledge economy" in his book "The Age of Discontinuity" (1969), where he also introduced the term "knowledge society", which Drucker used to describe a future dominated by societies (cities, megalopolis) based on "knowledge workers", those who have specialized greatly in generating information as a major output.

Later, different interpretations of these terms have surfaced, from some close to Drucker's concept --countries where a high percentage of the population is highly skilled-- to others that see knowledge as a tradeable commodity that can change hands and generate profits. Carl Dahlman (2007) favours a definition developed by the United Kingdom's Department of Trade and Industry (1999): "a knowledge economy is one in which the generation and exploitation of knowledge has come to play the predominant part in the creation of wealth".

Here, the issue of realm of application of the KE concept returns. The concept can be used both, at a macro and a micro level. At the macro level –country, region—the KE is a *planning tool* aimed at giving the country comparative advantage over others by investing in sectors where growth can be based on the capture and dissemination of knowledge: for example, unique indigenous knowledge that can become a valuable asset; new knowledge that can be developed internally; or knowledge developed elsewhere that can be adapted to generate wealth under the unique conditions of the country.

At the micro level –individual organization or enterprise—the KE is a *strategic growth choice* used to achieve greater effectiveness, efficiency or reach where growth is impeded by a "knowledge challenge": for example, existing knowledge that is yet untapped; gaps in required knowledge; or the need to adapt knowledge developed elsewhere to the specifics of the organization or enterprise.

An encompassing definition of the knowledge economy, then, conceives of it as an interconnected, *globalized* economy where knowledge resources such as *know-how*, expertise and intellectual property are as critical as other economic resources such as land, natural resources, or even manpower. Knowledge is recognized as a source of competitiveness, where value lies in new ideas, services, and networks, using technology as an instrument, not as an end in itself.

In this new economy, sustained use and creation of knowledge are at the centre of the economic development process. Knowledge and education can be treated as a business product, as educational and innovative intellectual products and services can be exported for high value return as productive assets. In a KE, knowledge is used to produce economic benefits, therefore making it an engine of economic growth. KE, thus, is the added non-monetary value that society accrues from increased access to data, information, and knowledge in the new, globally connected world.

Conceiving knowledge as a commodity leads to the appreciation not only of the value of acquiring it, but also of the cost of losing it. Today an un-quantified amount of knowledge is lost because management agents are not actively seeking to capture and retain it. People's knowledge is lost when employees move on; indigenous knowledge is often lost when new technology is introduced; institutional knowledge is drained when changes overrun existing operating systems; cultural knowledge is wasted when development goals are narrowly defined as economic gain. In most of the world, knowledge is not yet considered a commodity to be exchanged and thus its impact on today's "knowledge society" is grossly underestimated.

Much of the theory behind the KE implies the advent of a fundamentally new era in which economic activity is increasingly "abstract", i.e., not as connected as it has conventionally been to traditional production factors such as land, labor and physical capital (machines and industrial infrastructure). The growth of internet-based businesses and business models, as well as the expansion of businesses (trade, particularly, but also education and medical services, for example) that rely heavily on information availability and exchange, supports this contention. But the concept of the KE does not necessarily revolve around high technology or ICT. In fact, the instruments of the KE do not need to be technological; sometimes, knowledge-based gains can derive from the utilization of traditional means to collect, transmit and apply knowledge, which may be more effective than highly sophisticated systems to solve a particular development challenge.

A concept related to that of the KE which can be helpful in measuring progress towards attaining knowledge society status that has been developed more recently, is that of the Economic Complexity Index (ECI) (Hidalgo and Hausmann, 2009). The ECI measures the productive capabilities of large economic systems—like countries, explained by the amount of knowledge accumulated in its population. It is based on observation of the countries and the products they export, ranking their economic complexity according to the diversity of a country's export and their sophistication. For example: some countries may generate goods that are rare (low ubiquity) produced in highly diversified settings (high ECI countries), while other countries may produce products that are common in many places (high ubiquity) that are typically produced in places that are not very diversified (low ECI countries).

ECI is a more accurate predictor of GDP per capita growth than traditional measures of governance, competitiveness --such as the World Economic Forum's Global Competitiveness Index-- and human capital --measured in terms of educational attainment. ECI also shows a strong negative correlation with income inequality, suggesting that more knowledge intense productive structures are more inclusive in terms of income distribution, and providing a statistically more powerful explanation of cross-national variations in income inequality than more traditional indicators such as GDP.

THE ARCHITECTURE OF THE KE

The experience of Asia, which precedes the rest of the world in this path, shows that the successful transition to a KE typically involves long-term investment in education, development of indigenous innovation capabilities, modernization of information sharing infrastructure, and creation of a market environment that is conducive to knowledge-based-transactions.

The Asian example has led the World Bank and other international financial institutions that are active in this field to recognize the following elements as pillars that support the establishment of a KE framework as a country's economic strategy:

1. Economic incentives and institutional regime—i.e., economic policies and institutions that permit efficient mobilization and allocation of resources stimulate creativity and the dissemination and use of existing knowledge.
2. Educated and skilled workers—i.e., a labor force that continuously upgrades and adapts its skills to efficiently create and use knowledge.
3. An innovative institutional and entrepreneurial system—i.e., private firms, research centers, universities, consultants and other organizations actively involved in keeping up with the knowledge

revolution that tap into the growing stock of global knowledge, assimilating and adapting it to local needs.

4. A modern and adequate information infrastructure—i.e., means to effectively acquire, process, communicate and disseminate information and knowledge.

A fifth pillar or basic element to allow the KE to maximize its benefits can be added: social inclusion. While there is no universal acceptance on the insertion of this fifth "pillar", social inclusion is included in the description of KE's architecture in this publication reasoning that "development" can be considered successful when the beneficiary population not only achieves improved economic conditions, but also when those goods and opportunities are more fairly or equitably distributed.

When describing this architectural construct, emphasis is given to simultaneity. Gains are achieved most effectively through simultaneous investment in education, research, ICT, social inclusion and enabling policies—not in research and technology alone. Investments in activities that bring about these conditions are necessary to sustain the creation and adoption of knowledge as a factor in domestic economic production. Sustained use of knowledge leads to higher value-added goods and services. This in turn results in greater probability of economic success, and hence, greater, and sustainable economic development. Knowledge can make an enormous difference in a country's position within today's highly competitive and globalized world economy.

RELEVANCE IN A DEVELOPMENT CONTEXT

The "digital divide" is a phrase coined by Llyd Morrisett in the 1990s when President of the Markle Foundation described the perceived growing gap between those who have access to and the skills to use information and communication technologies and those who, for socioeconomic and/or geographical reasons, have limited or no access to those (Hoffman and Novak, 2000). In particular, the digital divide concept is used to raise the concern that the emergence of ICT could exacerbate existing inequalities in the access to information and that, thereby, certain groups could face additional disadvantages because of their geographic location, age, gender, culture, and social and economic status, among others. Moreover, the phrase reflects the prevalence of socioeconomic and structural inequalities at the regional, national, and local levels, which are characterized by insufficient ICT infrastructure, relatively high access costs, inappropriate or weak policy regimes, inefficiencies in the provision of telecommunication networks and services, lack of local content, and uneven ability to derive economic and social benefits from information-intensive activities.

Indeed, the use of ICT and technology innovation in general is creating new social and economic development opportunities for lower-income populations, by enlarging markets and facilitating greater access to information, public services, and economic activity. ICT and technology innovation solutions can facilitate the participation of lower income populations in the development process by tackling factors that hinder their integration to social and economic development. In particular: (i) limited knowledge and literacy which impairs access to skills and jobs; (ii) poor health and sanitary conditions limiting employability and risk-taking attitudes; (iii) lack of active involvement in civic life and strengthening of democratic process; and (iv) lack of access to high-paying jobs and other economic opportunities. In this respect, the evolution of modern ICT brings about concrete opportunities for enhanced provision of social services and poverty reduction through, among others, distance education and telemedicine solutions; improved connectivity; strengthened and transparent government operations (i.e., e-government). It also provides for the modernization and expansion of the micro-finance sector to effectively reach marginalized and less favoured populations through technology-based solutions and innovative financial services, thereby, creating economic opportunities at the local level.

Yet, these opportunities cannot be effectively and fully realized if left to market forces alone, and require the active participation of the public, private and civil society sectors under integrated efforts towards the development of an inclusive information society. The United Nations Millennium Declaration in its 20th resolution noted that efforts to make access available to all and harness the power of ICT can contribute toward the achievement of its goals by creating digital opportunities in development (United Nations, 2000). Such digital opportunities, when coupled with education, social inclusion, and the whole architecture of the KE can support development both directly and indirectly. Directly, by expanding the reach, scope and impact of social development programs, health services, and education and training programs, and providing opportunities for improving gender equality and citizen participation. Indirectly, by creating new economic opportunities and/or extending them to lift individuals, communities, and nations out of poverty.

A significant gap exists today between developed and developing countries in terms of access to the potential benefits of the KE. Least developed countries are at a great disadvantage because international trade and direct external investment flows do not favor them. Furthermore, trademark and intellectual property right systems are not well developed and do not adequately protect the smaller economies. Yet, developing countries might have a comparative advantage when it comes to tapping into local sources of original knowledge generated by traditional societies and put them to work as a factor in production or as a tradable good. In their efforts to tap the benefits of the KE, developing countries can not only seek to tap into existing knowledge; they can also seek to generate new knowledge; or even choose to adapt knowledge generated somewhere else to their needs or comparative advantages. It is possible that some countries would choose one path or the other, or that some may choose to undertake these paths sequentially.

A challenge has thus emerged for governments to build national capabilities, facilitate collaboration within and between businesses, and encourage competition. The transition towards a KE requires that the rules and practices that determine success in the industrial economy be rewritten. Economic valuation and accounting rules need to be redefined so that governments, industries, and organizations incorporate the value of knowledge and the added value that its innovative use would create. Accordingly, public policies must be redesigned to provide the conditions necessary to make knowledge a monetary asset. Public policies designed and implemented to support the KE must focus on how to generate public value out of knowledge existing or produced in the country, and how to make locally available knowledge a factor in the global economy. In other words, public policies must provide conditions to exploit the positive externalities of the global KE.

WHERE THE TOPIC FITS IN TODAY'S WORLD

Today, the world faces high challenges and dire prospects. Principal among them are the following, which are discussed in terms of their relevance for the sustainability of our planet and our way of life, as well as in reference to the Knowledge Economy's ability to exert positive influence over them.

Climate Change

As expressed by the Intergovernmental Panel on Climate Change (IPCC) in its August 2021 report, the earth's climate is changing in every region, at unprecedented rates, with some of the changes that have been set in motion considered irreversible over hundreds or thousands of years. Culpable of these changes are principally humankind's choices in the use of non-renewable natural resources, as well as the sheer weight of the planet's human population and its living habits.

The KE constitutes an alternative and a complement to natural resource-based economic models by creating wealth from the exchange of information and technology-based products and services. It can also contribute to make more efficient use of energy, transportation systems and household consumption services that are heavily dependent on non-renewable sources. Finally, products upon which the KE is built –information and communication technologies—are fundamental instruments to generate early warning, monitoring and evaluation systems that can help humanity better understand and manage climate-change processes.

Projections by Victoria University's Peter Sheehan et at in 2006 are well under way to become reality in 2030, and their projections for 2050 and beyond may also prove to be accurate:

"By 2030, many technologies – such as ultra-light weight hybrid or fuel cell vehicles, improved buildings systems, advanced fossil fuel power generation, carbon capture and storage, energyplexes and a wide array of renewable energy technologies – are likely to be commercially proven and will be increasingly used, especially in OECD countries. By about 2050 the most successful of these technologies should be mature, with growing market share in OECD countries and, in due course, in developing countries. Other technologies, such as advanced hydrogen technologies and possibly even nuclear fusion, are likely to become commercially viable in the second half of the century. However, the limiting factors that constrain the technology diffusion process – cost competitiveness, critical mass, slow turnover of capital stock, parallel advances in fossil fuel and renewable technologies and delayed adoption in the developing countries – will also persist, even under rising fossil fuel prices." (Sheehan et al, 2006).

Advances in technology, which can be highly beneficial to humanity, must be accompanied by a raise in awareness among the population as to the need to reduce consumption of noxious products, change attitudes and habits to adopt a climate-conscious minds, and participate actively in an economic growth model that depends less on carbon emissions and more on carbon-neutral activities such as the ones supported by the KE.

Poverty

The more widely accepted figure for a percentage of the world population that lives in extreme poverty (persons living on less than USD1.90 per day) is around 11.4% for 2020. The figures for 2020 are a reversal of a positive trend that saw those figures decrease consistently in the previous decade until 2019.

In fact, in 2020 approximately 100 million additional people entered the poverty threshold, mostly because of the COVID pandemic, which compounded pre-existing conditions such as the prevalence of armed and social conflict and the effects of climate change. In fact, the great majority of those in extreme poverty live in Sub-Saharan Africa and South Asia, where climate change is an acute threat, manifesting itself principally as high exposure to flooding.

Causal factors behind global poverty are many and complex; no single factor can be credited with creating the conditions that result in poverty, but the following are mentioned often: inequality in access to agricultural land, water, and sources of nutrition; lack of education and associated limited access to regular jobs; armed conflict, limited capacity of governments and corruption; lack of infrastructure to gain access to markets and employment.

Of these, the architecture of the KE attempts to tackle three elements: education, information and communications infrastructure, and strong government and enabling governmental policies. In fact, the Knowledge Economy sees action in these three fronts, when tackled simultaneously, as the path for a country's economic modernization based upon knowledge resources.

While the KE cannot be seen as a direct answer to the plight of the world's extreme poor, the application of its model has helped many countries to move up in the development ladder in relatively short periods of time. Perhaps the best example of this has been the Republic of South Korea, which converted its economy from agriculture-based to a technology and knowledge-based economy that saw its standing as a low-income country change to a rising star in the Asian continent. In the 1950s about half of its population was under extreme poverty, which declined to about 3.4% in the mid-1990s; today, only about 2% of its population is affected by extreme poverty. South Korea was the first country in the world to establish a Ministry of Knowledge Economy and its model has been replicated in other countries with positive results.

Crisis of Governance

Around the world governments, whether democratic, autocratic, or somewhere in between, seem to be having a particularly hard time. Even the least participatory government structures are seeing their grip on power decline or at risk. Citizen groups are demonstrating an uncanny ability to organize themselves and act against perceived slights or failures in government policy or management.

While there are several factors that are causing this effect –increase in levels of education and worldwide achievements to protect human rights, for example-- perhaps the one contributing factor that has changed most radically and swiftly in later years is the rise of the internet. Access to the internet has meant unlimited access to information and the ability to communicate globally on issues that transcend boundaries. Widespread availability of information has put in evidence the presence of corruption and abuses by government officials and has facilitated the ability of community leaders to communicate and call for action.

Some of these changes can be unequivocally termed positive, when it is citizenry protesting government abuse, as described before. However, there are some other phenomena that are eminently negative and which roots are traced also to the globalized access to social media. That is the case when such phenomena are fueled by "misinformation". For the average citizen, the written word has traditionally been equated to "truth", and for most it is difficult to distinguish true from false from a given piece of information; few will conduct detailed research to be able to make that distinction. As a result, strong social currents are now moved by disinformation and misinformation and now challenge government mandates and legislation as corrupt even when no real evidence exists to support that assertion. Therefore, in today's world the "rule of law", for centuries adopted as the one guiding principle to curb self-interest and abusive social behavior, seems to be opened to interpretation and to become optional.

A case in question is the onset of the COVID pandemic, which is wreaking havoc across the planet and has put every government to the test. Reluctance to get the vaccine is fueled in part by disinformation and misinformation. The impact of these individual decisions on a country's stability and economy are very significant and is one clear example of the power of social media on the world's governance. The

World Economic Forum in 2020 notes, when discussing the coronavirus crisis, that "the interconnected nature of our globalized society and economy, and the constant proliferation of information on a multitude of media platforms, have quickly morphed a public health event into a global political, economic, psychological and social crisis of epic proportions."

The governance crisis, of course, is a complex social issue and as such has no easy answers. Still, faith in the value of truth is fundamental to the health of society, and thus, it must be expected of governments to face this crisis by adopting a strong knowledge-based social communication policy and strategy, where citizenry is given the opportunity to check and balance information to regain confidence in their leaders or, conversely, understand when leadership truly must be challenged.

TARGET AUDIENCE

This book is directed specially to the following target audiences:

1. Decision-makers—government officials, industry leaders, managers of academic institutions, among others—who can understand the potential of the Knowledge Economy for their countries and their sectors and redirect the economy to benefit from their countries or sectors' comparative advantages; with their actions, decision makers can also tap into insofar underutilized local knowledge and value, deriving from these actions not only economic but also social benefits.
2. Development practitioners, who can benefit from their peers' experience in the application of KE instruments to solve development challenges, and who can become interested in sharing their own experiences and help others learn from them.
3. Researchers, who can identify gaps in knowledge areas and analytical tools that can facilitate decision-makers making the most out of the opportunities offered by the Knowledge Economy.
4. Students, who can find in the Knowledge Economy a new field of interest and study, drawing from the wide academic fields associated to this subject.
5. International finance organizations working in favor of developing countries, and willing to establish new investment sectors
6. Librarians and knowledge managers, who can help raise awareness among the general public regarding the value Knowledge has for their everyday life.

ORGANIZATION OF THE BOOK

The book is organized in chapters which discuss the topic of the KE as it applies to specific sectors of the economy or society, or as it is being applied to specific countries or regions of the world. The cases discussed here are examples of the challenges, benefits, and costs of using the KE concept in its entirety or some of the instruments that make up its architecture.

Section 1: Society

Chapter 1 describes the efforts by the Government of the State of São Paulo in Brazil to improve the lives and opportunities offered to persons with disabilities in their State, through the adoption of a technology innovation program. The program engages the private sector and academia, besides the government itself. The program aims at providing persons with disabilities access to technology innovation products and services that facilitate their participation in the labor force. In particular, the program supports educational organizations to provide training to develop marketable skills; connects those trained with potential employers; and supports the process with favorable government policies.

Chapter 2 discusses the results of an analysis of observed world-wide trends where lower income groups keep growing, the middle class is shrinking, while the higher income groups also grow. Disparities in income are traced to several causes, including different forms of discrimination. Access to sustainable employment is presented as the way to counter such disparities, and thus the need to develop adequate education and training policies.

Section 2: Health

Chapter 3 describes a methodology used to enhance patient performance in physical rehabilitation and analyzes the results of the practical application of such methodology by one laboratory in Brazil. The analysis describes how knowledge management has been used to re-structure the work of the different specialties involved in providing physical rehabilitation to patients, and how such instruments have improved results both at the medical as well as the psychological levels.

Chapter 4 focuses on transfusion medicine as impacted by the introduction of digitally-based systems to manage blood products and healthcare services more generally. The chapter provides a clear analysis of the interrelation between the healthcare systems and digital management systems.

Chapter 5 introduces the case of Ecuador in its fight against the COVID-19 pandemic and highlights the participation by a private entity in support of the government's effort to provide testing and later vaccines to the population. The ability of the private entity to enhance and widen its service capacity to encompass a much larger and growing number of patients hinged heavily on its ability to modernize its online platform, train its personnel, and devise patient/health provider interfaces that are client friendly.

Section 3: Education

Chapter 6 focuses on a very specific application of online education, one reaching out to persons with visual disability. ICT-based applications are found to be crucial in making distance-learning courses available to persons who would otherwise be denied the opportunity to improve their livelihoods by means of gaining access to employment and income-earning options.

Chapter 7 describes the usefulness of an online platform –the Learning Experience Platform—to empower people in least developed countries to enter new fields of education and training and thus gain access to new employment markets. The chapter supports life-long learning as a powerful tool to enhance a country's development through more active economic participation from groups that have little access to income-generating activities.

Chapter 8 discusses how civil society organizations have lent crucial support to making health care, medical services, and education available to disadvantaged groups –in particular young girls' education as well as persons with disabilities. The chapter describes digital systems used in providing these services, emphasizing the roles of civil society participation in the effort.

Section 4: Agriculture

Chapter 9 showcases knowledge transfer and technology innovation as tools in territorial development. The chapter describes an operational program working in public-private collaboration to strengthen producer's transition to an agroecological production system, a process that requires a significant adaptation in producer's practices, which in turn depends on the ability of the program to transfer relevant knowledge to its beneficiaries.

Section 5: Industry

Chapter 10 provides a comprehensive introduction to the applicability of the KE concept on a macroeconomic scale. The chapter focuses on the MENA region --comprised of Algeria, Bahrain, Egypt, Iran, Iraq, Israel, Jordan, Kuwait, Lebanon, Libya, Morocco, Oman, Qatar, Saudi Arabia, Syria, Tunisia, United Arab Emirates and Yemen; it describes how a KE-oriented policy can support the region's objective of strengthening its industrial structures and output, focusing on the acceleration of technological change, growth of ICT services, and intensification of worldwide integration.

Chapter 11 describes how growing demand for data storage is not being met by industry, as the latter tend to suffer from unstructured data resources. Well organized information infrastructure is depicted as fundamental to allow for ongoing and future growth in the use of 5G, artificial intelligence and the internet of things.

Chapter 12 puts forward a proposal for a south-south collaboration for the purpose of introducing ICT-based industrial innovation geared towards improving environmental sustainability of the industrial sector –the so-called "green ICT". Adoption of green ICT in industrial operations is heralded as a factor in improving industrial processes while at the same time minimizing or reversing environmental impacts.

Chapter 13 discusses the use of knowledge management and knowledge transfer to achieve a decisive change in attitude towards recycling among a population that was generating waste and creating a social and economic problem for the community and the local government. The program promotes good practices that demonstrate how knowledge transferred and managed can make a difference in support of environmental sustainability.

Section 6: Urbanization and Transportation

Chapter 14 showcases how internet-based data sharing and innovation in economic modelling can contribute to enhanced environmental awareness and lead to the adoption of environmentally sound industrial practices, in this case, the adoption of e-buses as a significant share of the public transportation system. Public opinion in favor of the adoption of e-buses, supported by a strong internet-based campaign, has encouraged the change in technology in this sector.

Chapter 15 supports the use of digital technologies to facilitate the planning and execution of urban restoration projects aimed at reversing long-lived trends that impede that public and private spaces fulfill the function for which they were conceived. Digital technologies contribute by making restoration projects more efficient and to achieve buy-into from project beneficiaries.

The cases presented in this compilation showcase but a fraction of what is being done in the world to make use of knowledge-based systems to improve people's livelihoods; make public investment more efficient; make private support more encompassing; make development more effective. There is need for further discussion and analysis of how KE instruments can be improved and made readily available elsewhere, and for that, the editors encourage development practitioners, students, researchers, organizations around the world to bring to public knowledge their experiences, learnings, and recommendations for others to follow. Furthermore, there are links and associations between the concept of Knowledge Economy and other areas of human development that must be explored and explained: Knowledge and the Arts, Knowledge and Sociology for example. Researchers around the world are encouraged to delve into those and other topics in their work.

Danilo Piaggesi
Knowledge for Development (K4D), USA

Helena Landazuri
Knowledge for Development (K4D), USA

Bo Jia
Tsinghua University, China

REFERENCES

Dahlman, C. (2007). The challenge of the knowledge economy for Latin America. *GCG: Revista de globalización, competitividad y gobernabilidad, 1*(1), 1.

Drucker, P. F. (1966). *The Effective Executive*. Harper & Row.

Drucker, P. F. (1969). *The age of discontinuity: Guidelines to our changing society*. Heinemann.

Hidalgo, C. A., & Hausmann, R. (2009). The building blocks of economic complexity. *Proceedings of the National Academy of Sciences of the United States of America, 106*(26), 10570–10575. doi:10.1073/pnas.0900943106 PMID:19549871

Hoffman, D. L., & Novak, T. P. (1999). The growing digital divide: Implications for an open research agenda. *Understanding the digital economy, 245*.

IPCC. (2021). *Climate change widespread, rapid, and intensifying – IPCC*. https://www.ipcc.ch/2021/08/09/ar6-wg1-20210809-pr/

Sheehan, P., Jones, R., Jolley, A., Preston, B., Clark, M., Durack, P., ... Whetton, P. (2006). *Climate change and the global knowledge economy: an immediate challenge*. Academic Press.

United Kingdom's Department of Trade and Industry. (1999). *Our competitive future: Building the knowledge driven economy*. Department of Trade and Industry, Her Majesty's Stationary Office.

United Nations. (2020). *United Nations Millennium Declaration*. https://www.ohchr.org/EN/ProfessionalInterest/Pages/Millennium.aspx

World Economy Forum. (2020). *Three lessons in crisis governance for the age of coronavirus*. https://www.weforum.org/agenda/2020/04/a-guide-to-crisis-governance-in-the-age-of-coronavirus/

Acknowledgment

The editors would like to acknowledge the help of all the people involved in this project without whose support this book would not have become a reality.

First, our sincere gratitude goes to the chapter's authors who contributed their time and expertise to this book.

Most of the authors also served as reviewers, in which case, they are doubly thanked. But several external peer reviewers also made a valuable contribution towards the improvement of quality, coherence, and content of the chapters. They were, alphabetically:

Dr. Mattia Bisconti, University of Molise, Italy

Master of Sciences (MSc). Physiotherapist specialized in sport and musculoskeletal physiotherapy. Lecturer at the Department of Medicine and Health Science "Vicenzo Tiberio", University of Molise. Senior physiotherapist at the University of Pittsburg Medical Center (UPMC) in Rome, Italy. Works on gender medicine and sex and gender-based approach in research, studying chronic pain. Health management expert, experienced in teaching and research.

Rodolfo Castillo López, Advisors to Enterprises S.A. (AESA) RATINGS S.A., Bolivia

Master of Business Administration (MBA) from The University of Texas at Austin, Texas, United States of America. President and Chief Executive Officer (CEO) of AESA RATINGS SA, a financial, industrial & telecom consulting firm with 35 years of experience, and an affiliate of FITCH RATINGS. Principal executive of the Andean Development Corporation (CAF) in Bolivia and of the Agency for the Development of the Information Society of Bolivia (ADSIB).

Mr. Vinicius Delgado Ramos, University of Sao Paulo, Brazil

Master's in Project Management. Research Support and Innovation Officer at the Physical and Rehabilitation Medicine Institute of the University of Sao Paulo Medical School & General Hospital, Sao Paulo, Brazil. Background in international relations, with an interest in international development cooperation and global health, and a focus on the rights of persons with disabilities.

Dr. Fabiano Mele, Lazio Regional Administration, Italy

Master's in Economics and Agrarian Sciences; graduated first class with honors. Professional agronomist. Researcher. Skilled in administrative capacity-building & assessment; development model shaping; and public/private policymaking.

Dr. Byron E. Price, Medgar Evers College, the United States of America

Doctor of Philosophy (Ph.D.) focused on public policy & administration from Mississippi State University. His research areas are mass incarceration, prison privatization, prisoner reentry, the school-to-prison pipeline, race, politics, social entrepreneurship, social reengineering, and social justice.

Dr. Giovanni Ruocco, Aurelia Hospital, Italy

Medical Doctor (MD). Surgeon. Plastic and reconstructive surgery. He specializes on microsurgery and hand surgery.

Dr. Nikola Trendov, Food and Agriculture Organization (FAO) of the United Nations, Italy

Doctor of Philosophy (Ph.D.) focused on digital agricultural technologies. Experienced in digital agriculture transformation, working in the field of digital agriculture strategies and digital innovation capabilities in countries of the European Union (EU) and developing countries. Expertise in digital skills, extension systems, rural development, and agribusiness; cooperation on digital transformation, agronomy, and youth programs for digital agriculture innovation.

Mr. Erik Van Ingen, Food and Agriculture Organization (FAO) of the United Nations, Italy

Master's in Business Process Management and Information Technology. Erik Van Ingen works as an innovation specialist on digital agriculture through frontier technologies such as blockchain, artificial intelligence, data analytics, IoT, and remote sensing in the FAO Office of Innovation.

Section 1
Society

Chapter 1
Technology Innovation for Persons With Disabilities in Brazil

Danilo Piaggesi
https://orcid.org/0000-0003-4610-174X
Knowledge for Development (K4D), USA

Helena Landazuri
Knowledge for Development (K4D), USA

Bo Jia
Tsinghua University, China

EXECUTIVE SUMMARY

The results of the Brazilian Census 2010 show that of a total population of 193 million people, approximately 46 million people of Brazil's total population have some kind of disability. Brazil is one of the world's leading IT markets and the largest IT market in Latin America. This chapter presents a program started by the Government of the State of Sao Paulo through its Secretariat for the Rights of Persons with Disabilities (SEDPcD) in 2013 that aims to promote the rehabilitation and social inclusion of persons with disabilities. Adopting the application of the concept and instruments of the knowledge economy as core strategy and through the application of ICT-based assistive technologies, the program develops solutions to a level where they can be applied massively in a cost-effective way.

PERSONS WITH DISABILITIES IN THE STATE OF SAO PAULO, BRAZIL

Definitions of Disability

The definition of Disability in the Convention on the Rights of Persons with Disabilities (CRPD) can be found in Paragraph (e) of the preamble of the Convention: *"Recognizing that disability is an evolving*

DOI: 10.4018/978-1-7998-8417-0.ch001

concept and that disability results from the interaction between persons with impairments and attitudinal and environmental barriers that hinders their full and effective participation in society on an equal basis with others". Article 1 further specifies that: *"Persons with disabilities include those who have long-term physical, mental, intellectual or sensory impairments which in interaction with various barriers may hinder their full and effective participation in society on an equal basis with others"*. (United Nations, 2008)
These definitions constitute the legal foundation of Accessibility Rights:

1. It confirms the abandonment of the traditional "medical" definition of disability which focused exclusively on a person's impairment;
2. It clearly establishes the "social" definition of disability which results from the interaction between persons with impairments and attitudinal and environmental barriers, a notion that emerged in the later part of the 20th century;
3. It affirms that the full and effective participation of disabled persons in society can only occur if those barriers are removed.

Accessibility Rights, including to Information and Communication Technology, are established to ensure that persons with disabilities enjoy a "full and effective participation in society on an equal basis with others" and become an integral part of Human Rights.

The "medical model of disability" – the model most widely understood and interpreted today – considers disability "a physical, mental, or psychological condition that limits a person's activities," linked to various medical conditions and viewed as a problem residing within the affected individual. While the medical model is the construct for disabilities that we are historically most accustomed to using, over time the international community has largely come to recognize that the medical model is not a sufficiently effective or empowering conceptual framework for promoting the full inclusion of persons with disabilities in society. As a result the paradigm of disabilities is expanding to include both the medical model as well as the more recently defined "social model of disability."

Unlike the medical model of disability, the social model of disability views disability as "arising from the interaction of a person's functional status with the physical, cultural, and policy environments," an approach which closely follows the work done by the UN Washington Group on Disability Statistics (more information is available at: https://www.washingtongroup-disability.com/).

According to the social model, disability is the outcome of the interaction of a person with his or her environment and thus is neither person- nor environment-specific. Within the social model, then, a disability results when a person attempts to communicate, yet does not understand or speak the national or local language. Similarly, a disability results when someone who has never before operated a phone or computer attempts to use one – with no success. In both cases, a disability has occurred, because the person was not able to interact with his or her environment.

Compared to the medical model of disability, the social model of disability inevitably encompasses more of the global population in more situations and under more circumstances. And it is based on the energetic and compelling leadership of the Washington Group on Disability Statistics and the World Bank's Disability and Development team, along with the United Nations' Declaration on the Rights of Persons with Disabilities in December 2006, that the disabilities paradigm – and the way we view accessibility - has begun to shift.

Persons With Disabilities (PwD) in Brazil

The results of the Brazilian Census 2010 show that of a total population of 193 million people, approximately 46 million people, or 24% of Brazil's total population has some kind of disability (See Table 1). The percentage increased by 10% compared with the 2000 census.

A series of press releases issued by the Brazilian Institute of Geography and Statistics (IBGE) described certain features of the results. Women and elderly were the majority in this group. Among the elderly, approximately 68% declared to have some kind of disability. Blacks and brown formed the groups holding the biggest proportions of disabled persons (27.1% for both). In all the color or race groups, there were more disabled women, especially in the black population (23.5% of men and 30.9% of women). (IBGE, 2012)

Among persons with disabilities, visual disabilities predominate. About 18.8% of the population had visual disabilities, 1.4% had intellectual disabilities, 7% had motor disabilities, and 5.1% had hearing disabilities. Rates of mental disabilities and hearing disabilities were higher among men than among women.

Table 1. Resident population, by kind of disability, according to sex and age group

Sex and Age Groups	Population (%)						
	Total	Type of Disability					
		At least One Type of Disability	Seeing Disability	Hearing Disability	Motor Disability	Mental or Intellectual	None of These Disabilities
Total	**100**	**23.9**	**18.8**	**5.1**	**7.0**	**1.4**	**76.1**
0 - 14	100	7.5	5.3	1.3	1.0	0.9	92.5
15 - 64	100	24.9	20.1	4.2	5.7	1.4	75.0
65 or more	100	67.7	49.8	25.6	38.3	2.9	32.6
Males	**100**	**21.2**	**16.0**	**5.3**	**5.3**	**1.5**	**78.8**
0 - 14	100	7.3	4.8	1.4	1.0	1.0	92.7
15 - 64	100	22.2	17.1	4.5	4.5	1.6	77.8
65 or more	100	64.6	47.3	28.8	30.9	2.8	35.4
Females	**100**	**26.5**	**21.4**	**4.9**	**8.5**	**1.2**	**73.5**
0 - 14	100	7.8	5.9	1.3	1.0	0.7	92.2
15 - 64	100	27.6	23.1	4.0	6.8	1.2	72.4
65 or more	100	70.1	51.7	23.6	44.0	3.0	29.9

Source: (Brazilian Institute of Geography and Statistics, 2010)

Participation of PWD in Brazil's Economy

Persons with disabilities are able participants in Brazilian society. Census 2010 data reveals their level of participation in two key life areas: education and employment.

Education

IBGE's 2010 census findings reveal that for persons with disabilities ages 0 to 4 years, attendance in daycare or school exceeded that of their nondisabled peers 38% versus 34% (See Table 2). For the 9 -14 years age group, the trend is reversed; attendance for people without disabilities is 97% versus 95% for persons with disabilities. Overall, the 16% attendance rate of people with disabilities see a 3% rise compared with 2000 census, while the rate for people without disabilities increased by 1%.

Table 2. Resident Population, with or without disabilities, by attendance in daycare or school

Sex and Age Groups	Total	Attend School or Daycare	At Least One of the Investigated Disabilities			None of the Investigated Disabilities		
			Total	Attend School or Daycare	%	Total	Attend School or Daycare	%
Total	190 755 799	59 565 188	45 606 048	7 333 130	**16%**	145 084 976	52 229 324	**36%**
0 - 4	13 806 733	4 661 218	385 303	145 740	**38%**	13 419 477	4 515 366	**34%**
5 - 9	14 967 767	14 234 497	1 147 368	1 080 258	**94%**	13 818 227	13 154 147	**95%**
9 - 14	17 167 135	16 562 084	1 926 730	1 828 482	**95%**	15 237 845	14 733 389	**97%**
15 - 19	16 986 788	11 610 342	2 017 529	1 395 804	**69%**	14 966 031	10 214 170	**68%**
20 - 24	17 240 864	4 331 498	2 215 799	615 178	**28%**	15 016 938	3 716 162	**25%**
25 - 29	17 102 917	2 446 915	2 376 938	387 461	**16%**	14 715 518	2 059 027	**14%**
30 - 39	29 632 807	2 794 524	5 038 527	531 754	**11%**	24 578 326	2 262 145	**9%**
40 - 49	24 843 143	1 530 248	8 560 642	551 577	**6%**	16 272 203	978 307	**6%**
50 or more	39 007 645	1 393 862	21 937 212	796 876	**4%**	17 060 412	596 611	**3%**

Source: (Brazilian Institute of Geography and Statistics, 2010)

In Brazil, according to IBGE's analysis, 95.2% of the children aged 6 to 14 with disabilities were attending school, 1.9 percentage points below the total of the population in this age group (97.1%). The North Region has the lowest schooling rate (93.3%), however, having the smallest difference between children with (94.0%) and without disability (93.3%). The biggest difference was found in the South Region, 97.7% and 95.3%, respectively. (IBGE, 2012)

The overall literacy rate of people without disabilities in Brazil was 92%; for persons with disabilities the rate was 82% (Table 3), while the date in 2000 are 87% and 71% respectively. Persons with disabilities' rates of literacy were lower than their non-disabled peers in every age group.

Table 3. People aged 5 years or more, with or without disabilities, by literacy level, according to age group

Age Groups	Total	Literate	At Least One of the Investigated Disabilities			None of the Investigated Disabilities		
			Total	**Literate**	**%**	**Total**	**Literate**	**%**
Total	176 949 066	158 311 433	45 220 745	36 964 660	**82%**	131 665 498	121 308 063	**92%**
5-9	14 967 767	10 589 797	1 147 368	781 590	**68%**	13 818 227	9 807 583	**71%**
9-14	17 167 135	16 567 640	1 926 730	1 764 021	**92%**	15 237 845	14 802 640	**97%**
15 - 19	16 986 788	16 659 025	2 017 529	1 894 162	**94%**	14 966 031	14 763 120	**99%**
20 - 24	17 240 864	16 801 664	2 215 799	2 069 238	**93%**	15 016 938	14 727 332	**98%**
25 - 29	17 102 917	16 446 213	2 376 938	2 188 584	**92%**	14 715 518	14 250 948	**97%**
30 - 39	29 632 807	27 722 439	5 038 527	4 469 700	**89%**	24 578 326	23 242 239	**95%**
40 - 49	24 843 143	22 428 677	8 560 642	7 405 914	**87%**	16 272 203	15 015 772	**92%**
50 or more	39 007 645	31 095 977	21 937 212	16 391 450	**75%**	17 060 412	14 698 430	**86%**

Source: (Brazilian Institute of Geography and Statistics, 2010)

In terms of level of education, persons with disabilities' level of achievement was less that of the population as a whole (Table 4). Out of the total persons over the age of 15 who had three years of education or fewer, 32.9% had some disability.

Table 4. People 15 years or older, with or without disabilities, according to level of education groups

Level of Education	Total	At Least One of the Investigated Disabilities	%	None of the Investigated Disabilities	%
	144 814 164	42 146 647	**29%**	102 609 427	**71%**
Uneducated and incomplete elementary school	65 043 145	25 766 944	**40%**	39 231 515	**60%**
Complete elementary school and incomplete high school	27 511 216	5 967 894	**22%**	21 537 500	**78%**
Complete high school and incomplete higher education	37 963 308	7 447 983	**20%**	30 509 053	**80%**
Graduated	13 463 757	2 808 878	**21%**	10 653 769	**79%**
Not determined	832 737	154 947	**19%**	677 590	**81%**

Source: (Brazilian Institute of Geography and Statistics, 2010)

Employment

According to the census, of the 86 million people aged 10 or over who constituted the working population of the country, 20 million were persons with disabilities (Table 5). The census found that the overall employment rate of persons with disabilities was lower than that among people without disabilities.

The rate of employment for people without disabilities was 56% while the rate for persons with disabilities was about 10% lower. Of the 20.4 million persons with disabilities employed at the time of the 2010 census, 10.9 million were men and 9.5 million were women. Thus, almost 57.3% of men with disabilities had work while 37.8% of women with disabilities were employed. The employment rate for women with disabilities increased significantly from 27.3% in 2000, while rate for man is 52% in 2000.

Table 5. People 10 years or older, with or without disabilities, by occupation condition, according to age groups

Age Groups	Total	With Occupation	Without Occupation	At Least One of the Investigated Disabilities			None of the Investigated Disabilities		
				Total	With Occupation	Without Occupation	Total	With Occupation	Without Occupation
Total	161 981 299	86 353 839	75 627 459	44 073 377	20 365 963	23 707 414	117 847 272	65 967 714	51 879 557
10 – 14	17 167 135	1 069 425	16 097 710	1 926 730	120 837	1 805 893	15 237 845	948 536	14 289 309
15 - 19	16 986 788	5 390 928	11 595 860	2 017 529	569 790	1 447 738	14 966 031	4 820 432	10 145 599
20 - 24	17 240 864	10 743 940	6 496 924	2 215 799	1 246 832	968 967	15 016 938	9 495 346	5 521 591
25 - 29	17 102 917	12 206 523	4 896 395	2 376 938	1 535 697	841 241	14 715 518	10 668 165	4 047 353
30 - 34	15 744 616	11 703 494	4 041 122	2 447 685	1 632 589	815 097	13 287 819	10 067 846	3 219 973
35 - 39	13 888 191	10 439 764	3 448 427	2 590 841	1 727 132	863 709	11 290 507	8 709 828	2 580 679
40 - 44	13 008 496	9 683 510	3 324 986	3 797 150	2 538 696	1 258 454	9 205 527	7 142 109	2 063 418
45 - 49	11 834 647	8 512 109	3 322 537	4 763 491	3 157 968	1 605 523	7 066 676	5 351 862	1 714 814
50 - 54	10 134 322	6 672 385	3 461 937	4 705 129	2 867 731	1 837 398	5 425 649	3 802 945	1 622 704
55 - 59	8 284 433	4 626 125	3 658 308	4 170 185	2 144 362	2 025 823	4 111 740	2 480 580	1 631 160
60 - 64	6 503 287	2 695 934	3 807 352	3 524 275	1 322 740	2 201 535	2 977 236	1 372 575	1 604 661
65 - 69	4 852 789	1 359 007	3 493 782	2 894 694	727 646	2 167 049	1 957 073	631 034	1 326 039
70 - 74	3 744 738	706 180	3 038 558	2 451 628	412 464	2 039 164	1 292 634	293 532	999 102
75 - 79	2 570 686	332 523	2 238 163	1 839 631	210 940	1 628 691	730 605	121 491	609 114
80 or more	2 917 391	211 992	2 705 399	2 351 671	150 540	2 201 131	565 475	61 433	504 042

Source: (Brazilian Institute of Geography and Statistics, 2010)

Poverty

Despite the lack of consensus on a definition and the variety of methods of data collection across the region, it is clear that disability is an important cause and consequence of poverty and exclusion. Recent census data show that Brazil, Chile, Ecuador, Nicaragua and Panama have disability prevalence rates higher than 10% (14.5%, 12.9% 12.1%, 10.3% and 11.3% respectively). According to the World Bank, around 82% of persons with disabilities in LAC live in poverty, and they are more vulnerable to exclusion from the economic, social, and political life, because of stigmatization and lack of access. In all Latin-American countries, the employment rates for persons with disabilities are lower than for those without and a high percentage work informally, or are underemployed. On average, 70% of persons with disabilities in the region are either unemployed or outside of the workforce. In Mexico, for instance, the general employment rate is 50%, while the rate for persons with disabilities is approximately 27%, and 22.6% of those who are working receive less than a minimum wage. Similarly, in Brazil, 30% of persons with disabilities receive less than a minimum wage, and in Chile only one-third of persons with disabilities who are employed have full-time work. In Bolivia, almost 40% of persons with disabilities are self-employed or work informally, and in Honduras 73% are self-employed or work for no pay.

State of Sao Paulo's Policy on PwD

In the State of Sao Paulo, the latest census showed that 7.29% of the State's population (3,008,617 out of a total population of 41,262,199) had some form of deficiency. Census data allows discriminating by type of deficiency, showing that distribution to be: 40% visual; 28.79% mobility; 16.72% mental/intellectual; and 14.49% auditory. 56.86% were women and 43.14% were men. The vast majority (96.17%) lived in cities. In terms of schooling, 70.52% had no schooling or had not completed elementary school. Only 4.94% had completed tertiary schooling.

Disability involves the interaction of a person's functional status with their physical, cultural, and policy environments. If the environment in Brazil is designed for the full range of human functioning and incorporates appropriate accommodations and support mechanisms, then people with functional limitations would not be "disabled" in the sense that they would be able to fully participate in society. Interventions designed to improve participation are not only targeted at the individual level, for example medical rehabilitation aimed at a specific impairment, but also at the societal level, for example the introduction of universal design to make ICT infrastructure more accessible, inclusive education systems, and community awareness programs to combat stigma. For purposes of social participation and the equalization of opportunities, the functional status – and how that impacts someone's life – is of interest and not necessarily the cause (medical or otherwise).

The implications for Brazil and Sao Paulo's Program related to the flexibility in this approach to disability, may be profound. If service provision is based on the disability prevalence, then clearly this would impact on policy, particularly in Brazil where essential resources and capital are scarce. However, one can ask "What are the implications of developing a national policy that provides AT or ICT services for 2.7% of the population if 13.4% require some service?" In the alternative, would it not be more appropriate and efficient to construct a long-term research agenda for AT and/or ICT technology targeted to the specific population that requires them? In Brazil, while 14.5% of the Census 2000 population, 67.6% had some visual impairment. Targeting specific sub-populations would be more cost-effective, and would provide for the equitable and efficient delivery of services. With the knowledge that many children with disabilities in Brazil do not attend school because of vision problems correctable by glasses, policy could be directed to target this specific sub-population, to provide necessary services and to rectify inequalities. A relatively minor and easily correctable functional problem that would have significant debilitating personal consequences could be avoided.

Regarding the use of ICT-based solutions, Brazil has committed itself to a digital inclusion effort for all segments of its population. Since 2005, the government of Brazil has invested significantly in digital inclusion projects. This activity has been developed and undertaken by the ministries of Communications, Planning and Science and Technology. In 2008, the Ministry of Communications invested $134 million in projects that include the deployment of Community Telecenters in cities around the country, as well as operating system access to broadband Internet. The Community Telecenters program is the federal government's effort to decrease the number of Brazilians who are excluded from the world of computing. The program involves the assembly and delivery of a computer center with Internet access, which serves a group of at least 10 people. Each telecentre kit consists of 11 computers - 10 terminals and a server - a laser printer, data projector and a router for Internet access; and, some furniture, including cabinets, chairs and tables.

The State of Sao Paulo's policy to provide for PwD is consistent with Brazil's Federal policy and the guidelines provided by the CRPD.

TECHNOLOGY INNOVATION FOR THE BENEFIT OF PwD

Brazil is one of the world's leading IT markets and the largest IT market in Latin America, representing more than 45% of the total investments for the sector in the region. According to Business Monitor International (BMI), it is projected to grow at a compound annual growth rate of 11% over the 2008-2013 periods. The total value of spending on IT products and services should pass US$30bn in 2011 and US$37bn by 2013. Brazil is a mature ICT market, with expenditure distributed between hardware, software and services in similar proportions than for large developed economies IT markets. PC penetration rate in Brazil, however, is less than 25% but the federal government has implemented programs to equip all elementary schools with computers. The number of mobile phones users reached 176.8 million in February 2010 and the market continues to show strong growth. By comparison, the number of landlines is approximately of 41.2 million.

One of the most important aspects of Brazil's ICT usage pattern from an accessibility standpoint is the rapid evolution of Internet usage. Brazil shows steady Internet usage growth, with the largest number of users in Latin America and 34% of its population using the Internet; persons with disabilities experience accessibility issues whether they have access to individual tools installed on a dedicated personal computer at home or at the office, or if they have access only to shared-access telecenters. Unlike the situation of the user of a dedicated personal computer at home or at the office, a user in a shared access situation cannot benefit from assistive technologies embedded in his or her equipment. These conditions have a bearing on how assistive technology can be made available to the greatest number of beneficiaries in Brazil.

ICT-based assistive technologies include a very diverse and complex group of equipment, software and services bringing accessibility solutions to PwD. It is a very fragmented industry worldwide and relies on a number of different channels for distribution, customer support and training. There are many definitions of Assistive Technology ranging from formal technical definitions maintained by organizations such as the WHO, to informal definitions generated by users themselves. The term "assistive technology" is closely related to "enabling technology", that is technology that enables access to information, communication or the environment. A broad definition is adopted here, that is, including technologies that enable access to other forms of technology, whether they be computers, phones, digital TV or home or office control systems or assistive technologies enabling and supporting Independent Living, personal mobility, working and communication (Piaggesi, et al, 2013).
ICT-based assistive technologies include:

- Palliative assistive technologies (ATs) aimed at compensating the lack of accessibility of mainstream ICT products and services to accommodate a person's access needs. Examples of such ATs would be magnifying software or contrast tuning add-on software when not included in an operating system. Such assistive technologies would not be needed with universally designed products, software or services. A significant number of assistive products and services can be considered as "palliative aftermarket products" which only exist because of the lack of universal design of mainstream products.

- Innovations driven by new ICT platforms such as embedded geo-positioning functionalities in a smart phone, enabling special applications servicing disabled persons such as path finding, proximity accessible services guides or emergency response functions. In such case, an innovative technology platform enables new assistive services for PwD which would not be possible otherwise. Those represent a large opportunity for cooperation between public and private sector, for CETI – D led consortia with the participation of service providers and product vendors.
- Condition-specific assistive technologies going beyond the scope of universally designed products and making it possible with a careful integration of products to develop solutions for persons with severe disabilities, for example using blue tooth technology and voice recognition to control house appliances from a single remote console or smart mobile phone; or embedding sensor technology in wheel chairs and a person's physical environment to enhance their maneuverability and safety. Those solutions tend to be developed by specialized enterprises and may include a significant amount of integration and support services.

PwD and their communities can derive enormous benefits from access to, and use of, assistive technologies (ATs) and information communication technologies (ICTs). ATs and ICTS can have a twofold impact on PwD. On the one hand, these technologies offer unprecedented potential for supporting innovative means of access and interaction to key aspects of life such as information, social exchanges, economic activity, education, and health. On the other hand, since access to these technologies is as relevant as physical accessibility, accessible AT and ICT solutions can constitute effective advantages for PwD. ICT-based assistive technologies can increase the possibilities for more participation of PwD in education, labor markets, and society at large. For instance, jobs in the technology sector do not depend on physical strength, but instead on intellectual knowledge and experience, meaning that someone with a physical disability can perform the tasks at the same level as a person without disabilities.

Regrettably, while it had been expected that more people would have access to information and knowledge as a result of advances in ATs and ICTs, for some segments of the world population the knowledge divide persists. Approximately 650 million people live with some type of disability, and with current trends in population, medical advances and an increasingly graying population, this number will only grow. PwD tend to be acutely vulnerable to exclusion. PwD are disproportionately poor and poor people are disproportionately disabled. Furthermore, there are an estimated 150 million children in the world with disabilities; about four-fifths of them in developing countries, as well as more millions live with disabled parents or relatives. Over 80% of PwD live in isolated rural areas in developing countries. Some 62 million children of primary school age have a disability; 186 million children with disabilities have not completed primary school, and fewer than 2% of children with disabilities in developing countries are in school. No society can ignore such a massive number of people and leave them to their own destiny. In addition to these circumstances, PwD also feel that they have very little to say in plans and programs that are supposedly provided for their welfare, for the improvement of their conditions. Any vision of empowering PwD must include the provision of access to information and knowledge, because that is the best way to empower people – to enable them to become productive citizens and to lead a life of dignity of their own (Piaggesi et al, 2013).

The Program described below tackles the challenge of making these technologies available to PwD in the State of Sao Paulo, supported by coordinated efforts with the private sector, academia and other sectors of society, following a pattern that is consistent with the architecture of the KE.

SEDPcD PROGRAM OF TECHNOLOGY INNOVATION FOR PwD

Objective

The Government of the State of Sao Paulo, through its Secretariat for the Rights of Persons with Disabilities (SEDPcD) started in 2013 a wide-ranging Program to promote the rehabilitation and social inclusion of PwD through the application of ICT-based assistive technologies, developing solutions to a level where they can be applied massively in a cost-effective way.
The Program is built upon three tenants:

- PwD have specific needs – transportation, communications, medical attention, public services, among others – of whose provision the whole society is responsible, not only the State;
- PwD have the potential to develop specific capabilities and specialized knowledge which must be developed through scientific research;
- Through social inclusion, PwD could make significant contributions to today's Knowledge Society and related Knowledge Economy

Specifically, SEDPcD's Program aimed to:

1. Attract high level Brazilian and international experts working in the various fields of interest for PwD, and offer them an environment where innovation and creativity are encouraged, in close interaction with the international community;
2. Conduct research to improve skills, particular conditions, and specific cognitive abilities of PwD, which could constitute attractive capabilities in the job market;
3. Produce knowledge about assistive technology for non-specialists and share it through different means (forums, blogs, guidelines, websites);
4. Act as a certifying agency for assistive technology;
5. Develop technological innovations, and their industrial applications, to generate products directed at facilitating the use of the specific abilities of PwD, improving their quality of life and facilitating their inclusion in society;
6. Develop technological solutions to improve rehabilitation and social inclusion for people with visual, hearing, physical and intellectual disabilities;
7. Conduct market research analysis to qualify demand and distribution channels;
8. Identify and develop job market niches able to utilize the specific capabilities of PwD in cooperation with private sector enterprises looking to pursue this new source of specialized labor force for the benefit of their own private companies;
9. Identify possible products, services and solutions that could be made in the main areas of interaction between PwD and the rest of society, in order to improve their social inclusion and quality of

life, starting from the architecture of housing and public services, to social communications and human relations;

10. Identify national and international financing mechanisms to support research; industrial innovation; education, training and job-generation; social structure adaptations and other proposals advanced by the Program with help from its support networks; and
11. Create communication mechanisms with organizations, councils of rights and public departments, to capture priority needs and share the projects developed.

Strategy

The Program will adopt as core strategy the application of the concept and instruments of the Knowledge Economy. For CETI-D, utilizing a KE strategy would mean to pursue a given concrete objective through simultaneous investment and work in the five areas that constitute the instruments of the KE (education, innovation, ICT infrastructure and enabling policies, complemented with social inclusion), not in one of them alone, but in all of them at the same time with highly focused purposes and doable targets.

Organizational Structure

For the implementation of the Program, the participation of a number of agencies and organization belonging to the public and private sectors is required.

Government, the host institution is the SEDPcD, the Government of Sao Paulo's Secretariat established in 2008 to promote the rights of persons with disabilities within the several levels of the public administration, aiming at prioritizing public policies that meet the demands of PwD, ensuring their inclusion into society and their participation in the sustainable development process. In line with the organizational structure of the State Government, the SEDPcD has the role of policy-maker, rather than an executive institution. To support actual rehabilitation activities, the SEDPcD goes through the Lucy Montoro Network, established also in 2008, for the purpose of providing rehabilitation services for patients with physical deficiencies.

The SEDPcD has pioneered the discussion of how to take advantage of ICT-based ATs into the work, not only of the Lucy Montoro Network, but more broadly, into the programming and budgets of many other public sector agencies in the State. Among those initiatives, the SEDPcD has funded the design and early development of the Program described here (at the time described as the establishment of a Center of Excellence for Technology Innovation in favor of Persons with Disabilities).

The SEDPcD counts on the support of the State Secretariat of Housing, through the participation of the Housing and Urban Development Company (CDHU) of the State of Sao Paulo. The State Law No. 905 of December 18, 1975, created CDHU as a State corporation linked to the Secretary of Housing of the Government of Sao Paulo, as the main promoter of social housing, being its mandate the execution of housing programs in the entire State of Sao Paulo, and aimed at lower income populations whose monthly household income range from one to ten minimum monthly wages. Also, as part of its property ownership regularization program, CDHU has been promoting since 1996, the provision of housing to families with PwD, allocating no less than 7% of the housing units raffled annually by the State under State Law No. 10.844. This includes the adaptation of housing units to guarantee the comfort, autonomy and accessibility of PwD, based on of State Decree No. 53.485 of September 28, 2008, which draws the policy of "Universal Rights" for PwD and housing. Such legislation has also established the framework for the "Terms of Cooperation" between SH/CDHU and SEDPcD of December 21, 2009. Sao Paulo's State Secretariat of Housing (SH) has instructed CDHU to further its involvement in creating better conditions for Persons with Disabilities (PwD) in social-interest housing, associating themselves to the efforts of SEDPcD. In the context of the Program, the Secretary of Housing and CDHU are expected to contribute with:

1. Identification of technology and innovation solutions to improve housing accessibility and functionality for PwD, and to form part of the specific line of financing within the CDHU in social housing;
2. Guiding the R&D activities of its Departments to cover the needs of specific projects selected by CDHU, which would later become products and services that would be part of its financing portfolio; and
3. Supporting technical oversight by CDHU of technology innovation projects contracted by CDHU but undertaken by third parties.

The Program also receives the support of the State Secretariat of Development. On December 21, 2009, the SEDPcD and the State Secretary of Development of the Government of Sao Paulo signed the "Terms for Cooperation" agreement which established the foundation for the implementation of CETI-D. Under such collaboration framework, the two State Secretaries agreed to:

1. Jointly developing and implementing technical cooperation projects aimed social inclusion, integration and support to persons with disabilities;
2. Exercise the necessary inter-institutional collaboration and coordination at the federal, state and municipal levels in the implementation of related programs and projects;
3. Provide specialized technical assistance and information in this field, towards the design and implementation of investment programs; and
4. Accompanying and validating the results of the projects and programmed activities vis-à-vis the joint objectives in the framework of the agreement.

Universities and Academia

The changing role of knowledge in society means that the research agendas of universities are increasingly defined through interaction with non-academic parties, in particular government and industry. As a result, the line between academic and non-academic realms is becoming blurred. Recent changes in the universities of developed countries suggest the emergence of an entrepreneurial model of academic research. The key feature of this model is acceptance by universities that they have a responsibility not only to provide teaching and carry out research, but also to contribute directly to the economic growth and social welfare of the society in which they are embedded.

Centers of Excellence for PwD

There is significant opportunity to engage in horizontal cooperation with centers of excellence for technology innovation around the world. Some of the most advanced are listed here:

- The Centre for Excellence in Universal Design (CEUD), Ireland, established in 2007 under the Disability Act 2005, is part of the National Disability Authority (NDA) of Ireland. NDA is the lead state agency on disability issues and universal design, providing independent expert advice to the Government on policy and practice. The Centre is dedicated to the principle of universal access, enabling people in Ireland to participate in a society that takes account of human difference and to interact with their environment to the best of their ability. The Centre focuses on three main areas of activity involving: standards development and promotion; education and professional development; and, awareness-raising.
- The Center for Assistive Technology and Environmental Access (CATEA), USA, is a multidisciplinary research and development center dedicated to promoting the health, activity and participation of people with all levels of ability through the application of assistive and universally designed technologies that enhance the usability, equitability and safety of real world products, environments, and devices.
- The Job Accomodation Network, USA is a service provided by the U.S. Department of Labor's Office of Disability Employment Policy, devoted to facilitating the employment and retention of workers with disabilities by providing employers, employment providers, people with disabilities, their family members, and other interested parties with information on job accommodations, entrepreneurship, and related subjects.
- The Mada Center for Assistive Technologies, Qatar, established in 2009 as an independent center to serve as a catalyst for research and development of ICT assistive technologies and to create public awareness around best practices and solutions. In addition to showcasing and facilitating the access to assistive technologies for PwD, the Center serves as a vehicle for cooperation with industry partners and to coordinate the efforts of existing institutions in Qatar and the region.

International Non-Governmental Organizations

SEDPcD has entered into cooperation agreements with two international NGOs to help the design of the Program, whose support could be important during project implementation as well:

1. Knowledge for Development (K4D), a US-based NGO devoted to providing project design and management support in subjects that pertain to KE applications; and
2. The Global Initiative for Inclusive ICTs (G3ICT), whose mission is to promote the rights of PwD in the digital age (https://g3ict.org/).

Both these NGOs have proven important in bringing the original project proposal and have subsequently collaborated with SEDPcD's activities in this area.

These organization can be useful in supporting the Program's promotion in international fora, supporting its search for international financial contributions, and promoting the participation of various academic, social, industrial, services, entrepreneurial and other sectors in the implementation of the Program.

Private Sector

SEDPcD engages the help of representatives from outstanding private companies and businesses in different areas of private investment, willing to participate voluntarily to support the work of the Program as it concerns its relations with the private, entrepreneurial, sector. Private sector participation is needed in order to:

1. Orient their R&D investment towards innovative industrial applications that facilitate access of PwD to public and private services, as well as products and services that foster the use of the specific abilities that are peculiar to people with disabilities and which could be highly useful in different industrial, commercial or service areas;
2. Strengthen the job market for people with disabilities where they can receive competitive wages and insert themselves in a productive cycle; and
3. Involve entrepreneurs to tap this underestimated potential regarding the fastest and cost-effective ways to incorporate people with disabilities in their everyday operations.

Program Components

Component 1: R&D in Specific Abilities, Innovation, Industrial Applications

The purpose of this component is to contribute to the fulfilment of three of the Program's objectives:

1. Attract high level Brazilian and international experts working in the various fields of interest for PwD, and offer them an environment where innovation and creativity are encouraged, in close interaction with the international community;
2. Conduct research to unveil and demonstrate skills, particular conditions, and specific cognitive abilities of PwD, which could constitute attractive capabilities in the job market; and
3. Develop technological innovations, and their industrial applications, to generate products directed at facilitating the activities of daily living of PwD, improving their quality of life and facilitating their inclusion in society.

In order to implement a significant R&D agenda, the Program works with private sector enterprises to tackle three complementary functions:

- Operate as a research and certification lab, where most promising projects are analyzed and their applications developed, and where products or services developed by other institutions could gain quality certification;
- Act as a clearing house for research and applied research projects conducted by others, establishing connections with organizations outside of Brazil; promoting peer reviews and other means of testing the proposals; and suggesting possible applications and development opportunities within CETI-D and through institutions to which CETI-D is associated; and
- Become a project funding mechanism if and when project proposals are deemed to have commercial or institutional value and could be subject to State, Federal or international financing.

Under this component, a number of activities are undertaken in close coordination with universities and research centers in Brazil and internationally, working in scientific and technological developments to prevent, deter, solve, or in any other way improve the conditions of people with disabilities. These activities are designed to create synergies, reduce duplication, and build critical mass in Brazil's and international research efforts directed towards meeting the needs of PwD.

Other activities under this component are directed towards acting to bridge the supply of technological innovation and its industrial applications, with the demand for such products and technologies useful to PwD. As part of this group of activities, the Program maintains direct communications between the supply and demand of technologically advanced products specialized in areas of interest of PwD. This interaction allows the Program to understand the workings of the market for these products and learn how to influence the market so as to include lower-income people with disabilities. Eventually, the Program would like to act as a "clearing house" for technologically advanced products which have been tested and approved by corresponding certifying authorities in their countries of origin.

Component 2: Job Creation, Education, Training and Business Services

This component contributes to the fulfilment of the Program's objective to identify and develop job market niches able to utilize the specific capabilities of PwD in cooperation with private sector enterprises looking to pursue this new source of specialized labor force for the benefit of their own private companies.

Through this component, the Program interacts with the academia and governmental and non-governmental organizations cooperating with the Program, to pursue activities in the fields of education and training, essential to develop the skill needed by PwD to participate effectively in the job market.

Under this component a number of activities are directed towards raising awareness among the public and private sectors of the potential job market value of people with disabilities, among them:

- Researches Brazilian and worldwide developments in education, professional qualification, and accessibility, aimed at improving the employability of PwD;
- Identifies new job opportunities for PwD, based on research, technological development and development of the job market;
- Develops campaigns to raise awareness among companies, entrepreneurs and academic institutions about the market's importance of the employability of PwD;
- Articulates and promotes partnerships among several society's areas to strengthen PwD's employability.

Additionally, this component aims to identify and contribute with the social transformation, based on equivalent opportunities, to ease the social inclusion of PwD. To do this, the component:

- Researches worldwide developments in culture, leisure, sport, urban design, housing, public services, and transportation infrastructure, to improve social inclusion of PwD;
- Develops campaigns to raise society's awareness towards an inclusive culture, that values diversity;
- Articulates and mediates PwD's priority needs, from society and public sector;
- Shares developed solutions and help train PwD and those serving PwD to use these solutions.

Component 3: Accessibility Infrastructure, Housing and Public Services

This component contributes to the fulfilment of the Program's objective to identify possible adaptations that could be made in the main areas of interaction between PwD and the rest of society, in order to improve their social inclusion and quality of life, starting from the architecture of housing and public services, to social communications and human relations.

Through this component, the Program brings in the cooperation of the various public sector agencies (State Secretariats, Municipalities, Federal Agencies, and others), whose collaboration will be needed to promote experimental projects in the fields of public transportation, housing and other public services.

One of the most promising activities undertaken under this component, is the cooperation between the SEDPcD and CDHU to insert technology innovations in social-interest housing. The central concept supporting this line of cooperation is that of "universal design", which refers to products, environments, programs and services to be usable by all people, to the greatest extent possible, without the need for adaptation or specialized design. "Universal design" shall not exclude assistive devices for particular groups of PwD where this is needed. In this case, universal design would be used to guide engineering and architectural strategies to provide public, low-income-housing with accessibility elements capable of ensuring the adequacy of the State's housing investment for the requirements of PwD.
Interaction with the Program:

1. Strengthens CDHU's capabilities for the conceptualization, design and implementation of technology innovation to improve accessibility and functionality for PwD;
2. Creates an incentive for specialized organizations, researches and innovators in the general public to device technology-based innovations applicable to housing units and urban complexes for the purpose of facilitating access and function for PwD; and leads the private construction sector to introduce similar innovations in housing developments elsewhere and raise the design and building standard to greater levels of accessibility and functionality for PwD.

Under this cooperation, the Program may fund:

- Innovations in design and functionality of access to housing units, including for example: electronic gate opening; automatic recognition and response devices; audio and other sensory guidance systems; voice-recognition activated devices; multi-modal signal, direction and orientation systems; multi-modal intercommunication systems;
- Development of technologies to improve functionality inside the housing units, including for example: modular design to enable flexible physical plant layout, adaptable to different needs; accessible fixtures and house electronics; voice-activated services (lights, stoves, showers, doors); multi-modal layout orientation devices; built-in multi-modal intercom systems; multi-modal automated alarm and response systems; built-in computer and internet services accessible to different disabilities;
- Development of innovations in urban public services to make them more accessible to PwD, including for example; accessible public transportation; multi-modal street layout message communications; multi-modal accessible public telecommunication centers; automated electronic urban service payment centers;

- Social inclusion mechanisms to foster integration of PwD in the urban context, including for example: recreation and fitness centers accessible to persons with different disabilities; job training for PwD to work in any of the service areas associated to the housing complexes and units; social communication skills tutoring and community awareness seminars; support and counseling services;
- Education, research, and inclusive policy development activities to support the above processes;
- Adaptation of all innovative technology designs to meet the demands of PwD belonging to different income groups.

Applied KE Structure

The Programs's simultaneous investments in research, technology, education, social inclusion and enabling policies – the main instruments of the Knowledge Economy—have direct application to the quest for greater and more productive inclusion of PwD in society. Implications for the Program's work can be found at the national-level (macro) and at the individual-level (micro).

At the macro-level, in order to bring PwD into inclusive knowledge societies, there are certain conditions that must be met, namely, the enabling of national policies and strategies. Capacity must be built so that people can undertake the activities that foster inclusion. This includes infrastructure development. If, for example, there is no ICT connectivity there is no access to content. In addition, even if there is ICT connectivity, there is also a need to develop capacity for generating local content in the language that people can understand. ICTs must be developed from the very beginning to be inclusive; otherwise, the cost of modifying the ICTs is going to be enormously prohibitive. Investments into research and development around ICT standards of services must be made available, otherwise it is not possible to guarantee and enable access to all.

At the micro-level, because disabilities involve functional limitations, it is often difficult or impossible for PwD to interact with their communities and societies without assistive technologies (ATs) and information communication technologies (ICTs). This technology can be highly technical and disability specific. Often, however, the provision of access for PwD to a mainstream technological innovation is more cost-effective than creating a specialized technology. For example, e-mail has revolutionized the communicative abilities of people who are deaf or hard-of-hearing at a fraction of the cost of the highly specialized communication equipment previously developed for their use; and personal computers, the Internet and e-mail have increased the social and economic access of people with impaired verbal capabilities in a similarly cost-effective way. Whether they be specially designed to meet the needs of PwD (e.g. Braille writers, prosthetic devices, wheelchairs and hearing aids) or innovative adaptations of mainstream technological innovations (e.g. e-mail, the Internet and personal computers), assistive technologies are vital to the process of providing social and environmental access to a significant cross-section of PwD.

In particular, this Program presents an innovative institutional and entrepreneurial system, where private sector organizations ensure that mainstream media and Internet are accessible and that specific services are developed for PwD. Additionally, areas of R&D opportunities for advanced condition specific ATs are identified in partnership with the private sector and universities. The latter are also active in providing education opportunities to feed the demand for specialized services in this field.

Finally, the leadership role adopted by SEDPcD and the participation of other crucial public sector entities ensure that enabling policies will be enacted, facilitated by suitable economic incentives and adequate institutional regime. The main lines of policy that must be developed jointly by these entities include:

1. Embrace and promote the "social" definition of disability "which results from the interaction between persons with impairments and attitudinal and environmental barriers";
2. Eliminate those barriers in cooperation with all relevant networks of stakeholders from both the public and private sectors;
3. Promote the role of disabled persons in society at all levels of responsibilities with role models, awareness raising and educational programs toward key influencers including employers;
4. Set new metrics in support of progressive inclusion strategies measuring their human rights, social and economic benefits;
5. Promote an effective Assistive Technologies eco-system by building critical mass via government procurement, standardization and consolidation of expertise and training via inter-agency coordination including science and technology, education, social services, health, housing and transportation services or the State of Sao Paulo;
6. Leverage Brazil's unique IT strengths by focusing R&D efforts on mobile phone applications and cloud based assistive technologies allowing disabled persons to access ATs free of charge and independently of the computer or point of access they use, including from any LAN House or telecenter.

Benefits and Obstacles

Benefits

In terms of benefits, the Program supports the Government of Sao Paulo's strategic agenda in the defense of the Rights of PwD forward into the realm of knowledge-based micro-economies; globalized services; state-of-the art technology and other means that would allow the State of Sao Paulo to promote the social inclusion of PwD as active and valuable members of society.

One of the difficulties for assistive technologies deployment, which IT industry service organizations are well aware of, is to make available a critical mass of competencies in various geographic areas for highly specific types of disabilities and in a variety of socio-economic contexts. While a fragmented approach cannot adequately serve the needs of PwD, consolidating expertise resources can be an important building block of an assistive technologies eco-system. The adoption of a far-reaching state-wide Program to tackle this complex undertaking, complete with inter-agency support, is bound to yield positive results in the State of Sao Paulo.

Obstacles

In terms of obstacles, developing AT and ICT products and services involves: a number of risks: research and development requires investment, some of which will not go into fruition; similarly, commercial application and production entail risk to the R&D center and to the user. A lot of it depends upon consumer and professional awareness, presence of guidance for product and service selection, which is not always present. Additionally, participants must have access to financing to acquire equipment and services, and cover service maintenance, repair and replacement. Finally, this endeavor requires the hiring of personnel and their training, and competing with the private sector for the highest skilled staff trained by the Program.

Many challenges, problems and obstacles relate to weaknesses in the market for ATs and ICTs. Sales may be limited by the small numbers of consumers and the lower than-average incomes of people with disabilities. Consumers and their families may not be aware of relevant product and service options, or may find them difficult to evaluate. Innovators and entrepreneurs may face high costs for manufacturing and distribution, as well as high research and development costs in relation to potential sales

Other obstacles are intrinsic to working in a governmental context, including difficulties in inadequacy of regulations and difficulties in inter-agency coordination, and financing. The Program attempts to lower these risks by engaging a full array of institutions and organizations, looking for society's support to sustain the effort.

REFERENCES

Brazilian Institute of Geography and Statistics. (2013). *Brazilian Census.* http://basededados.sedpcd.sp.gov.br/dadoscensitarios.php

IBGE. (2012). *2010 Census: number of Catholics falls and number of Protestants, Spiritists and persons without religion records increase.* https://censo2010.ibge.gov.br/en/noticias-censo?view=noticia&id=1&idnoticia=2170&t=censo-2010-numero-catolicos-cai-aumenta-evangelicos-espiritas-sem-religiao#:~:text=In%202010%2C%20the%20employed%20population,23.7%20million)%20were%20not%20employed

Piaggesi, D., Axel, L., Andres, G., Martin, G., & David, D. (2013). *Center of Excellence for Technology Innovation in Favor of Persons with Disabilities –CETI-D. Concept Paper and Schematic Proposal.* Framericas.

United Nations. (2008). *Convention on the Rights of Persons with Disabilities and Optional Protocol.* https://www.un.org/disabilities/documents/convention/convoptprot-e.pdf

Chapter 2
Visions of a More Sustainable Future of Work for the Underserved

JoAnn Rolle
Medgar Evers College, City University of New York, USA

EXECUTIVE SUMMARY

For generations, humanity has experienced socioeconomic disparities that are yet unresolved. Although education and training have transformed some individuals in society, they have not addressed the broader issues of sustainable employment for many underserved communities. Governments, corporations, policymakers, and numerous stakeholders have continued to address the problem, yielding disappointing results. Growing inequality in society continues to be a major concern. Vertical inequalities between the poor and the rich and horizontal inequalities between various groups of society have remained high for centuries. This chapter focuses on a variety of individual elements that outline the current challenges to humanity in an unequal society that certain communities continue to face, citing an unsustainable environment. Inequality and degradation negatively impact the future of work. Efforts continue to advance the future of work as a progressive, stable, and welcoming environment without the need for underserved communities to be marginalized.

"Struggle is a never-ending process. Freedom is never really won, you earn it in every generation." Coretta Scott King

"The future of work and entrepreneurship for the underserved is a struggle for humanity." J. D. Rolle

DOI: 10.4018/978-1-7998-8417-0.ch002

INTRODUCTION

Many areas shape the future of work. Recently, the focus has been on the impacts of the adoption of technologies and the augmentation of work tasks. However, that's not all. The future of work is also defined by five significant dimensions defined by the International Labor Office. These dimensions are job creation, job quality, social protection, wage and income inequalities, and social dialogue and industrial relations. These are considered integral elements of the 2030 Agenda for Sustainable Development (World Employment and Social Outlook Trends 2020 (2020)).

In the context of social protection, poverty and the poor have been with us for generations. In some cultures, there is no escape from class or the class system. In some cultures, race establishes a pseudo-class system by the historical and socioeconomic conditions that surround work and/or the lack thereof. It is no surprise that racism and poverty continue to plague the economy, especially for the majority who are poor.

The greatest share of the world's wealth has long been in the hands of a few men. None of this is new or surprising. What was surprising to us when we looked at the global data was that the middle class is shrinking—due not to gains of the bottom class, but to more gains of the upper-income class (Rolle et al., 2019). The income growth continues to be tilted to the upper-income class; hence, a greater share of aggregate income to the upper-income class indicates the share going to the middle to lower-income classes is falling. The share for middle-income households decreased from 61% in 1971 to 51% in 2019.

The increase is because middle-income families are more dependent on home equity as a source of wealth, whereas upper-income families have personal assets and business equity that provides a larger share of their wealth (Pew Research Center, 2020).

How then do we channel more of the lower- and middle-income class workers into jobs and/or entrepreneurial ventures that are more equitable and sustainable? How do we begin to take the gains from technology and use them as a force for equity? How do we transform informal economies into formal economies? Where do we start? There are many ideologies, abstract thoughts, and political strategies that have been executed in the past, yet for many demographics, such as Blacks in the U.S., the income and subsequent wealth gap are greater now.

In *A Handbook of the Future of Work and Entrepreneurship for the Underserved*, which posit different observations in different regions, a compelling one is in the beginning of chapter one, Social Innovation Strategies to Transform Slums Into Successful Neighborhoods in Latin America, by Mariano Bernardez. Bernardez and a team of researchers demonstrate that socioeconomic gains of the underserved can be achieved and as such the study is worthy of further review and discussion. Bernardez's work focuses on "nanoeconomics" and Roger Kaufman's Mega-planning, both of which have promising demonstrations of societal progress and success. They refer to their model as "The City Doctors framework, which organizes the goals and interventions around the neighborhood or city and its stakeholders." Their work suggests that bottom-up strategies starting from analyses within households are more powerful and provide more sustainable and equitable work and venture-based solutions for the future.

The focus of this study is to use these cited papers to examine the work presented, along with the use of other secondary sources, to determine sustainable socioeconomic and income gains for the underserved.

Hence the focus of this chapter is a brief examination of several related works. We intend that the review yields prospects for possible replication globally and as such produce sustainable socioeconomic and income gains for the underserved. As many of the world's most densely populated areas are in cities, Bernardez et al.'s potential solutions can help resolve some of the global income inequities that we continue to experience.

OBJECTIVES OF THE CHAPTER

The study will address the question of the future of work for the underserved in the following areas:

- Raise awareness of challenges of inclusiveness in the future of work for the underserved
- Frame the impact of the technology transformation on the underserved
- Build an ecosystem for an inclusive future for the underserved in the knowledge economy

METHODOLOGY

This study uses a literature review to compile information, discussion points, and conclusions on the subject matter of the future of the underserved. It is our intent that the literature review helps to assess collective evidence of other studies and research to form a basis of opinion or critique, a less systematic way of synthesizing previous research (Baumeister & Leary, 1997). A literature review can address research questions as a unique method that no other method or technique can. It also allows to identify or uncover areas that require further or future research (Snyder, 2019).

Selection of Research Method

The various research methods available cater to specific objectives. The chosen research area consists of analyzing and determining the future of work within the context of the knowledge economy, including any technological impacts on the underserved. The objective is to gain further insight as to the state of the knowledge economy with regard to those communities who continue to experience inequality and disparities, and seek to use the research method chosen to factually determine these disparities in greater detail.

We will strive to understand the disparities and challenges for the future work and also analyze the history of disparities and their impact on the general workforce environment, understand income shares, and finally, put forward some proposals for a more sustainable and equal workforce that promotes social protection and equality for all communities.

The analyses will be identified through secondary research material, and conclusions will be formed based on sources identified from the internet, such as peer-reviewed journals and textbooks. Gaps in existing knowledge will be analyzed to help support any arguments and conclusions drawn from the research.

LITERATURE REVIEW

Income Disparity and Its Impact on the Workforce

This element of the study focuses on the income disparities between Whites and Blacks, and men and women. Federico Cingano (2014) analyzed income inequality trends from the perspective of economic growth. Household incomes of the top 10% grew quicker compared to the poorest 10%. This has resulted in widening income inequality. The U.S. Internal Revenue Service used detailed tax data to show a pattern of income transfer. The United States has also seen a substantial widening of pay between males and females since the 1970s, and this trend is ongoing. Even as the economy continues to rise in one of the biggest countries in the world, people are accepting of low-wage jobs, even if they have middle-job skilled expertise. What's more, immigrant women are even more disadvantaged and have experienced more losses in employment opportunities than immigrant men.

A similar survey was conducted by Hersch (2017), who demonstrated male and female wage inequality between 1970 and 2004 within the labor market. While there has been a dramatic rise in female workers within the labor market, bringing them to 46% of the total workforce, the weekly earnings of female and male full-time workers are still unequal. By 2004, women were earning only 80% of men's wages. However, the differentiation of the labor market occupation categories could contribute to the larger wage for men (Hersch, 2017). From 2002 onwards, half of the roles within a professional capacity were covered by women, and females in the space of technical, sales, or administrative support constitute 60% of the labor workforce within these occupation types. While it can be said that the professional and managerial roles are contributing to a narrowing gap in wages, the results demonstrate that women continue to fare worse in pay compared to men within these occupations. The results of this study outline a global perception of female and male wage disparities but do not help us identify the cause of this wage disparity. It isn't only the wage structures set within those industries and roles, but the characteristics within those roles that are maintaining this unexplained wage disparity. Does this disparity have to do with discrimination, gender, and ethnicity, or is it simply biased towards women?

Figure 1. U.S. racial income gap

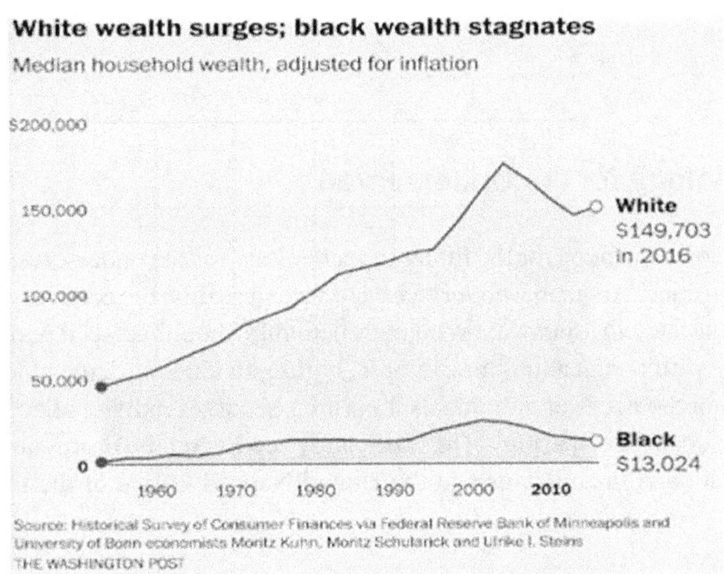

While there have been many civil rights laws, policies, and programs, the fundamental truth is that the gap between Whites and Blacks in the U.S. is greater now than at the start of the movement, as shown in Figure 1. The reasons vary but the root cause is that Blacks remain in lower-income yielding work without the same access to other income generation opportunities as other segments of the population (McKinsey & Company, 2019).

A report from the World Inequality Lab, specifically looking at the disparity between 2018 and 2020, found that wealth inequality largely remained the same.

In many regions, 10% of the population control over 50% or more of the wealth, as indicated in Figure 2. As the impact of the global pandemic continues to accelerate and exacerbate income inequities, so the United Nations' goal of eliminating poverty in our lifetime slips further into the oblivion of a future that is neither equitable nor sustainable. In the 2020 report whose results Figure 2 illustrates, the greatest disparities occur in Africa, Latin America, and Asia.

Figure 2. Worldwide income inequity

Source of World Map https://wid.world/world/#sptinc_p90p100_z/US;FR;DE;CN;ZA;GB;WO/last/eu/k/p/yearly/s/false/23.524/80/curve/false/country

Impacts of Technology for the Underserved

Rolle et al. (2019) explores the hope for the future of technology for the underserved. With technologies such as artificial intelligence, Amazon web services and virtual reality, the economy is rapidly changing, and Rolle et al.'s study states that innovation entrepreneurship should act as a pathway out of poverty. The use of technology within education, for example, highlights that on-demand learning will become a develop training to suit the needs of individuals. Learning becomes individualized without taking into account any racial and societal disparities. The 2019 study reports on the discussions between the Inter American Commission on Human Rights and the United Nations Office of the High Commission on

Human Rights. Their consultation was focused on combating racism, discrimination, xenophobia, and other forms of intolerance. The outcome was a recognition of the impossibility of changing "business and usual" solutions for those who are in poverty or jobless. The current experience continues to favor those who control capital and production to increase their share of market gains. As the world increases its technology pace, more undeserved communities are being left behind globally. While progress is being made, the result is that many underserved populations continue to be cast aside in an unequal economic system.

Another report from Dillahunt (n.d.) found that 1.6 billion people were "impoverished" with regards living conditions, health, and education, and identifies what needs to be done to reduce the disparities for those in poverty and classed as low-income families:

- Understand the specific needs of the underserved population to produce information and solutions that cater to them.
- Understand the constraints the underserved population face such as digital literacy, reading skills, and technological access.
- Address any social barriers that may hinder their ability, such as social and income inequalities.
- Create sustained technologies for limited-resources environments.

A study from Brunette et al. (2015) seeks to address technology within poor networking environments. With many struggling countries not having access to up-to-date information relating to health outbreaks, as an example, there is a necessity for the underserved to have access to a reliable data transfer and communication service which enables them to receive regular updates within limited-resource settings. A report from 2017 written by Van Winkle et al. (2017) explores digital injustice and barriers that continue to occur in the United States for the underserved. Their lack of healthcare access shows that digital innovation provides no incentives to support the underserved population.

Poverty and Environmental Degradation—A Major Constraint to Sustainable Development in the 21st Century

In this section, we intend to review how environmental degradation and poverty are correlated with a focus of the influence of their outcome on sustainable development.

Global institutions such as the U.N. and many developed countries, such as the U.S., are trying to achieve sustainability in terms of economic, ecological, and social well-being. More specifically, from the very start of this century, there have been efforts to control the uncontrolled consumption of natural resources by industrialized or developed countries. The unchecked practice of utilizing natural resources for meeting economic requirements has created a huge negative impact on the environment throughout the world, leading to its degradation.

What is more daunting is the effect of environmental degradation on the work force and poverty. Many studies have provided evidence for the argument that poverty and environmental degradation are correlated. (Cavendish, 2000; Samal et al., 2003). The impact of environment on the future of work will be significant. Global and local environmental degradation will cause job losses and will exacerbate working conditions and quality of work in developing countries. Its impact will be more prominent among the underserved and other vulnerable people (migrants, tribal people, etc.). It has the potential to turn environmental degradation into an issue of social injustice and inequality.

According to ILO (2018), in Asia, Africa, and the Pacific, about 1.2 billion jobs (40% of total jobs worldwide) are directly influenced by the environment. Moreover, most jobs throughout the world are highly dependent upon sustainable environment. However, the continuous exploitation of natural resources by developed countries over the years has put enormous pressure on the environment and its sustainability. Several authors agree that developing countries are net exporters of natural resources while developed countries act as the net importers of the natural resources (Tukker et al., 2014; Wiedmann et al., 2015). This has certainly become a strong reason for socioeconomic disparities between developed and developing nations. The carbon-extensive model adopted to meet economic needs has not only put ecological sustainability in jeopardy but has also created certain resource challenges for generation to come.

A specific illustration of what constitutes the three necessary dimensions of sustainability is provided by Besler (2009) in Figure 3.

Figure 3. The dimensions of sustainability.
Source: Besler (2009)

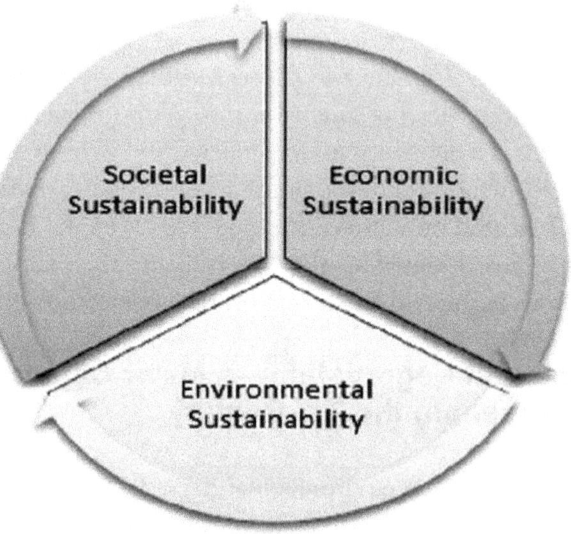

COMBATING ECONOMIC INEQUALITIES

In the previous section, we discovered how inequitably natural resources are employed, creating disparities in income and wealth. Income inequalities have been growing throughout the world primarily due to uneven distribution of natural resources and wealth between the so-called 1% and the remaining 99%. Even the top 1% shows huge within-group economic inequalities (Atkinson & Morelli, 2014). The significance of this issue can be gauged from the fact that reducing economic inequality has been treated as a U.N. Sustainable Development Goal. Economic inequality has led to a dramatic increase in extreme poverty in past years and is still on the rise. Future projections also predict that low-income communities will continue a trend towards extreme poverty by 2030. A graphical representation of extreme poverty scenario by the year 2030 in fragile or weak states is cited by Edward & Sumner (2013.

Figure 4. Scenario of extreme global poverty in 2030 in fragile states.
Source: Edward & Sumner (2013).

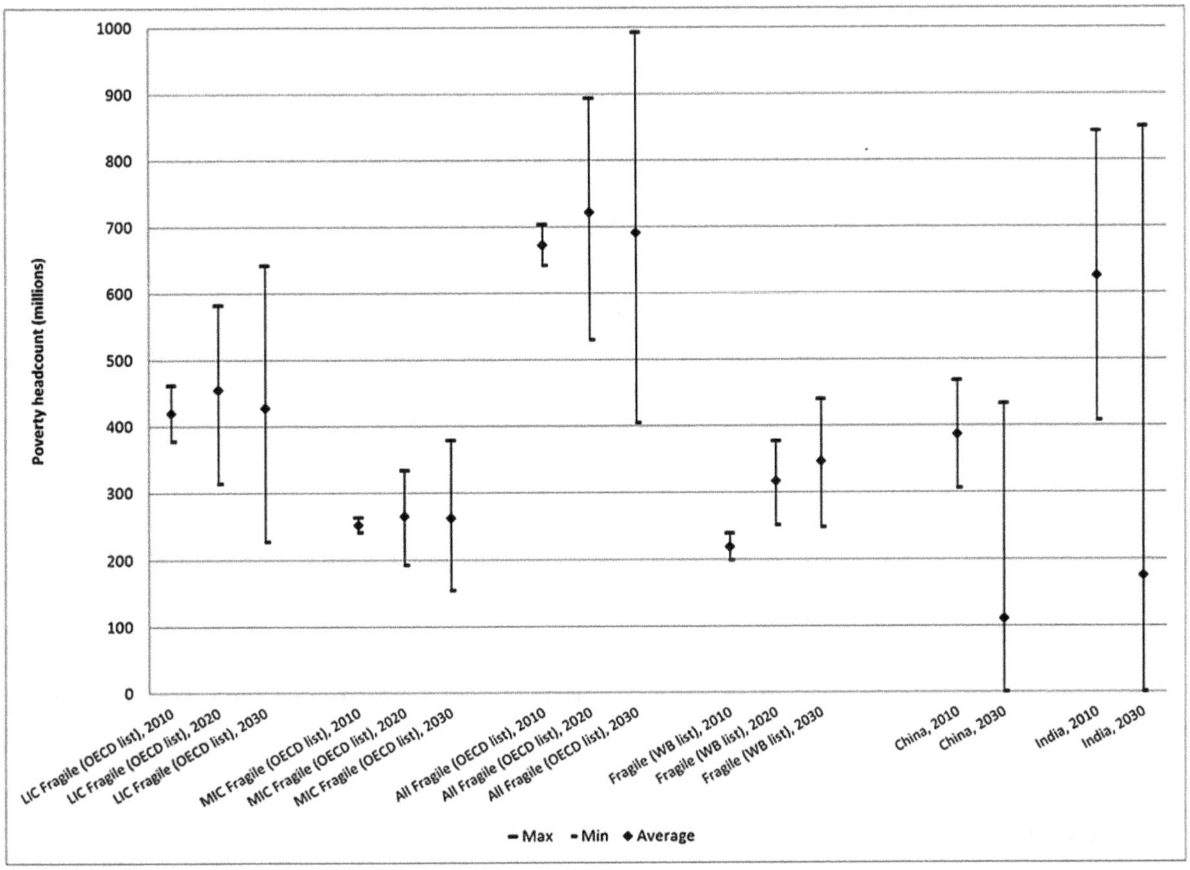

Under such a scenario, addressing inequalities between various groups has become pertinent. In this regard, "inclusive growth" is a concept that is worthy of more academic, social, and policy review. Inclusive growth advocates for fair and equitable distribution among economic participants, resulting in removing income disparities and reducing poverty. Instead of focusing on traditional models of economic outcomes, this concept explicitly concentrates on equity. A framework for policy action on inclusive growth developed by the Organization for Economic Co-operation and Development (OECD) is illustrated in Figure 5.

Figure 5. OECD framework for policy action on inclusive growth to tackle economic inequality.
Source: OECD (2018)

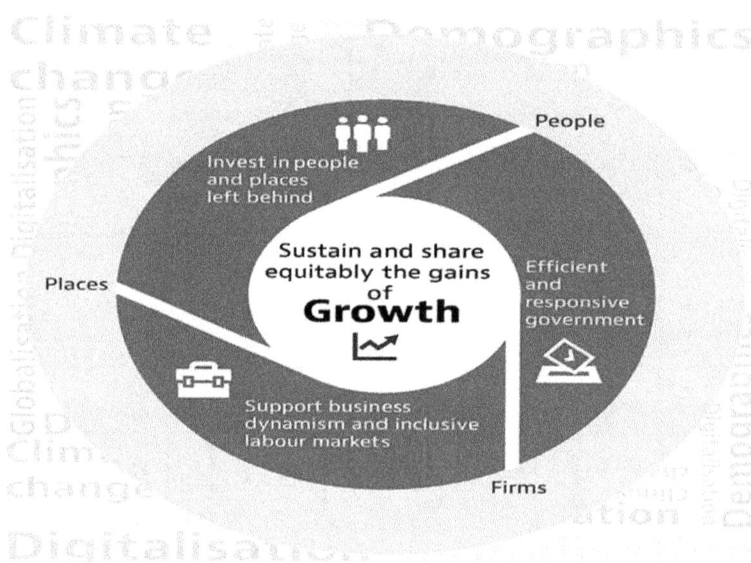

Moreover, as a general proposition, economic inequalities can be combatted as a byproduct of addressing global socioeconomic issues of racial discrimination and gender disparities, and by implementing innovative solutions such as job creation.

DISCUSSION

The Inclusive Need of a Community Engagement Strategy

The last section discussed the income inequity disparities that exist globally. This is extreme in regions such as Latin America. The Bernardez et al. (2018) Latin American work developed a framework to assess and address the multifaceted and complex challenges of inner-city slums. The study posits that multiple problems need multiple but coordinated solutions. The central focus of their work is community involvement and engagement in both problem assessment and systemic resolutions. They refer to their model as the City Doctors Framework (see Figure 6 below). Central to the framework is a shared vision that empowers community capacity building and yields sustained socioeconomic transformations. Central to urban transformation is an entrepreneurial ecosystem that supplies the needs of the city residents. Residents become venture owners and employers to meet the needs of the city. The workforce is developed internally through skill development and job creation. Private/public partnerships are developed to support the ecosystem. All systems work together to support the shared vision of sustained community development and economic growth.

Figure 6. City Doctors framework.
Source: Bernardez et al. (2012).

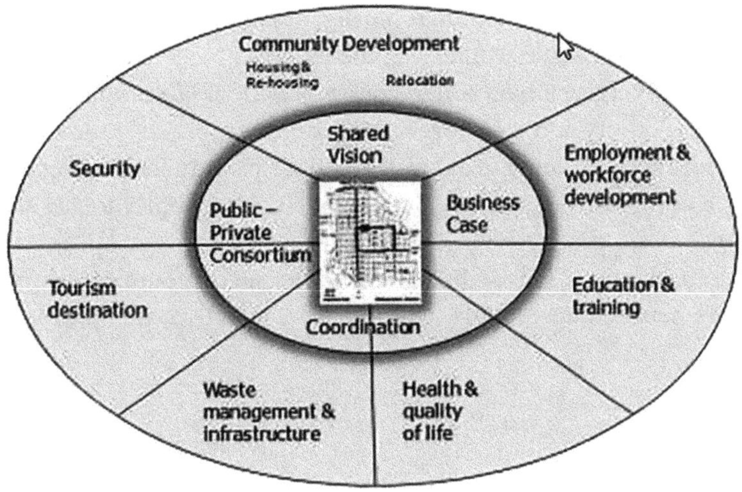

What makes the Bernardez et al. (2018) framework compelling is the demonstration that bottom-up, community-based strategies can be measured and analyzed for their impact on the social good.

Sustainability for Community and Capacity Building in the Future

Bernardez et al. (2018) share six concepts which address the issue of venture creation and employability among the underserved in city slums. Bagheri (2012) argues that slum neighborhoods are defined by four factors: health, poverty, unemployment and lack of economic facilities and unsuitable housing risks. These dangers may be caused by buildings that have experienced significant deterioration over time, that are located in a hazardous area, or that are exposed to harmful health conditions such as lack of safe drinking water or basic sanitation (Brooks, 2000). The high rates of poverty and unemployment among young people is a serious concern and undermines the security of the site and the adjacent township. As noted above, several disturbances prevented young people from achieving their ambitions. The lack of economic facilities and resources to pave the way for productive youth employment has not only contributed to the trend towards poverty but has also caused social damage like drug addiction among young people. And in terms of nutrition, people do not have a proper diet of foods rich in protein and vitamins.

Key factors for integrating and developing slum economies were cited in Bernardez (2021) in a chart on page 58. Bernardez took challenges and barriers in underserved communities and responded with social innovations that yielded community engagement, empowerment and improved prosperity.

Developing economies will likely be affected both positively and negatively by the latest developments in technology, including the Internet of Things, digital transformation, and big data analytics. Alonso et al. (2020) warn that developing nations face the possibility of greater income inequality since new technology shifts investments to wealthier countries where automation is already common. As automation threatens to replace rather than complement the rising labor force of less developed nations, it could have serious negative repercussions for jobs. To lessen the widening gap, developing-economy governments will need to implement measures to increase productivity and labor skills.

When new inventions and breakthroughs in technology arise, richer countries (such as the United States) tend to gain distance from less advanced countries (such as India). This is because new technology, like robots, tends to be less expensive than paying workers. There will also be more joblessness throughout the transition, and for some workers, in the long run.

It is impossible to stop divergence by a single course of action. Developing countries must invest in improving aggregate productivity and skill levels more urgently, because the technological revolution has made it necessary for them to compete against machines by complementing their workforce rather than by using robots to completely replace it. This is obviously simpler to say than do. In Alonso et al.'s (2020) model, total factor productivity is especially helpful, because it incentivizes more robots and physical capital accumulation. This is because it takes into account many institutional and other fundamental differences between developing and advanced countries that aren't represented by labor and capital inputs.

CONCLUSION

We shared a series of perspectives in our previous studies on the future of work and entrepreneurship; however, many others are asking similar questions, posing different factors and contingencies. Here, and in our 2019 paper, we focus on the future of work and entrepreneurship for the underserved.

We opened this chapter with a discussion of income inequity—which is why we are engaged in this work. We then presented one approach to address those inequities. We presented the first chapter of *A Handbook on The future of work and entrepreneurship for the underserved* which is one solution to address inequities in urban areas. The chapter demonstrates that there is hope to reduce disparities amongst communities to make way for multicultural, multigenerational, multidiscipline teams that are agile and resilient, and that persist through barriers both natural and man-made.

We discuss the pain of youth unemployment, small businesses, women-owned businesses, immigrant businesses, minorities, and elder work transitions. As a global society, we can no longer silently witness massive erosion of entire populations merely because they were born into a certain race, class, country, or region.

Other supported sources were used to understand the impact of technological challenges on the underserved. It is essential to understand the disparities in a world that is consumed with digital technologies, and what has been outlined in the 2021 Bernardez's study indicates that more needs to be done to ensure adequate infrastructure and coordination in all areas, especially for those who live in slums or can only afford to reside in lower-income residential areas.

Eventually, the pace and impact of technological innovations will flatten our once segregated socioeconomic boundaries, but it remains to be seen whether the innovations will reach all regardless of income and location (Daugherty & Wilson, 2018).

We intend that the work cited here and in our previous work will help stimulate further discussions and, more urgently, instigate action to help reduce humanity's challenges and create broader visions of coordination, collaboration, and community development for a more inclusive and sustainable global family.

REFERENCES

Alonso, C., Berg, A., Kothari, S., Papageorgiou, C., & Rehman, S. (2020). Will the AI revolution cause a great divergence? *IMF Working Papers, 2020*(184). doi:10.5089/9781513556505.001

AtkinsonA. B.MorelliS. (2014, March 8). Chartbook of economic inequality. SSRN. doi:10.2139/ssrn.2422269

Autor, D., Katz, L., & Kearney, M. (2008). Trends in U.S. Wage Inequality: Revising the Revisionists. *The Review of Economics and Statistics*, *90*(2), 300–323. doi:10.1162/rest.90.2.300

Bagheri, M. (2012, September). The Challenge of Slums: Socio-Economic Disparities. *International Journal of Social Science and Humanity*, *2*(5).

Baumeister, R. F., & Leary, M. R. (1997). Writing Narrative Literature Reviews. *Review of General Psychology*, *1*(3), 311–320. doi:10.1037/1089-2680.1.3.311

Bernardez, M. (2017, September 17). *Apps for positive social impact: From Uber™ to Neighbors™*. Retrieved from LinkedIn: https://www.linkedin.com/pulse/apps-positive-social-impact-from-uber-neighbors-mariano-bernardez/

Bernardez, M. (2021). Social Innovation strategies to transform slums into successful neighborhoods in Latin America. In J. A. Rolle, J. Kisato, & C. Kebaya (Eds.), *A handbook on the future of work and entrepreneurship for the underserved* (pp. 30–61). Centre for Business & Economic Research.

Bernardez, M., Arias Vallarino, C., Krivatsy, A., & Kaufman, R. (2012). City Doctors: A systemic approach to transform Colon City, Panama. *Performance Improvement Quarterly*, *4*(4), 41–60. doi:10.1002/piq.20125

Bernardez, M., & Perelrozen, M. (2019). Nanoeconomia del Barrio 31. *Performance Improvement Journal*, 12-18.

Besler, S. (2009). The effectiveness of the decision-making process and strategic consensus. *Journal of Public Administration,* 89 - 108. https://app.trdizin.gov.tr/publication/paper/detail/T1RFMk1qSXk=

Brooks, D. (2000). *Bobos in paradise: The new upper class and how they got there.* Simon & Schuster.

Brunette, W., Vigil, M., Pervaiz, F., & Levari, S. (2015). *Optimizing Mobile Application Communication for Challenged Network Environments*. Academic Press.

Cavendish, W. (2000). Empirical regularities in the poverty-environment relationship of rural households: Evidence from Zimbabwe. *World Development*, *28*(11), 1979–2003. doi:10.1016/S0305-750X(00)00066-8

Cingano, F. (2014). *Trends in income inequality and its impact on economic growth.* OECD Social, Employment and Migration Working Papers, No. 163, OECD Publishing. doi:10.1787/1815199X

Daugherty, P., & Wilson, J. (2018). *Human + machine: Reimagining work in the age of AI*. Harvard Business Review Press.

Dillahunt, T. (n.d.). *Technology for underserved communities; personal fabrication.* Association for Computing Machinery. http://www.tawannadillahunt.com/wp-content/uploads/2012/12/abridgedacmqueuearticle.pdf

Edward, P., & Sumner, A. (2013). *The future of global poverty in a multi-speed World: New estimates of scale and location, 2010–2030*. Center for Global Development.

Grero, M. L. (2018). *Mismatch between the education system and the job market in Sri Lanka with special reference to soft skills* [Unpublished doctoral dissertation]. AIMS College.

Hersch, J. (2017). Sex discrimination in the labor market. *Foundations and Trends in Microeconomics, 2*(4), 281–361. https://scholarship.law.vanderbilt.edu/faculty-publications/668

ILO. (2018), https://www.ilo.org/weso-greening/documents/WESO_Greening_EN_web2.pdf

McKinsey & Company. (2019, August 13). *The economic impact of closing the racial wealth gap*. https://www.mckinsey.com/industries/public-and-social-sector/our-insights/the-economic-impact-of-closing-the-racial-wealth-gap

OECD/European Union. (2015). *The missing entrepreneurs 2015: Policies for self-employment and entrepreneurship*. OECD Publishing; doi:10.1787/71b7a9bb-

OECD/European Union. (2018). *Meeting of the OECD Council at Ministerial Level*. OECD Publishing. https://www.oecd.org/mcm/2018/documents/C-MIN-2018-5-EN.pdf

Pew Research Center. (2020, January 9). *Most Americans say there is too much economic inequality in the U.S., but fewer than half call it a top priority* [Press release]. https://www.pewresearch.org/social-trends/wp-content/uploads/sites/3/2020/01/PSDT_01.09.20_economic-inequailty_FULL.pdf

Rolle, J., & Kisato, J. (2019). The future of work and entrepreneurship for the underserved. *The Business & Management Review, 10*(2), 224–234.

Samal, P. K., Palni, L. M. S., & Agrawal, D. K. (2003). Ecology, ecological poverty and sustainable development in Central Himalayan region of India. *International Journal of Sustainable Development and World Ecology, 10*(2), 157–168. doi:10.1080/13504500309469794

Snyder, H. (2019). Literature review as a research methodology: An overview and guidelines. *Journal of Business Research, 104*, 333–339. doi:10.1016/j.jbusres.2019.07.039

United Nations Department of Economic and Social Affairs. (2020). *World social report 2020: Inequality in a rapidly changing world*. https://www.un.org/development/desa/dspd/wp-content/uploads/sites/22/2020/01/World-Social-Report-2020-FullReport.pdf

Van Winkle, B., Carpenter, N., & Moscucci, M. (2021). Why aren't our digital solutions working for everyone? *AMA Journal of Ethics, 19*(11), 1116–1124. doi:10.1001/journalofethics.2017.19.11.stas2-1711 PMID:29168683

Wiedmann, T. O., Schandl, H., Lenzen, M., Moran, D., Suh, S., West, J., & Kanemoto, K. (2015). The material footprint of nations. *Proceedings of the National Academy of Sciences of the United States of America, 112*(20), 6271–6276. doi:10.1073/pnas.1220362110 PMID:24003158

World Employment and Social Outlook Trends. (2020). *ILO*. https://www.ilo.org/wcmsp5/groups/public/---dgreports/---dcomm/---publ/documents/publication/wcms_734455.pdf

World Inequality Lab. (2020). *2020 Report update*. https://wid.world/fr/news-article/global-inequality-data-2020-update

Section 2
Health

Chapter 3
Re-AbilityLab:
Innovation and Strategic Aspects of the Knowledge Economy - Innovative Elements in Rehabilitation

Linamara Rizzo Battistella
Faculty of Medicine, University of São Paulo, Brazil

Lilian Aparecida Treff
Faculty of Medicine, University of São Paulo, Brazil

EXECUTIVE SUMMARY

This study aims to show the methodology of implementation of the Skills Laboratories (Re-AbilityLab) at the Institute of Physical Medicine and Rehabilitation of the Hospital das Clínicas of the Faculty of Medicine of the University of São Paulo. These Skill Labs offer activities to maximize patient performance by promoting specific functional outcomes, which are described in the International Classification of Functionality. The activities are dynamic and carried out by a multidisciplinary team in the areas of health, education, and management. Innovation and strategic aspects of the knowledge economy are structured in the management of this project to enhance the achievement of purposes and results. The implementation process includes solutions adopted, definition of responsibilities, difficulties faced, benefits, functionality of the methods applied, and lessons learned. Mapping the process from the current scenario to the desired contributes to the transition from a care model (linear, refractory, obsolete) to an exponential model of care (intangibles, incremental innovation).

INTRODUCTION

The Institute of Physical Medicine and Rehabilitation of the Hospital das Clínicas of the Faculty of Medicine of the University of São Paulo is part of the Lucy Montoro Rehabilitation Network, which was created by the Government of the State of São Paulo, by decree 52,973, of 2008, regulated by Decree 55,739 of 2010 and amended by Decree 58,050 of 2012. The Lucy Montoro Rehabilitation Network

DOI: 10.4018/978-1-7998-8417-0.ch003

aims to provide the best and most advanced rehabilitation treatment for patients with disabling, motor and sensory-motor disabilities. The Network carries out specific rehabilitation programs, according to the characteristics of each patient. The treatments are carried out by a multidisciplinary team in the health area, including physical doctors, nurses, physiotherapists, nutritionists, psychologists, occupational therapists, social workers, physical educators, specific speech therapistsin theareaof management. Currently the Lucy Montoro Network has 6 units in operation, in the State of São Paulo. In addition to internationally promoting the Hospital das Clínicas (HC) brand and the increase in *networking* between the various actors of the state and municipal health value chain, and its integration into reference and counter-reference networks, which induce the robustness of the business and scientific fabric.

This article presents the implementation of the Skills Laboratories - Re-AbilityLab, focused on specific functional results, and the activities are correlated with the International Classification of Functionality - ICF, where the dynamics of knowledge requires the multidisciplinary team to develop conducts that contemplate creative exchanges between different specialties and areas of knowledge, horizontality of powers, co-responsibilities and self-organization.

These LABs aim to integrate activities through development trails and strengthen the rehabilitation process, valuing and expanding the functional capacity and autonomy of patients, to consolidate therapeutic objectives of patients in the units of the Lucy Montoro Rehabilitation Network. In addition, it describes the implementation process, solutions adopted, attributions and activities developed, difficulties faced, lessons learned, results and benefits. In addition to demonstrating the functionality of the methodology and its strategic formulation (Figure I), structured in agile project management.

Figure 1. Stages of the Strategy Formulation
(elaborated by the authors)

Thus, the re-abilitylab proposal is an approach centered on the individual's perception of its functioning in various areas of life, for example: physical, occupational, psychological and social aspects. In this context, it aims to help patients achieve better results, obtain functional independence, autonomy, improving and improving the post-rehabilitation process. It is possible, therefore, to consider part of the scope the modes of knowledge conversion, which aims at the transfer of knowledge and technologies produced by basic science research in new approaches of prevention, diagnosis and treatment to promote health.

In addition, the implanted post-rehabilitation service provide conditions for maintaining the physical and functional health status acquired in rehabilitation by patients. This prevents impairment of your motor and neurological capacity after therapy. Adaptability and technologies are considered the vital forces for this new model of generating health value. In view of this, innovation has added new features to day-to-day practice, to further improve service and make it advantageous for patients. Moreover, the management of knowledge, the valorization of tacit knowledge and the methods for outsourcing knowledge become focuses in the current scenario. The value of knowledge is not new, the novelty is the importance of knowledge as a decisive resource for organizations. Reiterating the statement stated by Davenport and Prusak (1998, p.6) "knowledge is produced in working minds". So much so that it can be found in the processes, practices and documentation of organizations. The role of knowledge management is to create means to transport, transfer, market or store knowledge. For both Earth (2000, p. 70) notes that:

Knowledge Management is thus intrinsically linked to the ability of companies to use and combine the various sources and types of organizational knowledge to develop specific skills and innovative capacity, which are permanently translated into new products, processes, management systems and market leadership.

To achieve effective, strategic and results-oriented management, the methodology presented was created based on agile project management, defined by groups of processes in project management: the main goal is divided into small and *short steps called sprints;* sprint planning *meetings (weekly)* covering aspects of management, monitoring and organization. Among the practices identified combination and outsourcing of knowledge providing shared greatness, application of perceptions through simplified processes, capillarity of knowledge at any levels of organizational operation, support to patient-centered care and adherence to the participatory management model. The concepts and models proposed by the authors privilege the interaction between people and use knowledge for the benefit of the Institution. Therefore, in the emphasis dedicated to the urgent need to identify and solve the problems that undermine the effective transfer of scientific progress and applied and useful knowledge, the structure of the knowledge economy was adopted in the generation of intangible assets and tangible resources. The challenge of converging efforts in the implementation of the Re-AbilityLab model through the generation, accumulation and application of knowledge, the metaphor of the Triple Helix (University, Government, Company) is useful as an analytical framework for understanding the processes of innovation and the proposition and implementation of public policies, aimed at expanding and supporting the interaction between the actors of the different helixes. The proposal is that the effectiveness of the activities carried out in the Skills Laboratories, be applied in a wholesome and simplified way, generating learning and new ways of thinking about post-rehabilitation practices. Thus, the process focuses on the results that can come from benefits for people with disabilities included in society, and for the community as a whole.

The Value Proposition of Skills Labs - Re-AbilityLab

In practice, skills labs are open to the public, coming from a Rehabilitation Program. Knowledge is acquired from technological tools and specific content. The activities proposed and developed in each LAB are correlated with the International Classification of Functionality - CIF, and are managed by a multidisciplinary team.

The *International Classification of Functioning, Disability and Health, more commonly known as* ICF, is a World Health Organization (WHO) classification of domains with health descriptions and health-related states related to body, individual and social perspectives. Since an individual's functionality and inability occur in a context, ICF also includes a list of environmental factors[1]. These Laboratories focus on attention, coordination, dexterity, memory and proprioception. In addition to valuing and expanding the autonomy and independence of the patient, in a stimulating, challenging and supportive environment. In parallel, recreational and cultural activities are integrated, focused on the leading role and social participation of the patient and they family.

In view of the questions mentioned, this work aims to evaluate the individual's perceptions about various perspectives of his life and not merely the disability itself. It is expected that this knowledge can contribute in several aspects: first, that allows an appreciation of the perceptions of people with disabilities in relation to the different dimensions of their lives; identify these multidimensional aspects to enhance independence, quality of life, well-being, mobility and functional improvement. Moreover, provide data to broaden the look of the rehabilitation professional; support plans and actions in society and public policy with a view to the functionality of these individuals and social inclusion. It is also notepoint that this has also been a global proposal that the WHO has presented as a perspective, including the elaboration of measurement instruments such as the ICF (used as part of this methodology) or for the evaluation of quality of life by the WHOQOL (BAMPI, GUILHEM, LIMA, 2008).

What Is the Function of These Laboratories and How Do They Impact Society?

The main function of LABs is to promote the maintenance and expansion of functional capacity and autonomy of patients. The spaces were designed so that the largest number of people with disabilities can have easier access to innovations, technological tools and contents that stimulate self-esteem and protagonism and recognize the value of one's own capacity. After all, it is from individual experiences that many ideas and projects end up becoming important in the generation of new businesses, valuing entrepreneurial behavior skills. Another goal is to encourage the culture of "getting your hands dirty", that is, to make more people interested in the development of products, services and actions — from self-care and health care, to a chair or packaging. Using the technological resources of the universe of robotics and electronics and reoperating with the help of more rudimentary techniques, such as joinery and crafts, new products and even new business can emerge. After all, the idea is to provide an inclusive environment for people with functionality restrictions and capacity limitations in the different lifecycles. All activities are offered after functional/global evaluation. The population that enjoys LABs becomes more empowered, learning to deal with new technologies and putting their ideas and plans into practice. Thus, it is possible to solve many everyday problems from the new businesses, products, solutions and actions created in the laboratories.

In the strategic formulation of the implementation phases of the LABs, we relate the process involved in the activities inserted in development trails, which is not only concerned with the acquisition of knowledge, but also with the gain of functionality by the patient, relating to the practical application of learning and indicating its degree of evolution, 'based on the International Coding of Functionality (ICF). This means that when walking the development trails, the patient will absorb knowledge and techniques that he will put into practice during the program, and in activities of daily living. With the purpose of evaluating the results, the Multidisciplinary Team will apply a Functional/Global Assessment that will contain the patient's clinical summary and the respective current objective (they jointly decide the main objective for the patient being treated). Having as a principle to measure how much the patient will perform during the execution of the activities allowing the care to be truly resolutive, an Intermediate Evaluation will be applied. After the end of the trail, a Final Assessment will be applied to assess and identify the patient's progress in relation to the degree of functionality. Thus, health professionals will have a stronger basis for strengthening actions with the patient, effectively contributing to their self-health and quality of life. Moreover, the development trails indicate a path based on the linear model where the patient in the execution of the proposed activities, is encouraged to be the protagonist of his development, and has as a pre-requisite to advance, complete the previous. And another path based on the grouped model where the patient is free to choose what he wants to perform in a sequence of experiments, as indicated in Figure II– Development Trail Model.

Figure 2. Development Trail Model
(elaborated by the authors)

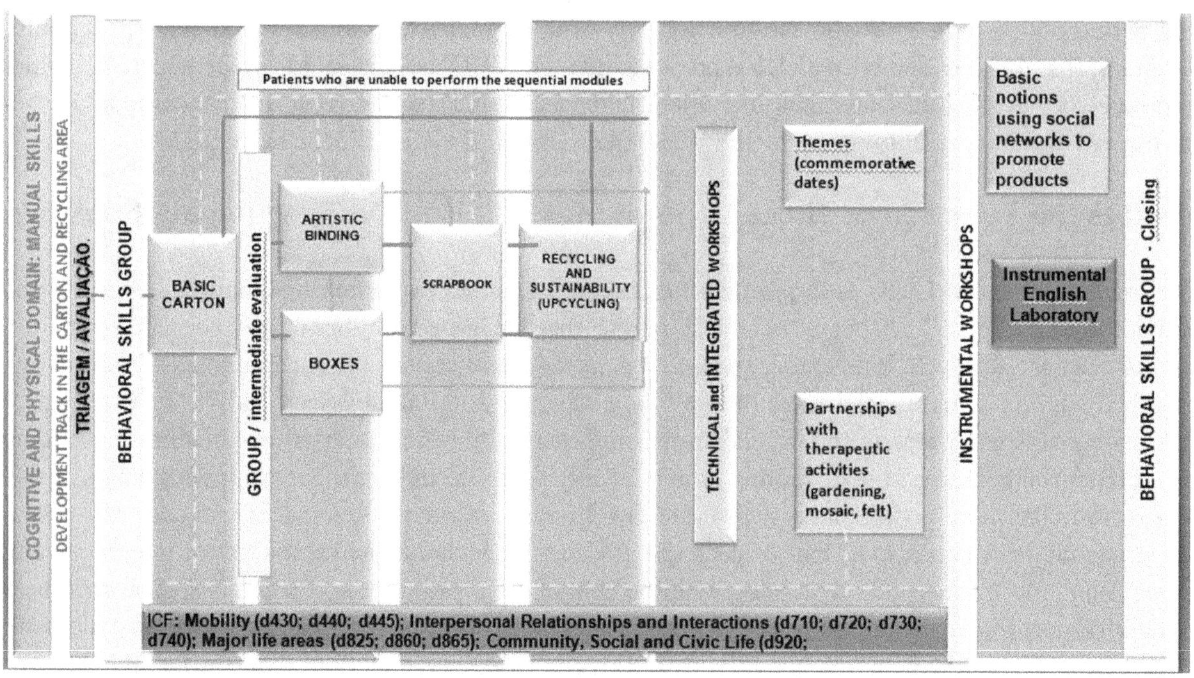

The Development Trails are inserted in the context of Skills Workers and present characteristics that enable continuous growth, which allows monitoring the needs and potential of the patient helping him to gain function, gain independence and autonomy through the production of care. In other words, the trails represent a path to be followed by the patient who, knowing the resources at they disposal, wants to improve they physical, motor and cognitive performance.

Skill Labs Offer

- **Activities of Daily Living and Practical Living** – aimed at improving complex motor activities, coordination in activities of daily living and in situations identified by patients and caregivers.
- **Independence and Self-care** - assists in the process of adaptation and maintenance of the orientations received during the period of treatment in rehabilitation.
- **Communication and Functionality** - offers alternative and playful solutions to make communication and the expand are verbal and non-verbal.
- **Global functionality** - for activities that require agility, balance and coordination. These activities produce qualitative changes that favor the quality of life, well-being and autonomy of people with disabilities, using a dynamic and systemic approach to rationalize a new process that guide evaluation and intervention, restoring the patient's functional gain.

General Objective

It was limited as the general objective of the work within the context of a Post Rehabilitation Program, the survey of information and development of studies to enable the implementation of the Skills Laboratories with all stages of detailed operation, valuing the functional condição of patients of the Lapa Unit, of the Lucy Montoro Rehabilitation Network.

Specific Objective

In addition, it is also intended to achieve the following specific objectives: to implement Skill Laboratories focused on specific functional requirements codified in the International Classification of Functionality - ICF; to describe the evolutionary path of the methodology in the implementation of the Re-AbilityLab model, based on the management of agile projects as a sustainability pillar; identify and analyze the main challenges for implementation, based on the evidence collected and examined, based on the expansion of the concept of value in health, placing the needs of the patient as the center of the process and the production of care; analyze the perception of the multidisciplinary team in relation to the evolution of the patient in an integral way, focusing on the best clinical practices with transdisciplinary approach (articulation between the various knowledge).

THEORETICAL APPROACHES ON INNOVATION AND THE ECONOMY OF KNOWLEDGE IN HEALTH SERVICES

The theoretical-conceptual framework was obtained through a literature review on quality services and innovation in the health area (models - methodologies), knowledge economy (knowledge conversion process) and patient-centered care (strategic guideline). We propose to provide the basis for strategic decisions and promote reflections that take into account various approaches, seeking in several sources elements that provide support for a vertical study of the issue.

The main challenge faced by the public sector is to provide quality services with scarce resources and limited operational capacity (Alberti & Bertucci, 2006). With regard to public health, the challenges faced are alarming: deficiency in the physical structure, absence of materials, equipment and medicines, in addition to the small number of employees, are problems that permeate most Brazilian health services. For Madeiro (2013), there is no doubt that public health in Brazil is in crisis. It is in this context that innovation has been considered as a strategic factor to improve the quality of public services for citizens, as well as to address social challenges and improve social well-being (Bloch, 2011). Through innovation, it is possible to increase the responsiveness of public services to local and individual needs by developing better ways to solve problems and use available resources. Although innovation is recognized as a key activity to improve the quality of public services, the number of innovations in public organizations is below expectations (Storey, 2000). In addition, research results (Resende Júnior & Guimarães, 2012) have drawn attention to the fact that only 5% of publications on innovations in services have focused on public sector activities, and more knowledge on the subject in question is needed (Lima & Vargas, 2012). In this sense, Gallouj and Zanfei (2013), Brandão and Bruno-Faria (2013) and Ferreira, Tete, Silva Filho, & Sousa (2015) state that there are important theoretical gaps regarding the elements that induce and inhibit innovation in the public sector, recommending that new research aligned with these themes is recommended. In an attempt to recognize the characteristics of the public sector, Koch and Hauknes (2005, p.9) present a definition of innovation that recognizes the context of the nature of its result: "Innovation is the implementation or performance of a new specific form or repertoire of social action, deliberately implemented by an entity in thecontext of the objectives and functionalities of its activities". On the differences in innovation in thepublic and private sectors, Roste and Miles (2005) and Bugge, Hauknes, Bloch, & Slipersaeter (2010) claim that the main one is motivation. While in the private sector the main motivation is the search for profit due to market conditions, to require the company to innovate to maintain its competitiveness, in the public sector the motivation is related to the enactment of new public policies, since any change in the political framework demands innovations of many kinds.

Given this perspective, there is no innovation without knowledge. The application of knowledge management to innovation management has high potential to contribute to results. In a definition of knowledge management we can find how to organize and systematize in all points of contact, the ability to capture, generate, create, analyze, translate, transform, model, store, disseminate, deploy and manage information, both internal and external and this information should be transformed into knowledge and distributed to stakeholders (COLLISON, 2001). This shows the appreciation of tacit knowledge and the effort to make it explicit for the common good. Thus, this study consists of exploring the potential of the Knowledge Economy approach as a perspective of interest in the post-rehabilitation process, based on the applicability of knowledge and its respective evidence to promote health. The underlying cause of the great transformation of the knowledge economy is the emergence of intellect and new management technologies as highly manageable assets. Once tacit knowledge has reached this state of explicitness, it can be shared and become part of a broader repertoire of knowledge that employees use to transform the design and supply of products and services. This allows tacit knowledge to be made explicit as we represent intuitive understandings in the form of "metaphors, analogies, concepts, hypotheses or models".

In 1998, a report by the Organization for Economic Cooperation and Development (OECD) stated that more than 50% of the Gross Domestic Product (GDP) of developed countries was the result of the use of knowledge (CAVALCANTI; GOMES, GOHETS PEREIRA, 2001). That same year, Robert Reich, in his article *The Company of the Future,* makes the following placement: Do you want to build a company that will survive a good pioneering idea? Create a culture that values learning. According to Choo, about 80% of the existing knowledge within a company is stored in people's heads (tacit knowledge) in the form of experience and not registered anywhere, and 20% remaining, only a fifth of it is stored in a structured way. (CHOO, 1988).

According to the conclusion of Nonaka and Takeuchi (1997), the success of organizations is the result of the ability and specialization in the "creation of organizational knowledge", the culture of managing knowledge through socialization to enable innovation both in the service and in the product offered, these organizations are pioneers and fundamental in innovation in a continuous, incremental and spiral way. Kanaane and Ortigoso (2010) refer to the age of knowledge, emphasizing that society is facing a universe of immense complexity and full of challenges, but affirm that education, training, information, training and the development of partnerships are pointed out as essential resources for organizations to succeed in this new scenario. The same authors also present the view on the importance of knowledge for companies to develop successfully, their activities:

Knowledge is the strategic insum of production and companies are increasingly becoming aware that it is necessary to treat it with appropriate methods, methodologies and tools so that the trinomial – processing data, processing information and managing knowledge – becomes the dynamic axis of personal and organizational results (KANAANE; ORTIGOSO, 2010, p. 56).

In relation to the age of knowledge, Stewart (1998) argues that the new economy will transform the old economy and reduce its relative importance, but it will not kill it. According to the author, no one can say with certainty that new forms of work and prosperity this revolution will create; because in a revolution, the only certainty is surprise. But it is already obvious, according to him, that success in a knowledge-based economy depends on new skills and new types of organizations and management.

From the definitions exposed, it can be understood that knowledge comes from the reasoning capacity of the human being, so this is a tool that only the same has and that if used, does not wear, does not lose purchasing value, does not depreciate, moreover, what occurs is the opposite of this, because through its insertion, knowledge makes any asset of the organization even more valued.

In view ofthis content, the methodology proposed in the implementation of Re-AbilityLab is the result of the role of knowledge in the knowledge economy, about the connections that can be established through organized propositions of facts or ideas, presenting an experimental result. Characterized by a constant flow, in a back-and-turn between the fundamental and the applied, between the theoretical and the practical. Knowledge can be created by professionals who facilitate a "spiral of interactions" between explicit knowledge - in terms of Nonaka and Takeuchi, information communicated orally or in written form - and the tacit knowledge they developed intuitively and naturalistically at work.

Despite conceptual discussions, there are studies arguing that health innovations can boost the expansion of access, as well as assist in the adequacy of the health system to the needs of the population, especially when advocating the impacts of Information and Communication Technology (ICT) on the reorganization and effectiveness of health systems. However, it is worth noting that the predicted social change would be radical, far-reaching and extensively changing the technological base. This implies that new technologies would not be used only to improve current approaches to health problems, but to change them (GREENHALGH, 2012). The continuous search for innovation can be considered as a means capable of enabling organizational adaptation, since it allows the reconfiguration of internal routines and external offerings, the valorization of resources, new products, services and processes (SALGE, 2012).

Thus, the Re-AbilityLab model aims to understand the points of dynamism of the generation and dissemination of innovations in health services for the ability to adapt the different elements of the health system, reproducing a transformation in the way of conducting the patient during the post-rehabilitation program. The activities offered are based on practice using the science, technology and innovation models in the development of new products and services. Interdisciplinary and transdisciplinary practices aimed at the constitution of unity or integrality without, however, losing multiplicity presupposes living with diversity, since they put in communication different ways of describing, analyzing, explaining and intervening in the patient's reality.

MAIN FOCUS

Dissemination of Knowledge and the Challenges of Innovation to Changes in Health Practice

Knowledge can be considered as the "valorization" of technical information incorporated through shared personal experience or not. For Davenport and Prusak (1998) the concept of knowledge is part of the difference between dado, information and knowledge consists in the combination of values, contextualized information and experiences that provide a framework for evaluating and incorporating new experiences and information. It originates in people's minds, but can dissipate in organizations through documents, databases, processes, practices and corporate standards. In the Knowledge Economy, knowledge isused to generate tangibleand intangible values. Drucker (1987), however, warn to some care that must be taken in relation to innovations, such as tuning innovation with strategic realities. Since the concept of innovation unfolds in other categories and its application for the analysis of services raises specific debates, scholars of the theme tend to converge around the need to problematize it, extending it and translating it to make it operational in the face of the singularities of health services.

Therefore, theoretical efforts focus on the elaboration of definitions that allow "transporting" classic concepts of innovation for health and health services (KALUZNY, 1970).

Notably through the implementation of the Re-AbilityLab methodology (Figure III), which based on a *framework of agile,* iterative and incremental projects, facilitated the transfer of knowledge in the execution of strategies. To this end, previous experiences were used to improve risk control and future decisions; application of new planning techniques; increased flow of information on the services offered; greater ability to introduce changes in the design of processes and definition of indicators; investigate causes and map potential solutions; treat barriers and deviations with agility; estimate theability to adapt to change: to view mistakes as an opportunity for learning - experimentation; manage the patient experience during all contact moments so that it can be mapped and optimized; to make thehands quickly and more frequently and with value tothe patient; respond quickly to changes, without losing the moment or vision; implement actions to correct the route and evaluate effectiveness.

Figure 3. Steps of the RE-AbilityLab Model Methodology
(Created by the authors)

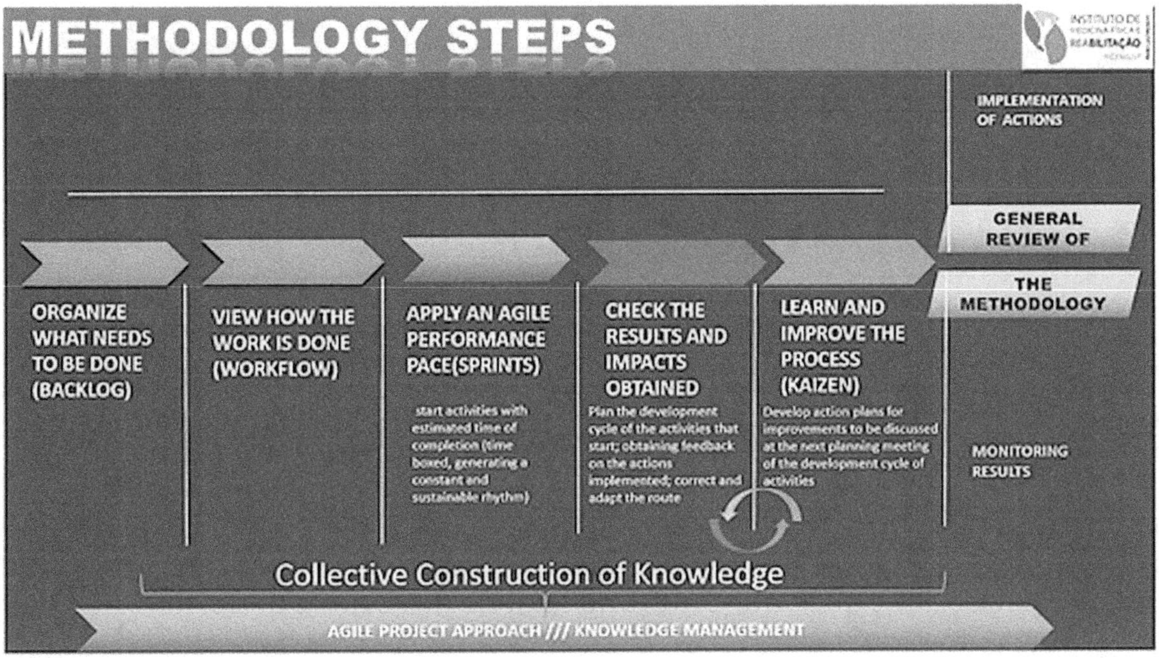

These initiatives are part of the culture of innovation in a highly collaborative environment, where trust is established in every action. From these organizational innovations, it is perceived the adoption of new working methods compatible with the new requirements in the health area and the availability of services to patients, qualifying the product, as well as the result of scientific research. It is *sine qua non condition* to think that users of the services are people! In view of this, we can sumarize the proposed methodology as something that puts people at the center, whether in the construction of systems solutions or organizational processes.

Consequently, we created the Re-AbilityLab Innovation Spiral (Figure IV), representing an iterative model. The goal is to allow you to revisit past phases in order to improve the next iterations (cyclic). Dividing the process into iterations allows the patient to be monitored throughout the course. All phases of the model add value, start the process defining the objectives of the current iteration, then evaluate and manage the risks (areas of uncertainty), evaluating the solutions, proceed to develop and test the product of this current iteration, as soon as tested the product, plans the next iteration, generating new ideas. In addition, it propitious the evolution of knowledge for the construction of new knowledge, based on evidence. The process is continuous and there will be validations of requirements, design specification, implementation and testing, where each cycle is planned and evaluated.

Figure 4. Innovation Spiral Re-AbilityLab
(created by the authors)

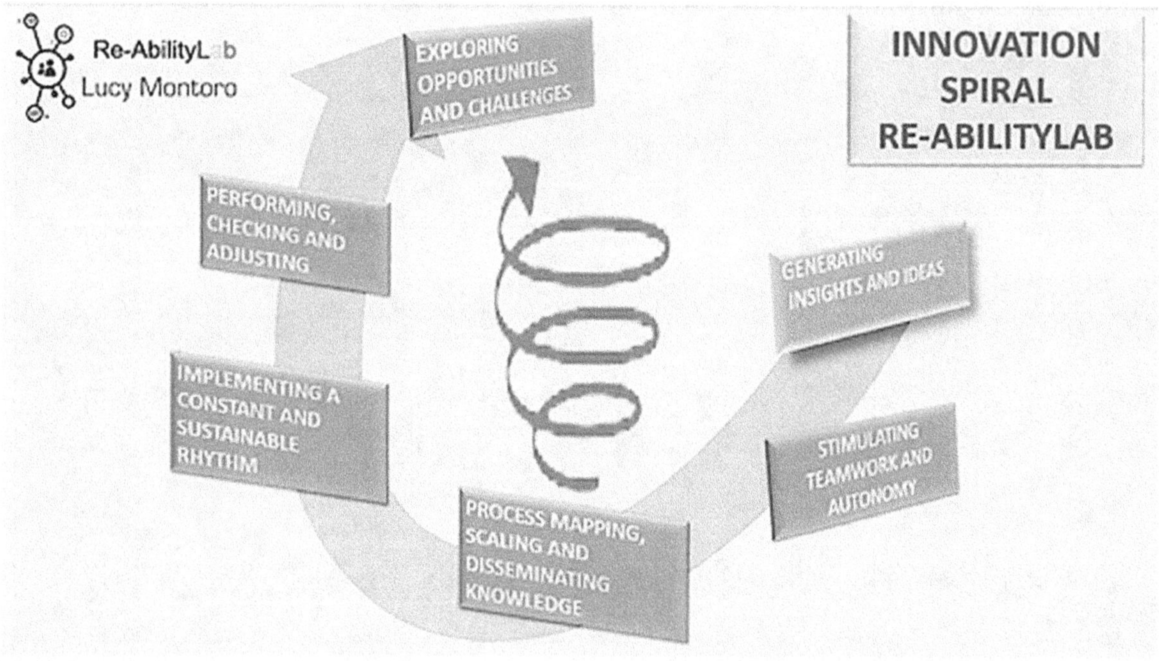

The efficiency of the Spiral impacts the user of the process, which is the object of the change, in this case the patient. Consequently, the combination of knowledge and experiences permite to the group changes course quickly, and more appropriate results can be produced. The focus is always on the best practices for process review: periodic meetings of critical analysis, team vision, integrative learning (amplify the apprentice), build with integrity, observe the whole, collaborative decision making and incorporation of rapid feedbacks to make the necessary adjustments.

Knowledge Management as a Source of Value Creation in the Re-AbilityLab Implemetnation Process

The experience and knowledge acquired by people are part of the organization's memory and are the basis for continuous improvement. According to DAVENPORT & PRUSAK (1998), the only competitive advantages a company has is what it collectively knows, the efficiency with which it uses what it knows, and the readiness with which it acquires and applies new knowledge. However knowledge, which is the ability to apply information to a specific work, only comes with a human being, his intellectual capacity and his ability, where the basic economic resource is no longer capital or natural resources or labor, but rather "knowledge", a society in which "knowledge workers" will play a central role. It is important to highlight one of the great characteristics associated with knowledge, which is the fact that it is highly reusable, that is, the more used and disseminated the greater its value. Currently, creating, disseminating, transferring and using knowledge promotes actions that serve as leverage, to achieve goals and solve a problem. An organization inserted in the Knowledge Society ceased to be characteristically linear and became dynamic, flexible, where it is not enough just to think, but mainly to act systemically. Additionally, the quality and speed in the sharing of information, experiences and practices, began to add value to the organizational strategy. Within this context, Skills Laboratories, when they adopt certain practices of knowledge management, generate insums for the achievement of excellence in the post-rehabilitation process.

In a statement, with the application of knowledge management practices in the re-abilitylab implementation process, building value with patient experience, the Institution benefited in several ways, among which we can highlight:

- Apply the quality tool PDCA (Plan, Do, Check and Act) in the project monitoring process, aiming not to repeat errors and learn from experience (clarity in the objectives outlined);
- Record the critical and essential knowledge of the multidisciplinary team, aligning the interests and expectations of the patient;
- Encourage the multidisciplinary team to record what they know, transforming individual tacit knowledge into collective tacit;
- Register and use the best practices developed during the execution of the project scope, using the Learned Lessons form - technique used for the leveling and dissemination of knowledge;
- Redesign new ways to provide health services, with the patient in the focus of business strategy.

Thus, we observed that this methodology focuses on generating health value in the development of its activities. In addition to opportunistic documentation of lessons learned, creating a knowledge bank that should be considered in measuring the process, results and technologies adopted.

From the change of the mental model, knowledge management appears as an important instrument in the creation of a shared vision with technology, generating learning and new ways of thinking about the post-rehabilitation process. And in this aspect the recommendation of the authors is to recognize the culture of the Institution and treat as an evolutionary process, *considering feedback* and learning. One of the results in the connection between knowledge, health services and economic development is the adoption of a design strategy for the implementation of public policies. However, that the political measures are driving forces of the necessary skills, ensuring the quality and qualification standards that can be "planned" to produce the desired set of results.

What are the Main Problems?

There are still several barriers that need to be transposed for the total consolidation of this post-rehabilitation model and the mass application of this type of health service. The confrontations arise in all instances of care, both for actors and for the institutions involved in the process that yearn for change and decrystallization of strongly instituted principles

The Challenges to Changes in Health Practice

Among the challenges faced, innovation is to be seen as a benefit of change, compatibility with values and past trajectory, complexity of the Re-AbilityLab methodology, its testing and ability to be observed; trust and encouragement of reinvention and adaptation; the provision of resources that favor change; leadership by example; the design of patient care and referral flowcharts; the process of making visible and, therefore, observable, patient performance during the execution of activities included in development trails; the reconfiguration of internal routines and external offerings (with new products, services and processes); the consolidation of an institutional competence with high value in the patient's experience.

The Challenge of Deploying the Method Until It Becomes a Habit

Even if the team has clear what values they want to implement, it is not enough to say that it is necessary to register and exercise the new principles every day. In addition to each team member being aware of their role in the process, focusing on collaboration, transparent communication and shared knowledge, so that the benefits of this organizational transformation positively impact all involved.

The objective of implementing the Re-AbilityLab methodology at this institution is to use the agile structure of projects to bring greater agility and efficiency to the processes, reflecting on continuous improvement in operations. Stimulating group discussions regarding problem solving and a set of ideas (diverge and converge), leading the *team to perform and initiate* deliveries of added value to the patient.

To support the transitions required by this initiative, a spread sheet of "ProcessTransition" (tasks from / tasks to) demonstrating the advancement of the current state to the future state, integrating people, operation and strategy. This structured and intentional approach allows the team to visualize the benefits of the transition process from a care model to an exponential model of care, and to take the new strategies required by this proposal.

In order to develop the capacity to respond to change and have strength in the adaptation process, before the implementation proposed, we linked the "Testing" phase that allows the review of the project plan and the development methodology adopted.

The Four Steps of the Re-AbilityLab Testing Phase

The proposal in this stage of "testing" is that each professional deepens more and more on the points to be improved, allowing to obtain more sophisticated and refined solutions, and that are shared in group meetings of Sprint Planning *(weekly),* exploring all the edges that involve the context of the problem.

The testing stage is fractionated into four (4) steps explained below, which contains the detailed functionalities directly linked to the attitude of the multidisciplinary team in doing well, the commitment to quality, the value proposition that will be delivered to the patient and the collection of feedback that *includes positive* points, negatives, ideas and doubts. Finally, this step will also help to keep deviations and non-conformities under control, without turning into emergencies or critical problems in the implementation phase. Therefore, during the monitoring of activities, one can act on a risk, altering or reducing its probability of materializing or its impact. This testing stage facilitates monitoring and ensures the success of the planned actions, in addition to qualifying the decision-making of which strategies will be adopted for the implementation phase.

Step 1: Alignment

Interview with patients to create a unified view. The first step is to build information in line with the new Re -Abilitylab proposal. Patients are asked about internal factors (goals to be worked on in the LAbs and respective therapeutic goals) and external factors (transportation support, family and/or social support) that can directly and indirectly affect their participation in the development paths.

Step 2: Deepening

The next step is to dive deeper into the factors that can facilitate or hinder the completion of the testing step. The factors that were previously mapped in the interview sessions need to be explored in more depth, in order to understand all the complexities and challenges underlying. Which patients, in fact, have the profile to adhere to the new Re-AbilityLab proposal. Apply global/functional evaluation with patients and the ICF questionnaire, using the Dr. Tis platform (Telemedicine) – a distance health solution that enables consultations through the Internet (connects patients, physicians and health institutions with practicality and safety). Finally, indicate the specific development path for each patient's evolution, stimulating the protagonism and sense of accountability.

Step 3: Consolidation

The third step focuses on applying the activities of the trails and monitoring the development of the patient during the course in the Re-AbilityLab program. It is important to align expectations with the patient's experience, and to expand their reach are throughout the organization and sequence of the process, for consolidation of therapeutic objectives.

Step 4: Monitoring

The final step is to monitor the success of on going activities, as the patient seeks to achieve a new *performance.* Clear performance indicators and guidelines should be established to monitor patient evolution over time by applying intermediate and final assessments based on chapters and domains of the ICF.

This testing step serves to refine ideas and solutions and learn more about the patient. These steps were defined with specific criteria, to ensure acquired knowledge standards and serve as an alternative measure to be used by the multidisciplinary team, in the evaluation of patients' performance during the post-rehabilitation program. More importantly, consider the fact that modernizing the learning process about the patient by emphasizing communication in relation to the exploration of information is increasingly the result of the adoption of a systemic position, where both sides: the health profissional and the patient should be able to quantify the value of the relationship and the recommended treatment. In this scenario the objective is to understand how the patient feels, to find out what benefits or problems he perceives, to recognize how he believes that this positively impacts his life. It is a new opportunity to learn, create empathy through patient observation and feedback, which can generate unexpected insights, create value and purpose for the solution. This, in fact, is the art of applying technical knowledge in clinical practice - Evidence-Based Medicine (EBM), with the aim of developing scientific reasoning, self-learning attitudes and the ability to integrate knowledge from different areas (transdisciplinarity), contributing to improve the quality of health services.

It is important to note that some relevant advantages in the construction of this methodology were the involvement of senior management; identification and mapping of the profile of *stakeholders;* definition of the functions and responsibilities of all those involved in the implantation process; integration, maximization and improvement of the use of existing resources; the institution's ability to adapt to the new model; formation of an *ad hoc committee* for monitoring and monitoring the activities of LABs, providing evidence-based decision-making and generating recommendations or working on a resolution. Moreover, it is worth mentioning the growing tendency to prioritize the autonomy of the team and shared knowledge in the construction of a culture of clear objectives, transparency in communication and in the design of strategies aimed at fostering innovations in the creation of a new organizational structure or practice, which facilitate the learning and production of new knowledge.

SOLUTIONS AND RECOMMENDATIONS

An Increase to the Solution Adopted

In order to apply the process of monitoring and control of the Re-AbilityLab Project (weekly meetings with stakeholders for presentation of results) we sought to create a sense of unity around the organizational purpose and evaluate the impacts caused by the activities of the LABs through the training of people, the improvement in the quality of the information of accountability and the methods and instruments that would support the management functions, aiming to ensure better results, constant review of decisions and eventual adjustments in the objectives.

As an increase to the solution adopted, to support the process of improvement and maturation of the "new health management model", through the application of the Re-AbilityLab methodology that reinforces the new paradigm in the post-rehabilitation process, and which adds new techniques and instruments used in the periodic critical monitoring and analysis of actions, the Critical Evaluation Cycle was established in the management of this project, which focuses on:

- The standardization of procedures for improving the processes of monitoring, evaluation and accountability of the services performed by *stakeholders;*
- The construction of indicators that contribute to the implementation of standardized practice of monitoring and permanent improvement of the accountability process, with a view to continuous improvement of performance and results of contracts and partnerships (Figure V - Systematic Monitoring and Evaluation);
- The definition of strategies, guidelines and procedures necessary for the Institution; training of the multidisciplinary team in monitoring and evaluating the results of the set of activities contemplated in each Skills Laboratory.

For the multidisciplinary team to be structures to follow a new business model, new experimentation practices were recommended, expanding the degree of adaptability. The resource used to adjust the route was constant dialogue, which stimulated the generation of reflections on progress, identification of errors and agility in decision making.

In this scenario of rebuilding new values it was necessary to focus on actions that impacted on process improvements, encouraging engagement and innovation. At this stage, it was essential to develop cognitive flexibility for a rapid adaptation to the constant changes in institutional practices. In addition to reinforcing the importance of the employee in every segment of change, and draw attention to the value of activating motivated behavior, consequently positively impacting the success of strategic objectives.

The big challenge is to make people understand exactly what the results of their efforts are, creating a culture of less politics, less subjectivity and more focus on planning and executing strategies.

Figure 5. Systematic Monitoring and Evaluation
(Prepared by the authors)

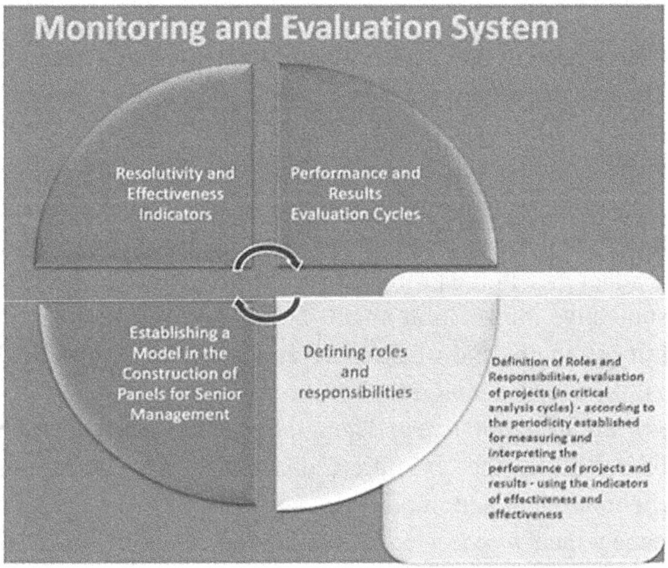

Results - Intangible Value of Business Generated

It is important to highlight that the activities offered in each LAB are services that aim precisely to tangibilize and evidence the results using the ICF to measure the degree of evolution of each patient. In the post-rehabilitation process it is possible to notice that despite the subtle variations the evolution of the patient occurs not only by the activity itself, and bythequality of the professionalswho perform the activities, but also by the perception that he has of his own progress. This simple observation is proof that intangible assets are extremely important in the participation of the real value of the products and services offered.
Thus, the Results already achieved are:

- Mobilization and Alignment of the Multiprofessional Team to meet the needs of change;
- Standardization of Procedures for Monitoring and Evaluation of Performance and Results;
- Commitment to the Ritual of Critical Analysis and Expansion of Participation and Dialogue between Stakeholders;
- Adequacy of Goals, Internal Processes and Work Plans;
- Identification and Implementation of Improvements, evolving the process and consequently making it more efficient - PDCA;
- Organization of the collection and treatment of relevant data for the generation of good indicators;
- Focus on measuring the effectiveness of work, with a view to promoting and evaluating public policies, requiring mechanisms of regulation, evaluation and weighing (indirect impact).

In verifying the effectiveness of the monitoring and evaluation system, the Expected Results are:

1. create a *culture of lifelong learning* favoring the training and training of health professionals in order to contemplate the exchange of knowledge and practices that do not imprison the work process in rigid structures;
2. contribute to the advancement of the applicability of the knowledge management cycle by favoring the socialization of knowledge among team members, promoting greater engagement and improvement of productivity;
3. encouraging the patient's good acceptance of his/her condition of disability and the recommended treatment;
4. meet the recommended deadline in the application of the global/functional assessment;
5. ensure the patient's adherence in the proposed activities;
6. capture the most subjective information about the relationship between expectation and patient experience, to identify strengths and weaknesses and continue improving the solution;
7. have as its final goal the social reintegration of the patient;
8. measure the results through quantitative and qualitative indicators that will be processed, analyzed, interpreted and validated during the "execution" phase of the project, to point out what is important and what needs to be monitored and improved;
9. change the micromanagement *mindset,* to encourage the autonomy of the team and strengthening talents and,
10. modify the power relations established by the medical paradigm, so that they are horizontal relations in the search for comprehensive and humanized care.

The above-mentioned expected results follow three pillars:

- Improve the patient experience;
- Increase the capacity of the health network through the provision of continuous services;
- Create innovative solutions and prepare the Digital Health workforce.

In view of this perspective, for this stage, therefore, it is essential to review and systematically synthesis based on evidence, which will allow and support the formatting of protocols and guidelines to be used in the post-rehabilitation process. In a statement, it is considered that the definition of metrics in the rehabilitation process inserted in the development trails, will allow the achievement of its purpose in measuring the functional advancement of the patient through the ICF, facilitating its adaptation and adherence to the program.

FUTURE RESEARCH DIRECTIONS

Future and Emerging Trends

In recent decades we have witnessed a process of transformation and technological innovation unprecedented in the area of health. As a consequence, the differentiation of health services in their sub-publicand market sectorsis deepened, both in patient care, as in work scales, prescription, results report and prevention systems. Therefore, in the knowledge society, under accelerated scientific and technological development (technoscience) and a real frenzy for the new (innovation), one would expect that the health sector would be strongly impacted by this process. With this, the new trends of Information and Communication Technology (ITCs) has been one of the biggest drivers of this process of change and are bringing direct and indirect benefits to Health Management. Technological transformations in the health sector are becoming faster and at every moment different techniques and more modern devices appear in the market with innovations that integrate solutions, making alignment with the business.

Following this technological evolution, the advance of the use of *tablets* and smartphones in the Brazilian *market* and the adoption of these personal devices in the work environment (consumerization) allowed health professionals to have access to the clinical information of their patients, stored in the solution of electronic medical records, through a wireless network. In view of the above, the concept that seems to prevail is that technology is the result of processes implemented from daily experience and research, for the development of a set of knowledge that enables the construction of products and services for a given practical situation.

For the continuity of a business model, the establishment of different processes that reflect on different solutions is important in the development of management practices added to the incorporation of new ICTs, processes and tangible results. Thus, technology can act as legitimizing the professional health act and the institution that adopts it, being used as a criterion for evaluating the quality of its services provided.

The choice and adoption of technologies is not something isolated, because there are decision variables, among them: policies, economic and social that bring with them many opportunities and also challenges due to the renewal of human values, need for cultural transformation, breaking paradigms and consequently changing the mindset.

In view of the above, the Re-AblityLab project suggests future opportunities for study and research to expand this theme. Innovations instigate profound changes in work processes and socio-professional categories. In particular, new competencies are required and, consequently, new challenges arise to explore the potential of subjectivity. With these transformations, there is, therefore,a need to knowthose related to operation, production techniques, the regulation of work and the formulation of norms and protocols. All this requires adaptation, ingenuity, further studies and new debates.

CONCLUSION

The data presented allow us to conclude that the Institution uses management information and indicators for monitoring results and goals, and there is an understanding of the multidisciplinary team on the importance of applying these indicators to evaluate patient performance in the development of activities proposed by the Skills Laboratories.

This process implies a change of mentality that involves a systemic approach, and that aims to integrate products and services in a methodology that privileges innovation. Finally, it highlights the importance of managing knowledge and understanding how processes related to work management to health changes are established.

Patients needs are reviewed and social interactions are an opportunity for growth and development, expanding the range of knowledge to be developed and the connection between health agents.

We present a new model of generating value in health, in a changing world with new requirements and technologies. The organization that learns, values the generation of knowledge, allows learning and the sharing of information that facilitates the discussion of unusual problems: errors, failures, quality issues, adopting collaboration as *modus operandi.*

It is important to point out that the lessons learned, extracted in the day-to-day interactions between team members, translate into individual and collective learning, that is, in the harmonic combination of organizational processes, skills and individual competencies for the generation of new knowledge. The use of knowledge throughout the organization generated from collective learning, leads to better decision-making, besides creating sustainable advantages that ensure the efficiency rate in the implementation of the project for delivering value in health, in the proposition of scientific and technological advances in human skill. It is noteworthy that the LABs included in the Development Trail focus on comprehensive care, considering individual aspects as well as those of disability, which requires a multidisciplinary team that points out biological, psychological and social aspects (biopsychosocial model) that influence the program rehabilitation of the patient, ensuring the best use of resources and continuity of care.

Teamwork, we have no doubt that it is what effectively sustains the good management of the project, and we should explore what is best each has, in a differentiated way, making them feel valued from the moment that their suggestions for improvements are accepted and make a difference for consolidating the main information of the project. Because people (stakeholders) havebecome the most expensive asset of organizations, they are the ones who make the "wheel spin" and that determine the success or failure of the project.

Moreover, the factor of knowledge production has never been valued so much, so it is necessary to attention to the retention of intellectual capital and to record the lessons learned adequately structured, assimilated, evaluated and disseminated in the Institution, where shared tacit knowledge is converted to explicit knowledge in the form of a new concept or an operational mechanism, in the case of abstract innovations or as a new corporate value. Finally, intangible heritage is tangibilized by the new technologies that make them accessible and shareable and together activate networked society and its forms of organization. Certainly, this movement of knowledge can help leaders to measure the performance of projects in the generation of a learning-oriented environment, capable of capturing the variables of innovation of social technologies by outlineing a new model in the Health System.

FINANCING INFORMATION

This survey did not receive any specific grants from any funding agency in the public, commercial or non-profit sectors.

REFERENCES

Araujo, O. (2010). *SWOT Analysis (Strengths, Weaknesses, Opportunities, Threats) or (Strengths, Weaknesses, Opportunities and Threats).* Available at: http://www.dearaujo.ecn.br/cgi-bin/asp/analiseSwot.asp

Bukowitz, W. R., & Williams, R. L. (2002). *Knowledge Management Manual.* Bookman.

Cassapo, M. F. (2011). *What We Understand Exactly by Tacit Knowledge and Explicit Knowledge.* Available in: www.sgbc.org.br

Choo, C. W. (2006). *The Knowledge Organization: How Organizations Use Information to Create Knowledge, Build Knowledge, and Make Decisions* (2nd ed.). Sao Paulo: Senac São Paulo.

Collison, C., & Parcell, G. (2001). *Learning to Fly*. Capstone.

Dai, X. C. (2001). *The role of the project management office in achieving project success* (Doctoral thesis). The George Washington University.

Davenport, T. H., & Prusak, L. (1998). *Business Knowledge How Organizations Manage Their Intellectual Capital*. Campus.

Dinsmore, P. C. (1999). *Winning in business with enterprise Project management*. Amazon Books.

Drucker, P. F. (1998). *Managing in Times of Great Change*. Pioneer.

Flowers, S. P. (2005). *Knowledge Management: Competitive strategies for the creation and mobilization of knowledge in the company: discover how to leverage and multiply intellectual capital and knowledge of the organization*. Qualitymark.

Greenhalgh, T. (2012). The organization vision for telehealth and telecare: Discourse analysis. *BMJ Open, London, 2*, 1–14.

Greenhalgh, T. (n.d.). Five biases of new technologies. *British Journal of General Practice, 63*(613), 425.

Kaluzny, A. D. (n.d.). Diffusion of innovative health care services in the United States: a study in hospitals. *Medical Care, 8*(6), 274.

Kanaane & Formigari. (2010). Manual of training and development of human potential (2nd ed.). São Paulo: Atlas.

Kerzner, H. (2002). *Project Management Best Practices*. Bookman.

Melo, L. E. V. (2003). *Knowledge Management: Concepts and Applications*. Erica.

Nonaka, I., & Takeuchi, H. (1997). *Creation of Knowledge in the Company How Japanese Companies Generate the Dynamics of Innovation*. Campus.

Peter Senge, M. (1998). *The fifth discipline: art and practice of the organization that learns*. Sao Paulo Beste Seller.

PMBOK® Guide Project Management Body of Knowledge. (2021). *Project Management Institute, Global Standards* (7th ed.). Newton Square, PA: PMI.

Probst, G. (2002). *Knowledge Management - The building elements of success*. Bookman.

Salge, T. O. (2012). The temporal trajectories of innovative search: Insights from public hospital services: Insights from Public Hospital Services. *Research Policy, 41*(4), 720-733.

Santos, A. R. (2001). *Knowledge Management: An Experience for Business Success*. Champagnat University.

Silva, R. V. (2004). *Company Management in the Age of Knowledge*. Serinews.

Silva, S.L. (2004). Knowledge management: A critical vision guided by the approach of knowledge creation. *Information Science, 33*(2).

Stewart, T. A. (1998). Intellectual capital: The new competitive advantage of companies. Rio de Janeiro: 11. Ed. Campus.

Treff, L., & Battistella, Lr. (2013). *Innovation in Project Management in Public Administration*. Brasport.

Vargas, R., & Nir, M. (2014). *Building Highly Effective Teams*. Brasport.

World Health Organization. (n.d.). Available in: https://www.who.int/classifications/icf/en/index.html

Yin, R. K. (2011). Case Study – planning and methods (2nd ed.). Porto Alegre: Bookman.

ADDITIONAL READING

Cooper, H. (1982). Scientific Guidelines for Conducting Integrative Research Reviews. *Review of Educational Research, 52*(2), 291–302. doi:10.3102/00346543052002291

Ontario, O. (2002). *The Ontario Cardiac Rehabilitation Pilot Project. Report and recommendations.* Ontario Cardiac Rehabilitation Pilot Project.

Scottish Executive. (2007). *Co-ordinated integrated and fit for purpose. The Delivery Framework for Adult Rehabilitation in Scotland.* Scottish Executive.

WHO. (2004). *CBR. A strategy for rehabilitation, equalization of opportunities, poverty reduction and social inclusion of people with disabilities: Joint position paper.* World Health Organization.

WHO. (2011). *World Report on Disability*. The World Bank.

KEY TERMS AND DEFINITIONS

Activity: The execution of a task or action by an individual.

Activity Limitations: Difficulties that an individual may encounter in performing activities.

Agile Project Management: It is a light and minimal intervention approach to project management. That is, the project is all divided into smaller steps, called iteration, which usually last from 2 to 4 weeks and at the end of each step there is a reassessment of the project priorities.

Body Functions: The physiological functions of body systems (including psychological and social functions – bio-psycho-social model).

Deficiencies: Problems in the functions or structures of the body as a significant impairment or loss.

Disability: Is a comprehensive term for deficiency, activity limitations and participation restrictions. It denotes aspects of the interaction between an individual (with a health conditions) and the contextual factors of that individual (environmental and personal factors).

Functionality: Is a comprehensive term for body functions, body structures, activities and participation. It denotes the positive aspects of the interaction between an individual (with a health conditions) and the contextual factors of that individual (environmental and personal factors).

Hospital das Clínicas of the Faculty of Medicine of the University of São Paulo (HCFMUSP): Is a hospital complex located in the city of São Paulo and an autarchy of the government of the state of São Paulo, linked to the State Department of Health for administrative coordination purposes, associated with the Faculty of Medicine (FM) of the University of São Paulo (USP) for the purposes of teaching, research and provision of health actions and services for the community.

ICF: International Classification of Functionality, Disability and Health, known as ICF, has as general objective to provide a unified and standardized language as a system of description of health and health-related states.

Institute of Physical Medicine and Rehabilitation of the Hospital das Clínicas of the Faculty of Medicine of the University of São Paulo (IMREA HC FMUSP): Is an entity of the State government, whose objective is to serve people with physical, transient, or permanent disabilities, in need of rehabilitation care, developing their physical, psychological, social, professional and educational potential. IMREA integrates the academic structure of the Faculty of Medicine of USP through the Department of Legal Medicine, Medical Ethics, Social Medicine and Labor and also integrates the Lucy Montoro Rehabilitation Network, governed by Decree No. 55,739 of April 28, 2010.

Lucy Montoro Rehabilitation Network: Is a health center for the care of people with physical disabilities or potentially disabling diseases. It was created in 2008 by the Government of the State of São Paulo, through the Departments of Health and The Rights of Persons with Disabilities, and launched by Decree 52.973/08. Its name is a tribute to the former first lady of the state of São Paulo Lucy Montoro, who has done numerous social works at the head of the Social Solidarity Fund of the State of São Paulo - FUSSESP.

Multiprofessional Team: Formed by professionals from different areas. These professionals interrelate and promote a differentiated treatment, seeing the patient as a whole and providing a humanized care.

Participation In: Involvement in situations of daily life.

Project Methodology: It is the path that will be followed throughout the project execution, the planning implementation of what needs to be executed and in what order.

Rehabilitation: Rehabilitation is a process of consolidation of therapeutic objectives not characterizing an area of professional exclusivity, but rather a proposal of multiprofessional and interdisciplinary action, composed of a set of measures that help people with disabilities or about to acquire disabilities to have and maintain an ideal functionality (physical, sensory, intellectual, psychological and social) in the interaction with their environment, providing the tools they need to achieve independence and self-determination.

Restrictions of Participation: Problems that an individual may face when engaging in life situations.

ENDNOTE

1 Perspectives in Information Science, v.15, n.3, p.131-154, Sep./Dec. 2010 continuity of care.

Chapter 4
Knowledge Economy and Its Impact on the Development Progress of Transfusion Medicine in Poor Economic Nations

Cees Th. Smit Sibinga
University of Groningen, The Netherlands

Yetmgeta E. Abdella
WHO Office for the Eastern Mediterranean Region, Egypt

EXECUTIVE SUMMARY

The chapter will provide a global situation analysis, describe the key elements of knowledge economy in the healthcare and transfusion medicine field, and analyze the impact of the knowledge economy on the pace of development progress of national blood supply and transfusion structures. The authors will provide examples to illustrate the case of applying knowledge economy principles to advance the safety and availability of blood products in clinical healthcare and hence the economy of care. Recommendations on how to improve will be described.

INTRODUCTION

Since the first World Health Assembly (WHA) Resolution on blood safety and availability in 1975 WHA28.72 'Utilization and Supply of Human Blood' (WHA, 1975) and the mapping of the blood supply and transfusion in the world in the 1980s (WHO, 1988), much has been done and achieved. Further exploration of the existing situation in the healthcare and supportive services, however, disclosed major gaps in the low- and medium human development index (HDI) (UNDP, 2020) group of countries, home to close to 84% of the global population. Apart from the weak governance and regulatory structures, the

DOI: 10.4018/978-1-7998-8417-0.ch004

fragmented blood procurement and supply structures, a major gap disclosed is in the existing knowledge and the approaches to knowledge economy.

The 2018 United Nations Development Program statistical update report 'Human Development Indices and Indicators' (UNDP, 2018) presents clearly that the lower the HDI the greater the decrement in secondary and particularly tertiary (higher education, medical school, university) education enrolment. Tertiary education in the very high-HDI countries shows 72% enrolment, where enrolment in the medium and low HDI parts of the world, respectively is only 24% and 8%, and enrolment in the high HDI countries is 50% (Table 1).

Table 1. UNDP (2018) education enrolment rates of school-age populations (%) in the 4 HDI groups for primary, secondary and tertiary education

Human Development Groups	**Education Enrolment Ratio**		
	Primary **School-Age Population (%)**	*Secondary* **School-age Population (%)**	*Tertiary* **School-Age Population (%)**
Low HDI	*98*	***43***	***8***
Medium HDI	*110*	***73***	***24***
High HDI	103	96	**50**
Very-High HDI	102	106	72

Most vocational and medical schools and universities (higher and tertiary education) in a large proportion of developing countries are relatively young and date back to the last part of the colonial era, the second half of the 19th and the first half of the 20st century. This illustrates the impressive paucity in education, hence knowledge and a weak economy of available and accessible knowledge.

The root cause analysis discloses a major area of attention to bridge and narrow the existing knowledge gap. Education in these countries has been focused almost exclusively on vocational education of laboratory skills (testing and processing) with limited theoretical attention (knowledge), and rudimentary attention to topics such as governance, human capacity investment and appropriate clinical use of blood (WHO, 2017). The World Health Organization (WHO), over the past three decades, has designed a series of useful educational materials, the Distance Learning Material (DLM) (WHO, 2021b) and an excellent Quality Management Training (QMT) (WHO, 2015) material focused on the various elements of the blood supply and clinical use to improve on knowledge and initiate development. Many other organizations and institutions have also contributed to the spread of knowledge and skills through countless workshops, seminars, courses, and short-term consultations. The Education Subcommittee of the AABB Global Transfusion Forum recently published the outcomes of two surveys (Al-Riyami et al., 2021; Rambiritch et al., 2021). The first focused on undergraduate medical school students among 32 medical schools in 18 countries belonging to the medium-, high- and very high-HDI categories. The second focused on laboratory professionals who attended a vocational school in 6 countries in Africa, belonging to the low-, medium- and high-HDI categories and representing 10 blood establishments and 2 blood banks. These outcomes justify the conclusion that education needs an environment and climate to grow into an effective knowledge economy at primary, secondary and tertiary education level, and contribute to advancing progress and improvement of quality and transfusion practices in the healthcare available and accessible to all, no one excluded (Smit Sibinga et al., 2021). This environment can only be created and developed when countries establish a national structure, institutional environment, and a competent management cadre. That depends on the existence of a well-educated and motivated cadre of 'intelligentsia', competent and responsible policy makers and governors, and the creation of an inviting and inspiring education climate, irrespective the level of knowledge to be acquired (Smit Sibinga et al., 2021).

KEY ELEMENTS AND CHARACTERISTICS OF KNOWLEDGE ECONOMY

Knowledge economy is a system of consumption and production that is based on intellectual capital. It is an economy where knowledge is acquired, created, disseminated, and used effectively to enhance economic development whether for profit or not for profit, private or public (Hayes, 2021).

It has been found that successful transition to knowledge economy typically involves elements such as long-term investments in education, developing innovation capability, modernizing the information infrastructure, and having an economic environment that is conducive to market transactions (Chen & Dahlman, 2006). These elements have been termed by the World Bank as the pillars of the Knowledge Economy and together they constitute the Knowledge Economy framework defined according to four pillars:

1. An *institutional and economic incentive regime* that provides good economic policies and institutions that permit efficient mobilization and allocation of resources and stimulate creativity and incentives for the efficient creation, dissemination, and use of existing knowledge.
2. *Educated (knowledge) and skilled workers* who can continuously upgrade and adapt their skills to efficiently create and use knowledge.
3. An *effective innovation system* of institutions, research centers, universities, consultants, and other organizations that can keep up with the knowledge revolution and tap into the growing stock of global knowledge and assimilate and adapt it to local needs e.g., healthcare.
4. A *modern and adequate information infrastructure* that can facilitate the effective communication, dissemination, and processing of information and knowledge e.g., the development of artificial intelligence (AI).

This knowledge economy framework thus asserts that investments in the four knowledge economy pillars are necessary for sustained creation, adoption, adaptation and use of knowledge in domestic economic processes, which will consequently result in higher value-added goods and services as exemplary for the blood supply and consumption in the healthcare.

Knowledge economy is focused on the essential importance of human capital in the economy of the 21st-century (Hayes, 2021). The rapid expansion of knowledge and the increasing reliance on computerization, big data analytics, and automation are changing the economy of the advanced world to one that is more dependent on intellectual capital and managerial skills, and less dependent on the technical production process, adding on to the existing knowledge gaps in the world. The emphasis is on specific knowledge and skills, data analysis and measurable performance, and strategic management by objectives. The knowledge economy is characterized by the presence of a higher percentage of highly skilled employees whose jobs require advanced and special knowledge and skills. Unlike in the past, when the economy depended heavily on low- and unskilled labor jobs and consisted primarily of producing physical goods, the modern economy is comprised more of services and jobs that require thinking and analysis of data produced by robotics and computerized processes and procedures. The modern economy is also known as the post-industrial economy or the information economy – a reference to the importance of information and communication technology (ICT) and artificial intelligence (artificial neural networks, deep learning and machine learning) in the economies of advanced nations, and an important platform for applied research and science to build on evidence (Chen & Dahlman, 2006).

In the new knowledge economy, the most valuable assets that an organization or institution owns are often intangible assets – such as service, experience, commitment, awareness, or proprietary software or processes. It is in contrast to previous economic epochs of the 19th and 20st Century – e.g., the agrarian economy, where the primary asset usually was land, and the industrial economy, where mechanical manufacturing plants and equipment were key assets for most industries. The knowledge economy both supports, and is fueled by innovation, research, and rapid technological advancements such as artificial intelligence (AI). An overwhelming majority of the younger generation working in the current knowledge economy settings are extremely computer literate and skilled at handling and manipulating data and creating data monitoring and evaluation models. There is an increasing emphasis on quality data collection and analysis, and on the development of algorithms and artificial intelligence (AI) through deep learning artificial neural networks and machine learning principles. The knowledge economy is considered the primary driver of the massive expansion of what is known as 'science, technology, engineering, and mathematics' (STEM) jobs (Giffi et al, 2015). Careers within the STEM fields – which includes occupational paths such as computer science, engineering, chemistry, biology, and medicine – are where many of the greatest opportunities for career advancement, higher compensation, and top-level executive positions can be found. These STEM fields show a rapid expansion in operational size allowing a high degree of standardization, quality management and economic efficacy. However, the bottom line is that knowledge provides the foundation for the necessary technical expertise, data collection and analysis skills, and innovative management practices that enable non-profit organizations and institutions such as blood establishments to compete in the modern global economy. Specialized knowledge and skills may serve as either productive asset to deploy, or as products to offer and market on a cost-recovery principle, e.g., pathogen reduction and inactivation technologies, cellular engineering, and cellular therapies.

Another characteristic element of the knowledge economy is the development of consolidation of essential processes such as mandatory safety testing and processing of collected human blood of smaller non-viable blood banks into larger economies of scale, centered in a strategic geographic area and affiliated to e.g., a university or one or more large tertiary healthcare institutions, clustering available knowledge and skills, offering better effectiveness (WHO, 2021a).

In summary, the knowledge economy, which today has become the primary economy among advanced nations, is an economy dependent on human capital and intangible assets, such as service and trust or proprietary technology. Knowledge economy has placed the ICT and AI science and industries at the forefront of overall economic growth through larger and faster computing capacities. Skill sets that include data analysis, creating and working with cost-recovery financial models, and the ability to innovate, based on well-structured higher and academic vocational and professional education systems, are highly sought after in the modern economy, a change in knowledge and skills requirements and a shift in assets through a different approach in customer orientation and appreciation, both with the community as well as with the healthcare organizations. It adds another valuable dimension to quality culture.

IMPACT OF KNOWLEDGE ECONOMY ON DEVELOPMENT OF THE BLOOD SYSTEM

Knowledge is gained and acquired through education and experience or learning. Knowledge is offered as information to be received and stored, perceived and interpreted, and converted into signals for action – recognition, behavior, action, expression, understanding, thinking, moods, etc. This chain of events starts with birth and builds up during life. To order and standardize a basic amount of knowledge, teaching and learning systems, processes and curricula have been developed and are continuously further developed; contextual, operational, and technical through e-learning concepts. Depending on the intelligence and IQ level of an individual, education could be adapted and adjusted to what maximally can be perceived and understood or interpreted. The more exposure and repetition the better the perception, storage, interpretation and understanding. In principle there are three successive layers of structured education – primary, secondary, and tertiary besides for each a system of continuous education and stimulation to improve and expand on existing knowledge, optimizing the economy of knowledge. As explained in the introduction, education, and the school-population enrolment rates from primary into secondary and from secondary into tertiary education form one of the human development index indicators used by UNDP (UNDP, 2018). These illustrate the growing quantitative knowledge economy gaps between education levels in the HDI groups. However, more important is the quality of knowledge offered and perceived. Education is neither limited nor restricted to what structurally is offered. Living creatures are continuously exposed to information, visual and pictorial (objects, light and darkness, colors, movement, postures, reading), audible (sound and music, soft and loud, harmonious, and dissonant, attracting and warning), touchable (size, shape, surface, smooth and sharp), smell and taste (sweet, bitter, salt, rotten and challenging), senses like temperatures and pain, balance, and speed; most come in combinations and environmental dimensions. The personal perception, interpretation, storage, and triggers to action are part of the individual knowledge economy with its levels of alertness and awareness, comfort and discomfort, risks, and safety perceptions (Thomas & Thomas, 1928). The intensity of experience is part of common life knowledge economy.

The 2018 UNDP data reveal impressive differences in acquiring structured knowledge economy and consequently the value added to education in different parts of the world (UNDP, 2018). This means that knowledge economy is very fundamental and relates closely to the need to survive because of poor economics. The lower the HDI, the greater the decrement in enrolment rates into secondary and even more prominent into tertiary education. The lower the HDI the smaller the intelligentsia cadre and opportunities to offer quality education to a broader group of the community, developing knowledge levels and economy. On the more specific Transfusion Medicine scale, the availability of expertise and/or training programs in the low and medium HDI countries are much lower compared to the higher HDI countries (Smit Sibinga et al., 2021). Currently, technology allows us to bridge this gap to an extend by having blended teaching and online learning programs, ideally developed, and presented jointly by local and international experts, at relatively low cost with no great need for travel, thanks to online teaching platforms.

Operations and Management of Blood Systems

Blood supply systems are *de facto* manufacturing institutions (Smit Sibinga & Jansen van Galen, 2020). The demand (market) is created by the patient in the hospital and translates into a tailor-made supply of safe and clinically efficacious blood products. These are manufactured from a crude source material, a human blood donation that finds its roots in the community. This vein-to-vein chain needs specific knowledge to be acquired and used economically to develop into a patient-oriented blood transfusion organization of adequate economy of scale to secure consistency, quality and competency, operational and managerial.

Analyzing the needed vocational and professional education backgrounds of staff to be employed in any part of the vein-to-vein Transfusion Medicine chain, at primary, supportive or steering process level, the following picture develops as shown in Table 2.

Table 2. Analysis of the vocational and professional backgrounds of staff to be employed in any part of the vein-to-vein Transfusion Medicine chain

Primary processes

1) Procurement/supply

- Donor issues/blood collection
  - o Social worker (public awareness, motivation, mobilization, and retention)
  - o (para-)Nursing (donor handling/care, selection, phlebotomy)
  - o Medical (medical responsibility, supervision – donor eligibility, adverse events, and donor vigilance)
  - o Ancillary support (administration, cleaning/waste, refreshments/canteen)
- Blood processing/component production
  - o Medical technical (medical or pharmaceutical responsibility)
  - o Ancillary support (administration, cleaning/waste)
- Testing/Quality Control (QC) (Laboratory)
  - o Medical technical (medical or laboratory medicine/pathology responsibility)
  - o Ancillary (administration, cleaning/waste)
- Storage and distribution (cold chain)
  - o Medical technical (medical or pharmaceutical)
  - o Ancillary (drivers/runners; cleaning/waste)
  - o Clinical consultation (medical responsibility)

2) Clinical use

- Ordering (diagnosis, indication, alternatives, decision, informed consent)
  - o Medical
  - o Nursing/midwifery
  - o Ancillary (administration, cleaning, runners)
- Component selection and immunohematology testing (blood group serology, antibody screening and identification, quality testing, crossmatching)
  - o Medical technical (medical or pathology responsibility)
  - o Ancillary (administration, cleaning/waste, runners)
- Transfusion (bedside)
  - o Medical
  - o Nursing/midwifery
  - o Ancillary (administration, cleaning, waste)

Supportive/secondary processes

- Human Resource Management and education
  - o Qualified HRM (vocational HE)
- Maintenance and engineering (building, equipment, vehicles)
  - o Qualified mechanic or engineer (vocational)
  - o Mechanics
- Domestic services (cleaning and hygiene, waste disposal, laundry, canteen, wellness)
  - o Qualified domestic economy
  - o Primary or secondary education personnel
- ICT (equipment, network, barcoding, printing, programming, logistics, inventory management, management information systems, artificial intelligence)
  - o Qualified ICT officers (vocational)

Steering processes

- Top management
  - o Medically qualified competent leader
  - o Secretariat (qualified secretary, secondary education)
- Quality Management
  - o Qualified quality management officer (vocational/academic)
  - o Quality management trained personnel (document management and control)
  - o Ancillary (secretariat, secondary education)
- Costing and financing of the vein-to-vein activities in blood establishments and hospital blood banks
- Clinical consultation service
  - o Medical (preferably clinical specialist – internist, hematologist, clinical transfusion medicine specialist)

This analysis illustrates the need for a specific knowledge pool to be deployed economically. Personnel with, in principle, a secondary education background exposed to continued education at a higher (HE) and academic (tertiary) level to graduate as a vocational professional. These vocational professionals then form the pool of (graduate) trainees for an operational or managerial position within a blood establishment (procurement institute) or hospital transfusion service (laboratory or bedside). The goal is improving patient safety, preventing avoidable harm and health outcomes (WHO, 2021c) through optimal knowledge economy.

Unfortunately, the pool of these graduates is limited in medium and low HDI countries (enrolment ratios 24% and 8% resp.) and marginal (enrolment ratio 50%) in high HDI countries (UNDP, 2018). That brings along a serious competition for a job at that professional level in the blood supply institutions and hospitals and the risk for a drain of well-equipped professionals away from the smaller blood supply institutes or Blood Banks to larger establishments and hospitals with a larger and more diverse and occasionally more advanced transfusion programs, e.g., pathogen reduction and inactivation technologies, cellular engineering, cellular therapies, and plasma fractionation.

The analysis also illustrates that the educational or knowledge acquisition focus and emphasis points to three integrated groups or categories of health professionals to be educated – doctors, nurses and (bio-) medical laboratory professionals; supported by ancillary personnel who do not need a specific Transfusion Medicine education and knowledge. Most ancillary personnel require a primary or secondary education background and may receive structured apprentice or work integrated education and training related to the professional behavior (professionalism), institutional values, hygiene and cleanliness, and basic risk prevention and management, in line with their respective roles and responsibilities. Knowledge on professionalism and stewardship is essential at early stage of entry and training, appropriate to the role and function of the various ancillary personnel (Rambiritch & Smith-Tolken 2019).

Knowledge Economy and Development

While progressing towards the second quarter of the 21st Century, annually a quantity of around 120 million blood donations is collected globally. Around 40% of these are collected in high-income countries, home to only 16% of the world's population. Consequently around 72 million blood donations are annually collected in the World Bank categories of low- and medium-income countries, home to 84% of the global population and indicating a protracted shortage in many of these countries (WHO, 2020).

There is a marked difference in the level of access to blood and its effect on the quality of the healthcare between low- and high-income countries. Based on samples of 1,000 people, the blood donation rate as an indicator for the general availability of blood and blood components in a country; 31.5 donations in high-income countries, 15.9 donations in upper-middle-income countries, only 6.8 donations in lower-middle-income countries and just 5.0 donations in low-income countries; 62 countries reported collecting fewer than 10 donations per 1,000 people. Of these, 34 countries are in the WHO African Region, four in the WHO Region of the Americas (South and Middle America), six in the WHO Eastern Mediterranean region, three in the WHO European Region, six in the WHO South-Eastern Asian Region, and nine in the WHO Western Pacific Region. All are low- or middle-income countries.

In low-income countries, up to 54% of blood transfusions are given to children under 5 years of age with severe anemia (malaria, helminthic and parasitic infections), whereas in high-income countries, the most frequently transfused patient group is over 60 years of age, accounting for up to 75% of all transfusions and largely indicated for supportive care in cardiovascular and transplant surgery, massive trauma, and therapy for solid and hematological malignancies, and cellular therapies. Only 55 of 171 (32%) reporting countries produce plasma-derived medicinal products (PDMP) through the fractionation of plasma collected in the reporting country; mostly upper-middle and high-income countries. Of the remaining 116 countries, 90 countries reported that all PDMP were imported, 16 countries reported that no PDMP were used during the reporting period, and 10 countries did not respond to the question.

From 2013 to 2018 an increase of 7.8 million voluntary non-remunerated blood donations has been reported by 156 countries; highest increase of voluntary non-remunerated blood donations was in the Region of the Americas (25%) and Africa (23%). Globally, 79 countries collected over 90% of their blood supply from voluntary non-remunerated blood donors. However, 56 countries collected more than 50% of their blood supply from family/replacement or paid donors, where a number of these countries interprets family/replacement as being voluntary non-remunerated.

Of the donations in high-income and upper-middle-income countries respectively 99.8% and 99.9% are screened following basic quality procedures, as compared to 82% in lower-middle-income countries and 80.3% in low-income countries, expressing a degree of safety for transfusion. The prevalence of transfusion-transmissible infections in blood donations in high-income countries is considerably lower than in low- and middle-income countries (Table 3). The lower the prevalence the safer the blood supply reflecting an important knowledge economy aspect. The higher the general education the better the general knowledge and the more effective knowledge economy.

Table 3. Prevalence of transfusion-transmissible infectious agents in blood donations [Median, Interquartile range (IQR)], by World Bank income groups

Income Group	HIV	HBV	HCV	Syphilis
High-income	0.001%	0.01%	0.06%	0.01%
	(0 – 0.01%)	(0.003 – 0.13%)	(0.002 – 0.05%)	(0.002 –0.11%)
Upper middle-income	0.10%	0.29%	0.18%	0.34%
	(0.03 – 0.23%)	(0.15 – 0.62%)	(0.06 – 0.35%)	(0.11 –1.08%)
Lower middle-income	0.19%	1.96%	0.38%	0.69%
	(0.03 – 0.77%)	(0.76 – 5.54%)	(0.03 –0.80%)	(0.16 – 1.25%)
Low-income	0.70%	2.81%	1.00%	0.92%
	(0.33 – 1.66%)	(2.00 – 4.50%)	(0.50 – 2.23%)	(0.60 – 1.81%)

These differences reflect the variation in prevalence among populations eligible to donate blood, the type of donors (such as voluntary non-remunerated blood donors from lower risk populations) and the effectiveness of the system of educating and selecting donors. It also reflects the differences in exposure to proper education and knowledge, including the accessible quality of the knowledge and outcome of the education process leading to awareness.

Unsafe transfusion practices and unnecessary transfusions expose patients to the risk of serious adverse transfusion events and transfusion-transmissible infections. Unnecessary transfusions also reduce the availability of blood products for patients who are in need. It is recommended to develop systems and benchmarking tools, such as hospital transfusion committees (HTC), patient blood management (PBM) and hemovigilance, to monitor and improve the safety of clinical transfusion processes.

The WHO global database (WHO, 2017) shows 128 countries that do have national guidelines on the appropriate clinical prescription and use of blood: 32 countries in the African region (74% of reporting countries in the region), 22 in the Americas (67%), 13 in the Eastern Mediterranean (68%), 33 in European (80%), nine in the South-East Asian (90%), and 19 in the Western Pacific (76%). Hospital Transfusion Committees (HTC) are present in 50% of the hospitals performing transfusions: 65% in hospitals in high-income countries, 35% in upper-middle-income countries, 31% in lower-middle-income countries and 25% in low-income countries. Systems for reporting and documenting adverse transfusion events are present in 57% of the hospitals prescribing and performing blood transfusions: 76% in hospitals in high-income countries, 35% in upper-middle-income countries, 22% in lower-middle-income countries and 18% in low-income countries, where 49% of reporting countries have a hemovigilance system. The European region, where in the 1980s hemovigilance started, has the highest percentage of countries with a hemovigilance system (83%), followed by the Western Pacific (48%), the Eastern Mediterranean (47%), African (40%), South-East Asian (40%), and the Americas (21%).

These situation analysis data provide a quantitative and qualitative idea of the state of development of the blood system in the World Bank development categories of countries, illustrating huge differences, where today knowledge is much more easily accessible as compared to the immediate post World War II decades. However, the UNDP 2018 Report (UNDP, 2018) together with the 2020 eLearning Africa/ EdTech^{Hub} report on the 'Effect of COVID-19 on Education in Africa and its Implication for the Use of Technology (ICT)' (EdTech and eLearning Africa, 2020) illustrate the problems to get access to structured quality education and applicable knowledge in an adequate quantity of years of exposure. In the low- and middle-income world there are too few professionals who could contribute to an effective economy of knowledge. That is one of the fundamental reasons for the still existing knowledge gap as a lock without a key to development. The more knowledge is acquired and treasured, the better the economy and the faster a structured and evidence-based development will be achieved. Knowledge provides the 'green fuel' for development, applied science and professionalism, needed to accelerate the stepwise moving forward. Economies of adequate scale provide the climate for effective knowledge economy, doing things better with less effort and an effective use of all resources, especially the human intellectual knowledge driven resource.

World Bank Knowledge Economy Pillars and the Blood System

When benchmarking development in blood systems against the mentioned four World Bank knowledge economy pillars (Chen & Dahlman, 2006) –

1. Institutional structures that provide incentives for entrepreneurship and the active use of knowledge.
2. Availability of competent (knowledge and skills) labor and a good education system.
3. Access to and exchange of information and communication technology (ICT, AI) infrastructures.
4. A vibrant innovation landscape that includes academia, the private and governance sectors, and civil society.

the following could be observed and implemented –

Ad 1 - Institutional Structures That Provide Incentives for Entrepreneurship and the Active Use of Knowledge

The institutional and economic regime of an economy like the healthcare and integrated blood system needs to be such that governance and leadership have incentives for the creation and efficient use of knowledge, and thus should have well-grounded and transparent macroeconomic, competition and regulatory policies. A 'knowledge-conducive' regime in general is one that will be free from various protectionist policies to foster development through healthy competition, which in turn will encourage entrepreneurship. Government expenditures and budget deficits should be sustainable, and inflation should be stable and low. The exchange rate should be stable and reflect the true value of the currency to allow uninterrupted imported supplies of consumables and reagents/test kits, and equipment. The financial system should preferably be one based on cost-recovery, able to allocate resources to sound investment opportunities and redeploy assets from failed enterprises to more promising ones through consolidation and creation of effective operational economies of scale.

Ad 2 - Availability of Competent (Knowledge and Skills) Labor and a Good Quality Education System

A well-educated and skilled population is essential to the efficient creation, acquisition, dissemination, and utilization of relevant knowledge, which tends to increase total productivity and hence economic growth and prevention of shortages. Basic/primary education is necessary to increase peoples' capacity to learn and to use information. On the other hand, technical secondary-level education, and higher education in engineering and scientific areas is necessary for technological innovation. The production of new knowledge and its adaptation to a particular economic setting is generally associated with higher-level teaching and research. Secondary-level education is also required for the process of technological adaptation of foreign technologies for use in domestic production processes such as the manufacture of blood products. Such training is necessary to monitor technological trends, assess what is relevant for the blood supply, and assimilate new technologies. A more educated population also tends to be relatively more technologically sophisticated and competent. This generates a local quality sensitive demand for advanced blood products, which in turn tends to stimulate blood establishments to innovate and design technologically sophisticated products and production techniques such as pathogen inactivation and cellular therapies.

Ad 3 - Access to and Exchange of Information and Communication Technology (ICT and AI) Infrastructures

Information and communication technologies (ICT and AI) infrastructure in an economy refers to the accessibility, reliability, capacities and efficiency of computers, phones, television and radio sets, and the various networks that link them. ICT consists of hardware, software, networks, and media for collection, storage, processing transmission, and presentation of information in the form of voice, data, text, and images. Apart from increasing the supply of information and knowledge, ICTs can overcome geographic boundaries.

ICTs are the backbone of the knowledge economy and in recent years have been recognized as an effective tool for promoting economic growth and sustainable development. With relatively low usage costs and the ability to overcome distance, ICTs have revolutionized the transfer of information and knowledge around the world. Over the past decade, there has been a series of studies that show that both ICT production and ICT usage have contributed to economic or operational growth. One of the most obvious benefits associated with ICT usage is the increased flow of information and knowledge. Because ICTs allow information to be transmitted relatively inexpensively, fast, and efficiently (in terms of cost), ICT usage tends to reduce uncertainty and transactions costs of participating in transactions. This, in turn, tends to lead to an increase in the volume of transactions leading to a higher level of output and productivity. Moreover, with the increased flow of information, technologies can be acquired and adapted more easily again leading to increased innovation and productivity as well as reduction in errors and unwanted deviations from standards.

Ad 4 – A Vibrant Innovation Landscape that Includes Academia, the Private and Governance Sectors, and Civil Society

Economic theory indicates that technical progress is a major source of productivity growth, and an effective innovation system is key for such technical advancement. An innovation system refers to the network of institutions, rules and procedures that influences the way by which a country acquires, creates, disseminates, and uses knowledge. Institutions in the innovation system include universities, healthcare institutions, public and private research centers and policy think tanks. Non-governmental organizations and the government are also part of the innovation system to the extent that they also produce new knowledge.

An effective innovation system is one that provides an environment and climate that nurtures research and development (R&D), which results in new products and services, new processes, and new knowledge, and hence is a major source of technical progress and development. Currently, most of the technical knowledge is produced in the advanced countries: More than 70% of production of scientific and technical publications are accredited to researchers in advanced countries. The disparity in the production of technical knowledge per capita between advanced and developing countries is even greater than the disparity in income. However, domestic technological innovation is not the sole source of generation of technical knowledge. There are many ways for developing countries to avoid reinventing the wheel and tap into, adopt and adapt technical knowledge that was created in advanced countries. A key element of a developing country's innovation strategy is to find the best ways to tap into the growing global knowledge base and to decide where and how to deploy its domestic R&D capability to strengthen existing systems and structures and accelerate the pace of development.

CONCLUSION AND RECOMMENDATIONS

From the analysis the most essential key elements of knowledge economy are in the establishment of

- a well-constructed and sustainable education environment, climate and adaptive radiation structure.
- a well-balanced and designed education scope and quality of knowledge.
- intellectual property, stewardship, and ownership.

These should be supported and accompanied by a genuine curiosity, continued exploration and a healthy appetite to science and evidence-based knowledge that drive development and determine the pace of acceleration towards advancement and improved effectiveness – safety, availability, accessibility, affordability, equity, and equality.

The available and expanding knowledge in the broad and comprehensive sense of the word should actively and purposeful be shared and exchanged through integrity-based collaboration and cooperation, away from dubious charity and knowledge colonialism. The quantitative statistical data presented (UNDP, 2018), whatever the reality of the quality of these data, unveil the enormous differences in UNDP indices and indicators state of development brought about by weak and brittle governance, regulations, leadership and stewardship structures and cultures in an impressively large part and population in the world.

These elements need a high, sustained, and devoted prioritization in the development to which economic spending, sharing and exchange of knowledge is paramount. The economy is not in the first place financial but depends on awareness and understanding of those who have the knowledge, willing to share and exchange, and convinced that such attitude is the missing key needed to unlock and access knowledge as a common human intellectual property to development and progress improvement.

REFERENCES

Al-Riyami, A. Z., Louw, V. J., Indrikovs, A. J., Nedelcu, E., Bakhtary, S., Eichbaum, Q. G., & Smit Sibinga, C. Th. (2021) Global Survey of Transfusion Medicine Curricula in Medical Schools – Challenges and Opportunities. *Transfusion, 61*, 617-26.

Chen, D. H. C., & Dahlman, C. J. (2006). The Knowledge Economy, the KAM Methodology and World Bank Operations. World Bank Institute.

EdTech[Hub] & eLearning Africa. (2020). *The Effect of Covid-19 on Education in Africa and its Implications for the Use of Technology. A survey of the experience and opinions of educators and technology specialists*. doi:10.5281/zenodo.4019774

Giffi, G., Dollar, B., Gangula, B., & Rodriguez, D. (2015). Help Wanted. American manufacturing competitiveness and the looming skills gap. *Deloitte Review, 16*, 97–113.

Hayes, A. (2021). Knowledge Economy. *Investopedia*. Accessible at https://www.investopedia.com/terms/k/knowledge-economy.asp#:~:text=The%20knowledge%20economy%20is%20a,is%20based%20on%20intellectual%20capital.&text=In%20a%20knowledge%20economy%2C%20a,workers'%20knowledge%20or%20intellectual%20property

Rambiritch, V., & Smith-Tolken, A. (2019). The imperative of teaching professionalism to biomedical technologists. *AJHPE, 11*(4), 139–144. doi:10.7196/AJHPE.2019.v11i4.1101

Rambiritch, V., Vermeulen, M., Bell, H., Knox, P., Nedelcu, E., Al-Riyami, A. Z., & Callum, J. (2021). Transfusion medicine and blood banking education and training for blood establishment laboratory staff: A review of selected countries in Africa. *Transfusion*, 1-10. doi:10.1111/trf.16372

Smit Sibinga, C. T., & van Galen, J. P. (2020). The Blood Supply – A special manufacturing process. Manufacturing Systems: Recent Progress, 165-186.

Smit Sibinga, C.T., Louw, V. J., Nedelcu, E., Al-Riyami, A. Z., Bakhtary, S., Johnson, S. T., Rambiritch, V., Seoraj, V., Callum, J., Berg, K., Vermeulen, M., Barrett, C. A., & Eichbaum, Q. G. (2021). Modelling Global Transfusion Medicine Education. *Transfusion*, *61*(10), 3040–3049. doi:10.1111/trf.16641 PMID:34469008

Thomas, W. I., & Thomas, D. S. (1928). *The Child in America*. Alfred Knopf.

UNDP. (2018). *2018 Statistical Update: Human Development Indices and Indicators*. Accessible at http://hdr.undp.org/en/content/human-development-indices-indicators-2018-statistical-update

UNDP. (2020). *Human Development Index*. Accessible at Wikipedia https://en.wikipedia.org/wiki/Human_Development_Index#:~:text=The%20Human%20Development%20Index%20(HDI,four%20tiers%20of%20human%20development

WHA. (1975). *Resolution 28.72 Blood Safety and Availability*. Accessible at https://www.who.int/bloodsafety/en/WHA28.72.pdf

WHO. (1988). *GBSI/GPA/2E Global Blood Safety Initiative background paper*. World Health Organization.

WHO. (2015). *Quality Management Training for Blood Transfusion Services*. Accessible at https://www.who.int/bloodsafety/publications/qmp_toolkit/en/

WHO. (2017). *Global Status Report on Blood Safety and Availability 2016*. Accessible at http://apps.who.int/iris/bitstream/handle/10665/254987/9789241565431-eng.pdf;jsessionid=1349FE91E41956276C864FB396ABF158?sequence=1

WHO. (2020). *Blood Safety and Availability. Key Facts*. Access at https://www.who.int/news-room/fact-sheets/detail/blood-safety-and-availability

WHO (2021a). *Guidance on Centralization of Blood Donation Testing and Processing*. Licence: CC BY-NC-SDA 3.0 IGO.

WHO. (2021b). *Safe Blood and Blood Products: Distance Learning Materials*. Accessible at https://apps.who.int/iris/handle/10665/61622

WHO. (2021c). *Global Patient Safety Action Plan 2021-2030. Towards eliminating avoidable harm in health care*. Accessible at https://www.who.int/docs/default-source/patient-safety/global-patient-safety-action-plan-2021-2030_third-draft_january-2021_web.pdf?sfvrsn=948f15d5_17

Chapter 5
Telemedecine the the Context of COVID-19 in Ecuador

Danilo Piaggesi
https://orcid.org/0000-0003-4610-174X
Knowledge for Development (K4D), USA

Helena Landazuri
Knowledge for Development (K4D), USA

Bo Jia
Tsinghua University, China

EXECUTIVE SUMMARY

The improvement in the delivery of healthcare services in geographically remote and rural areas is one of the most promising and clearly demonstrated applications of information and communication technology (ICT) in sustainable development. ICT provides considerable benefits and capabilities when applied to disease prevention and response efforts during epidemics and pandemics. The expansion of the COVID-19 outbreak that began in Wuhan, China alerted all the countries of the world from the beginning of 2020 and reached Latin America in mid-February 2020. In this chapter, VERIS, an Ecuadorian successful practice of telemedicine during the COVID-19 times, is presented. VERIS allows remote consultation with a certified doctor, following the WHO protocol, and other relevant services provided also remotely. The VERIS experience is particularly relevant during the present COVID-19 pandemic because it eliminates the risks of contagion deriving from visiting hospitals in person and could be particularly useful for emerging economies with practical implications for mature ones.

DOI: 10.4018/978-1-7998-8417-0.ch005

THE COUNTRY UNDER COVID-19

Impact

The expansion of the COVID-19 outbreak that began in Wuhan, China, alerted all the countries of the world from the beginning of 2020 and reached Latin America in mid-February 2020. Ecuador, in the northwest corner of South America, has a population of 17.6 million; it has so far (May 2021) had around 410,000 cases of COVID-19 (2.36% of its population), with 20,000 deaths (0.12% of its population).

In Ecuador the announcement of the first COVID-19 case occurred on February 29, 2020 by the Ministry of Public Health, dealing with a 71-year-old woman, who arrived in the country on February 14 2020 from Madrid, Spain. Since then, there has been a progressive increase in cases (See Table 1).

Table 1. COVID-19 Situation in Ecuador

	July 23 2020	October 17 2020	May 23 2021
Confirmed cases:	79,940	151,659	417,840
People recovered:	5,900	128,134	354,499
Deaths:	5,489	12,357	20,180
Dropped cases:	107,235	265,959	922,652
Hospital discharges:	10,555	20,249	43,745

Source: (Ministry of Public Health and Worldometers, 2021)

Of those infected, around 45% are women and 55% are men. By age groups close to 60% are between 20 to 49 years of age, 22% of 50 to 64 years of age, 15% of those over 65 years of age. For several months at the onset of the pandemic, Ecuador was considered the hot spot of COVID-19 in South America.

The rapid spread of COVID-19 took the international medical community, authorities, and the population by surprise. Governments and even international health organizations initially treated the pandemic as a sectoral health emergency. The impact of the pandemic quickly developed serious socio-economic and political implications due not only to the direct effects of the disease (number of persons affected) but also due to the impact of prevention and mitigation measures adopted to prevent and reduce transmission upon the productive sectors. Principal among them has been the partial or total shutdowns that have affected practically all sectors of the economy in countries around the world, both at the national and the at community levels.

UNDP estimates that in 2020 Ecuador has suffered losses of close to USD6.5 billion, nearly 6% of its nominal GDP in 2019 (UNDP, 2020). Some sources project the COVID-19's impact on Ecuador's economy will grow to 11% of its GDP by the end of 2021 (Statista, 2020). As Ecuador ranks seventh in terms of nominal GDP in the context of LAC, COVID-19's impact will be devastating to its economy, and it will put its health system to the limits of its capacity.

UNDP estimates that the COVID-19 pandemic has caused the number of the poor in Ecuador to raise by over 50%, reaching to close to 40% of the population. The middle class was also impacted, with over 10% leaving the middle-class category to enter the poverty category. Concomitantly, as a consequence of the pandemic, some 13% of the population currently face food insecurity. As in the rest of the world, the socio-economic groups worst affected by the pandemic prevention and remediation strategies are the young –loss of education and employment opportunities—and the old –lack of access to medical services and loss of social network support.

Also UNDP estimates that over 80% of economic losses corresponds to the private sector and the rest to the public sector. A full two-thirds of those losses were borne by the productive sector, which showcases the need for a comprehensive socio-economic recovery strategy.

Response of the Medical Establishment: Capabilities and Limitations

Ecuador's Constitution guarantees the right to health and permanent, timely and inclusive access to comprehensive health promotion and care services through economic, social, cultural, educational and environmental policies. 2018 data revealed an 8.1% gap in the effective access to health services, that families invest in health up to 39% of the value of the sector budget, and 2.4% of the Ecuadorian population has been pushed below the poverty line by catastrophic health expenditures (WHO et al., 2020).

In Ecuador, the health sector is made up of five subsystems: four public and one private. The four public subsystems are led by the Ministry of Public Health and include three social security institutes, one for the general population, one for the military and the last one for the police. The public subsystem service provision is articulated through the Comprehensive Public Health Network, which follows a Comprehensive Health Care Model which in turn includes health promotion, disease prevention, health recovery and rehabilitation, and palliative care, pain management and accompaniment in good death.

In 2018, there were 4,165 health establishments in Ecuador, of which 80% belonged to the public sector and 20% from the private sector. Eight nine percent of public sector facilities do not have in-patient care, while the private sector has more hospital centers (64%) with 39% of the beds (INEC-RAS, 2018).

The public health care subsystems are assigned a budget that constituted approximately 5% of GDP in 2020. The ratio of medical personnel to population is 23 per 10,000 inhabitants, a minimum standard defined by PAHO; the ratio nurses to population is 15 per 10,000 inhabitants. The shortage of hospital and Intensive Care Unit beds at the beginning of the emergency, (1,183 available between public and private, equal to 7 beds per 100,000 inhabitants) was evident during the pandemic.

The private sector includes for-profit hospitals, clinics, physicians' offices, pharmacies and prepaid health care organizations. There are also non-for-profit private outfits offering health and medicine services, including non-governmental organizations (NGOs), social service associations and other popular health service providers. To this, private health insurance companies must be added, although their coverage is only around 3% of the population. (Iturralde, 2015)

In May 2020, the United Nations Secretary General alerted nations to the implications of the pandemic and called for structuring, among other measures, a large socio-economic response based on five pillars; insisting that actions during and after this crisis must have a strong focus on building more equitable, inclusive and sustainable economies and societies, more resistant to pandemics, climate change and other global challenges (UNDP 2020). The pillars are:

- Protecting existing health services and strengthening the capacity of health systems.
- Helping people cope with adversity through social protection and basic services.
- Protecting jobs, supporting small and medium-sized enterprises, as well as workers in the informal sector.

- Guiding the necessary increase in fiscal and financial stimulus for macroeconomic policies to benefit the most vulnerable populations.
- Promoting social cohesion and investing in community resilience and response systems.

On March 12th 2020, Ecuador's Ministry of Health declared a sanitary emergency affecting all medical establishments that are part of the National Health System originally for 60 days, which the government has been extending ever since. Besides issuing regulations concerning the use of different tests to detect the virus, and measures to protect workers' benefits and manage access to public services, transportation and other administrative issues, as well as directives to affect the behavior of the population, the government has not issued a policy document to deal with the emergency. Policy is being issued through public communication channels, and decisions taken daily in response to changing circumstances.

The state of emergency facilitated the adoption of measures to respond to the health emergency through personal, family and community prevention and care, reprogramming of budgets, assignment of responsibilities to the institutions of the system, procurement of equipment and drugs, approval of protocols, organization of human effort, information management and other key aspects.

The country has made a significant effort to tackle the pandemic. In less than 2 months, the capacity to process COVID-19 tests in the country tripled; by the end of April 2020 there were 42 public hospitals and 35 of the private sector specifically dedicated to attend to COVID-19 cases. Up to now, the Health Ministry's online reporting system has managed close to 1,986,392 calls, has followed up through phone calls 471,058 to confirmed patients, and has provided remote services (teleconsultation) to 137,541 cases. (Ministry of Public Health, 2021)

Despite this effort, the demands imposed by the pandemic overcame the ability of the established medical system to give an adequate response. The following limitations have been apparent:

- The pandemic altered the operation and budget of the sector as a result of the increase in the number of prehospital, emergency, primary and hospital care services for COVID-19, with the use of laboratories, imaging and drugs; the drastic reduction of regular patient care in the public network; the substantial reduction of health promotion and disease prevention programs; the referral of patients from the public network to the complementary private network; and the increase in the number of COVID-19 deaths.
- Limited diagnostic capacity for the detection, isolation and timely care of COVID-19 cases: There is one laboratory certified as the National Liaison Centre and National Reference Laboratory certified by the WHO in the city of Guayaquil, for the collection and processing of samples by COVID-19 by using PCR tests. The laboratory has expanded its capabilities to other major cities; however, demand has exceeded response capacity. The National Institute for Public Health Research (INSPI) with the support of the National Institute for Public Health Research (ARCSA) is reviewing the certification of 22 private laboratories whose installed capacities, however, would not be enough.
- Lack of health personnel for epidemiological surveillance actions and timely case care at all levels of care: 400 doctors, nurses, epidemiologists, and health workers have been infected by COVID-19.
- Shortage of personal protective equipment (PPE), equipment and supplies at the national level, as well as suppliers at the international level to supply the demand: Because all countries are experiencing outbreaks of COVID-19, there is a shortage of personal protection equipment, medical

equipment and supplies to meet the country's demands; this factor makes the provision of health services for patients with severe and critically ill conditions difficult.

- Difficulties in caring for patients who require hospitalization and critical care: In the cities of Quito and Guayaquil, which concentrate the largest number of COVID-19 cases, health care service providers have been overwhelmed in their response capacities, which makes it difficult to attend to all cases that require assistance at the third level of care.
- Difficulties in handling fatalities: Due to the increase in the average number of deaths per day there has been a reduction in the capacity of funeral homes in the public and private sectors to respond to the growing demand for these services. The operational guidelines for the management of dead bodies by COVID-19 and the limited capacity to put them into practice also contributed to deficiencies in the timely and technical management of the deceased (United Nations, 2020).
- Prevention of hospital infections to protect healthcare personnel from possible COVID-19 contagion: It is estimated that at least 10% of the total number of people infected with COVID-19 correspond to health personnel. The lack of protective equipment and the application of infection prevention and control standards has led to contagion by health personnel, who are also among those population groups with the greatest capacity to spread the disease.
- Disruption of access to sexual and reproductive health: Evidence from past epidemics, including Ebola and Zika, indicate that efforts to contain outbreaks generally divert resources from routine health services including prenatal and postnatal care, contraceptives, and sharpen access to sexual and reproductive health services. In addition, access to critical care such as clean and safe delivery, treatment of complications in pregnancy, treatment of sexually transmitted infections (STIs), availability of contraceptives, and supplies for the clinical management of rape, have all suffered (United Nations, 2020).

TELEMEDICINE AS A VIABLE OPTION TO TREAT DEMAND FOR COVID-19 MEDICAL SERVICES

There is considerable literature concerning the usefulness of ICT in the delivery of health services. In fact, the improvement in the delivery of health care services in geographically remote and rural areas is one of the most promising and clearly demonstrated applications of ICT in sustainable development. ICT is often credited for the deliverance of positive social and economic impacts that help solve some of the most stringent development problems.

Indeed, telemedicine solutions can facilitate the participation of lower-income populations in the development process by directly tackling aspects that hinder their social integration and economic development, for example limited literacy which impairs knowledge of available services and limited access to preventive health contents, which results in poor health and sanitary conditions. In this respect, the digital transformation brings about concrete opportunities for enhanced provision of social services and poverty reduction. It also provides for the modernization and expansion of the private health sector to effectively reach marginalized and less favored populations through effective technology-based solutions.

In practical terms, at the level of a country, the application of ICT to the field of medicine and health services provides the opportunity to harness some of that potential and put it to use generating numerous benefits, At this level, telemedicine can be credited with facilitating:

1. Dissemination of public health messages and disease prevention techniques, particularly important in disease prevention during epidemics and pandemics;
2. Fast distribution of healthcare services with the support of wireless connections to hospitals, clinics, pharmacies, and front-line health workers, as well as expanding mobile networks and newer broadband wireless networks and solutions;
3. Ability to reach wider audiences;
4. Attainment of real-time monitoring of the disease, rapid response to disaster hot spot areas and health emergencies, and timely restocking of medicines;
5. Improvement in the operational efficiency of public and private health care systems through knowledge management and process automation, streamlining medical procurement or creating and managing patient records;
6. Expansion of national telemedicine efforts through both, remote screening and diagnosis, and live consultations with national or international experts on serious cases and, thereby, improvement in the standard of care in many smaller towns and remote villages;
7. Implementation of inexpensive digital distribution networks for public health information, including easily updated video and audio segments or inexpensive devices in every clinic and in many schools and community centers.

At the level of the patient, evidence suggests that improved health outcomes have been achieved through various applications of ICT solutions. In particular, ICT is being used in many developing countries and communities to facilitate:

1. Access to information to educate patients regarding preventive medicine, nutrition and other associated topics;
2. Access to personalized medical advice in remote rural areas, where medical services are otherwise unavailable;
3. Remote consultation, diagnosis and treatment through the use of digital cameras to download images onto a computer and transfer them to doctors in nearby towns, which can have the added benefit of involving shorter consultation time;
4. Access to information and data to support online medical services to facilitate follow-up and periodic monitoring for the patient;
5. Access one's medical records of procedures undertaken in different times and locations, and ability to compare and analyze, share and store such records;
6. Access to immediate support and response in case of emergencies;
7. Lower individual costs as opposed to in-person treatments, given lower fixed costs than those associated to in-person services infrastructure;
8. Positive psychological effects of peace of mind resulting from quick return diagnosis and the ability to establish immediate communication with a doctor to pose questions and receive quick answers;
9. Collaboration and information exchange among physicians;
10. ICT-based medical research through the use of a network of satellites and ground stations to submit data for clinical trials;
11. Medical training through ICT-enabled delivery mechanisms; and
12. Access to centralized data repositories connected to ICT networks that enable remote healthcare professionals to keep abreast of medical knowledge.

The disruption of COVID-19 has accelerated technological innovation and pushed forward policy changes related to telehealth in Latin America. The tele-monitoring segment accounted for 25% of the Latin America telemedicine market share in 2019. Additionally, the call centers segment represented 40%. Several platforms in the region have emerged and demonstrated rapid growth. For example, the Colombian telehealth company 1Doc3 is aggressively addressing the issue of access to healthcare in Latin America with its all-in-one telemedicine platform. It is currently Latin America's largest telemedicine provider. Since the onset of COVID-19, its platform has experienced a seven-fold increase in consultations, serving 300,000 patients in May 2020 and projecting a 50% growth in demand in June 2020. Similar experiences are present in Peru and Mexico, among others. (Pierce et al., 2021)

Untapped opportunities exist to replicate, multiply and scale up successful practices and approaches in the deployment of ICT to contribute to the fight against the COVID-19 pandemic. Of interest are those opportunities that further the potential of ICT for sharing knowledge, generating synergies and economies of scale, adapting to local conditions, and facilitating access to preventive and curative health by low-income communities.

Naturally, changes in a country's infrastructure need to take place before this potential is seized. For telehealth innovation to take hold and gain scale, several elements of telecommunications infrastructure, adequate connectivity and access to technology equipment would need to be provided. Internet literacy needs to raise, and overall literacy will also need to be widespread to make effective use of internet contents.

Internet connectivity, in particular, is crucial to support the expansion of telemedicine. In fact, the Pan American Health Organization recommends that any online interactions between a clinician and a patient for the purpose of providing diagnostic or therapeutic advice through electronic means should be conducted over fast and stable Internet and broadband connections, including asymmetric digital subscriber line, fiber optic, cable, or 4G, with at least 1 MB/300 kb. (Pan American Health Organization, 2021)

The economic crisis derived from the pandemia affecting developing countries in particular will inevitably limit governments' ability to make the necessary investment in the short term. The role of the private sector becomes crucial under these circumstances.

VERIS, A SUCCESSFUL CASE OF PRIVATE SECTOR FUNDED TELEMEDICINE APPLIED TO COVID-19

Context

During COVID-19, the world is experiencing how to learn, work, socialize, shop, and collaborate in different ways. Many people are doing all this virtually particularly in the provision of medical services, because remote services eliminate the risks of contagion deriving from visiting hospitals in person. The pandemic is therefore a watershed moment for the digital transformation of people's lives. Humanity relies more today on harnessing the power of digital transformation to create new value and experiences. Looking at it this way, COVID-19 is a shared opportunity for improving the quality of people's lives and that of services rendered by the public and private sectors as a by-product of tending to the emergency.

Successful companies are seizing the opportunity to advance a new trajectory for digital transformation that aligns with the changing role of business to become powerful enablers of long-term value creation for its stakeholders. The case presented here showcases the increasing and evolving role and relevance of digital transformation in medicine, presenting a successful practice of telemedicine in Ecuador at the hands of an innovative private enterprise.

In July 2020 the Government of Ecuador, through the Ministry of Public Health issued a Protocol to foster the use of telemedicine to support the government's efforts to combat the pandemic; the Minister of Health emphatically invited all health service providers to make extensive use of it. While public sector hospitals and health centers received some form of support from the government to start offering telemedicine services –mainly in the form of equipment and training--, private sector outfits had to make the investment.

By the end of 2020, there were slightly over 300 private health establishments participating in the provision of services associated to the COVID-19 pandemic. As per government regulations, their participation is so far limited to sample collection and testing (Calidadsalud, 2020).

Ecuador's newly elected President has vowed to vaccinate some 9 million people against COVID-19 between March and September 2021. He plans to do this by partnering with private sector health providers to distribute doses from various vaccine manufacturers, for which the government is setting aside $200 million to purchase vaccines from seven companies including Pfizer Inc (PFE.N) and BioNTech SE. Vaccination would concentrate on the adult population, starting with inoculation of senior citizens in shelters and medical personnel working in hospitals that treat COVID-19 patients.

Ecuador expects to have about 400 distribution centers, including primary care centers in rural areas, and 10,000 vaccination points such as pharmacies, universities and even companies whose facilities include medical offices. Ecuador will carry out the vaccinations in phases that will depend on supply deals negotiated with the manufacturers. Ecuador also forms part of the World Health Organization's (WHO) COVAX vaccine initiative intended to oversee equitable access to the protection against COVID-19, and has recently announced agreements with Russia to gain access to the Sputnik vaccine (Reuters, 2020).

Among private providers, VERIS stands out for its commitment to make full use of technology inputs coupled with open lines of cooperation with the public sector and academia. VERIS is used here as an example of how vertical and horizontal integration utilizing elements of what is known as the KE architecture can help a private company succeed in a context where the "public good" is the overarching objective. The case of VERIS shows these potential benefits as applied during the present COVID-19 pandemic in Ecuador, a developing country. This experience could be particularly useful for emerging economies, with practical implications for mature ones. This case has been selected based on the company's service strategy, availability of its operational and financial records, and its willingness to provide the data for this paper.

VERIS' Objective

The objective VERIS pursues in the current context of COVID-19 pandemic is to provide faster, cheaper and safer diagnostic and treatment services to the community in Ecuador, by modernizing its technological tools, training its staff, adjusting costs to reach lower-income groups, and working with central governmental strategies that support telemedicine and related aspects.

Organization

VERIS allows remote consultation with a certified Doctor, following the WHO protocol, and other relevant services provided both in person and remotely. VERIS is a private enterprise registered in

Ecuador; established in 1999 under the name "Punto Médico Familiar" (Family Medicine Point, PMF) with the goal to offer health services to Ecuadorian families; PMF opened its first centre in the north of Guayaquil city, which was followed by a second centre in the same city in 2001, and a third one in Quito. This effort adopted the name VERIS In April 2013, with a view to continue to provide health services to more patients and grow its supply of services. Currently, VERIS has 12 medical centres, 12 clinical labs and more than 1,280 people working.

In 2018, the VERIS Online project was launched. VERIS has invested heavily in acquiring state of the art technological capabilities, emphasizing web-based platforms and online consultation services. In this area, VERIS is pioneer in Ecuador, and to a great extent, in the rest of South America. Today, VERIS offers services that include:

1. Personalized and monitored accompaniment for the patient in both medical and administrative procedures;
2. Full range of services besides medical attention, including imaging, dentistry, optical, physical therapy and pharmacy;
3. Complete integration of online medical services such as laboratory analysis and results check and video consultations, which are accompanied by an efficient system of home collection and delivery services;
4. Offer of preventive plans for all pathologies or chronic diseases that includes monitoring and periodic controls;
5. Strategic alliances with private entities;
6. Work with numerous insurance companies, national and international;
7. Low carbon footprint;
8. Landing page system (web page) and complete App; and
9. Online payment service that is economical, safe and practical.

VERIS has experienced significant growth over the past three years. Revenues increased from US$35M in 2016 to US$50M in 2019, primarily due to its retail expansion strategy, which included adding 3 new centre locations in the most populous cities in Ecuador. These new centres contributed to expanding its client database from 258,000 clients at the end of 2016, to almost 390,000 in 2019.

As patient volume increased, VERIS revisited its pricing strategy, aligning it to its business and marketing plan, focusing on attaching more value to the VERIS brand by pricing its services within the market but fairly above of lower-priced competitors.

The company also put in place consistent actions to increase cost efficiency at retail centres, including renewed negotiations with larger-scale suppliers, introducing statistics analysis in capacity planning, and implementing budgetary discipline and control, which all contributed in generating important savings in VERIS sales and operational costs.

Additionally, significant investments in information systems and technology, helped VERIS contain its General & Administrative expenses (G&A) during this expansion effort. G&A expenses/Revenues ratio was reduced from 11.5% in 2016 to 8.4% in 2019. All these efforts combined, helped consolidate the Earnings Before Interest, Taxes, Depreciation and Amortization (EBITDA) which grew from US$2.6M in 2016 to US$4.1M in 2019; and VERIS Net profit margin grew from 1.5% in 2016 to 3,9% in 2019.

Intervention

Early Period

Before the start of the pandemic, VERIS online assisted about 10 patients per day and that line of service was growing very slowly, around 1 or 2% per month. Even during the weeks immediately before the pandemic, online assistance followed the same pattern; in fact, in the first two weeks of March VERIS had a total of 145 patients assisted through 154 appointments, that is close to 10 per day.

However, from March 16 –the day the Ecuadorian government made the onset of the pandemic official-- to April 1st, there were 4,812 patients assisted through 5,813 online appointments; in just 15 days VERIS online service grew more than 3000%, which was the largest growth in a service in the history of the company. After this initial peek, online services continued to increase In April for an additional 290% with 12,495 patients assisted through 16,988 online appointments, thus reaching the highest peak of consultations provided through this service. During that period VERIS provided online assistance to an average of 800 patients per day. In May 8,207 patients were assisted through 10,979 online appointments and in June 5,052 patients were assisted through 6,740 appointments. The average fell by around 180%, of course, due to the drop in demand because there are fewer patients with suspected COVID-19.

There was a significant increase in cases of COVID-19 in the months of April (18,253 cases) and July (26,000 cases) up to October (30610 cases). The first is explained by a peak of new cases in the Province of Guayas (mostly Guayaquil city, the epicenter at the beginning of the pandemic in Ecuador; the second, in turn, is associated to a peek in cases for the Province of Pichincha, where the city of Quito became the new epicenter of the pandemic in the country.

In July the trend began to increase again since 6,015 patients were registered and assisted through a total of 8,420 medical appointments. By the end of July, VERIS online was treating 330 patients daily. 40% of patients reserve their medical appointments through VERIS digital platforms. As of 20th of November, 180 thousands attentions were generated through the Virtual Medical Center.

From the onset of the pandemic in Ecuador (March 2020) to date (November 2020), VERIS has provided medical attention to a total of 585,214 patients, with an average of 3 appointments per patient. Of these, 45,344 corresponds to patients suspected of being infected with COVID-19. Out of these, 11,069 were positive to COVID-19, which represents 5.7% of all confirmed cases nation-wide. VERIS' share of the number of cases found positive is an impressive coverage for a relatively small, recently established private outfit (See Table 2).

Table 2. VERIS coverage of COVID-19 cases during the pandemic

Month 2020	Patients	Suspected of COVID-19		Positive to COVID-19		Video-Consultation
		Cases	% of Total Patients	Cases	% of Suspected Cases	% of Suspected Cases
March	80,151	2,653	3.31	696	26.26	52.82
April	19.130	6,034	31.64	2,084	34.54	62.88
May	32,819	5,796	17.66	1,731	29.87	38.84
June	57,871	4,676	8.08	1,065	22.78	28.00
July	64,556	6,704	9.92	1,431	21.36	36.20
August	77,144	6801	8.82	1652	24.29	33.88
September	80,396	4,225	5.26	845	20.01	26.62
October	88,794	4,101	4.62	735	17.93	26.92
November	84,353	4,354	5.16	829	19.05	29.35
Total	585,214	45,344	7.75	11,069	24.41	Aver. 37.28

Source: (VERIS, 2020)

Since the start of the pandemic, VERIS has carried out 23,440 RT-PCR tests through VERIS Molecular Biology laboratory, around 15% being positive, 75% negative, 6% being inconclusive and 4% remaining are in processing. 69,160 rapid tests have also been carried out, of which 28.19% have been positive, 66.96% negative and 4.83 are in process. VERIS has also performed 3,110 high-resolution chest tomographies, of which 39.40% have obtained a positive reading for COVID-19 and 33.10% have negative results, 27.49% in the process of reading.

Adaptation and Innovation

Before the pandemic, VERIS had a basic virtual medical appointment service used often but in much lesser extent than the conventional face-to-face system. With the onset of the pandemic, the online service system had to be strengthened, as presential appointments were to be discouraged given the heightened risk of contagion they represent. Demand for online services also multiplied itself greatly. The majority of VERIS doctors agreed to make virtual appointments.
Main modifications to the earlier virtual medical appointment system included:

- New licenses were requested for the zoom program for doctors who joined the modality.
- Almost double the number of consulting rooms provided for online care were enabled.
- Doctors who were new to the online service were trained to carry out the service from home.
- Through the "MI VERIS" app the patient can self-manage their queries and procedures from Schedule and pay their appointments, to receive lab results.
- Virtual appointments are offered at a 25% discount over in-person appointments (this discount was increased to 50% during the peak of the pandemic in April 2020).
- Payment system was strengthened through the use of digital portals, website and the app MI VERIS.

- At-home laboratory sample collection was offered, to avoid the patient entering into contact with other patients possibly affected by COVID-19. Technicians make appointments and pay a house visit to the patient; samples are collected and conserved in cold packaging. VERIS offers same day laboratory results for most tests and 48-hour results for COVID-19, which is extraordinary in most medical facilities in the country. Since the onset of the pandemic, the laboratory has processed 14,000 orders sent by doctors associated to the online service.
- Prescription management was also automated through a system that detects when a patient is given a medical prescription and sends a pharmacy request via WhatsApp; VERIS also offers home delivery of those prescriptions –in the last 5 months, the pharmacy service has filled over 10,000 orders derived from online appointments.

ICT Infrastructure

VERIS web site (www.veris.com.ec) focuses on the patient; it is organized in two sections: the first offers medical services, directing the patient to establish his/her appointment, use the laboratory facilities or open the patient's account and records; the second offers a host of preventive medicine plans with clear price tags associated to each and detailed descriptions of what they entail; a third section concentrates on providing information on COVID-19 and guidance on how to avoid contagion. There is also a chat option in case the patient requires help accessing any of these services.

The platform that VERIS uses is based on cloud technology designed in order to exploit any service or component of the internet cloud. Its architecture promotes the efficient use of resources such as servers, web services, micro services, containers, among other digital solutions available to innovate products or health-oriented technology services in the shortest possible time.

Based on a business architecture model, the platform is structured in three layers: infrastructure, data, and business. These interact as a platform composed of interconnected micro services; each process or component is specialized, which ensures high performance, agile and efficient maintenance of the business layer, greater control of functionalities and version administration.

Figure 1. Transformation of the structure of the VERIS platform
Source: (VERIS, 2020)

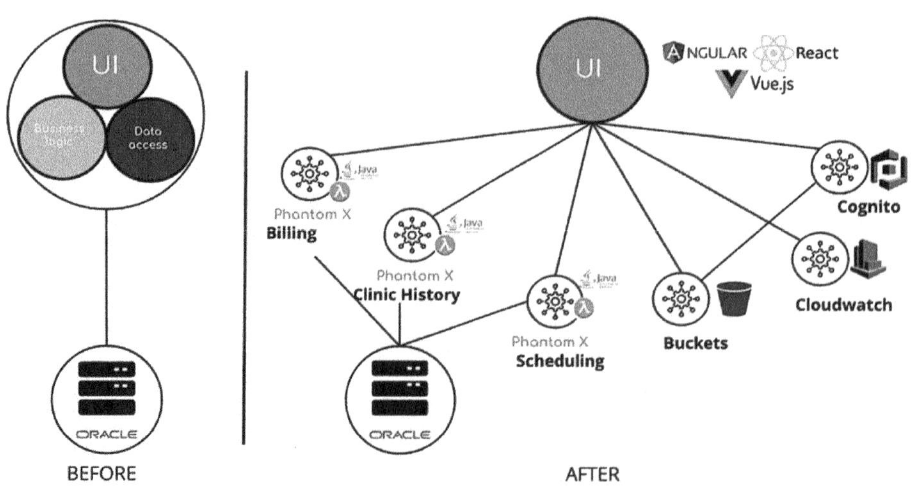

The current platform is the evolution of an integrated monolithic system to a composite system (see Figure 1). Information security is one of the most developed chapters of this model, since being a native CLOUD platform, the vulnerability points are more critical. This situation has led to the implementation of components integrating high security and accesses for data protection.

The VERIS digital platform contains a data warehouse and data lake that stores all the information from the electronic medical record and its dimensions, which are complemented by Artificial Intelligence and Machine Learning. The platform allows feedback to internal and external users with information and insights that guide actions taken to improve the service experience.

Applied KE Architecture

The VERIS model is based on:

- A highly trained staff, drawing from a pool of close to 200 specialists distributed among the various specialties, all of whom were diverted to supply initial and follow-up online consultations during the pandemic.
- A state-of-the-art technological model that follows international (WHO) protocols and service models adapted to the needs and requirements of Ecuador,
- A modern and evolving ICT infrastructure, that has been adapted to providing online/remote services, utilizing means that are highly advanced but at the same time accessible to a general public that is only gradually getting used to utilizing web-based platforms;
- A will to reach all groups of society, lowering costs when necessary;
- Support to and from the central government's pandemic and telemedicine tactics.

The ability to adapt to the circumstances and take advantage of a technology niche that is particularly apt to be of effective service in the current global emergency, all coupled with an aggressive financial strategy, makes of VERIS a clear example of how the combination of the elements that make-up the KE can work to the benefit of the enterprise and to the benefit of the country at the same time.

Benefits and Obstacles

Benefits

Principal benefits derived from VERIS's strategy include the ability to reach a higher number of beneficiaries, provide cheaper service, train personnel in a new way of doing things, and developing a model that can be replicated.

Its principal tool, online consultation, has been a crucial tool to provide diagnostic and preventive care during the time of isolation and quarantine; this way, VERIS has not only helped patients avoid the risk of contagion, but has also provided patients with a sense of security of being accompanied during a time of crisis.

The COVID 19 pandemic is devastating in developing countries where the health-system is suboptimal. VERIS case during the COVID-19 pandemic in Ecuador shows that, by using the elements of the KE architecture, it has been able to provide comprehensive services during the pandemic: by accompanying and monitoring affected people; providing health services, education and care through virtual tools; making available opportune information to qualified professionals; and contributing not only to the physical but also emotional well-being of its patients.

While not rigorously evaluated yet, the combined physical and emotional benefits of readily available health and medicine care under circumstances as stressful as the COVID-19 pandemic could be analyzed to derive useful learnings. VERIS itself come easily become a best-practice model to be replicated elsewhere.

Challenges and Obstacles

This successful undertaking has not gone without its share of challenges and difficulties, principal among them the fact that online services are a relatively new concept in Ecuador and patients were not very keen on using them. It took the pandemic and associated disincentives to in-person services, to popularize VERIS remote consultation services. VERIS hopes the community will remain attracted to online servicing even after the emergency passes, to justify the investment made in ICT infrastructure and services.

A second difficulty faced by VERIS has to do with the necessity to utilize remote insurance and payment processing; both, private health insurance and credit/debit card payment are not as extended in Ecuador as they are in other areas of the world; some patient have had to adapt to those new instruments before they could take full advantage of VERIS.

Focusing all medical specialists to provide diagnostic and treatment services for COVID-19 symptoms has been quite a challenge; it required providing those specialists with training not only on the medical aspects but also on getting used to the online interaction with the patient, including the ability to read patient reactions and understand their fears, needs and preferences; all this under pressing circumstances.

Additionally, reliance on a highly advanced technological model is a competitive advantage; in the context of a for-profit private sector enterprise, there is little incentive to export the model and structure. Also related to the private sector nature of this endeavor, the willingness to embrace a model complex as the one described here depends on the management's appetite for innovation and risk taking. These characteristics are not widely-spread.

Finally, while the company showcased here has made a concerted effort to make its services widely available (see above) affordability remains an issue, as the great majority of Ecuador's population is poor. Private sector practitioners must derive a profit from this line of service, and the private health and medicine sector is a competitive one. At this point in time, surely the central government will cover the costs of vaccination when asking the private sector to support the public sector efforts, but in the long term, the private sector cannot depend on subsidies to develop. Additional research is needed to learn if privately offered services will remain an option for the majority or at least a wide share of the population.

Despite these challenges and obstacles, VERIS has come through with a successful, popular and, most importantly, relevant and timely service package for the Ecuadorian society. The ability the company has shown to adapt to a changing market and nimbly modify its business model can be an interesting lesson to others facing similar conditions, particularly as VERIS is also remaining financially sustainable in a developing country context.

Thanks in part to VERIS efforts, Ecuador now stands a wide breath away from its neighbouring countries like Colombia, Peru, Chile and Brazil that are among the worst hit by the COVID-19.

REFERENCES

Calidadsalud. (2020). *Private health establishments participating in the provision of services.* http://www.calidadsalud.gob.ec/wp-content/uploads/2020/10/22-10-Privados.pdf

CoronavirusEcuador. (2020). *Official information on the pandemic affecting Ecuador.* https://www.coronavirusecuador.com/

INEC-RAS. (2018). *Actividades y Recursos de Salud.* https://www.ecuadorencifras.gob.ec/actividades-y-recursos-de-salud/

Iturralde, P. (2015). *Privatización de la salud en Ecuador Estudio de la interacción pública con clínicas y hospitales privados.* Quito: Plataforma por el Derecho a la Salud/CDES.

Ministry of Public Health of Ecuador. (2021). *Situation of COVID 19.* https://www.salud.gob.ec/el-ministerio-de-salud-publica-del-ecuador-msp-informa-situacion-coronavirus/

Pan American Health Organization. (2021). *Teleconsultations during a pandemic.* https://iris.paho.org/handle/10665.2/52006

Pierce, W., Schroeder, D., & Suchecki, R. (2021). *Telehealth in Latin America: Progress, challenges, and opportunities in the face of COVID-19.* Telehealth and Medicine Today.

Reuters. (2020). *Ecuador prepares for COVID-19 vaccination campaign with private sector.* https://www.reuters.com/business/healthcare-pharmaceuticals/ecuador-prepares-covid-19-vaccination-campaign-with-private-sector-2020-12-16/

Statista. (2020). *Impact of the novel coronavirus (COVID-19) on gross domestic product (GDP) growth in selected countries in Latin America.* https://www.statista.com/statistics/1105099/impact-coronavirus-gdp-latin-america-country/

UNDP. (2020). *In Ecuador, COVID-19 could cause 11 percent dive in GDP this year.* https://www.undp.org/content/undp/en/home/news-centre/news/2020/Ecuador_COVID-19_cause_11_percent_dive_GDP.html#:~:text=The%20COVID%2D19%20PDNA%20for,term%20total%20US%242.7%20billion

UNDP. (2020). *Socio Economic Assessment COVID-19 PDNA. March-May 2020.* https://www.undp.org/content/dam/undp/library/covid19/Ecuador-Eval-Soc-Econ_EN.pdf

VERIS Ecuador. (2020). www.veris.com.ec

WHO, OECD & World Bank. (2020). *3rd Joint IMF-OECD-World Bank Conference on Structural Reforms.* https://www.oecd.org/economy/reform/joint-imf-wb-oecd-conf-structural-reform-2020/

Worldometer. (2020). *COVID-19 Coronavirus pandemic.* https://www.worldometers.info/coronavirus/

Section 3
Education

Chapter 6
The Knowledge Economy and Social Impact

Fabian Koss
KC Social Impact Lab, USA

Giulia D'Amico
KC Social Impact Lab, USA

EXECUTIVE SUMMARY

There is not a one-size-fits-all definition of "social impact." In fact, in a Google search for "What is social impact?" more than 400 results appear. This chapter will highlight global initiatives led by OneSight, an NGO that is utilizing new technologies to combat the vision care crisis, and CanopyLAB, a software company that has teamed up with over 120 NGOs around the world to create and provide online courses utilizing artificial intelligence.

INTRODUCTION

The Knowledge Economy which has seen the rapid growth in technological advances has made our planet much smaller, and more connected. The NGO global community and the private sector are taking advantage of these constant advances to improve lives in the most needed and neglected communities around the world. This chapter highlights how international NGOs and a software company which all have social impact in their DNA are using Information and communications technology (ICT) as tools to improve lives throughout the globe.

THE CURRENT GLOBAL VISION CARE CRISIS

Vision is considered by many the strongest of our senses. Without vision one finds it difficult to learn to move, read, attend school and to earn a living. Raising awareness and engaging all sectors of society is fundamental in combating the vision care crisis. Deloitte and OneSight(OneSight, n.d.) joined forces

DOI: 10.4018/978-1-7998-8417-0.ch006

to develop the *The Bringing Vision Care Crisis Into Focus* (Wong et al., 2016) study which concluded that many barriers including physical, economic and cultural prevent 1.1 billion people on the planet (1 out of every 7) from receiving a basic eye examination. One of the key findings was that no age group is untouched by this crisis. Vision impairment is intergenerational and impedes children, adults and the eldery from focusing on their daily activities. In October of 2019 the World Health Organization published its first *World Report on Vision* specifically targeted at Ministries of Health, Researchers, Development Agencies, Practitioners, the NGO community and policy-makers dedicated to the field of eye care. The report was produced to assist the international community develop a shared global agenda on vision. The aim of this report is to provide stakeholders support in the massive challenge to improve eye conditions and reduce vision loss to achieve the Sustainable Development Goals (SDGs), particularly SDG target 3.8 which is focused on universal health coverage.

APPLYING NEW TECHNOLOGIES IN COMBATING THE GLOBAL VISION CARE CRISIS 80% OF LEARNING IS VISUAL

An analysis of the *Vision To Learn* model to determine its effectiveness conducted by the Mattel Children's Hospital at UCLA (Slusser & Dudovity, 2013) in 2013 found that 80% of classroom learning is visual. In addition, over 20% of students have a vision problem that can be identified by screening and over 80-90% of those defects can be corrected with glasses. In the United States and around the world, low-income and minority students are disproportionately affected by untreated visual impairments. This segment of the population also has limited to no access to corrective lenses.

The *Lancet Global Health Commission on Global Eye Health: VISION Beyond 2020 (Lancet Global Health Commission, 2021)* a commission of 73 experts from 25 countries globally conducted research in eye health concluded that improving eye health is essential to achieving the United Nations Sustainable Development Goals. Their report clearly states that vision enables better educational outcomes, and increases work productivity, reducing inequality. Eye health is a global public priority, transforming lives in both poor and wealthy communities.

OneSight, an independent NGO, is mobilizing the latest technologies to combat the global vision care crisis. They do this through two successful models which include free charitable vision clinics that manage a specific community need lasting 1-2 weeks, as well as more permanent self-sustaining vision centers. Both sides of their programming require the latest technology to allow them to make the glasses that people need to see clearly. OneSight deploys state of the art equipment and develops new virtual tools to continue its mission of eradicating the vision care crisis for good.

To date they have impacted over 45 million people in 53 countries, and have operated nearly 2,000 charitable clinics serving refugee camps, indigenous populations and low income families that face barriers in accessing vision care resources. These models have provided immediate access to eye exams and glasses, and have established 197 sustainable centers, creating jobs, educational opportunities, and permanent access to vision care. Innovation and technology play an instrumental role in reaching people in need in the most remote areas of the world.

In June of 2018, an expedition team of 46 OneSight volunteers embarked on a mission to the most remote areas of the Amazon River in Brazil to provide vision care to 2000 people in the villages of Muritinga, Cuia, Iguapenu, Sao Felix and Sissaima. OneSight transformed small boats into portable vision treatment centers that navigated the river to perform checkups and tests on board using cutting-edge technology while maintaining direct and constant contact with specialists on the mainland via satellite communication. The expedition relied on small medical kits and used portable Kaleidos screening tools for vision testing that provided the specialists results in seconds. The Kaleidos screening devices were specially designed to perform eyesight tests under any environmental condition. Developed by Adaptica (Adaptica, n.d.), these tools have contributed to the visual screening of thousands of people who otherwise would have never reached optical centers which are too far from their villages and communities.

In April, 2020 in response to the COVID pandemic OneSight developed and launched a free online Vision Check to provide parents an opportunity to check their families vision at home during the lockdown period. This new virtual tool was designed to determine whether a refractive error exists, as well as assessing color vision. Another key objective of rolling out this new tool was to raise awareness of the importance of vision care especially as people were spending more time in front of screens during this time.

THE FUTURE OF LEARNING AND HOW ARTIFICIAL INTELLIGENCE MAKES KNOWLEDGE AVAILABLE THROUGH NGOS AROUND THE WORLD

Bridging the Knowledge Gap

Over the last two decades, technology in education has been one of the major topics for teaching and learning which is constantly being debated globally. Technology in and for education has shown us 3 main outcomes:

1. Ignites powerful learning in and out of school: the number of hours students engaged in learning activities increases due to access to much more content available at their fingertips. Today, students are exploring and discovering instead of being spoon fed with information. This learning philosophy well known as –constructionism- is at core of what (Papert, 1980) Papert had been describing in his publication *"Mindstorms: Children, Computers and Powerful Ideas"* (1980). His definition in a proposal to the National Science Foundation titled *Constructionism: A New Opportunity for Elementary Science Education* was advocating:

"The word constructionism is a mnemonic for two aspects of the theory of science education underlying this project. From constructivist theories of psychology we take a view of learning as a reconstruction rather than as a transmission of knowledge. Then we extend the idea of manipulative materials to ***the idea that learning is most effective when part of an activity the learner experiences as constructing a meaningful product",***

2. Promotes positive change to specific school practices: project based learning, personalized and blended learning are becoming common practices and easier to implement especially in schools with multi-age classrooms. As described by Michael Horn, Co-founder and Distinguished Fellow at Clayton Christensen Institute for Disruptive Innovation, a US-based non-profit think tank, "Students suffer from the Swiss cheese effect in education" (Horn, n.d.). What Horn refers to is

related to existing education that delivers content to students and then tests to see whether they have assimilated it. He described this as the Swiss cheese problem, resulting in "holes" in learning, as opposed to a personalized approach, project based and blended form of learning, delivered through online modularity content.

3. Enables the transformation of schools from "funnels of received information" to "engines of knowledge construction and appropriation". Schools are becoming centers to spark creativity by introducing new ways of delivering learning outcomes: from teaching students to work in teams, to initiating competitive creative challenges, and focusing more and more on competency and less on curriculum. Competency-based learning as described by Michael Horn in his book -The Blended Workbook: Learning to Design the Schools of Our Future- *is the idea that students must demonstrate mastery of a given subject, including possession, application, or creation of knowledge, before moving into the next one.*

LAPTOPS ARE THE PENCILS FOR THE DIGITAL AGE

Though Innovation is a Process, not an Event, Canopylab Has Found a Way to Disrupt This Process

Founded in Copenhagen in 2015, CanopyLAB (CanopyLab, n.d.) is a Danish EdTech company that is changing the way that people learn and teach by combining adaptive and blended learning in a social network structure. Although it is a commercial company, social impact and the Social Sustainable Goals (SDG's) exist at the core of the company. CanopyLAB is an online digital platform that offers both white label solutions for educational institutions and organizations as well as a free, global learning tool for NGOs and teachers worldwide to be able to share their content. The available content focuses on Climate Action & Sustainability, the SDGs, Health, Sexual & Reproductive Rights, Entrepreneurship and Democracy. It is a global library of resources created by hundreds of organizations around the world. Canopy LAB is the best example of shared and participatory knowledge.

CanopyLAB has a strong footprint in Latin America with offices in Lima, Peru and Bogota, Colombia. In Peru, CanopyLAB joined forces with CARE to develop the Girls with Opportunities Program. The main goal of the program is to support 1 million girls to complete a higher education by 2021. CanopyLAB is supporting Girls with Opportunities in adapting the program's content and in-person workshops into interactive online educational tracks available on a personalized learning platform, making it available at their fingertips.

Through the platform girls are taking classes on sexual and reproductive rights, entrepreneurship, social abilities and other important topics that expand their horizons and empower them to seek out greater opportunities beyond schooling. Furthermore, the platform provides a social space for girls to connect with one another, engage in conversations and learn from each other. The goal is to remove any geographical and economic barriers and connect the 100,000 girls from all corners of Peru through technology. This partnership also aims to create tracks for teachers and parents who will be equipped with knowledge and resources needed to reach NGO' s mission in their own classrooms and homes to further support the girls in every aspect of their lives.

Through a collaboration with the state, education institutions, families, teachers and students, the program changes the lives of under-resourced young women through initiatives that provide them with the life skills and knowledge to break them and their families out of the poverty cycle.

Uruguay: A Shift of a Nation: From a Rural-Based to a Knowledge-Based Society

The vision that Nicholas Negroponte had at the MIT Media Lab 15 years ago of an inexpensive network computer in classrooms was realized in One Laptop per Child (One Laptop per Child, n.d.).

Prior technologies for education experiences in other countries have demonstrated tremendous gains in learning, more time spent on schoolwork, development of technological fluency, and a stronger sense of inclusion among the students. While the majority of prior experiences have been in wealthier countries, the experience in a rural country like Uruguay exemplifies the potential. In 2007, the then President of the country, Tabarez Vasquez, announced that Uruguay was committing to deploying the first 100,000 laptops of One Laptop per Child (OLPC) through a program called Plan Ceibal. One Laptop per Child's mission was to provide educational opportunities to the world's poorest children by providing a low cost device, connected to the Internet.

Launched in late 2005 by Nicholas Negroponte, Founder of the MIT Media Lab, the program's vision to provide connected laptops to children in developing countries seemed unrealistic. While technology was relatively expensive in western geography, Negroponte insisted not only in making it affordable and accessible to billions of children left behind, but he focused on a more profound concept: learning how to code.

When the Uruguay President engaged with Nicholas Negroponte, he had in mind to deliver educational opportunities to his young population, by introducing the OLPC laptops. The real outcome was a way more profound experience that changed the course of the nation.

«All of us in Uruguay should not only be equal in the eyes of the Law, which is important, but also equal in life.» (Presidency of the Republic, 2006) (UNESCO, 2008)

Plan Ceibal was focused on three main principles:

1. equity, social inclusion and equality in access to technology;
2. technology as a means to achieve these goals;
3. education, universal law that aims to equal opportunities.

The project started by focusing in the rural areas as a way to promote equalities and rights for the overall population. CEIBAL has shown how powerful is the aspect of social value creation through technology which enabled economic wealth, shifting the country from a rural economy into knowledge based one. Not many years later, Uruguay became the first country in the world to have reached full saturation 1:1, where every single student in pre-school, primary and secondary school personally owned a connected device.

CONCLUSION

2020 was extremely difficult for the world. The COVID-19 pandemic robbed us of many lives and impacted the wellbeing of countless others. Yet, Social Impact is increasingly evident, and growing in today's Knowledge Economy (Schwartz, 2017).()()

Chapter 7
Case Studies on Applying Knowledge Economy Principles for Economic Growth in Developing Nations:
CanopyLAB Implementing LXPs in Digitally Challenged Areas

David E. Pines
CanopyLAB, USA

Natalia Bernal Restrepo
CanopyLAB, Colombia

EXECUTIVE SUMMARY

The authors demonstrate through specific case studies, representative of Civil Society in Least Developed Countries (LDCs), how user-acquired knowledge has the potential to impact both economic growth and economic development. In the interconnected, interdependent 21st century world of full participation as envisioned in UN Agenda 2030, it is essential to equip the people of developing nations with the tools to participate, grow, and develop themselves. This chapter both illustrates the importance of education and lifelong learning as well as highlighting the potential of a robust learning experience platform in geographies in which issues of infrastructure, connectivity, and access are some of the greatest challenges to overcome.

DOI: 10.4018/978-1-7998-8417-0.ch007

INTRODUCTION

The objectives of this chapter are:

1. To demonstrate the efficacy of asynchronous remote pedagogy based on learner curiosity and commitment as well as host (instructor) developed content.
2. To illustrate the potential long term economic impact implied by a more learned population in LDC's as well as rural communities.
3. To illuminate the challenges of disparity in equity between developed and less developed nations and showcase potential solutions through online learning communities.

BACKGROUND

"The most valuable assets of a 20th-century company were its production equipment. The most valuable asset of a 21st-century institution, whether business or non-business, will be its knowledge workers and their productivity." -Peter F. Drucker

Everyone should be afforded the opportunity to become a more valuable asset for both themselves and their organization. Lifelong learning is now possible for any individual who is interested in acquiring or deepening their knowledge, grasping an understanding of what, who, where, when and why, on any subject that is relevant to them. The information revolution began to highlight the vast quantity and disparate quality of that knowledge which was, and is, available to be acquired. Anyone with an intention and commitment to acquire knowledge and learn something that they did not know, should be afforded the opportunity to do so anytime and anyplace to further their personal growth and development.

Brick and mortar institutions of Higher Education have been part of Western culture since the European Gymnasia. In Least Developed Countries (LDCs), these institutions are mainly a result of colonial presence. The organic nature of learning in developing nations has always been centered more on necessity and immediate need. In a globally connected world learning beyond walls and borders can be viewed as an essential 21st Century necessity for all people. The high costs associated with creating infrastructure, building schools, distributing books and even paper can be prohibitive in many rural, as well as urban areas in the developing world. We need to innovate and transform the learning and teaching experience in LDCs.

MAIN FOCUS OF THE CHAPTER

"Economic activity is currently undergoing a process of profound transformation, which we can summarize as the migration from an industrial economy towards a new structure characterized by the decisive importance of knowledge flows. This change can be attributed to a triple feedback interaction: first of all, a process of technological revolution led by investment and the massive use of digitization technologies; second, by virtue of the dynamics of the space–time extension of the economic flow (globalization);

and third, because this global-knowledge environment interacts with other intangible assets, especially human capital and organizational innovation."[1]

The focus of this chapter is twofold. In the first section, the authors consider two of the four pillars of the Knowledge Economy as defined by The World Bank[2]. In the second section the authors provide specific Case Study examples of how implementing a Learning Experience Platform supports local NGO's in educating people both in the classroom and beyond.
The Four Pillars of the Knowledge Economy are:

- Institutional structures that provide incentives for entrepreneurship and the use of knowledge
- Availability of skilled labor and a good education system
- Access to information and communication technology (ICT) infrastructures
- A vibrant innovation landscape that includes academia, the private sector, and civil society.[3]

This chapter highlights two key elements of the cornerstones of the Knowledge Economy: access to information and innovative education. The authors demonstrate through specific case studies, representative of Civil Society in LDC's, how user acquired knowledge has the potential to impact both economic growth *and* development. By meeting these challenges, people in remote communities can become part of the vibrant innovation landscape so essential to the success of SDG 8 (Decent Work and Economic Growth) and Agenda 2030.

PART I: THE ESSENTIAL ELEMENTS OF THE KNOWLEDGE ECONOMY

Economist Peter Drucker distinguished the concept of the "Knowledge Economy" in the mid-20th century (The Effective Executive (1966), & The Age of Discontinuity (1969)). The evolutionary economic shift from Agrarian to Industrial to Knowledge was not a linear progression but encompassed transformational shifts in the economic basis of an increasingly globalized society. As rural farmers migrated to industrialized communities, basic education became central to economic growth. Public education systems were designed to enhance basic literacy, economic opportunity, and ultimately the productivity of workers. These systems, created in the 19th Century, remained relatively unchanged well into the first decade of the 21st Century, even as, in the second half of the 20th Century, knowledge began to equate with power. Knowledge brought educated people the power to innovate, invent and grow a new global economy. The (developed) world became connected, interconnected and increasingly interdependent.

Harvard Business School professor, Michael Porter, the creator of Porter's Five Forces Model for business analysis, argues that in today's economy, the ability of a business to develop and maintain a competitive advantage in the marketplace is more and more dependent on its ability to quickly adapt to an ever-changing world by using continual innovation in its processes and business systems. It is also important to understand that any business is made up of people. The more educated a person, the more valuable they become to both the business and community.[4]

The World Bank model, based on Drucker's concept, is a four-pillar framework for investment and development to support underdeveloped nations in joining the global Knowledge Economy.

Figure 1.

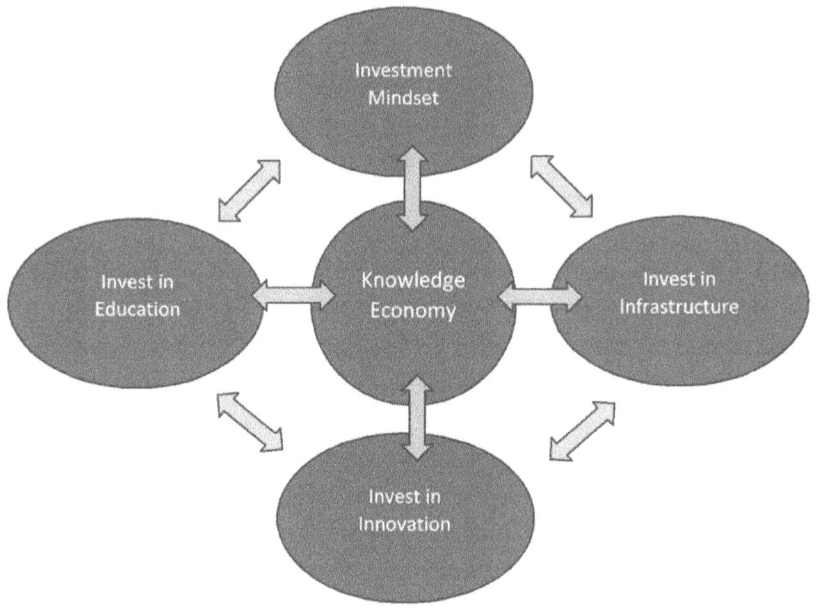

- **An Institutional regime with a "mindset" that creates incentives for entrepreneurship and the use of knowledge:** Mobilizing and investing in resources (governments and international development organizations) which encourage innovation and entrepreneurship with the application of new knowledge.
- **An educated and skilled labor force**: The establishment of a strong knowledge-based economy requires workers to have the ability to continuously learn and curate their knowledge acquisition efficiently.
- **A dense and modern information infrastructure:** Easy access to the information and communication technology (ICT) resources to facilitate the effectiveness of interacting, disseminating and processing information and knowledge resources.
- **An effective innovation system:** Keep up with the latest global technology and intelligence for adaptation and application in a domestic economy.

"Institutional Mindset"[5] may be best illustrated by Kenya's commitment to becoming the "Silicon Savannah" by 2030, leapfrogging other African nations. "This elevated status owes to a number of advantages in the form of a thriving tech ecosystem, digitally skilled talent, geographical positioning endowment, and ICT centric policies. The country boasts of dedicated government ministries, authorities and programs along with the existence of widespread digital infrastructure. These fundamentals have elevated Kenya in the region, and attracted both regional and international attention, capital, networks and resources."[6] The aligned commitment to becoming a regional technology leader is the mindset required to capitalize on this opportunity and build a knowledge-based economy. Later in this chapter the authors present a case study of one such Kenyan NGO with a bold commitment to bring change.

Current State in Least Developed Countries

According to the United Nations the gap between developed and less developed nations began to increase at a more rapid pace as the divide between connected and not connected widened.[7] "...The lack of high-speed connectivity in LDCs poses a major challenge. Inadequate connectivity prevents access to the most promising broadband applications for education, health, finance and other sectors, as well as to global and regional knowledge networks. Most LDCs face great difficulties in making broadband Internet access available and affordable for all. Digital technologies have great potential to bring economic and social development benefits to these nations."[8] Bringing the collective commitment of developed nations to resolve this disparity can bridge the gap.

Growth vs. Development; Not Mutually Exclusive

Economic growth is distinct from economic development. Growth implies economic gain primarily through increased production while maintaining cost. Development has more complex and subtle connotations, including the interconnections between and among the economic, social, political, and environmental spheres." Economic development, defined as the improvement in living conditions and the satisfaction with life for *all* people, is accepted by economists to be a worthy goal...."[9] Agenda 2030 presents the possibility of just such a world. The seventeen Sustainable Development Goals (SDGs) were conceived and created to concisely focus on what matters in having the world work for everyone with no one left behind. The offspring of the marriage of growth and development, now within reach by a mobile device, can be the transformational force needed to create equity and parity between all nations for all people-access to information through digital learning.

Knowledge/Learning as Opportunity

Every learner has a wide range of potential opportunities in front of them. Creating a "discovery mindset," the basis of which is curiosity and inquiry, will set a learner on the path of discovery which can lead to creativity and innovation. When one acquires new knowledge, and learns new things, one has the possibility of thinking new thoughts and discovering new horizons. Their world opens beyond the limits of what they already know into a whole new world of what, for them, isn't yet.

In his paper on the role of education in knowledge economies in developing countries, Alan Weber cites M.A. Peters, "Knowledge production and dissemination requires the exchange of ideas and such exchanges, in turn, depend upon certain cultural conditions, including trust, reciprocal rights and responsibilities between different knowledge partners, institutional regimes, and strategies and the whole sociological baggage that comes with understanding institutions....There is not one prescription or formula that fits all institutions, societies, or knowledge traditions."[10]

Focus on Least Developed Countries; Economic Potential

The 47 least developed countries are low-income nations that suffer from severe structural handicaps to growth, particularly low human resources and high economic vulnerability. In 2017, the combined population of LDCs stood at roughly 1 billion. Projections posit an increase by 33% between 2017 and 2030 reaching a projected population in LDCs of 1.9 billion persons in 2050.[11] Many of these people are mobile, not by choice, but because of circumstances such as famine, war, civil conflict, or perceived lack of potential economic opportunity. Many nations in Africa present a graphic demonstration of the extent of the crisis.

According to the Global Business Coalition for Education[12] Uganda hosts the largest number of refugees in Africa – an estimated 1.3 million people, half of whom are children. These young people face some of the harshest living conditions without access to basic needs. More importantly, without access to safe, reliable, quality education and learning materials, these children face the risk of becoming part of a "lost generation" who fall further behind in learning and productivity.

Online platforms that host digital educational content can be an effective solution to overcome the challenges of distributing up-to-date textbooks and other printed educational materials to rural and remote communities. However, for regions that do not have stable access to broadband connectivity, it is not presently feasible for online solutions solely to deliver the desired impact. The opportunity to leapfrog hard wired infrastructure challenges and deploy innovative tech solutions can, and will, provide access for new users in remote, unconnected communities.

Leapfrogging With Technology

"The application of modern technologies will have the most significant impact on the growth trajectories of most African economies. Specifically, the greatest opportunity for growth will come from technological innovation and the adoption of new technologies in services sectors, such as banking, insurance, health, education, and agriculture. New opportunities have arisen that make it possible for low-income economies to leapfrog other countries by adopting technologies that are suitable to their specific circumstances. Those countries that embrace and invest in technology will be able to sustain growth and be competitive regionally and internationally moving forward."[13]

"In the past, it took decades for a technological breakthrough to spread across countries. Diffusion and adoption were slow and there were considerable barriers. The process is different for many new technologies. Mobile phones, for example, reached billions of people worldwide in less than 20 years. Today, nearly 70 per cent of the world's population uses mobile phones not only to communicate, but also to read news, check weather, make payments and sell products. These devices have become an indispensable feature of modern existence, regardless of where we live or what we do for a living. The Internet is another technological advance that more than half the world's people use every day. These are great examples of enabling technologies used by communities and societies to bypass or 'leapfrog' a linear path of progress. Frontier technologies open new windows of opportunity for communities and countries to catch up and accelerate development."[14]

The World Economic and Social Survey 2018: Frontier Technology for Sustainable Development[15] (WESS 2018), from UN DESA, outlines technologies that can support the eradication of hunger and poverty and improve the quality of life for millions. The UN report highlights the breakthrough potential for communities and societies to "adapt and adopt frontier technologies" with relatively low upfront investment. Technology being affordable, replicable, portable and reliable can level the playing field for LDCs. The report goes into depth on the necessary investment in Human Capital to realize the potential. The opportunity is clearly in education. Nearly 20 million children in LDCs are not enrolled in any formal education. Even then, in those countries with higher levels of educational enrollment, the student/teacher ratio is as high as over 40-1. Yet, now mobile technology makes digital educational experiences for learners accessible with a click. While in 2017 only 18% of African homes were connected to the

Internet, the rate of mobile broadband connection is outpacing much of the world. By 2022 it is expected that 1.07 billion Africans (over 75%) will be connected to the digital world.[16]

The opportunity afforded education in 2019 and 2020 as a consequence of the global health crisis was itself transformational in nature. Present and future generations will know the power and possibilities of learning online, acquiring information and knowledge on virtually any topic of interest. These "native technologists" will navigate this new environment with ease. And there will be a lot of them. The World Bank projects that the population of students engaged in some form of "formal" education is expected to be over ½ billion in the next 10 years, with rural Asia and Africa growing most rapidly.[17] Not having to invest solely in brick-and-mortar infrastructure opens the potential for increased institutional and governmental investment in lower cost innovative access solutions.

Institutions, be they government or educational, can only do so much in isolation. They need partners in both the private and NGO sectors. There are thousands of organizations working independently on local issues of health and wellness, sustainable agriculture, renewable energy, increasing prosperity, education for all, as well as issues of all of the SDGs. They can coalesce to create pathways to successfully develop both their people and their communities.

Summary of Part I

Building a Knowledge Economy in and among developing nations takes vision, commitment and investment of resources. When opportunity is present, people will naturally engage and participate in growing both themselves and their community. Turning an idea into a new reality takes the aligned resolve of groups of individuals with similar commitments. Investment and innovation are essential elements of the formula for bringing equity and parity among all nations, large or small. Turning now to practical approaches to both economic and social development, the authors present three examples of people in civil society, from organizations with very different missions, utilizing technology to support learners in developing and enriching themselves to be more valuable assets to their communities and organizations.

PART II CANOPYLAB OUTREACH; THE LAB

What Is CanopyLAB?

The LAB is a free open online learning experience platform. It was conceptualized by the co-founders and CEO as the Corporate Social Responsibility Project of CanopyLAB. With a very strong belief that everyone deserves equitable and quality education, The LAB was formed to establish partnerships around the globe that allowed organizations to have free access to a social learning platform, providing reliable content and courses for users. Early adopter partners were easily accessible local NGOs due to location and proximity to CanopyLAB. With the onset of the pandemic in 2020, the opportunity to rapidly grow and make this opportunity available for developing countries became a top priority.

CanopyLAB developed a unique social learning platform powered by Artificial Intelligence with strong learning principles. These same pillars apply to NGOs in The LAB, offering all the advantages of community building as in the commercial platform. Innovative education must focus on a student-centered approach, developing skills and competencies so that the engaged learners can excel in a variety of scenarios. Students are valued as individuals, each with a potentially different learning style. Rather than having only one exercise and one way of showing their learning, CanopyLAB provides more than 55 different ways of approaching knowledge transfer.

Outreach to NGOs

The first challenge was to find NGO's, organizations and institutions willing to share their knowledge and content and saw value in the possibility of entering a global partnership. The LAB is a free, open and growing "organization" with more than 120 partners providing courses on topics related to the UN Sustainable Development Goals [18], Mental Health, Sexual and Reproductive Rights, Entrepreneurship, Sustainability, Technology and Humanity and much more. Enrollment has grown to over a million users from 90 different countries taking courses in English, Spanish, Portuguese, Danish and Arabic. Participation in The LAB is continuing to grow exponentially.

Who Are We Committed to Reaching?

Young people over the age of 13, who are eager to learn and grow, are the primary beneficiaries of courses in The LAB. Traditional education, and most curriculum, centers on the same topics of traditional subject matter that have been taught in the same ways for more than a century. The organizers of The LAB felt a compelling need to include diverse young voices and provide them a forum in which thought provoking conversations could take place. They felt the need to create an innovative space where youth could learn and discuss about often neglected (and even taboo) topics in their cultures. The LAB provides a global platform of reliable resources through registered NGOs, committed to Agenda 2030, who want to freely connect with a wide range of young people.

Entrepreneurship is a major area of focus in The LAB. empowering young people (and especially young women) with tools that can help them find and create business opportunities and give them economic advantage in their countries. The LAB found organizations that were aligned with these principles and wanted to provide free learning experiences for young entrepreneurs.

Acquiring NGO Partners

The LAB began an aggressive outreach strategy that involved social media and independent research utilizing NGO databases, Instagram, and Facebook posts. A massive email campaign sparked interest to schedule a first meeting. Working in geographic regions, The LAB team began taking demo meetings with dozens of NGO leaders in LDCs. Many organizations felt overwhelmed and burdened by the thought of additional work to "get online." Every conversation began with the commitment of The LAB team and their belief in the power of the platform and connecting it to each NGO's mission, vision and objectives. Many NGOs were struggling during 2020 just to stay alive due to the pandemic. Many more had closed their workshops, operations and programs. Some even had to shut down for months. The LAB provided both a solution and a support system that allowed them to maintain their impact and their presence in the community.

Big Challenges

One big challenge was that many people in LDCs didn't feel that they had the digital skills necessary to start this process. They thought that it would involve hours of planning, learning new skills and adding endless tasks to their daily routines. The commitment of The LAB's staff was to have one-on-one conversations where they could express this fear and demonstrate how easy the platform was to navigate. Organizations normally spend a considerable amount of time creating material. Having existing content was all that was needed. Once the material is ready, the platform works on "auto-pilot" as a self-building course. The LAB provides an extraordinarily strong network of both technological and pedagogical support to the unique needs of each partner organization.

On-boarding Partners

Partners were able to have meetings in which the goals for the partnership were established. There was a strong focus in helping the NGO fulfill its mission while reaching more users through applied technology. The platform allowed these organizations to move beyond the local scope to a more regional, national and in some cases even global reach which would not be possible without technology. Once the goals were established, often their materials had to be modified to transform into a successful online user experience.

Innovative Solutions

CanopyLAB's team created a specific NGO process of templates for course creation and self-guided stages of development, the basics platform of The LAB. In some cases extensive support was necessary and involved the creation of graphics, guidance on how to make videos, and content creation. The aligned outcome was courses from which any user, even in remote communities, could learn, become more knowledgeable and productive.

The second big issue was connectivity and access to the platform. Many of the organizations felt that it would be difficult for users to engage with a platform that required high-speed internet and advanced technological devices. The LAB team explained that all the courses and content were cloud-based which meant that there was no need for downloading a program. The platform could be accessed from any computer, laptop, or smartphone. Initially, many meetings were a "no-show" in some nations due to the lack of power or internet connection. Perseverance paid off. People joined.

Crisis as Opportunity

Before the onset of the global pandemic, The LAB had 40 partners and 83 courses. With the growth of eLearning as a result of Covid-19, there has been a significant increase in the number of students, partners, and course offerings. The result was individuals and institutions choosing CanopyLAB's two products—the Canopy and The LAB—to ensure the continuation of digital learning and development. In the first 12 months, The LAB experienced 3x growth in organizations and content with 120 partners and 365 courses available through our growing community.

The LAB provides a unique space for creating, understanding, sharing, and empowering the new learning behaviors. Growth in 2020 and 2021 is a reflection of the ability to understand the new and emerging markets in these sectors and pivot quickly to provide needed resources and information to empower peoples' choices. At the conclusion of 2019, no one could envision the magnitude of the crises 2020 brought to the world. And The LAB stood strong in the face of these circumstances.

The LAB's team worked diligently to find course opportunities, partnerships and continue to engage users in all the functionalities of the platform. Courses are constantly reviewed and updated responding to the necessities identified by the team. There is a strong sense of the need for quality for 2021 and so, partners will continue to be given not only technological but pedagogical support in service of our commitment to SDG 4, Quality and Equitable Education.

Empowering Youth Entrepreneurship

Youth should have the opportunity to gain access to materials, tools, content and ideas that may help them have a greater economic impact in their local communities. The LAB creates learning spaces for all, rather than specifically for the traditional student receiving their education in Business Administration from a University. They focused on young students still in school, curious college students, independent learners and women to find a place where they could learn from real-life experiences for free. There has been an increase in the interest for these topics from non-traditional sectors.[19] The LAB and its partners respond to that creative learning demand.

The LAB created courses which provide some basic tools, using the CanopyLAB journey as a startup for inspiration. They share the struggles, the hard work, and all that creating a successful company entails. The inspiring story of co-founder and CEO Sahra-Josephine Hjorth, who created a company in an industry predominantly managed by men[20] was a primary example of committed actions in the face of challenging "norms."

After creating these courses, The LAB began to look for partners who would make this offer more attractive with diverse professional content and a specific focus on youth entrepreneurship. The LAB team works with partner organizations to create courses for specific demographics on topics they care about. The following Case Studies illustrate the experience of a robust e-learning platform helping foundations and organizations in developing countries continue to fulfill their mission. We discuss Partners in East Africa, Cambodia, and the Corporate Social Responsibility program of CanopyLAB.

THE LAB: CASE STUDIES

Case I: Dream Rise Foundation- Kenya[21]

Dream Rise Foundation's commitment to the fulfillment of Sustainable Development Goal #4 and all the actions that they take towards it was noticeable from the first conversation. There was synergy with their mission. Providing them with the platform support and pedagogical tools for online learning could be a game changer for them.

This East African youth-led foundation believes in the empowerment of young people. The LAB wanted to provide them with a robust tool to help them meet their goals. Co-founder and CEO Royford Mutegi states:

"We are focusing on Transformative Mentorship to achieve a Transformative Leadership within the society. Through this, we will be focusing on nurturing a generation of youths whose mindset will be

aligned to transforming self, by being within the boundaries of what is morally acceptable, to inspire this transformation in others".

They faced struggles during 2020 because of COVID restrictions. Like many others, they were forced to shut-down their face-to-face work and move to an online learning environment. The partnership with CanopyLAB seemed like a great opportunity to learn about possibilities with online learning and create their first courses. They also needed to keep the connection they had already established with their users as well as generate a broader reach. The LAB began to work with Dream Rise Foundation in facing some difficulties of access to internet connection and becoming a potentially international player. Team meetings by phone and online outlined the project and course creation. The LAB's partnership included support to provide pedagogical tips to review and suggest the best ways to create a successful user earning experience.

Dream Rise began to notice a trend that The LAB experienced with many NGOs, especially those from LDCs. This related to the way that learning was perceived in an online environment. What has been done and taught traditionally has been a very independent model. Typically, users are expected to go through materials and learn by themselves, sometimes with some guiding exercises but with very limited options. This can make the learning process one that is very lonely and thus gives little motivation to stay on task. The social aspect of The LAB's platform solved this problem and a very high percentage of their users stayed engaged.

The First Course

Existing content and course materials from Dream Rise were informed by their mission and values. These were designed as face-to-face workshops aimed to promote discussion amongst students, debates, and peer to peer conversations. The perception was that this content was difficult to translate into a digital remote learning space. The CanopyLAB team introduced the concepts of social and collaborative learning, pillars of The LAB's learner experience, and began with examples of how this type of learning could take place inside the platform. It began a mindset shift for the foundation.

The LAB's team aided in finding new materials to enhance the learning program and complement the guides that were created in the project. This resulted in the creation of their first course for the platform entitled "Introduction to Personal Development." This course consists of four different units that take the user through a personal journey regarding strengths, areas of improvement and it also provides very specific tools that promote personal development. The course complements the mission of Dream Rise Foundation as it reflects the foundation of the four pillars in their model. This course has been taken by learners worldwide, bringing many new users (and "Followers") into the Dream Rise sphere.

In addition to helping research materials, the team suggested exercises that invited users to interact with others through the platform, make personal reflections, and think about their own learning process. All of the exercises came from the CanopyLAB database with incorporating innovative ways of learning including elements of individual, social and collaborative learning. The NGO acquired different tools and new ways of approaching their students. To successfully launch the course, several meetings took place to clarify the objectives of the course and be sure the essence of the NGO remained the same, while providing new elements and experiences to the end users.

Innovative Outreach

Once the course was launched, the analytics showed some minor difficulties with regard to the recurring users. The LAB team began to provide support with instructions on how to use their webpage and social media (SO-ME) to promote the course as well as how to access it. Dream Rise began to train their users in using the platform. They began to be self-reliant and sustainable, using SO-ME to best suit their unique needs. They have an unlimited number of courses and can use their page as their "official" website where they can communicate with their users, post announcements, and provide content. While the programs and courses of Dream Rise are in the formulation stage of development, their message is clear and bold. With their commitment to youth empowerment and leadership, they are a potential voice of change in Africa and worldwide.

The partnership with Dream Rise Foundation continues to grow. They plan to launch more courses. Mr. Mutegi belongs to CanopyLAB's Innovation Council in which several NGOs discuss their challenges and share potential solutions. They have more than 800 students currently and plan to reach many more. They demonstrate the advantages of online learning reaching beyond their students in Kenya to potentially hundreds of thousands of users around the world available on a smartphone free of charge. Check them out in The LAB.

Case II: The Red Road Foundation -Cambodia

Garrett and Rachel Riggio co-founded The Red Road Foundation with a very clear motto "Addressing critical global issues, such as waste and education" and work for the welfare of villages in Cambodia in which they have developed a program that involves interns, volunteers and the close work with local communities.

"We are seeking inspired minds to make long-term, sustainable impacts. We offer an internship focusing on Leadership, Impact Business and Sustainable Development that utilizes the talents, skills, and passions of all involved to build a more conscious world"[22]

The work with this NGO, with offices in both the United States and Denmark, had some interesting challenges because this is an organization that has its main focus abroad but develops their programs and projects in a different location. They faced challenges related to the pandemic but were able to keep their people thinking about creative ways in which their programs could pivot and function in an online environment.

The First Course

The LAB team showed all the functionalities of the platform and all the possibilities that it opened for people all around the world. They saw the potential to grow and develop online and keep their internship program. The organization created materials for students and offered personal mentors to discuss course content and what students had learned. Their first course, called "Leadership in Sustainability, Communication, & Development," has three different units including materials, videos and a very hands-on approach to the exercises. This course allows students to reflect on their perspective of leadership and empowers them to become better leaders ultimately thinking about the importance of giving back, thinking outside the box and unlocking the potential of each individual.

Global Reach Is Within Reach

The LAB team and The Red Road Foundation worked together to discuss elements of online learning, explore social and collaborative learning, see the possibilities within the platform and develop the courses step by step. They are committed to growing their organization into an international presence through expanding their reach in LDCs using innovative technology to enhance their face-to-face experiences.

Case III: TeacherLAB /DocenteLAB

As a result of COVID-19, teachers globally had to change their primary method of teaching overnight. This inspired CanopyLAB's CEO to create a free channel specifically designed for teachers that could help the global community of educators with the struggles they were facing. Teachers are continually reinventing how they work and teach while figuring out what types of content and software will engage their students in continuing to grow and learn. Docente/TeacherLAB equips teachers with new knowledge, skills, and tools to make their job easier, more rewarding, and less chaotic.

Growing Teacher/DocenteLAB

The LAB is designed on a platform that helped alleviate many pedagogical challenges. Teachers could freely access it on their tablets, computers, and smartphones without downloading data-heavy programs. The Cloud holds all of their profiles, work and courses. Teachers have their own portfolios in their pockets, using CanopyLAB and The LAB for support. During 2020 Teacher and Docente LAB hosted webinars both in English and Spanish in order to complement the courses and engage more directly with teachers. Learning sessions such as, "Tools to assess your students work digitally" had over 700 teachers from around the world online learning about tools that they could access for free to provide them with more opportunities for timely feedback and increased student engagement.

Docente/TeacherLAB is an open learning platform made by teachers for teachers with original produced digital content focused on educators at all levels including primary and secondary schools, colleges, universities, and teachers at Lifelong Learning institutes. The platform is in both English (TeacherLAB) and Spanish (DocenteLAB). In addition to the social network designed specifically for educators, these free interactive platforms give teachers engaging courses designed to empower them in mastering new tools, online pedagogy, and much more. Each course is designed by expert designers (teachers themselves) who have spent considerable time curating material and finding the best tools. Teachers are supporting teachers in this global community which reaches many thousands of teachers worldwide.

TeacherLAB is a case study for the implementation of robust e-learning experiences because it has given the opportunity for teachers from around the globe to learn asynchronously and follow their own learning path while learning from other teacher's experiences. It is a place where teachers can share academic content, concerns and projects. The largest number of users come from Nigeria, Pakistan and India for our English content platform and Colombia, Venezuela and Argentina for our Spanish speaking teachers. Each of these countries are facing issues of access to technology, lack of infrastructure in rural areas on top of a crisis in education due to the pandemic.

Both Teacher and Docente LAB continue to grow at an unprecedented pace as teachers have to cope with the lasting impact of the pandemic and the transformation of pedagogy and the user experience.

SOLUTIONS AND RECOMMENDATIONS

Lessons Learned

The work with these organizations and all the partners that became part of The LAB in 2020 provided several important lessons for deploying digital learning platforms in challenging environments. Some key lessons learned are:

1. Embrace diverse voices. In many situations, groups working together on an aligned outcome can achieve greater results. Diverse groups bring the best minds together to talk through issues and challenges to create innovative solutions.
2. Listen. The LAB team listened to the challenges that many NGOs were facing related to economic, socio-cultural and health barriers. While their focus was providing software solutions to NGOs, they learned to listen to the people who had to deal with many issues before they could get to designing courses.
3. Work together. There can be many diverse pathways to success. Working together to create a partnership mindset of possibility and opportunity can open new avenues of collaboration to achieve goals. The Mandarin language characters for the word "Crisis" are made up of symbols for both Danger and Opportunity. Collaboration can mitigate the danger and present opportunity.
4. Face the hard things. The year 2020 was a year of challenges, dangers, and opportunities throughout the world. Nearly every nation has been impacted by the global health crisis, social unrest, political polarizations, systemic educational upheaval, and emotional distress. The LAB has seized the opportunity to bring possibility to the world through our AI powered collaborative learning platform for NGOs.

PART III THEREFORE.......

Future Research Directions

With increased investment by governments, institutions, private corporations and Regional Development Banks, the technology gap could, and should, begin to close. The World Bank and the United Nations both fund research opportunities to study the efficacy of current programs and solutions. Beyond universal connectivity, it can be important to study the impact of social learning environments among NGOs and institutions as they co-create solutions to pressing global issues. Research may include areas such as:

- Rates of adoption of technology in LDC's
- Infrastructure needed in order to provide more accessibility in rural areas,
- Survey of technology strategic plans of Ministries of Education around the world.

CONCLUSION

In the beginning of this chapter the authors stated the following learning objectives: 1) to illuminate the disparity and challenges of ICT in Least Developed Countries; 2) to illustrate the potential impact of knowledge economy in LDC's and rural communities; and 3) to demonstrate the possibility and potential of learner-based pedagogy.

The authors have presented a compelling case for investing in two specific aspects of the Pillars of the Knowledge Economy, technology and people. Adhering to these principles can support any nation, large or small, in developing the most valuable asset in their borders- their people. Creating a culture among any population of life-long learning, a mindset of curiosity, and a commitment to find out about new things makes people in that culture more innovative and creative. The authors demonstrate through specific Case Study examples how the resolve and actions of committed people can, and will, overcome the barriers of disparity and inequity. They fly the banner that says, "Resources Follow Commitment."[23]

Aggressive and thoughtful investment by donor nations, innovative corporations, global and regional economic institutions, such as the World Bank and the InterAmerican, Asian, and African Development Banks, can provide the opportunity for those in least developed countries to leapfrog from the 19th into the 21st century.

The NGO community has demonstrated their commitment to Agenda 2030 and achieving the 17 Sustainable Development Goals on time and in full. Having a robust learning platform provides new educational opportunities, access to new information, the possibility of collaboration on common issues that cross geographies, and greater global reach.

Overcoming the challenges of infrastructure, access, and connectivity will provide people everywhere with the opportunity to learn and grow anytime from anywhere. Having access to information on every area of interest or concern empowers people. People who know can participate in the Knowledge Economy, enhancing themselves and their value to their communities, both business and social. As Peter Drucker so presciently said, "...The most valuable asset of a 21st century institution, whether business or non-business, will be its knowledge workers and their productivity."

Make It Real

The authors invite potential investors to meet this global challenge head-on. Invest in access to knowledge and people. Connecting the world and empowering people is possible. We request they demonstrate their commitment making this possibility reality.

REFERENCES

Chen & Dahlman. (2006). *The Knowledge Economy*. The KAM Methodology and World Bank Operations World Bank Institute.

Dweck, C. (2006). *Mindset, The New Psychology of Success*. Ballantine Books.

Hanushek & Woessmann. (2015). *The Knowledge Capital of Nations: Education and the Economics of Growth*. MIT Press.

Kemp, S. (2018). *2018 Global Digital Report*. We Are Social.com.

Kimenyi & Moyo. (2011). *Leapfrogging Development Through Technology Adoption*. Brookings Institution.

Peters. (2008). Education and the Knowledge Economy. Academic Press.

UN-OHRLLS. (2020). *LDCs in Facts and Figures, 2018. 'Utoikamanu, F. UN Chronicle*. Closing the Technology Gap in Least Developed Countries.

VanDen Berg. (2017). *Economic Growth and Development* (3rd ed.). World Scientific Publishing.

World Bank. (2021). *EdStats Database*. Author.

World Bank Group. (2019). *Kenya Digital Economy Assessment. Summary Report*. World Bank.

World Economic and Social Survey. (2018). Department of Economic and Social Affairs of the United Nations Secretariat (UN/DESA).

Zhenmin. (2019). Frontier Technologies: A window for Leapfrogging. *UN Chronicle*.

ENDNOTES

1 Prof. Dr. Joan Torrent-Sellens, Faculty of Economic and Business Studies, Open University of Catalonia, Barcelona, Spain; Prof. Dr. Jorge Sainz-González, Applied Economics, Universidad Rey Juan Carlos, Madrid, Spain

2 The Knowledge Economy, The KAM Methodology, and World Bank Operations, Chen & Dahlman. World Bank Institute, 2006.

3 The World Bank. "The Knowledge Economy, The Kam Methodology, and World Bank Operations," Pages 5-8. Accessed Jan. 22, 2021.

4 The Knowledge Capital of Nations: Education and the Economics of Growth, Hanushek & Woessmann, MIT Press, 2015.

5 Dweck, C. "Mindset, The New Psychology of Success". Ballantine Books, 2006.

6 World Bank Group. 2019. Kenya Digital Economy Assessment. Summary Report. Washington, DC: World Bank. License: Creative Commons Attribution CC BY 3.0 IGO.

7 UN Chronicle.

8 UN Chronicle; Closing the Technology Gap in Least Developed Countries. 'Utoikamanu, 2020.

9 "Economic Growth and Development, Third Edition." VanDen Berg, World Scientific Publishing, 2017.

10 "Education and the Knowledge Economy." Peters, M.A. Cheltenham, 2008.

11 UN-OHRLLS; LDCs in Facts and Figures, 2018.

12 https://youtu.be/xKcxjxSVtTM

13 "Leapfrogging Development Through Technology Adoption." Kimenyi & Moyo, Brookings Institution, 2011.

14 "Frontier Technologies: A window for Leapfrogging." Zhenmin.. UN Chronicle. 2019.

15 The World Economic and Social Survey 2018. Department of Economic and Social Affairs of the United Nations Secretariat (UN/DESA).

16 Digital in 2018, Simon Kemp. 2018 Global Digital Report, We Are Social.com.

17 World Bank EdStats Database 2021.

18 https://sdgs.un.org/goals

19 https://www.frontiersin.org/articles/10.3389/fpsyg.2020.01557/full

20 https://canopylab.com/about/

21 http://www.dreamrisefoundation.epizy.com/about.html

22 https://theredroadfoundation.org/

23 David E. Pines, M. Ed.

Chapter 8
Educational Development in Hadhramaut

John M. Mulholland
Friends of Hadramaut, USA

Sultana Feroze al-Qu'aiti
Friends of Hadhramaut, UK

EXECUTIVE SUMMARY

This chapter will define the goals and describe the methods of Friends of Hadhramaut's (FOH), a UK-based charitable trust, efforts to nurture the seeds that will evolve to embrace the goals of the knowledge economy (KE) in Hadhramaut. As a charitable organization, FOH focuses its support on the health/medical and educational sectors of society. FOH has made additional strides to focus on girls' education and on those who have what we call "learning disabilities," a label which covers a broad range of dysfunctions. This chapter will focus on FOH's methodology and achievements in the educational sector.

INTRODUCTION

The reader will likely ask, "Where is Hadhramaut"? As shown in the map (Friends of Hadhramaut Newsletter, 2021) below, it is the largest of Yemen's 17 provinces (also frequently referred to as "Governorates") and found on the south coast of the Arabian Peninsula on the Indian Ocean as shown in Figure 1.

DOI: 10.4018/978-1-7998-8417-0.ch008

Figure 1. Map of Yemen and the Hadhramaut
(Friends of Hadhramaut Newsletter, 2021)

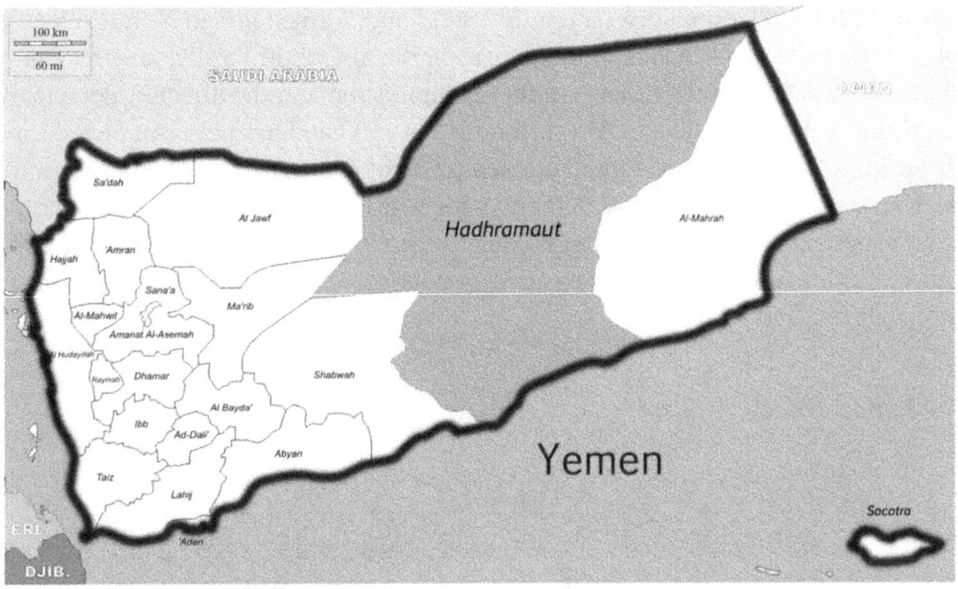

This chapter will define the goals and describe the methods of a UK based Charitable Trust's, "The Friends of Hadhramaut" (FOH), efforts to nurture the seeds that will evolve to embrace the goals of the Knowledge Economy (KE). Embracing the goals does not necessarily mean achieving them. Let the reader be under no illusion. Yemen is a desperately poor country by any measure. Undoubtedly its one bright spot is that the Civil War in the mountainous western part of the country has not moved to the eastern part of the country where Hadhramaut is located . . . yet. As a charitable organization the FOH focuses its support on the health/medical and educational sectors of society (Friends of Hadhramaut Newsletter, 2021) though recently the situation has become so dire that the FOH has imported foodstuffs. In the educations sector the FOH has made additional strides to focus on Girls' education and on those with what we call "learning disabilities," a label which covers a broad range of disabilities. This chapter will focus on the FOH's methodology and achievements in the educational sector.

Background

In order to better understand the current situation in Hadhramaut, let us, for a moment, take a short trip back through history. Although hardly a household word in the West today, the Hadhramaut has enjoyed moments of glory and recognition over the thousands of years of its historical existence. The Hadhramaut was perhaps first noted in history as part of that long swath of land along the Arabian Peninsula's south coast called the "Land of Frankincense and Myrrh" during Greco-Roman times (Disto, 2021). It also became associated with the Kingdom of Saba (of Queen of Sheba fame). Because of its poverty Hadhramis emigrated abroad as far back as perhaps 700 BC. Hadhramis became famous for creating an arc of Hadhrami colonies around the Indian ocean from India down the East Africa Coast and, later populating Indonesia (Wikipedia, 2021). In fact, many prominent businessmen, especially in the Arabian (Persian) Gulf countries are descendants of Hadhrami immigrants. In modern times the Hadhramaut came under the rule of the Qu'aiti dynasty (Wikipedia, 2021) in the middle of the 19th C under British protection. In 1967 the British left, the Qu'aiti ruler was expelled and the Hadhramaut became part of South Yemen, a short-lived Communist nation. In 1990 South Yemen joined North Yemen to form the Yemen Republic. However, it is thanks to the efforts on the al-Qu'aiti family, now residing in exile in Saudi Arabia, which has created the Friends of the Hadhramaut under the direct leadership of the exiled Sultan's wife, Sultana al-Qu'aiti. The FOH was founded in 1993 and has now completed approximately 120 small to medium projects in the aforementioned fields of health/medical and education.

Today the Hadhramaut consists of 192,000 km^2 with an estimated population of 2.3 million (Friends of Hadhramaut Newsletter, 2021). Its capital is Mukalla, on the seacoast, and hosts 3 inland UNESCO nominated cities: Tarim, Seiyun and Shiban, made famous for their clay mud skyscrapers as shown in the pictures of figures 2 and 3.

Figure 2. The Kathiri Palace in Tarim

Figure 3. The city of Seiyun

Sadly, today, the Hadhramaut is a desperately poor province in an even poorer country, Yemen, which, in turn is being torn asunder by a civil war. The evidence of this civil war is shown regularly on international TV complete with bombed-out buildings and children literally starving to death. This war is taking place mainly in the western part of Yemen. While this war is not the subject of this paper, its effects are, in as much as they affect the large eastern province of the country, the Hadhramaut. While in the eastern part of the country there has been little to no actual civil war, the region has become infested with cells of al-Qaeda fighters who have reeked their own havoc, vengeance, and terror on Hadramaut. *ISIS related groups have also established themselves throughout the region and wantonly attacked various towns and institutions* (Wikipedia, 2021).

Even before the current fighting, the Hadhramaut has always been a poor province (the principal reason for its overseas migration as mentioned above) with only artisanal industries, insufficient agricultural in the wadis, fishing, and remittances from its vast diaspora abroad to sustain it. Although the Hadramout hosts 80% of the oil and gas production in Yemen, this income has been cut-off by the war. The authors were unable to obtain GDP per capita figures for the Hadhramaut but for Yemen, as a whole, it's $1910/yr compared to the U.S. which is $65,118/yr (Wikipedia, 2021) It is hard to believe that this region, today known as Yemen, was historically known in the West for centuries as *Arabia Felix* (Happy Arabia).

The Friends of Hadhramaut

A group of knowledgeable and concerned individuals visited the Hadhramaut in 1993 and returned to the UK realizing how desperately the province required support if it were to ever begin to achieve its development goals. This group founded a charity called "The Friends of the Hadhramaut" (FOH).

The "Knowledge Economy" consists of several principles: education, innovation, ICT infrastructure, social inclusion and enabling policies. It is hoped that the contribution of this chapter will be to demonstrate that well directed charity works, no matter, how humble in origin, if based on defined objectives, and guided by sound principles, can indeed make a significant contribution to improving and achieving the KE principles, 'pillars" if you will, of education, innovation, ICT infrastructure, social inclusion and enabling policies. In this book the reader will read of large organizations which have made scientific analysis of a given society's needs, invested significant resources (including the "triple helix" approach) to achieve its stated goals, and then used defined metrics to measure the success or failure of the invested resources, especially as they relate to the Knowledge Economy" (KE). In the case herein presented, the efforts of the "Friends of Hadhramaut," are not so sophisticated but, as will be shown, has been at least somewhat successful in achieving its goals which, in large measure coincide with the so-called "Pillars" stated above. In short, it is the authors' belief that this study is pertinent to the overall KE goals because it embraces these goals in an environment lacking in many of the prerequisites usually associated with attaining KE goals. Just contemplate for a minute a place of deplorable poverty, omnipresent hunger, and, effectively, no Internet in the region. Needless to say, there is no help or support of any kind from the central Yemen government for the citizens of the Hadhramaut.

Perhaps the best way to view this study as it applies to the KE principles is to make a comparison to Bangladesh. Bangladesh's war of cessation ended in December 1971, with a death toll estimated by some to be as many at 3 million and, by any standard, one of the poorest countries on earth. Yet, 50 years later Bangladesh has surpassed its "mother" country, Pakistan, in per capita GDP and is quickly catching India as well. Women as a percentage of the work force have risen from 3 to 36% in 50 years. 98% of Bangladeshi children complete primary school (The Economist Magazine, 2021). Amazingly, this success is not a result of good governance but, rather, in spite of it. Much credit must go to the efforts of charitable people such as:

Zafarullah Chowdhury who dropped out of university in Britain to set up a charity to distribute cheap generic drugs and contraceptives (The Economist Magazine, 2021). .

Fazel Hasan Abed who sold his flat in London returned to found BRAC to teach mothers how to rehydrate children suffering from diarrhea, turning it from a deadly sickness to a nuisance. Immunization rates rose from 2% to 80% (The Economist Magazine, 2021). .

The results have been amazing:

One of the poorest countries on earth in 1971, today Bangladesh has surpassed Its "mother" country, Pakistan, and is quickly catching India in per capita GDP (The Economist Magazine, 2021).

98% of Bangladeshi children complete primary school (The Economist Magazine, 2021).

As a percentage of the work force the female rate of participation has risen from 3 to 36% in 50 years (The Economist Magazine, 2021).

The analogy is that Bangladesh is on the threshold of joining the world's Knowledge Economies as a result of educated, capable, well-intentioned people who believed in their country and wanted to help it and, most importantly, did so. In the same spirit the FOH hopes its modest efforts can, with time, affect similar changes in Hadhramaut. This chapter is a study of those efforts.

In addition to the lack of infrastructure in Hadhramaut to advance formal learning for both boys and girls, the society as a whole is under significant pressure from lack of resources, lack of work, no income, skyrocketing prices for foodstuffs and physical safety which have put the whole population at risk to one degree or another. The 2019 Humanitarian Overview by the UN, though dated, sums up well the dire situation even before the arrival of COVID 19:

In Aden, Lahj, Hadhramaut and Al Maharah (provinces of South Yemen) 54 per cent of surveyed households reported at least one vulnerability, including a medical condition, physical disability, being a single parent or caregiver, or GBV concerns. About 15 per cent of households reported at least one member with legal or physical protection needs. Due to extreme hardship, persons of concern increasingly resort to negative coping mechanisms that exacerbate risks, including begging and forcing children to drop out of school to beg or work. A UNHCR assessment found that more than 80 per cent of male refugee children and more than 70 per cent of female refugee children (referring to internally displaced Yemenis because of the civil war) who do not go to school either do nothing or engage in begging. Parents have complained that youths are prone to recruitment by fighting forces. Focus-group discussions revealed that refugee children feel inhibited and anxious and are under severe psychological stress. A third of male respondents reported arbitrary assaults and arrests, most frequently in Al Jawf, Hudaydah, Hadhramaut, Shabwah, and Sa'ada (UN Humanitarian Overview, 2019).

FOH Methodology

The methodology of the FOH is straight forward and, basically, quite simple.

1. **Project Prioritization:** Through the partners on the ground in the Hadhramaut of the FOH, prioritized Lists of needs are created in the health/medical and education fields. The FOH Has also prioritized education for girls and special needs students, realizing that These groups are the most discriminated against by local customs. Frequently these defined needs go beyond the supply of construction materials, learning supplies and computers but to include more basic needs such as toilets and ceiling fans. In fact, as will be seen, for the first time the FOH is delivering food supplies through the administration it originally set-up up to prioritize, deliver and implement educational requirements. The FOH realizes that neither teachers nor students can function when they are starving.
2. **Accounting Responsibility:** In a place and situation of nearly unlimited needs matched against the limited means of a charity, accounting and cost controls must be imposed and rigorously enforced. The costs of materials, supplies, and manpower to support each projects are carefully calculated. The FOH raises funds through events sponsored by its various chapters around the world. FOH funds are dedicated 100% to its projects. No member of the FOH management team in the UK, nor its team on the ground in the Hadhramaut receives any financial compensation.
3. **Local Participation:** The FOH confers with its team in Hadhramaut to select for the coming year which projects will be supported. Every attempt is made to utilize locally supplied materials and manpower. Nonetheless, nearly every project requires the importation of certain critical items such as computers and textbooks. This may seem obvious but the delivery of supplies and materials to Hadhramaut has proven to be extremely challenging. As an example, the FOH, at a time before the beginning of the Civil War, determined the most efficient method of delivering supplies was by ship to Jeddah and then overland by truck to Hadhramaut. Although the FOH supplies a local project manager, it is a requirement that the recipient participate in the project, usually by contributing manpower, supplying locally supplied materials and/or sharing in the funding when possible.
4. **Project Administration:** Once a project is started, it is supervised and monitored by the FOH team on the ground and from the UK office to assure that bottlenecks and unforeseen impediments are overcome and that the project is successfully completed, at, or under, budget and on, or under, time. To the extent possible the FOH tries to obtain contributions from the local schools and cities. Every attempt is also made to involve the recipient school in the investment in the subject project. This can be in the form of a cash contribution but often comes in the supply of materials and labor.
5. **Follow-up:** Finally, to the extent possible, the FOH follows-up on each project to assure that the benefit to the local society is achieved. This is where this report is at its weakest. While there is no lack of appreciation by the administrators, teachers and students for the contributions and donations by the FOH, it has been impossible to follow-up systematically on the long-term impact of the FOH's projects as measured by KE principles. What can be supplied are some specifically known success stories and infer the greater impact from these anecdotes. For further details the reader is invited to read the "Project Results" in the summary chart below (Figure 4) and expanded the in the "Conclusions" part of this chapter.

Project Summary

See Table 1 and Figures 4-8.

Table 1.

Year	Project Name/ Location	Project Goal(s)	Project Description	Project Results
2004 - 2013	Primary and Intermediate School, Ghayl BaWazir	Upgrade existing facilities and expand or add to them.	2004 Educational items, 2006 inauguration of 10 completely renovated classrooms and 10 new lavatories. 2010, classroom roof repaired after floods. 2013, one classroom repainted, roofs renewed of two classrooms with new fans and electric wiring.	This is one of the FOH's major educational projects. The British Ambassador in Sanaa drove to Ghayl BaWazir (a long and very difficult trip) to inaugurate the new facility. It has allowed the pupils to enhance their learning experience through enjoying 10 new refurbished classrooms and 10 new lavatories. The Riyadh Group of British businessmen who had partly funded this project were amazed to see the high standard of reconstruction and renovation in spite of the very limited budget. This project fulfilled two of FOH's core aims, as laid out in our charter: support education and improve health facilities where it can.
2005	Community College, Mariama, Seiyun	Provide English teaching materials throughout the Hadramaut.	Provided English teaching manuals for 65 teachers throughout Hadhramaut	While the FOH has not been able to survey objectively the results of this investment, the news regarding this project anecdotally has been positive and most encouraging. This project was funded by the British Council in Yemen.

Continued on following page

Table 1. Continued

Year	Project Name/ Location	Project Goal(s)	Project Description	Project Results
2008	Tariq bin Ziyad Primary School, Asnab, Wadi Khonab	Supply Teaching materials and construct expanded facilities.	2008: 3 new classrooms, 4 lavatories, a teacher's office, storeroom and a perimeter wall. 2009, desks, chairs, tables, a water cooler, teaching materials (e.g., maps) and a loudspeaker system. 2014, new printer .	The education of all children against all odds is truly inspirational. The dedication of all involved is admirable. It was very rewarding to distribute school items which friends had carried from their homes and a world map donated by a FOH member to give the staff and villagers in this very remote barren wadi (valley) some idea of the geography of the world. The staff and pupils found it hard to believe that somebody really cared for them from so far away. The laborers and craftsmen were very appreciative that their hard and excellent work was recognized by visiting foreigners dignitaries. The FOH is proud of having rebuilt this school in the sandy wastes of the Hadhramaut, especially given the extremely difficult rural location and the problematic logistics of delivering construction material to the site.

Continued on following page

Table 1. Continued

Year	Project Name/ Location	Project Goal(s)	Project Description	Project Results
2008 - 2009	Tariq bin Ziyad Primary School, Asnab, Wadi Khonab	Classroom and lavatory construction, furnish selected teaching materials.	2008: Three new classrooms, four lavatories, teacher's office, storeroom and a perimeter wall. 2009, desks, chairs, tables, a water cooler and a loudspeaker. 2014, new printer, large map. See figures 4 and 5 below.	The education of all children against all odds is truly inspirational. It was very rewarding to distribute school items which friends had carried from their homes and a world map donated by the FOH gave the staff and villagers in this very remote barren wadi (valley) some idea of just how far England was from their school. There was a palpable sense of joy felt by all the staff and pupils who found it hard to believe that somebody really cared for them to such a degree. The laborers were beaming as FOH reps walked around the school, proud to see their hard work appreciated by these foreigners. FOH is proud of having rebuilt this tiny school in the sandy wastes of Hadhramaut. Given the extremely difficult rural location and the problematic transportation and logistics of delivering construction material to the site.
2010	Bayn al-Jabaal School (Jol) and Ras Mahal School (Jol)	Supply 200 blankets. Install flooring and generator	200 blankets, linoleum, and a generator. The area where the schools are located is northwest of al-Mukalla where it is extremely cold in winter.	The schools bring Bedouin and orphan children from different areas to study there. The Jol is the large crystalline limestone plateau covering ninety percent of the landmass of Hadhramaut. The schools are far from the paved road and can only be accessed via a dirt track.

Continued on following page

Table 1. Continued

Year	Project Name/ Location	Project Goal(s)	Project Description	Project Results
2010	Zahrah Primary School for Girls, al-Mukalla	Installation of floor matting.	Floor matting was installed.	The floor matting provided by FOH was very much appreciated by the pupils as they could finally sit on a clean surface. The dearth of proper suitable classroom furniture is a problem throughout Hadhramaut. It is believed that the new flooring material will enhance the students' learning ability.
2011	Rawdat al-Amal Kindergarten, al-Qatn	Supply of educational materials and installation of a protective shelter and fans.	Educational games and toys 2011; playground equipment 2014; protective shelter and six new fans.	The FOH built protective shelters for several schools across Hadhramaut. These are greatly appreciated by the pupils as it allows them to play outside protected against the scorching sun of hot Hadhrami summers. The children also benefit from exercise, fresh air and, in the process, also get some vitamin D.
2012 - 2019	Al-Khansaa' Secondary School for Girls, al-Qatn	Facilitate girls' learning in al-Qatn	Al-Qatn was the site of one of FOH's first projects and one that evolved into a multi-stage and multi-year project. FOH built 6 lavatories in 2012; a storeroom in 2014; two verandahs and 6 classrooms were renovated with new blackboards, doors, fans, windows, electric wiring, and desert coolers in 2016. In 2017 FOH repaired classrooms' roofs; in 2018 five classrooms were repainted; in 2019 work was undertaken on maintenance of the floors outside the classrooms and renovation of all six roof surfaces. See Figures 6 and 7 below.	The chronic shortage of classrooms in al-Khanasaa' greatly limited the opportunity for girls' education in the town. FOH undertook building additional ones to enable more girls to be educated at the secondary level from the surrounding areas. The ultimate of seeing graduates go on to tertiary education is already starting to be fulfilled.

Continued on following page

Table 1. Continued

Year	Project Name/ Location	Project Goal(s)	Project Description	Project Results
2014	Primary School, Uqran, Shibam	Facilitate girls' learning IAW one of the major goals of the FOH. Given the conservative nature of Hadhrami society, most families do not like their daughters to study in a mixed environment, and therefore remove them from primary school after completing Grade 3 or 4. To encourage these families to enroll their daughters back at school, it is imperative to provide extra classrooms to enable these girls to continue their education.	The FOH built 4 new classrooms, a teacher's room, a perimeter wall, a tiled courtyard, a sewage well 4 lavatories for 150 to 200 girls, also raised the height of the perimeter wall and built a new storeroom door. These girls had to stay at home after completing Grade 3 due to the lack of school facilities. Uqran is a large village approximately 10 kilometers from the UNESCO World Heritage city of Shibam and serves 3 nearby villages	The goal to enable these girls to continue their education has proved successful. The construction work in this school was greatly appreciated by the local communities as the girls were able to resume their studies after staying at home for quite a while.
2014	Madrasat al-Mustaqbal, al-Aneen	To facilitate outdoor sports for the school's pupils.	FOH built a protective shelter in the playground.	The FOH built protective shelters for several schools across Hadhramaut. These are greatly appreciated by the pupils as it allows them to play outside protected against the scorching sun of hot Hadhrami summers. The children also benefit from exercise, fresh air and, in the process, also get some vitamin D.
2014	Kathiba al-Mallahi School for Girls, Ghayl BaWazir		FOH built a protective shelter in the playground.	The FOH built protective shelters for several schools across Hadhramaut. These are greatly appreciated by the pupils as it allows them to play outside protected against the scorching sun of hot Hadhrami summers. The children also benefit from exercise, fresh air and, in the process, also get some vitamin D.

Continued on following page

Table 1. Continued

Year	Project Name/ Location	Project Goal(s)	Project Description	Project Results
2014	Madrasat al-Huda, al-Muraqqadah, Wadi Hadhramaut		FOH built a protective shelter, levelled the playground, and raised the railings on the verandah for security.	The FOH built protective shelters for several schools across Hadhramaut. These are greatly appreciated by the pupils as it allows them to play outside protected against the scorching sun of hot Hadhrami summers. The children also benefit from exercise, fresh air and, in the process, also get some vitamin D.
2014	Primary School for Girls and Boys, Wuaylat, Zekaykah, Wadi Hadramaut	To encourage reading, creating small plays and acting in them.	Renovated four classroom floors with tiles to enable better use of the floor space for pupils and a small stage was erected for school performances and local performances.	Exciting result of increased reading, script preparation and acting.
2015	Al-Istiqlal School for Girls and Boys, Hidye, Wadi Hadhramaut	Local custom is to separate the sexes in the schools after the 5th grade. The added classrooms allowed girls to continue their studies in this small village.	Constructed 2nd floor consisting of 5 new classrooms and an adjoining balcony. Used traditional mud brick (madar), indigenous materials and local stone. FOH also installed fans, electricity, doors and windows.	These additional classrooms have enabled girls to continue their studies after grades four and five.
2016	Omar bin AbdulAziz Primary and Intermediate School, an-Naqah, Ghayl BaWazir	Supply of teaching and student materials, student uniforms, electrical wiring, and lighting.	FOH provided chalkboards, chairs, fans, sockets, switches, and tube lights to the school in 2016. Aid was provided to 36 pupils on their graduation. In addition, FOH supplied stationery, satchels, school shoes, uniforms, and miscellaneous school items due to the inability of families to cope with the ever-increasing expenses.	Another example of how the supply of basic necessities can facilitate learning.
2016	Saif bin Dhi Yazen Secondary School for Boys, al-Qatn, Wadi Hadhramaut	Renovation of lavatories		FOH renovated the old lavatories in this school. The situation regarding lavatories in schools throughout Hadhramaut is to be deplored, many schools having no toilet facilities whatsoever. FOH policy is to always construct lavatories alongside classrooms. More often than not, existing lavatories have to be completely renovated due to their dilapidated state

Continued on following page

Table 1. Continued

Year	Project Name/ Location	Project Goal(s)	Project Description	Project Results
2017	Al-Shatie School for Girls, Qusair	Supply of educational materials.	This school on the coast in eastern Hadhramaut was supplied with educational items by FOH.	The impoverished community eking out a subsistence existence based on fishing is in a sorry state. The hope is that the FOH's contribution will help facilitate future learning for its youth.
2018	Saeed ibn al-Museeb School for Boys and Girls, Wadi Araf, al-Shihr Directorate	Construct new and renovate old lavatories.	Constructed 7 new toilets and a new sewage tank. The Local Coordinator was approached by the Director of this school to renovate 7 old lavatories and build a few new ones based on the excellent renovation and construction of lavatories by FOH in al-Barh.	This school comprises 750 pupils from a catchment area of 14 villages. This is further evidence of FOH's reputation and standing in this remote and underdeveloped area.
2018 - 2020	Al-Tumooh al-Nahidh, The Society for Rising Endeavour and Aspiration, Al-Shihr	Help and assist children with disabilities and special needs.	2018: The FOH provided locally made items designed to help children with disabilities. 2020: The FOH supplied educational equipment. This center serves those children who have special needs and those with disabilities in the area. It is a private initiative started by female volunteers, including the mothers and relatives of those needing special care. Parents are asked to pay minimal fees as the organizers seek financial assistance from the local community to run the center. The manufacture of locally made purpose-built chairs funded by the FOH are designed to help the local craftsmen. Fidget blankets made by Friends in the UK were also supplied.	The donation of equipment and Fidget blankets facilitated learning for these disadvantaged children. It also reminded them that people care for them although half a world away.
2019 - 2021	Sports, Youth and Culture Club, al-Qatn, Wadi Hadhramaut	To provide sports facilities to encourage healthy sports and to discourage anti-social activities such as the chewing of "qat" (a mild stimulant) and smoking "shisha."	This was a 3-year project. Initially, 3 rooms were constructed, and a perimeter wall built around the volleyball and basketball courts. Later painting and marking of the volleyball and handball courts was undertaken and in 2021 a purpose-built cafeteria with 5 toilets were constructed.	This club is going from strength to strength. By encouraging its members to participate in handball, volleyball, basketball, ping pong, football and athletics, it has successfully discouraged the youth from indulging in anti-social activities, while improving their health. The number of boys who train and practice is increasing by the day due to the superb facilities that FOH has provided.

Continued on following page

Table 1. Continued

Year	Project Name/ Location	Project Goal(s)	Project Description	Project Results
2019 - 2020	Madrassah al-Iradah for Girls and Boys, al-Qatn, Wadi Hadhramaut	The FOH believes that extreme heat discourages learning and sports. This project objective was to ameliorate those detractions.	Installed 11 solar fans with roof solar panels. In 2020 a large protective outdoor canopy for the playground was supplied and erected. The school serves several villages in the area. which were specially arranged. The local FOH rep was able to convince a store owner in al-Mukalla (the capitol of the Hadhramaut) to donate a foosball table.	The fans and canopy achieved their goal judged by the jump in new students attending the upgraded school.
2019 - 2020	Al-Zahra Primary School for Girls, al-Qatn	Facilitate girls' education	In 2019 FOH built a protective shelter and outdoor stage. The stage was highly appreciated by the school administration as it could be used by the local community for events and festivals. In 2020 FOH installed electrical equipment and provided a wheelchair. Due to the Ministry's inability to provide sufficient textbooks for the school, FOH were able to meet this requirement in 2020 by getting the relevant textbooks printed.	In the challenge to garner support for the school the stage provided an unexpected "hook" to involve the town fathers with the school. While still early to judge results the FOH is pleased to report already a significant increase in girls' attendance in 2021.
2019	Yemeni Society for Rehabilitation of the Physically Handicapped, al-Mukalla	Assist physically handicapped children.	The FOH donated numerous pieces of rehabilitation equipment. See Figure 8.	Significant improvement was noted during 2020 in the ability of many handicapped children in their movements and ability to take care of themselves.

Figure 4. Pupils studying in the open in Asnab as they await the new classrooms promised by Friends of the Hadhramaut

Figure 5. New school, gate and perimeter wall surrounding courtyard, Asnab

Figure 6. Inspecting new FOH constructed school for girls in al-Khansaa'

Figure 7. A new wing of the al-Khansaa' School for Girls

Figure 8. Physiotherapy equipment donated to The Yemeni Society for Rehabilitation of the Physically Handicapped, al-Mukalla

RESULTS / CONCLUSION

"In a knowledge economy, highly skilled jobs require excellent technical skills and relational skills such as problem-solving, the flexibility to interface with multiple discipline areas as well as the ability to adapt to changes as opposed to moving or crafting physical objects in conventional manufacturing-based economies.

The Knowledge Economy is closely linked to the information economy. While FOH agrees with these absolutely vital objectives of the KE, FOH would humbly submit that the first and primary goal to achieving a KE is to instill in students the ability to use rational and objective thinking. It is in the achievement of this goal in the middle and high schools that FOH has dedicated its efforts in creating nests of learning even in the most remote and poor villages of the Hadhramaut; 22 schools, in fact. FOH has always aimed its efforts towards those schools with the greatest need.

At the time of the creation of this chapter the situation (see "Future" below) in Yemen continues to deteriorate. Children arrive at school so hungry that they cannot concentrate on their studies. That is why, during the past 8 months, FOH has swung its efforts to supplying boxes of food directly to communities to assure, at least, one good meal a day for families. Perhaps such basic assistance is not generally considered part of the Knowledge Economy, but FOH believes that without food assistance, there will be no "rational and objective" leaders of the future given the current circumstances in the Hadhramaut and the Yemen, in general.

In spite of such impediments the FOH can point to certain factual and measurable accomplishments:

1. As mentioned above, 22 schools of various types have received aid in one form or another from Friends of Hadhramaut. Anecdotally FOH has had its aspirations of assisting young Hadhramis to gain access to better education confirmed through hundreds of written and verbal expressions of gratitude which are obviously sincere.
2. While FOH is of the opinion that its aid assists all students, however, it is particularly proud of the aid that it has specifically directed to support education for girls and students with "special needs." There can be no doubt that in a time of crises, such as now, these children would have lost all opportunity for a formal education without FOH assistance.
3. One measure of progress is the number of students who have graduated from middle schools and gone on to the Mariama Community College in Seiyun. The school has achieved a staggering 88% graduation rate, mostly by students who studied in schools which were recipients of FOH's programs. It should be noted that there are ten universities in Yemen including the Hadhramaut University of Science and Technology in the capital, al-Mukalla (Imka, 2021). It is reported that some Hadhrami students have been able to go to the UAE and Egypt for further education, but FOH has no specific details.

THE FUTURE

The various Yemeni stakeholders' success in resolving the country's Civil War has been limited, they have not managed to resolve tensions in the country, though they have dampened them. Nonetheless, officials have still succeeded in providing some form of regional consensus regarding key priorities and areas of political convergence in the Hadhramaut. These priorities include several that have essentially been achieved, including preventing regional and national power struggles from escalating, shaping the political vision of the governorate; and securing 20 percent of the revenue from oil extraction in the governorate. Additional goals, which have yet to be achieved, include unifying the local security apparatuses and unifying the governance structures (2021, International organization of Migration).

Moving forward, such locally rooted processes will be vitally important. Regardless of what shape post-conflict Yemen takes, it is undeniable that the heavily centralized governing systems of the past are gone. Bottom-up efforts to determine how local governance will function—and how various parts of the country will interact with each other—appear to be the best recipe for stability in the near future. In that sense, the processes that have emerged in the Hadhramaut—rooted, as they are, in the governorate's particular history and in its diaspora—represent a potential model to be followed (Out of Hadhramaut, 2006).

The model of local governance that is emerging in the Hadhramaut is starkly different from the top-down implementation of federalism that has traditionally been attempted in Yemen. Any top-down approach also belies the emerging dynamics on the ground in governorates like the Hadhramaut. Feeling underrepresented—given its vast size and its oil—locals in the Hadhramaut have long demanded far more economic and political authority and autonomy. The power vacuums that the ongoing conflict have caused have granted Hadhramis an opportunity to take action — albeit cautiously, at least thus far (Out of Hadhramaut, 2006).

Peace does not lie only with the representatives of al-Hadi and the Houthis. There is also the Southern Transitional Council, which didn't exist in 2015, but by 2019 the STC held President al-Hadi's temporary capital of Aden, a city it continues to control. The STC advocates for an independent south Yemen and is backed by a number of affiliated military units, many of which were established, trained, and armed by the UAE. Convincing the STC to give up its dream of an independent state will not be easy, but ignoring STC desires or denying it a seat at the negotiating table is a nonstarter. The STC, by virtue of both its support in the south as well as its affiliated fighters, has an effective veto over the peace process. It can subvert any settlement it feels does not adequately represent its interests (Out of Hadhramaut, 2006).

There are similar issues in Marib, Shabwa, and the Hadhramaut. These governorates, Yemen's so-called "triangle of power," account for most of Yemen's oil and gas exports. All three governorates have also acquired a significant degree of political and economic autonomy over the course of the war, as roughly 20% of oil and gas revenue is now channeled back to local governments, instead of being deposited with the central government like it was before the war. Perhaps nowhere is this more acute than in the Hadhramaut, which has long advocated for greater local rule (Baron and Basalama, 2021).

This chapter is about the future of the Knowledge Economy in the Province of the Hadhramaut. However, the authors felt it important to paint a comprehensible picture of the challenges and hopes for a stable government in the future. Hadhramis have a long track record of being successful under extremely trying conditions. The authors of this chapter are of the opinion that the intelligence, resourcefulness, and ingenuity of the Hadhramis will find a way to assure a positive and successful future for its people.

REFERENCES

Baron & Basalama. (2021). *The Century Foundation World Report: "The Case of the Hadhramaut: Can Local Efforts Transcend Wartime Divides in Yemen?"* Academic Press.

Distro. (2012). *Travel to Eat: Myrrh and Frankincense.* https://traveltoeat.com/myrrh-and-frankincense-1/

Friends of the Hadhramaut. (n.d.). http://hadhramaut.co.uk/

Harpan & Draghici. (2014). Debate on the Multilevel Model of the Human Capital Measurement. *Procedia: Social and Behavioral Sciences*, 170–177.

Imka. (2021). *Yemen's 10 universities "My Top Schools".* Academic Press.

International Organization of Migration (IOM) Yemen. Ma'rib Response. (2021). https://www.iom.int/sitreps/yemen-marib-response-28-april-15-may-2021

Out of Hadhramaut. (2006). https://hadhramouts.blogspot.com/2006/01/know-hadhramaut.html#:~:text=There%20are%20no%20recent%20population%20census%20of%20Hadhramout%3B,very%20fertile%20Wady%20Hadhramout%20and%20along%20the%20Coast

The Economist Magazine. (2021, Mar. 27). Bangladesh turns 50. *The Economist Magazine.*

UN. (2021). *Humanitarian Overview*. UN.

Wikipedia. (n.d.a). *Hadhramaut, Hadhrami Diaspora.* https://en.wikipedia.org/wiki/Hadhramaut

Wikipedia. (n.d.b). *Hadhramaut, History, Modern.* https://en.wikipedia.org/wiki/Hadhramaut

Wikipedia. (n.d.c). *Hadhrami Insurgency*. https://en.wikipedia.org/wiki/Hadramaut_insurgency

Section 4
Agriculture

Chapter 9
Connect the Dots:
Sustainable Territorial Development and the Knowledge Economy

José Amaral Wagner Neto
São Paulo State Government, Brazil

Zoraide Amarante Itapura de Miranda
Independent Researcher, Brazil

EXECUTIVE SUMMARY

This chapter presents a case study of the Connect the Dots Project, which encompasses a coordinated and connected set of actions aimed at sustainable territorial development, under the prism of the knowledge economy. The project, held in São Paulo City, Brazil, was awarded with the first place at the contest Mayors Challenge 2016, organized by the North American institution Bloomberg Philanthropies. Connect the Dots is a project aimed at strengthening producers and support their transition to an agroecological production system, as a way of protecting the rural landscape, conceived within the scope of the 2014 São Paulo Strategic Master Plan. The name of the project, an allusion to a puzzle game, has its inspiration in the fundamental connections between public and private actors. Its foundation is in the development of technological innovations, education collective actions, and decisions based on data and evidence typical of the knowledge economy.

INTRODUCTION

This chapter presents a case study that encompasses a coordinated and connected set of actions aimed at sustainable territorial development, under the prism of the Economy of Knowledge. The project, held in the City of São Paulo in Brazil, is called Connect the Dots.

Connect the Dots is aimed at promoting ecological agriculture as a way of protecting the rural landscape. Besides developing tools and methodologies to encourage and help local farmers to transition from traditional to ecological farming, the Project also focused on helping them commercialize their organic production, being responsible for the development of a regional value chain for agricultural products.

DOI: 10.4018/978-1-7998-8417-0.ch009

In addition to receiving help to make the transition mainly through technical assistance and inputs compatible with agroecological farming, the farmers could increase the value of their crops, receive managerial and entrepreneurial training, improve their access to buyers and set partnerships with restaurants and local markets.

The Location of the Project

Approximately 12 million people live in São Paulo City and 20 million in the Metropolitan Region. The municipality of São Paulo has an area of 1,500 km^2. The rural area of São Paulo Municipality – target area of the project - is 420 km^2, representing 28% of the municipality´s total area. This rural area is in the south region of São Paulo City comprising Parelheiros, Marsilac and Grajaú Districts. They are poor districts inhabited by people living in rural areas, small towns and slums that suffer the impact of the expansion of São Paulo City in detriment of rural and environmental protection areas.

This is a strategic area of environmental protection because it contains the main water supply of Great São Paulo (the largest metropolitan region in South America), in addition to important remnants of the Atlantic Forest biome. This extensive area of native vegetation provides relevant ecosystem services for the metropolitan region, such as the production of water for public supply, climate regulation and biodiversity conservation.

Agriculture occupies less than 5% of this territory and it is mainly represented by families that use a conventional farming system.

This region has been a focus of state and municipal public policies for environmental protection for a long time. The first laws to protect public water supply sources for the metropolitan region of São Paulo date back to the 1970s. Most of these regulations are of the command-and-control type which have brought deleterious side effects as the abandonment of areas and the spreading of irregular urban occupations without any basic infrastructure and sanitation. Miranda addressed the theme of the deleterious effects of urban sprawl over rural areas in her 2002 works (Miranda, 2002a and b).

The Goals of the Project

Considering the strategic and environmental value of this area, the lessons taken from previous unsuccessful efforts to preserve the Atlantic rainforest biome and the need to assist the rural communities to adopt sustainable farming, Connect the Dots Project developed a set of innovative solutions to address this challenge, based on the guidelines of sustainable territorial development and Economy of Knowledge.

Among these solutions is promoting ecological agriculture as a way of protecting the rural landscape and helping local communities of farmers to transition from traditional to ecological farming. Besides enabling them to improve their income and quality of life, the project´s goal is to transform them in guardians of nature, preservers of the strategical land where they live.

All technological innovations, systems and methodologies developed by the project are based on data and evidence, something characteristic of the Economy of Knowledge. Thus, its replication effort should be smaller for other cities in Brazil, Latin America and even in Europe.

The Implementation of the Project

The project started its implementation in 2018 and had its main expansion period between 2019 and 2020, spending U$ 2 million (R$ 12 million) from a prize won in 2016, in addition to the resources of the city hall of São Paulo Municipality.

The City Hall of São Paulo Municipality conceived this project in 2016, going through the development of methodologies in 2017 and finally the pilot phase (first phase) of implementation in 2018.

So far, the project has three phases of execution: 1st) January/18 to June/19, 2nd) July/19 to June/20 and 3rd) July/20 to June/21. For each phase of the project, qualitative and quantitative goals were established together with the City Hall of São Paulo City and the private funding companies.

This chapter will report the different phases of the implementation of the project, its main actions and results, especially during its major period of expansion (2019-2020), when the authors of this chapter participated of Connect the Dots.

Private and Public Partnership

Fundamental to the success of Connect the Dots has been the partnership between the Municipality of São Paulo and some important private institutions, both providing technical knowledge, equipment and supplies to local farmers and other actors in this value chain, trying to empower them against the advances of a socially and environmentally harmful urban sprawl.

Besides farmers and the public and private sectors, this value chain involves markets and restaurants that consume the farmer´s products together with rural, ecological, and educational tourism agents, among others.

Fundamental to this project was the contribution of Bloomberg Philanthropies (BP) that not only funded, but also contributed to the management of the project, incorporating strict criteria for monitoring project and actions, and releasing resources for each of the project's development phases. To this end, BP hired two organizations: Delivery Associates, based in England, for technical assistance, and Vital Strategies, based in the US, for financial management, responsible for contracts made through public processes. To get an idea of the complexity of the project management process, at the end of 2020 there were more than 90 ongoing initiatives.

It is also worth noting that during this period a great effort was made to build a robust governance for the project. This structure was coordinated by São Paulo Mayor's Cabinet, with the participation of important public actors of the project´s value chain: the Municipal Secretariats of Urban Development, Economic Development, Environment and Agriculture. Supporting the public team, there also were actors from organizations belonging to national and international networks operating in this value chain. The most important one is Bloomberg Philanthropies (BP) responsible for the resources that are transforming this project into reality. Besides BP, the project counts with the academic partnership of the School of Public Health of the University of São Paulo (FSP/USP) and with the technical advice of the Brazilian Micro and Small Business Support Service (SEBRAE).

The support of international partnerships was also relevant, such as the World Resources Institute (WRI) through its Cities for Forests initiative, and Ellen MacArthur Foundation through its Food Circular Economy initiative (2021).

The Future of the Project

So far, the project has gone through three phases of execution: 1st) January/18 to June/19, 2nd) July/19 to June/20 and 3rd) July/20 to June/21 when the resources from BP cease. Necessary for the approval of Phase 3, in June/20, actions were organized into three main axes: project expansion, sustainability of project actions and replicability of these actions, all of them fundamental for the search of a new private partnership for the project.

As an important step two evaluations of the project were carried out in the first half of 2020, which allowed the identification of strengths and weaknesses and to improve the project´s course. One carried out by an institution hired by Bloomberg to assess the actions already developed and those still to be developed. The other one was contracted by Porticus Institute to seek new strategies to continue funding the project. This second contribution is important for the continuation of the project after BP´s prize resources end, foreseen to happen in June 2021.

Final Considerations

This project was awarded with the first place at the contest "Mayors Challenge 2016", organized by the North American institution Bloomberg Philanthropies (BP). This competition gathered projects presented by Latin American city halls that showed the adoption of technological innovations to deal with important challenges in their cities. Reports on the prize and the agreement were published on the websites of Bloomberg Philanthropies (2016) and São Paulo City Hall (2017).

The inspiration for the project's name comes from a puzzle game, as an allusion to the necessary action to connect the dots of this complex value chain, including private and public agents, where urban development is always pressing on the resources of remnant rural areas, bringing social, economic, and environmental challenges.

This case study exactly addresses this reality and encompasses a coordinated and connected set of actions aimed at sustainable territorial development, through promoting ecological agriculture as a means of protecting rural landscape and strengthening local farmers. We are sure it can be replicated everywhere.

BACKROUND OF THE PROJECT

Historically, the development of rural territories has been one of the main objects of national public policies and state governments. The local government is responsible for providing rural areas with basic education, health, social assistance, and road maintenance. Nevertheless, the development of rural areas is generally ignored or not considered in city programs aimed at supporting the development of rural areas, whether due to the urgency of urban demands or to the lack of fiscal resources.

On the contrary, over the past thirty years there has been a real race in Brazil to expand the urban perimeters of municipalities, often to meet the demands of the real estate market for cheaper, more distant and with less access to urban infrastructure lands. This process of urban sprawl occurs in detriment of rural and environmental protection areas. The result is the spreading of urban occupations evicting agriculture to more distant regions and the loss of social and economic contact of local populations with the productive rural landscape and natural resources that provide ecosystem services to the city.

When preparing the 2014 São Paulo Strategic Master Plan, this gap was identified and in an innovative way, the city government proposed the recreation of the rural zone that had been formally incorporated into the urban zone in the past.

For a city like São Paulo, whose urban growth model has reached a point of irreversibility, this proposal was widely accepted by representatives of society who participated in the collective construction of the Master Plan approved by the City Council. However, the inclusion in rural territory of areas that still preserve the typical characteristics of the rural landscape (mosaic of productive areas and natural vegetation) demanded the development of a set of strategies, as an imperative for the future sustainability of the Metropolis.

The 2014 Master Plan went beyond the simple formal recreation of the rural area (which is not a small thing in the current context). It establishes a specific land use zoning and a Sustainable Rural Development Plan, a Plan for Payments for Environmental Services and Recovery of Degraded Areas, among others, and the definition of the necessary resources for its implementation.

Consequently, São Paulo city sought innovative ways to support and promote sustainable rural development in what is nowadays the largest metropolis in Latin America and probably the one with the greatest challenges in urban policies for housing, mobility, social inequality, among others.

It is in this context that Connect the Dots Project was born, a pilot project that seeks to connect a peripheral territory, in every way, with its city and its urban population as a strategy for a sustainable future. The results achieved should illuminate new urban public policies with a more holistic vision.

To ensure the continuity of the Connect the Dots Project, which has not yet reached its full maturity, it is essential to strengthen its governance system, not only through the partner secretariats, but also with the participation of municipal councils for urban, rural, and economic and environmental development and institutions such as Bloomberg Philanthropies, Ellen MacArthur Foundation, World Resources Institute and Porticus, among others. This multi-sector governance has allowed different public policies affecting the territory of the southern rural zone to act in a more integrated manner, seeking to support farmers so that they start to adopt more sustainable practices, both from an environmental and economic point of view. It is worth to reaffirm that is of fundamental importance for the city that these farmers remain in the region, with better living conditions and income, producing food and conserving the rural landscape and the ecosystem services that exist there.

EXECUTION OF THE PROJECT

The project started its implementation in 2018 and had its main expansion period between 2019 and 2020, investing U$ 2 million (R$ 12 million) from a prize won in 2016 from Bloomberg Philanthropies (BP), in addition to the resources of the city hall of São Paulo Municipality.

So far, the project has gone through three phases of execution: 1st) January/18 to June/19, 2nd) July/19 to June/20 and 3rd) July/20 to June/21 when BP´s resources come to an end.

The focus of this chapter is to report these three phases of implementation and their actions and results, especially during its main period of expansion (2019-2020), when the authors of this chapter participated of Connect the Dots. Phase 1 is reported individually, while Phases 2 and 3 are reported together due to the duration and nature of their actions.

PHASE 1: IMPLEMENTATION OF THE PROJECT

January 2018 to June 2019

It should be noted that the 2019-2020 expansion of the project would have not been possible without the work developed by the City Hall of São Paulo City, since its conception in 2016, going through the development of methodologies in 2017 and finally the pilot phase (First Phase) of implementation in 2018. During this Pilot Phase a farmer data base was done and a pilot group of about 60 farmers was selected to receive Technical Assistance and Rural Extension.

Most of the farmers of this pilot group belonged to the only cooperative in the region whose focus is agroecological conversion and organic certification of its members (Cooperapas, 2021). Conventional farmers were also included in this pilot group.

After the project's Pilot Phase experience and the creation of the database, Connect the Dots was responsible for expanding the project´s reach from 60 to 160 producers. These farmers were registered, analyzed, and encouraged to adopt good agricultural practices to convert their farms into agroecological and/or organic production units. Emphasis was placed on increasing the preservation of the rural landscape, forest remnants and watercourses.

Agricultural Producers' Registration

Before the implementation, Connect the Dots reviewed the existing Data Base and organized this information. After this a new survey was hired to update and deepen the knowledge of the farmers of the region. "The unit of analysis adopted was the Agricultural Production Unit, similarly to the other surveys carried out, including the Agricultural Census of the Brazilian Institute of Geography and Statistics - IBGE and the Census Survey of Agricultural Production Units (LUPA Project), from the State´s Government Department of Agriculture and Supply.

Only the production units that met the following requirements were considered eligible for the application of the data collection questionnaire: a) commercialization of production in the last 12 months or b) production commercialize to at least 20 people per month. This cut-off criteria eliminated from the data base many properties listed in the first phase, corresponding to the cases of backyard vegetable gardens or domestic production for their own consumption" (São Paulo City Hall, 2020b, pp. 1 and 2).

Originally, 1,692 rural properties were listed. Through criteria aiming at prioritizing those farmers producing for sale, 428 Agricultural Production Units (UPAs) were chosen and identified their main characteristics and weaknesses. In addition to this register, the field work allowed to expand the project's database from 428 to 515 UPAs, all of them georeferenced. Access to data of the UPAs is available in two websites: GeoSampa and Sampa+Rural, both from the City of São Paulo (São Paulo City Hall, 2020a, 2020b, 2021a and 2021b) and in an open format.

Profile of the Farmers

It's worth noting that most of the registered UPA's are smallholder farmers who don´t make more than one monthly minimum wage (R$ 1,000.00 = U$ 200.00) of income from their agricultural production. Most of their production are leafy vegetables with low added value, reduced use of technology and considerable logistical difficulty.

The following is the profile of the farmers:

- Land ownership: 65% are owners, 20% lessees, squatters, or assignees.
- Size of the production unit: 68% with less than 5 ha (1 ha = 10,000 m^2), of which 41% have less than 0.5 ha, 9% between 0.5 and 1 ha, and 18% between 1 and 5 ha.
- Crops: 23% are vegetables and/or grains, 23% tubers and 19% ornamental.
- Commercialization: 62% sell their production, 38% produce for self-consumption.
- Agricultural income: 47.3% of those who trade obtain monthly income below R$ 1,000.00 (U$ 200.00), 32% obtain between R$ 1,000.00 and R$ 3,000.00 (U$ 600.00), and only 20% obtain more than R$ 3,000.00. These low-income forces 41% of them seek other sources of income outside the productive unit, a frequent characteristic to rural peri-urban areas. Graziano da Silva (2002) explored this topic in his work about the *New Brazilian Rural*.

The information collected showed that the farmers of this region are very poor, have very small properties and that despite selling their production their income is still very low. This farmer profile was fundamental for the development of actions and aid programs aimed at empowering needy farmers to transition to agroecological farming. Some of these actions were devised on Phase 1 and implemented in Phases 2 and 3.

Further Details of the Farmer's Profile

79% of the registered farmers declared they have a small fruit orchard in their backyard. This information was a useful indicator for the implementation of the project's fruit-growing program. The second example shows that 50% of the production units have hen farming for self-consumption. This information was an indicator for the development of the Demonstrative Unit Project to encourage free-range commercial chicken farming.

The farmers registry also allowed to identify that organic production occurs only in 8% of the production units. However, 39% of them showed interest in improving their knowledge on it and adopting agroecological production practices. This data supported the implementation of the Conversion to Agroecological/Organic Productive Practice Program, which is particularly important both for environmental protection and for increasing the producer income. Despite organic products are more expensive, São Paulo City can afford it as it represents the largest consumer center for organic and agroecological products in the country.

Regarding the adoption of technology by farmers, it is worth mentioning that the scenario found is that 42% of respondents report that their UPAs has a computer, 79% of them have a cell phone and 67% have already used the internet.

About the producer's degree of organization, 79% reported not belonging to any cooperative or union. As mentioned before, there is only one cooperative in the region (Cooperapas, 2021) that is focused on agroecological and organic production. This cooperative has few members and many difficulties to maintain itself. This information was relevant to guide project actions to strengthen cooperation among farmers. Thus, a consultancy was hired to support the professionalization of the cooperative's management, with the structuring of a business plan to implement product processing systems and optimize product distribution logistics, to add value to products and increase producer income.

The data also shows that part of farmers sell their products 'at the farm's gate', a modality that usually pays less for the product. Another part of them with more structure sell at fairs, markets, and restaurants, some of them far from their production units. Some of the Connect the Dots actions were aimed at shortening the links of this chain, such as actions to strengthen the cooperative of producers so that sales can be made through this channel to allow for fairer prices. The other actions are based on supporting the creation of conscious consumption groups, detailed below, with actions to raise awareness of people's role as co-producers.

It is noteworthy that this survey identified that 33% of those responsible for the units are over 60 years old, 40% between 45 and 59 years old and 27% under 44 years old. This characteristic puts at risk the permanence of the land as a productive unit. The region requires policies that can attract younger people to live in the productive units and reverse the aging process of those areas. This is the wish expressed by most producers who would like to see their children and grandchildren continue their work. Perhaps the effects of the pandemic could accelerate a trend of young families migrating from urban to rural areas seeking more quality of life. A recent publication in the O Estado de São Paulo Newspaper (2021), records the movement of two young families now living from agriculture in the rural district of Parelheiros and who receive support from Connect the Dots project.

From education level perspective, 43% attended secondary or higher education and 45% only attended elementary school or are illiterate, indicating the need to improve the access to education, and technical information for the adoption of agroecological and organic practices and technologies.

Finally, it is worth noting that, still from the data and evidence pillar, booklets, technical notebooks and reports were produced on the project's actions, available on the Connect the Dots Sampa+Rural platform (São Paulo City Hall, 2021b) and website (São Paulo City Hall, 2021d), to allow access to relevant information and to support the replication of those actions to other cities, which is a city's commitment to Bloomberg Philanthropies.

PHASES 2 AND 3: ACTIONS OF THE PROJECT

July 2019 to July 2021

Transitioning From Traditional to Ecological Farming

After choosing 160 farmers, Connect the Dots centered its efforts in offering technical assistance and rural extension for the adoption of farming practices compatible with the preservation of the soil, the springs, the natural vegetation, and the biodiversity.

To achieve these goals, all necessary support for the transition to an agroecological and organic production system was offered to the farmers. The São Paulo State Secretary of Agriculture offered the Agroecological Transition Protocol to farmers as a step towards the various existing modalities of organic certification.

The goal established for the approval of Phase 3 of the project (July/20 to June/21) was to reach 80 producers with an agroecological protocol or an organic certificate by June 2021, representing 50% of the 160 assisted farmers.

It is worth noting that in mid-2018, there were 34 farmers and in mid-2020, 61 farmers with a protocol or certificate. Despite being slow, costly, and difficult, the process to obtain and maintain these certifications still has a significant positive impact on the farmer's income.

The actions of Phases 2 and 3 are grouped into Transitioning Actions, Commercialization Actions and Other Actions. Considering the large number of initiatives of the project, only the most relevant, successful, and replicable were chosen for this chapter.

Technical Actions to Support Transitioning

The following are actions implemented to provide the 160 farmers selected by the project with information, inputs, and technical assistance to facilitate their transition to agroecological practices. The goal of these actions is to persuade farmers to obtain a certification that enables them to increase their outcome and protect the rural landscape at the same time. Once persuaded, the Project supports them with Technology, Plant Nutrition Programs, demonstrations and biweekly technical visits.

SisRural: Technical Assistance Methodology Developed by Connect the Dots

To support field activities, the project developed the Rural and Environmental Technical Assistance System, called SisRural (São Paulo City Hall, 2020c). It is an innovative tool for managing technical assistance, which allows field technicians to feed the system with information about their visits to the farmers. They can insert guidance, specifications, photos, and videos. The system allows real-time monitoring and the definition of policies and programs in a standardized way.

The system not only contains technical assistance protocols for agroecological or organic production, but also for the implementation of the Payment for Environmental Services Program (PESP) (São Paulo City Hall, 2020g). The system allows to create other protocols oriented to regenerative agriculture and low carbon agriculture.

The development of this SisRural was based on the checklists of the questionnaires applied in Phase 1. These checklists assess the adoption of good agroecological practices and the capacity of the productive unit using an index that varies from 0 to 10. In the pilot phase of 2018, when the project supported about 60 farmers, this index reached less than 4; at the end of 2019, when the project started to support 150 farmers, it was 4,3; in May 2020 it was 5,3, and in June 2021 it reached 6,3. Periodic updating of this data takes place through field notebooks on biweekly technical visits to the farmers.

Two years of accumulated experience allowed the development of SisRural, which has been used by field technicians since the second half of 2020. The success of this system is such that it is being implemented by the States of São Paulo and Paraná for agricultural areas. This is an unprecedented achievement and a replicable outcome from Connects the Dots. SisRural uses open code so that other agents can adopt it through an agreement with São Paulo City Hall.

PESP

Besides SisRural, Connect the Dots developed the Payment for Environmental Services Program (PESP). This tool is contemplated in the 2014 Strategic Master Plan of São Paulo City and the project supported its formulation and legal regulation. This is an important program aimed at supporting owners and also farmers with resources from the São Paulo City Hall Special Fund for the Environment (São Paulo City

Hall, 2020g) which supports the conversion of conventional family farming into organic and/or agro-ecological agriculture, in addition to paying for environmental services provided for the maintenance, recovery, restoration of springs, riparian forests, permanent preservation and legal reservation areas, and assignment of an area for the release of wild animals.

Parelheiros Agroecology School: Inspiring Farmers to Transition

The project also supported the Parelheiros Agroecology School, managed by the Municipal Green and Environment Secretariat, by purchasing equipment and furniture for courses. Demonstrative showcases with simple and low-cost sustainable techniques were installed in the school's space, so that farmers and other residents of the region could learn about them and replicate in their areas, such as water pumps, composters, filtering gardens, etc. As a pilot project, the school hosted courses on Non-Conventional Food Plants (PANCs), native bees and native fungi from the Atlantic Rainforest, with video production classes available in the Sampa+Rural platform library.

Besides this partnership with Parelheiros Agroecology School, demonstration activities to explain the benefits of equipment and techniques for plasti-culture and for irrigation systems were also carried out.

The organization of technical trips of groups of farmers to visit developed organic production areas was another initiative aimed at encouraging them to transition.

Demonstration Units

To persuade farmers to adopt agroecological practices, the project was responsible for the installation of five Demonstration Units of technology adapted to family farming: i) free-range chicken, ii) fungiculture (mushroom production), iii) rainwater collection and storage systems for rural purposes, iv) shed for storage of inputs and v) solar energy systems. Producers who received these DUs were selected in a public process with the condition to open their properties to receive other producers interested in knowing the systems and replicating them on their farms.

Agroecological Plant Nutrition Assistance

Supported by SisRural and costs covered by the project, the field team implemented technical actions to teach the farmers assisted by the project how to fertilize their crops in a compatible way with agro-ecological farming.

Soil sampling campaigns were carried out to assess fertility, evaluate the composition of the soil, identify the need of specific nutrients and determine a fertilization protocol for each plot and crop based on the technical guidance given by the field team.

The Project not only diagnosed the soil but also supplied organic inputs and limestone to fertilize the soil according to the nutritional programs previously determined, it was a demonstrative activity.

Besides the purchase of fertilizers, Connect the Dots developed a specific Fruit Program which supplies fruit seedlings (citrus, passion fruit and strawberry) grown for commercialization. The goal is to reduce dependence on short-cycle cultivation with low added value.

The Project is responsible for purchasing agricultural equipment and supplies to support the farmers.

Demonstration Units

To persuade farmers to adopt agroecological practices, the project was responsible for the installation of five Demonstration Units of technology adapted to family farming: i) free-range chicken, ii) fungiculture (mushroom production), iii) rainwater collection and storage systems for rural purposes, iv) shed for storage of inputs and v) solar energy systems. Producers who received these DUs were selected in a public process with the condition to open their properties to receive other producers interested in knowing the systems and replicating them on their farms.

Empowering Field Technicians

Connect the Dots developed courses to empower city hall technicians serving at the Agroecological Office (CAE). They are responsible for assisting the farmers of the south rural area in Parelheiros District.

The project funded improvements in CAE facilities enabling technicians to work and attend farmers more comfortably

The construction of a shed for the storage of inputs and machinery in the CAE space.

Actions to Support Commercialization

The following are actions executed to help transitioned farmers to sell their agroecologically produced crops. Connect the Dots identified the lack of managerial and entrepreneurial skills to run the new businesses, the farmer´s difficulty to reach buyers and their struggle to finance the transitioning costs.

Sampa+Rural Platform: Helping Farmers to Reach Buyers

Besides SisRural and PESP platforms, Connect the Dots developed another technological tool: Sampa+Rural platform. This platform connects farmers with consumers of products and services from the rural area of São Paulo city, such as restaurants, markets, fairs and rural and ecological tourism agents.

The objective is to bring information on sustainable rural development, tourism, environmental awareness, and healthy food, encouraging citizens to explore and discover the treasures of the rural areas of São Paulo. In a simple way, it is possible to find information on where to buy local products, who are the city's farmers and who sells their products. The platform also highlights natural attractions and rural tourism. Sampa+Rural Platform is an example of how partnerships between civil society and public authorities can directly benefit citizens and connect the city to sustainable practices. (São Paulo City Hall, 2021b).

The project also developed Sampa+Rural stamps for establishments that produce and markets and restaurants that sell the products of the region, with the aim of connecting the establishments to the platform. The stamps have information such as the establishment's name and a Quick Response Code (QRCode) that accesses the establishment's virtual profile.

CSA: Aid for Transitioning Farmers

Many farmers don´t have enough resources to transition to agroecological agriculture. To help them, Connect the Dots developed a specific project: The Community that Sustains Agriculture (CSA, 2021h)

program. It is a form of commercialization that allows the producer to have a guarantee of sales to pay for technical assistance and support during agroecological transition.

Groups of about 50 people were formed, connected to producers who want to make their transition to agroecological production and/or organic certification. Within this concept, consumers become "co-producers", and they commit themselves to be part of the group for at least one semester or one year.

Each group pays around R$ 100.00 to 200.00 per month (U$ 20.00 to 40, for half or an entire basket) and in exchange they receive weekly baskets of vegetables produced by a transitioning farmer who can afford the costs of agroecological conversion of his production (or obtain organic certification), receiving technical assistance and paying the transportation cost to a distribution point where co-producers will pick up their baskets. With the support of new electronic media, it is possible to organize groups on the internet, hold virtual meetings between the group and the producer and arrange transport and distribution points.

Partnership With Adesampa: Entrepreneurial Training for Farmers and Local Agents

Offering technical assistance IS not enough as many farmers don´t know how to run their own businesses and have no entrepreneurial and management skills. To solve this, a virtuous partnership with the São Paulo City Development Agency (Adesampa) of the Municipal Secretariat for Economic Development, Labor and Tourism was done. Entrepreneurship courses were offered to 206 local agents with businesses pre-acceleration of 20 and acceleration of 8 community-based businesses, with mentorships and prizes of R$ 35,000.00 (U$ 7,000.00) for each one of the 8 businesses.

Within the scope of the partnership with Adesampa, a consultancy was hired to help a group of producers structure a value chain for their products. Another consultancy was hired to improve the management of the rural co-working space – TEIA Parelheiros (São Paulo City Hall, 2021f) created and equipped by Adesampa with computers, beamer and space for meetings, mentoring and courses.

Regarding the lack of farmer associations necessary to overcome logistical and product distribution bottlenecks, Connect the Dots hired the development of a business plan for the only agroecological cooperative operating in the southern rural area of São Paulo (Cooperapas).

Other Actions

Pedagogical Agrotourism: Shaping the Mindset of Future Generations

Parelheiros, Marsilac and Grajaú Districts, the field of work area of Connect the Dots, is struggling with the loss of their younger population that prefers to move to São Paulo looking better opportunities, than continue relying in agriculture. Therefore the project developed the program "Pedagogical Agrotourism" formerly known as "Receptive School Producer" (São Paulo City Hall, 2019a). This program, developed in 2019 in partnership with the municipal secretariats of Education and of Environment was an educational action very well received by the community. The initiative took students from municipal public schools to a day of rural experience.

They visited a rural producer in the morning who explained them its history and production. The students also collected products, like lettuce, that were consumed during the students' lunch. In the afternoon, they visited a natural park with remnants of the Atlantic Rainforest. To do so, the City Hall covered part of the costs (travelling and reception) and the Project paid the amount given to the producer.

Connect the Dots seeks ways to finance this action so that it becomes permanent, allowing the producer to significantly increase its rural income. 15 production units were adapted for this reception, based on the experience in educational tourism of the Welcoming Colony Association (Associação Acolhida na Colonia) in Parelheiros, São Paulo (2021).

Land Use Cartography

A cartographic survey of the region was hired by Connect the Dots to support fieldwork and other public policies, such as environmental one. From 2019 high-resolution satellite images at the 1:5,000 scale, three maps were generated: i) Ground coverage map, ii) Map of environmental interest areas, including all categories of Permanent Preservation Areas defined by Federal Law 12,650/2012 (New Forest Code), Conservation Units, parks, the Indigenous Land and Atlantic Forest remnants; and iii) Agricultural capacity map, which identifies suitable areas and those with partial or total restriction for agricultural activity.

Indigenous Land Agriculture

Connect the Dots hired an unprecedented study of the Agriculture of the Guarani Tenondé Porã Indigenous Land (São Paulo City Hall, 2020c). It is worth noting that this indigenous land occupies other cities of the region, and in São Paulo city represents 1/3 of this rural south zone of the municipality of São Paulo. This Connect the Dots initiative is focused on supporting public policies to this territory. This study also serves to make non-indigenous people (Juruá in the Guarani language) aware of the cultural wealth that exists in the metropolis and to support the efforts of the region's Guarani leaders to rescue their traditional practices of cultivation and consolidation of their territory. Just to illustrate this information, 81 swiddens with about 190 plant species were registered, including vegetables, annual and perennial crops, shrubs, and trees.

Rural Sanitation

Another relevant information from the data base is that 85% of the production units have more precarious or non-existent sewage treatment systems.

Samples of water used for irrigation and washing products were collected and analyzed to support educational actions to improve the quality of these waters' sources. In addition, a study of the sanitary sewage conditions of the productive units was carried out to assess the farmers' willingness to pay for the implementation of isolated sewage treatment systems. This diagnosis can not only subsidize field work to reduce contamination problems, but also public water security policies with a view to implementing isolated sewage treatment systems to improve the quality of water in the region, the health of farmers and consumers of their products.

The COVID-19 Pandemic

It is important to remark the strong impact of COVID-19 Pandemic on the project since March 2020, forcing it to restrict, delay or cancel important actions oriented to reach the established goals. Between March and June 2020, all field work was suspended. The experience of remote work for field actions had low efficiency, considering the nature of the activities and limited access of farmers to the internet. Since July 2020, with the adoption of preventive health measures, field work has been progressively resumed.

It´s worth noting that on the second half of 2020, Connect the Dots supported two local initiatives to supply food for vulnerable social groups amid the pandemic. One of them is called Campo Favela (Field Slum), an initiative coordinated by professors from an education institution called INSPER (INSPER, 2020). They organized donations, bought food from small agricultural producers who were struggling to sell their products, and donated or sold them for a symbolic price to people in slums. The second initiative, called Faces and Sustainability, already finished, was coordinated by the Public Attorney´s Office (Ciclovivo, 2020; São Paulo City Hall, 2020d). They hired a social institution to buy fresh food from vulnerable family farmers and hired cooks and kitchen assistants from groups of migrants in vulnerable conditions to prepare meals. They produced 1,000 lunchboxes per day to be delivered to people from poor communities in Paraisópolis, Brasilândia and Vietnam neighborhoods.

CONCLUSIONS OF THE PROJECT

Outcome of the Project

Let´s remember that Connect the Dots is a project aimed at promoting ecological agriculture as a way of protecting the rural landscape. Through technical and commercialization initiatives, the Project carried out several initiatives (listed above) to help farmers to transition from traditional to ecological farming.

In addition to receiving help to make the transition mainly through technical assistance and inputs compatible with agroecological farming, the farmers could increase the value of their crops, receive managerial and entrepreneurial training, improve their access to buyers and set partnerships with restaurants and local markets.

Considering the strategic and environmental value of this area, the lessons taken from previous unsuccessful efforts to preserve the Atlantic rainforest biome and the need to assist the rural communities to adopt sustainable farming, Connect the Dots Project successfully carried out this challenge.

Number of Farmers Who Transitioned

In mid-2018, Phase 1 of this project, there were 34 farmers with an agroecological protocol or an organic certificate. Two years later, in mid-2020, 61 farmers had already obtained a protocol or a certificate. In July 2020 a new goal was set for the approval of Phase 3 (July/20 to June/21): to reach 80 producers with an agroecological protocol or an organic certificate by June 2021, representing 50% of the 160 assisted farmers.

More than 160 farmers and their families had their lives changed. Besides having access to a higher income, they became models for other farmers of their community, inspiring others to migrate to sustainable farming. Considering the lack of education and poor conditions of these farmers, the project has been a life changing experience.

After three years of public and private joint effort, Sao Paulo´s rural area now counts with a new generation of more than 160 guardians of nature, preservers of the strategical land where they live.

Technological Contributions and Replicability

Sis Rural: To support field activities, the project developed the Rural and Environmental Technical Assistance System, called SisRural (São Paulo City Hall, 2020c). It is an innovative tool for managing technical assistance, which allows field technicians to feed the system with information about their visits to the farmers. They can insert guidance, specifications, photos, and videos. The system allows real-time monitoring and the definition of policies and programs in a standardized way.

The success of this system is such that it is being implemented by the States of São Paulo and Paraná for agricultural areas. This is an unprecedented achievement and a replicable outcome from Connects the Dots. SisRural uses open code so that other agents can adopt it through an agreement with São Paulo City Hall. This platform could be used to set production programs for any crop and in other rural communities.

Sampa+Rural Platform: Helping Farmers to reach buyers: This platform connects farmers with consumers of products and services from the rural area of São Paulo city, such as restaurants, markets, fairs and rural and ecological tourism agents. The objective is to bring information on sustainable rural development, tourism, environmental awareness, and healthy food, encouraging citizens to explore and discover the treasures of the rural areas of São Paulo. In a simple way, it is possible to find information This platform has been extremely useful and can be replicated in any other area.

CSA: Aid for Transitioning Farmers: Many farmers don´t have enough resources to transition to agro-ecological agriculture. To help them, Connect the Dots developed a specific project: The Community that Sustains Agriculture (CSA, 2021h) program. It is a form of commercialization that allows the producer to have a guarantee of sales to pay for technical assistance and support during agroecological transition. This initiative can also be replicated and helped many farmers to migrate to agroecological farming.

PESP: The Payment for Environmental Services Program (PESP) was also developed by the project. This is an important program aimed at supporting owners and also farmers with resources from the São Paulo City Hall Special Fund for the Environment (São Paulo City Hall, 2020g) which supports the conversion of conventional family farming into organic and/or agroecological agriculture, in addition to paying for environmental services provided for the maintenance, recovery, restoration of springs, riparian forests, permanent preservation and legal reservation areas, and assignment of an area for the release of wild animals. It can be replicated in other areas as a source of funding for agroecological transitioning.

Questionnaires, checklists, and all necessary elements to know farmers better and build a database are available and can be easily replicated to be used in any other place.

Knowledge Economy as an Inspiration

It is a fact that all Connect the Dots methodologies and actions were inspired and set within the scope of the Economy of Knowledge, as an important factor of empowering social production in the city and its rural areas. The 160 farmers assisted by the project had access to technical, entrepreneurial and commercialization knowledge

The more access different actors have to knowledge that qualifies their productive activities, the greater their empowerment to develop socially and economically. In this context, it is possible to cite the work of David Guille (2008) that refers to the implications of the Economy of Knowledge in Education.

From the perspective of our modern network society, in the terms of Manuel Castells (1996, cited by Guille, 2008), knowledge, as the generation, processing and transmission of information, has supplanted land, labor and capital as the fundamental source of productivity and power. It is possible to infer that

Guille stresses greater emphasis on collaboration and communication as fundamental aspects of the education required to live and work in a Knowledge society/economy. According to Guille, Castells emphasizes the importance of technological application of science. Consequently, policy makers must be committed to education and the Economy of Knowledge.

In another paper, Castells (2005) highlights that, in the adoption of knowledge and information as central elements in society, what´s new is the growing adoption of technological networks to provide new capabilities to different forms of social organizations.

So, it is possible to infer that the actions to strengthen smallholder farmers and other agents of this value chain, developed by the Connect the Points Project, could subvert the old evolutionary vision of humanity's progress. In the words of Castell (2005, pg. 18), for whom "humanity, commanded by reason and equipped with technology, moves from the survival of rural societies, through industrial society, and finally to a post-industrial/information/knowledge society, the resplendent mountain where Homo Sapiens will finally realize its dignified state".

Economy of Knowledge Implemented in the Project

Connect the Dots is a project based on information and knowledge. It began with an effort to deepen knowledge of the region and its agents, through surveys, registrations, and mappings. In parallel, fieldwork was started together with meetings with different public and private actors to implement the project. And then, collaboratively, created ways of accessing knowledge aimed at providing productive activities more autonomy. In other words, seeking ways to overcome constraints and expand access to knowledge that generates new social and economic production possibilities.

Tools like SisRural, PEPS and Sampa+Rural, all developed by Connects the Dots, are examples of how knowledge can contribute to the development of specific technological tools based on the needs of the farmers. The analysis of the project´s database was the starting point for all these tools. Knowledge on technology and science were used to develop technological and communication platforms aimed at promoting decision making on the farm and the formation of networks to foster commercialization. Following the guidelines of the Economy of Knowledge is essential to this project, especially for communities like ours, left out geographically and socioeconomically of public policies and unable to leverage their creative capacity.

Still in the context of the knowledge economy, it is important to cite the study coordinated by Instituto Escolhas (2020), with support from Porticus, called "Closer than you think: the challenges of food production in the metropolis of São Paulo". The published document points out important issues that somehow have been contemplated by the project, such as:

The importance of strengthening short commercialization chains, reducing the distance between producers and consumers, not only geographically, but also the number of intermediaries, as a way of reducing costs and improving prices for both. In this sense, it is possible to identify actions of the project supporting the local Cooperative and to create Community Groups that Sustain Agriculture (CSA), as experiences of strengthening short circuits. Sampa+Rural, a technological platform created by the project is another example connecting buyers and sellers shortening the chain.

This document also addresses financing capacity as an important restriction to organic production transition. Connect the Dots faced this problem and to solve it developed a specific project: The Community that Sustains Agriculture (CSA, 2021h) program. It is a form of commercialization that allows a producer to have guaranteed sales during a period, in order to pay for technical assistance and support during agroecological transition.

The Importance of the Public Sector

As stated by Castells (2005), it is worth highlighting the importance of the public sector as a decisive actor in developing and shaping our modern network society. In this publication, Castells states that, although it may be considered backward in the adoption of new communication technologies and, therefore, dependent on reforms and modernization, the public sector has an important role in commanding fundamental collective actions for the dissemination and governance of the Economy of Knowledge. This includes citizen participation and political decision-making.

It is a priority of Connect the Dots to strengthen the project's governance, as well as the project's links with instances of social participation, such as the municipal councils for rural development and environment, among others. The role of Sao Paulo´s city hall and all its departments were crucial not only to fund the project, but to actively participate in the creation of the first farmer data base and to contribute to the implementation specially in Phase 1.

It is also worth noting that during this period a great effort was made to build a robust governance for the project. This structure was coordinated by São Paulo Mayor's Cabinet, with the participation of important public actors of the project´s value chain: the Municipal Secretariats of Urban Development, Economic Development, Environment and Agriculture. Supporting the public team, there also were actors from organizations belonging to national and international networks operating in this value chain. The most important one is Bloomberg Philanthropies (BP) responsible for the resources that are transforming this project into reality. Besides BP, the project counts with the academic partnership of the School of Public Health of the University of São Paulo (FSP/USP) and with the technical advice of the Brazilian Micro and Small Business Support Service (SEBRAE).

Importance of the Private Sector

Fundamental to this project was the contribution of Bloomberg Philanthropies (BP) that not only funded, but also contributed to the management of the project, incorporating strict criteria for monitoring project and actions, and releasing resources for each of the project's development phases. To this end, BP hired two organizations: Delivery Associates, based in England, for technical assistance, and Vital Strategies, based in the US, for financial management, responsible for contracts made through public processes.

The support of international partnerships was also relevant, such as the World Resources Institute (WRI) through its Cities for Forests initiative, and Ellen MacArthur Foundation through its Food Circular Economy initiative (2021).

International networks have generated important opportunities for the project and its key actors. The cooperation between Connect the Dots and Glocull Project ("Globally and Locally sustainable food-water-energy innovation in Urban Living Labs"), through the Public Health School of University of São Paulo (FSP/USP), puts the project team in contact with a network of cities in seven countries (Austria, Brazil, Germany, Netherlands, South Africa, Sweden, and the United States). The research FSP/USP is developing deals with water, energy-and food interactions. In São Paulo, the researchers are evaluating the impacts of Connect the Dots for the regional water springs (São Paulo City Hall, 2019b).

The opportunity to present Connect the Dots at international network events gave the project visibility. Examples can be identified as early as Bloomberg Philanthropies award, in mid-2016, when São Paulo City Hall presented Connect the Dots at the International Architecture Biennale in Rotterdam, Netherlands. It was also a rich opportunity to present the project at the 1st Latin American Forum of the Milan Pact signatory cities network, whose opening speech from Graziano da Silva, United Nations World Food Program General Director, highlight that "city and countryside must be engaged to transform food-security, nutrition, and climate change global commitments in local realities. Therefore, it is necessary to preserve our natural resources and, above all, the planet's biodiversity, integrating sustainable and responsible actions from the production to the consumption of food" (United Nations World Food Program, 2019).

It is remarkable the participation of Connect the Dots in the construction of the Municipal Agenda for the Implementation of Sustainable Development Goals, completed in December 2020, which has several references to the project's actions (São Paulo City Hall, 2021e).

On May 25, 2021, Connect the Dots was chosen as the winner of the Innopolis Urban Innovation 2020 Contest of the Inter-American Development Bank (2021).

THE FUTURE OF THE PROJECT

As it was already cited, the partnership with Ellen MacArthur Foundation, brought to the project in February 2020 the prospect of a partnership with a new and promising funder, Porticus Institute.

Connect the Dots actions depends on new types of funding, private and public, which can be supported, at least in part, by resources from the Payment for Environmental Services Program (PESP) and by the success of the negotiations with Porticus.

ACKNOWLEDGMENT

No work is done without the support of many people. So, it is nice to register, without writing names and eventually missing someone, the contributions of those who had the patience to review the text and specially of those who dedicated themselves to make this project a reality.

REFERENCES

Castells, M. (1996). *The Rise of the network society, the Information age: Economy, society and culture, 1*. MacMillan.

Castells, M. (2005). A Sociedade em Rede: do Conhecimento à Política. In *A Sociedade em Rede: do Conhecimento à Política*. Universidade Federal de Santa Catarina. Retrieved 06/09/21. https://egov.ufsc.br/portal/sites/default/files/a_sociedade_em_rede_-_do_conhecimento_a_acao_politica.pdf

Cooperapas. (2021). *Cooperativa dos Produtores Rurais e de Água Limpa da Região Sul de São Paulo*. Retrieved 06/09/21. https://www.instagram.com/Cooperapas/?fbclid=IwAR1VtnVdgaYAH7f8kQ7euOvlNHEeCB4LkTWble00mtduKPrNAnEYyFqo1BI

Ellen MacArthur Foundation. (2021). *Economia circular do alimento em São Paulo*. Retrieved 06/09/21. https://youtu.be/hsxrPxFwWMA

Estado de São Paulo Newspaper, O. (2021). *Agricultores orgânicos de Parelheiros: eles vivem de cultivar a terra na cidade de São Paulo*. Retrieved 06/09/21. https://sustentabilidade.estadao.com.br/noticias/geral,produtores-organicos-de-parelheiros-eles-tentam-encurtar-o-caminho-da-roca-para-o-centro,70003729084

Graziano da Silva, J. (2002). *O novo rural brasileiro*. Instituto de Economia, Universidade Estadual de Campinas (Unicamp). https://www.eco.unicamp.br/images/publicacoes/Livros/pesquisa/O-novo-rural-Brasileiro.pdf

Guille, D. (2008). O que distingue a economia do conhecimento? Implicações para a educação. *Cadernos de Pesquisa*, *38*(135), 611–636. doi:10.1590/S0100-15742008000300004

INSPER. (2020). *Projeto Campo-Favela*. Retrieved 06/09/21. https://www.insper.edu.br/noticias/crowdfunding-projeto-campo-favela/

Inter-American Development Bank. (2021). *Innopolis Urban Innovation 2020 Contest: resultados da competição*. Retrieved 06/09/21. https://convocatorias.iadb.org/pt/rede-de-cidades/innopolis-concurso-inova%C3%A7ao-urbana-2020

Miranda, Z. A. I. (2002a). *A incorporação de áreas rurais às cidades: estudo de caso sobre Campinas* (Doctoral thesis). Universidade Estadual de Campinas (Unicamp), São Paulo, Brazil. Retrieved 06/09/21. http://www.repositorio.unicamp.br/handle/REPOSIP/286485

Miranda, Z. A. I. (2002b). As terras que a cidade engoliu. In: *Livro Verde: desafios para a gestão da Região Metropolitana de Campinas*. Instituto de Economia, Universidade Estadual de Campinas (Unicamp), São Paulo, Brazil. Retrieved 06/09/21. https://www.eco.unicamp.br/colecao-geral/livro-verde-desafios-para-a-gestao-da-regiao-metropolitana-de-campinas

Philanthropies, B. (2016). *City of São Paulo Selected as the 2016 Grand Prize Winner in Bloomberg Philanthropies' Latin American and Caribbean Mayors Challenge*. Retrieved 06/09/21. https://www.bloomberg.org/press/city-sao-paulo-selected-2016-grand-prize-winner-bloomberg-philanthropies-latin-american-caribbean-mayors-challenge/

São, P. C. H. (2014). *Plano Diretor Estratégico 2014*. Retrieved 06/09/21. https://gestaourbana.prefeitura.sp.gov.br/marco-regulatorio/plano-diretor/arquivos/

São, P. C. H. (2016). *Connect the Dots Project*. Retrieved 06/09/21. https://sampamaisrural.prefeitura.sp.gov.br/uploads/post/file/21/1415b14e-b1f0-4265-9cfd-e3e2b50b5ed5.pdf

São, P. C. H. (2019a). *Projeto Produtor receptivo de escolas*. Retrieved 06/09/21. https://www.youtube.com/watch?v=QS8q4PRc43o&t=41s

São, P. C. H. (2019b). *Prefeitura de São Paulo e USP vão estabelecer parceria para o desenvolvimento sustentável da zona rural sul da cidade*. Retrieved 06/09/21. https://www.prefeitura.sp.gov.br/cidade/secretarias/licenciamento/noticias/?p=289284

São, P. C. H. (2020a). *Ligue os Pontos: Relatório da Fase 1*. Retrieved 06/09/21. https://gestaourbana.prefeitura.sp.gov.br/wp-content/uploads/2019/01/RELAT%C3%93RIO_SITE_PTBR.pdf

São, P. C. H. (2020b). *Ligue os Pontos: Relatório da Fase 2*. Retrieved 06/09/21. https://ligueospontos.prefeitura.sp.gov.br/wp-content/uploads/2020/12/LoP_Relatorio2.pdf

São, P. C. H. (2020c). *Os agricultores guarani e a atual produção agrícola na Terra Indígena Tenondé Porã, Município de São Paulo*. Retrieved 06/09/21. https://sampamaisrural.prefeitura.sp.gov.br/uploads/post/file/38/05144f1a-44a8-4495-b5d1-a5f5b69ce86c.pdf

São, P. C. H. (2020d). *Imigrantes e refugiados preparam marmitas saudáveis com alimentos de produtores rurais de Parelheiros*. Retrieved 06/09/21. https://ligueospontos.prefeitura.sp.gov.br/imigrantes-e-refugiados-preparam-marmitas-saudaveis-com-alimentos-de-produtores-rurais-de-parelheiros/#:~:text=O%20Projeto%20Ligue%20os%20Pontos,conex%C3%A3o%20dessa%20cadeia%20de%20produ%C3%A7%C3%A3o.&text=O%20Projeto%20apoia%20a%20log%C3%ADstica,Hotec%2C%20regi%C3%A3o%20central%20da%20cidade

São, P. C. H. (2020e). *Informe Urbano nº 45: Quem são os produtores agrícolas da Zona Sul de São Paulo?* Retrieved 06/09/21. https://www.prefeitura.sp.gov.br/cidade/secretarias/upload/desenvolvimento_urbano/arquivos/45_IU_PRODUTORES-AGRICOLAS_2020_final.pdf

São, P. C. H. (2020f). *Transcrição da 152ª Reunião Plenária Ordinária do Conselho do Fundo Especial do Meio Ambiente (CONFEMA), realizada em 26 de Junho de 2020*. Retrieved 06/09/21. https://www.prefeitura.sp.gov.br/cidade/secretarias/upload/meio_ambiente/ATA%20DA%20152%2026%20DE%20JUNHO%20DE%202020.pdf

São, P. C. H. (2020g). *Plano Municipal de Pagamento por Serviços Ambientais (PMSA)*. Retrieved 06/09/21. https://ligueospontos.prefeitura.sp.gov.br/wp-content/uploads/2020/08/PMSA-web.pdf

São, P. C. H. (2021a). *GeoSampa*. Retrieved 06/09/21. https://gestaourbana.prefeitura.sp.gov.br/noticias/geosampa-prefeitura-disponibiliza-a-visualizacao-de-lotes-no-mapa-digital/

São, P. C. H. (2021b). *Sampa+Rural: sobre*. Retrieved 06/09/21. https://sampamaisrural.prefeitura.sp.gov.br/sobre

São, P. C. H. (2021c). *SisRural*. Retrieved 06/09/21. https://ligueospontos.prefeitura.sp.gov.br/agricultura-familiar/sisrural/

São, P. C. H. (2021d). *Ligue os Pontos*. Retrieved 06/09/21. https://ligueospontos.prefeitura.sp.gov.br/

São, P. C. H. (2021e). *Agenda Municipal 2030 para o Desenvolvimento Sustentável*. https://www.capital.sp.gov.br/noticia/prefeitura-publica-agenda-municipal-2030-para-o-desenvolvimento-sustentavel-da-onu

São, P. C. H. (2021f). *Adesampa: TEIA Parelheiros*. Retrieved 06/09/21. http://adesampa.com.br/teia/work/teia-parelheiros/

São, P. C. H. (2021g). *Comunidade que Sustenta Agricultura (CSA vídeo)*. Retrieved 06/09/21. https://www.youtube.com/watch?v=2XnCUW_Suu0&t=7s

São, P. C. H. (2021h). *Comunidade que Sustenta Agricultura (CSA site)*. Retrieved 06/09/21 https://sampamaisrural.prefeitura.sp.gov.br/explorar?term=comunidade%20que%20sustenta%20agricultura

São Paulo State Government. (2021). *Conexão Mata Atlântica*. Retrieved 06/09/21 https://www.infraestruturameioambiente.sp.gov.br/conexao/

United Nation World Food Program. (2019). *Fórum Regional das Cidades Latino-Americanas Signatárias do Pacto de Milão reúne especialistas para debater políticas de alimentação urbana*. Retrieved 06/09/21 https://www.fao.org/brasil/noticias/detail-events/pt/c/1196064/

Vargas, F. G. (2015). *Pagar por serviços ambientais*. Centro de Estudos da Sustentabilidade. https://pagina22.com.br/2015/02/27/pagamento-por-servicos-ambientais-impoe-desafios/

Vivo, C. (2020). *Refugiados preparam marmitas saudáveis com alimentos de Parelheiros*. Retrieved 06/09/21. https://ciclovivo.com.br/covid19/refugiados-marmitas-parelheiros/

Welcome in Colony Association. (2021). *Acolhida em Parelheiro*. Retrieved 06/09/21 https://acolhida.com.br/viajar-para/sao-paulo/acolhendo-em-parelheiros/

World Resource Institute. (2021). *Cities for Forest*. Retrieved 06/09/21 https://www.wri.org/our-work/project/cities4forests

Section 5
Industry

Chapter 10
MENA Countries Face the Challenge of the Knowledge-Based Economy

Olfa Boussetta
PS2D & FSEGT, University of Tunis El Manar, Tunisia

Najeh Aissaoui
LARIME & ESSECT, University of Tunis, Tunisia

Fethi Sellaouti
PS2D & FSEGT, University of Tunis El Manar, Tunisia

EXECUTIVE SUMMARY

The growing interest in the knowledge economy raises many questions about its effect on economic growth. The study aims to position a set of MENA countries in the context of the knowledge economy compared to developed countries. It also detects theoretically and empirically the knowledge effect on economic growth. To do this, the authors have estimated an endogenous growth model, using the dynamic panel data technique, for a sample of 16 MENA countries over 1995-2014. The results show that, despite the significant improvements that have registered in the knowledge economy pillars, the selected countries are still lagging compared to developed countries. Far from international comparisons, the internal effects of these knowledge pillars (education, innovation, ICT, institutional regime) on growth are positive and highly significant.

INTRODUCTION

Traditional development mechanisms based on classical factors are no longer effective in a complex global context of increasingly tough competition. This context imposes its imperatives of competitiveness and sustainability on competing markets. As a result, natural and human resources are increasingly insufficient (Andersson and Djeflat, 2013) and even have the opposite effect on economic growth (Sachs and Warner, 1997, 2001), and are losing importance to a renewed dimension that is none other than

DOI: 10.4018/978-1-7998-8417-0.ch010

knowledge. This phenomenon is supported by the revolution in information and communication technologies (ICTs), which suggests a new direction that specifies the new growth paradigm, characterized by the strengthening of education, innovation, the development of ICTs and learning.

In March 2000, the participants of the Lisbon European Council decided "*to make Europe the most competitive and dynamic knowledge-based economy in the world, capable of sustainable economic growth with more and better jobs and greater social cohesion*"[1] by 2010. This is how knowledge regains its scope in a larger framework. According to Karagiannis (2007), the Lisbon Strategy contains structural reforms for all European economies to ensure Europe's insertion in the new information context, strengthen innovation and R&D activities, and focus on improving the education system. In general, the aim is to implement favorable policies to boost growth.

As for the Arab world, the attributes of the MENA region determine and subsequently influence the evolution of its level of growth and its possibilities of integration into the knowledge economy. This area has long suffered from a tense geopolitical climate due to successive wars and conflicts and the absence of democracy, the pervasiveness of corruption in all areas and the lack of accountability on the part of the state, social and economic problems including high unemployment, enormous natural wealth without achieving stable growth and many other problems. This begs the question, will these characteristics affect MENA's economic growth, its integration into the knowledge economy, and its position in relation to other regions of the world?

In the light of the above, the motivations that motivate us to deal with this issue are summarized, first of all, in the growing interest attributed to the emergence of the knowledge economy as the primary source of wealth creation, based on innovation, skills training, use and dissemination of ICT, in an economic and institutional framework suitable for the implementation of these dimensions. Moreover, previous research has been limited to determining the elements of the knowledge economy in relation to growth, such as human capital and growth, ICT and its effects on economic growth, etc., separately. At the same time, we seek to examine the impact of all aspects, taken together, of knowledge on growth. And finally, the position of MENA countries in relation to other countries in this field and the little work devoted to this topic.

The purpose of our reflection is to position MENA countries in the context of the knowledge economy compared to developed countries and detect the effects of knowledge on economic growth in the region. Therefore, we first attempt to present a conceptual approach that summarizes the notion of the knowledge economy, its foundations and characteristics, and the measurement approach adopted (section 1). We then move on to a theoretical description of the implications of the knowledge economy for the level of growth through the study of the different links between each pillar and growth (section 2). And we finish with the descriptive analysis and econometric modeling, which try to answer the questions related to the place of the MENA region in the knowledge context and the relative performance on each dimension and the effects of this new relay on economic growth (section 3).

1. THE KNOWLEDGE-BASED ECONOMY, A NEW RELAY: A CONCEPTUAL APPROACH

The phenomenal potential that governs modern economies is to ask about the new deal that contributes to creating wealth and thus influences economic growth. However, according to the OECD (1995), economics has so far been unable to provide a comprehensive understanding of the forces that influence long-term growth. In fact, in the history of economic thought, neoclassical theory is the most dominant, and the core of this theory is the production function, which relates output to the quantities of factors of production employed. This traditional neoclassical growth model (Solow, 1956) focuses on labor and capital and assumes the exogeneity of technical progress. However, these classical factors alone are no longer the basis on which an economy in transformation can be built following the acceleration of technological advances, the insertion of information and communication technologies (ICT) in all areas of life and fierce global competition.

Hence, the birth of the notion of the knowledge economy or the knowledge-based economy (KBE). Although, the notion of knowledge has been present for a long time, its growing importance in economic development has only been recognized in recent years. This importance appears as a result of changes in the qualification of the labor factor, in the forms and methods of production, in the activities of exchange and consumption. Citing "*the observation made by all that knowledge is becoming an invaluable asset for development, growth and competitiveness*" (Djeflat, 2008, p 2), we begin by defining the concept of the knowledge economy while briefly proposing a historical overview of the emergence of this new economy. We then put forward the attributes that characterize this new phase of the modern economy and, towards the end, we introduce the measures relating to this new concept.

1.1. Conceptualization

Recently, we are experiencing the advent of a knowledge-based economy, a consequence of the profound changes in the economy. Previously, the precursors of the classical economy were mainly concerned with tangible material goods. In contrast, in the framework of this new economy, the interest is based on intangible elements related to the production of knowledge, science, technical skills, and human capital.

The beginnings of this concept seem to go back a long way since knowledge was the main stimulant of economic growth for a long time. Drucker (1968) considers that «*Knowledge is now becoming the one factor of production, sidelining both capital and labour* ».

Nevertheless, this concept has gained new momentum, especially towards the 20th century and the 21st century. Several previous versions have appeared, notably the new economy, the economy of the immaterial, the digital economy, and finally, the notion currently adopted and widespread, the knowledge economy or the knowledge-based economy. The OECD (1996, p 7) defines knowledge-based economies as "*economies which are directly based on the production, distribution and use of knowledge and information*". In the same perspective, Foray (2000, p 1) considers that "*the knowledge-based economy corresponds essentially, in each country, to the sector of production and service activities based on knowledge-intensive activities. These are usually identified by combining knowledge production and management indicators, such as research and development (R&D) expenditure, the employment rate of graduate workers, and the intensity of use of new information technologies*".

However, economists are now questioning the new dimensions of this new economy, which were at the origin of a radical change in the productive structure, notably innovation, the use and diffusion of ICTs and skilled labor. Amable and Askenazy (2003, p. 1) affirm these statements in contributing to a study led by UNESCO on constructing the knowledge economy. These authors define the knowledge economy "*as a stage of capitalism where a particular productive model is generalized, organized around organizational and technological complementarities between ICTs, the human capital of agents likely to use these technologies and a reactive organization of the firm that would allow the full use of the productivity potential of the first two elements*".

Before further analyzing, the major characteristics of a knowledge-based economy, it is necessary to question the elements circulating in the electronic channels; is it knowledge or information? (Winter, 1987, Dossi, 1988, Foray, 2000, David and Foray, 2002). David and Foray (2002, p 17) predict that "*To possess knowledge in any domain is to be capable of intellectual or manual action. Knowledge is thus fundamentally a cognitive capacity*". Whereas "*information is a set of data, structured and formatted, but inert and inactive as long as they are not used by those who know to interpret and manipulate them*".

This distinction between information and knowledge refers to a double configuration of knowledge, among others, tacit/implicit knowledge and codified/explicit knowledge (Polanyi, 1966, Djeflat, 2008). The first form reflects the whole of intangible knowledge, personal to each individual, it calls upon skills, know-how and experience, and it is difficult to convert into a codified form. Hence, the difficulty of making it explicit, transferring it and exploiting it by other individuals. However, part of the knowledge can be made explicit and expressed in a formal and structured language. It can be presented in the form of an electronic document, material support, a paper document; the main thing is that it is easily disseminated due to its real character.

After a short historical perspective on the extent of the role of knowledge in economic growth, which has led to the emergence of a knowledge-based economy, it is interesting to trace the essential characteristics that have underpinned this new economy.

1.2. The Foundations of the Knowledge Economy

The attention given to the knowledge economy raises many questions about the milestones that have led to this new phase of the contemporary economy. In fact, among the characteristics often mentioned, we can cite the acceleration of knowledge production, the importance taken by intangible capital, the technological revolution and the rise of ICT, the dominance of innovation activity and a more rigorous valuation of human resources, in other words, more qualified human capital (Kendrick, 1994, Foray, 2000, David and Foray, 2002, Djeflat, 2007, 2008, Dutraive, 2008).

As a first element, it is, therefore, necessary to consider the expansion of investments in knowledge-intensive activities as an essential aspect at the origin of the advent of the knowledge-based economy. An acceleration in the creation and accumulation of knowledge is evident, especially in high-tech industries, marked by significant scientific and technological progress. This trend encompasses several sectors, including computer and space, ICT, and financial and service sectors. This trend also refers to the increased investment rate that improves education, training, R&D activities, and innovation. These orientations were at the origin of the increase in the share of intangible/immaterial capital to the detriment of physical capital, "*Thus, the growth of physical capital per hour worked represented two-thirds of the growth in labor productivity during the second half of the 19th century and only between one-quarter and one-fifth in the 20th century*" (Diallo Demba, 2006, pp 11-12).

Thus, the second element refers to the importance acquired by intangible assets. For a long time, physical capital and natural and material resources (tangible capital) were the factors with the most significant explanatory capacity for disparities in productivity and economic growth between different countries. Nevertheless, during the 20th century, we have witnessed an increase in the share of intangible capital in GDP at the expense of tangible capital, and this thanks to improvements in investments either linked to the creation, production and transmission of knowledge (education, training, R&D, information and coordination), or investments aimed at improving the physical state of human capital (health)

(Kendrick, 1994, Foray, 2000). Thus, Lévy and Jouyet (2006, p. I) affirm that *"a new component has emerged as a determining engine of economic growth: the intangible".*

A key reference on the question of the increase in the share of intangible capital in GDP (see Table 1) was developed by Kendrick (1994) over a period of more than half a century (1929-1990) in the United States. The stocks of intangible capital investments started to increase in the late 1970s at the expense of tangible investments. This increase is essentially centered on knowledge embodied in individuals, or human capital, notably education and training, followed by investments in health and safety and R&D investments.

Table 1. Gross real capital stock in the United States (in billions of dollars, 1987)

	1929	1948	1973	1981	1990
Tangible capital	6075	8120	17490	22365	28524
Structures & equipment	4585	6181	13935	17963	23144
Natural resources	1222	1468	2555	3149	3843
Inventories	268	471	1000	1253	1537
Intangible capital	3251	5940	17340	23777	32819
Education & training	2647	4879	13564	18730	25359
Health & safety	383	692	2081	2791	4371
Mobility Expenses	184	200	446	596	762
R&D	37	169	1249	1660	2327

Source: Kendrick (1994, p 6)

Although the creation and production of knowledge is partly a matter of education, training and learning, then its transmission and dissemination require significant investments in information and communication technologies (ICT). A reiteration of Foray's (2000) definition of the knowledge-based economy, supported by the one later proposed by Godin (2006, p. 20), who argues that «*the term knowledge-based economy referred to at least two (supposed) characteristics of the new economy. Firstly, knowledge would be more quantitatively and qualitatively important than before. Secondly, applications of information and communication technologies (ICT) would be the drivers of the new economy* ». In addition to the increase in investment and knowledge-intensive activities, both agree that another element that requires attention is the revolution in knowledge production and transmission techniques.

Thus, the rise and diffusion of ICTs have led to the emergence of a new paradigm of knowledge-based growth (Foray and Lundvall, 1996). Brousseau (2001, p. 2) states: *"ICTs appear to be the emerging part of a phenomenon of the reorganization of our economies around a new growth regime based on information and innovation".*

Various approaches conceive that ICTs are the main factor of mutations and changes in the economy (Perez, 1983, Romer 1986, 1990, Lucas 1988, Foray, 2000, Steinmuller, 2002, Chen and Dahlman, 2005). This relationship between growth, on the one hand, and the acceleration of progress, use and diffusion of ICT on the other, will be further developed in the following sections.

Various authors have focused on the potential effects of these technologies on the dynamics of the knowledge economy. The properties of knowledge are primarily influenced by ICT. So that the acceleration of the diffusion speed and the universal access to ICTs make them challenging to control, which can favor the appearance of knowledge externalities, despite all the measures taken to protect the appropriation of knowledge. The convenience of imitation and reproduction gives a particular aspect of non-rivalry to knowledge.

However, this transfer of knowledge remains dependent on its degree of codification. Thus, ICTs transform tacit knowledge into information in the form of computerized databases, immediately accessible to users and therefore reducing their transmission costs (Djeflat, 2007). This codification makes it possible for individuals to access information and even knowledge at a distance through the transmission of digitized information, but also interactive distance training, distance learning (David and Foray, 2002) and the mutual exchange of knowledge and experience between researchers making it possible to make progress in R&D and thus supporting the innovation process (Chen and Dahlman, 2005).

Qualified as generic technologies, ICTs constitute a factor of acceleration of the innovation pace allowing to realize of product and process innovations. Moreover, the interaction between different actors thanks to these technologies in a globalized world leads to an accumulation of knowledge through sharing and exchange, thus generating new cognitive resources. Thus, ICTs strengthen the skills of individuals in the field of education and training by updating learning methodologies and updating the tools adopted, the development of distance learning, including the virtual university, teleconferencing ... etc.

Several works recognize the primacy of the role played by innovation in the emergence of a new paradigm based on knowledge (OECD, 1996, 2001, 2005, Foray, 2000, Encaoua et al., 2004, Chen and Dalhman, 2004...). Encaoua et al. (2004) establish a specific link between ICT and innovation, they argue that "*A booming ICT sector serves local markets and is often a source of local innovation and dynamism*". Nevertheless, this one-sided relationship is not very convincing since it is true that the diffusion of ICT accelerates the innovation pace. Moreover, the intense knowledge mobilization through R&D and innovation activities are likely to assist in producing new technologies. This is the finding of Powell and Snellman (2004) in their analysis, which asserts that the imperatives of offering new products and processes at the firm level and even in the economy as a whole, and the need to overcome the phenomenon of obsolescence of technologies and knowledge, require technological innovation and the intense mobilization of knowledge. This is how innovation has become an element of competitiveness, as David and Foray (2002, p 14) state, *"The need for innovation is becoming stronger since innovation tends to become the almost unique way to survive and prosper in highly competitive and globalized economies"*.

Another aspect is closely related to the process of innovation concerning R&D activities. R&D expenditures, considered among the leading indicators of the knowledge economy, have increased considerably, which necessarily impacts innovation intensity. For example, in 1998, total R&D expenditure in OECD countries ranged from 3.8% to 0.4% of GDP, with an average of 2.2% (OECD, 2001). This expenditure grew steadily, more slowly than in the second half of the 1990s, by 4.8% per year (in real terms) between 1995 and 2000, but only by 1.8% per year between 2000 and 2003 (OECD, 2005). As for innovation, more than 40,000 families of patents were granted in 1998 in the OECD area, increasing 32% compared to 1991. These investments in knowledge impact the growth of trade in high-tech products, including computers, planes, pharmaceuticals, and scientific instruments. They increased from less than 20 percent in the early 1990s to more than 25 percent of world trade between 2000 and 2001 (OECD, 2003).

The accumulation of know-how and the qualifications obtained are tacit knowledge and, thanks to the codification facilitated by ICT, they will be disseminated in a geographically fragmented world. Thus, companies become "learning organizations (OECD, 1996). Thus, the collective management of knowledge requires the interaction between different actors, grouped in networks, within the framework of an innovation system, which brings together firms, public and private research centers, universities, governmental organizations, etc. (Chen and Dalhman, 2004).

The awareness of the importance of innovation points to other dimensions that take precedence in this respect, notably human capital. Technological innovation, in particular, dramatically accentuates the role of human capital, especially specialized skills (Dutraive, 2008). This renewed interest in human capital is justified by the world economy's transformations, submerged by information and communication technologies (Paul and Suleman, 2005). Thus, human capital is a factor in creating new knowledge and application (Harris, 2001).

Measures have been taken by the economies involved in this new global context, especially after the declaration of the European Council of Lisbon in March 2000, notably the development of a system of lifelong learning defined as *"any learning activity is undertaken at any point in life, to improve knowledge, skills and competences, in a personal, civic, social and/or employment-related perspective"* (Le Douaron, 2002, p 573), the improvement of the level of education through investment in education.

An educated and qualified population is the duty of educational institutions and research institutes following a vocation devolved by governments. A high level of education helps get an idea about the technological trends, acquire the most relevant technologies for the company or the economy and adapt them for use in the local production process (Chen and Dahlman, 2004). Moreover, changes in the productive system have led to shifts in wages and employment in favor of the most skilled workers. The distribution of income and the associated divergences are closely linked to the level of education (Korres et al., 2002, Powell and Snellman, 2004, Léné, 2005).

According to some analyses (Foray, 2000, David and Foray, 2002), this new model of the economy, based on knowledge, constitutes continuity of the processes of economic growth that we experienced until the end of the 1970s. However, knowledge's importance for more than twenty years makes us wonder about the attributes of this new trend towards a new growth pattern. Essentially, we have cited the technological revolution and the enormous progress of ICTs, the strong position of innovation to guarantee a more competitive economy and a more rigorous valuation of human resources.

1.3. Indicators for Measuring the Knowledge Economy

Considering that knowledge is produced in all economic sectors raises many problems regarding its measurement and the evaluation of the contribution of knowledge-based activities to growth since the immaterial is challenging to quantify. Nevertheless, some international organizations, such as the World Bank and the OECD, have keenly interested in this new concept and have presented different evaluation frameworks. Therefore, we will try to list all the measurement indicators according to the approach adopted by the World Bank.

1.3.1. The World Bank's Knowledge Assessment Methodology (KAM)

As part of its "Knowledge for Development" (K4D) project, launched in 1999, the World Bank aims *«to raise awareness among national policymakers of the powerful growth effects of knowledge, to encourage economic actors to combine global and local knowledge to accentuate comparative advantage, and to help leaders to build institutions that foster, rather than discourage, individuals' attempts to exploit the competitive opportunities available to knowledge-powered enterprises. »* (World Bank, 2008, p 3). Accordingly, it has developed an assessment method called Knowledge Assessment Methodology (KAM).

This method allows countries to assess their positioning by comparing themselves to neighboring and/or competing economies in terms of the knowledge economy. It brings together a range of variables within the framework of four pillars.

1.3.1.1. The Pillars of the Knowledge-Based Economy

To successfully transition to a knowledge-based economy, several works have supported the requirement of investing more and more in the four pillars designed by the World Bank (Chen and Dahlman, 2004, 2005, Driouchi et al., 2006, Djeflat, 2007, 2008, Sundać and Krmpotić, 2011, Tocan, 2012). These pillars are as follows (see Table 2):

- Economic incentive and institutional regime
- Education and Human Resources
- Innovation system; and
- Information and communication infrastructure.

Table 2. The four pillars of the knowledge economy

Pillar 1 The Economic and Institutional Regime	**Pillar 2 Education and Skills**	**Pillar 3 Information and Communication Infrastructure**	**Pillar 4 Innovation System**
The country's economic and institutional regime must provide incentives for the efficient use of existing and new knowledge and the flourishing of entrepreneurship.	The country's people need education and skills to create, share, and use it well.	A dynamic information infrastructure is needed to facilitate the effective communication, dissemination, and processing of information...	The country's innovation system—firms, research centers, universities, think tanks, consultants, and other organizations—must be capable of tapping the growing stock of global knowledge, assimilating and adapting it to local needs, and creating new technology.

Source: World Bank (2010)

To make the pillars mentioned above more explicit, we will briefly review these different elements and try to identify their contributions to the development of the national economy in a more globalized world economy. Following Chen and Dahlman's (2005) analysis, it is appropriate to put them into perspective:

Economic incentive and institutional regime: this pillar ensures an economic and institutional environment conducive to better mobilization and allocation of resources to stimulate the creation, use, and dissemination of knowledge. On the one hand, an appropriate economic regime has a minimum number of price distortions, fiscal sustainability to maintain fiscal space for the state to pay its fees, low and stable inflation, prices free of controls and protectionist policies, a stable exchange rate, and thus an excellent financial system that can efficiently allocate resources for investment opportunities. Furthermore, a favorable institutional regime is characterized by a compelling government free of corruption and a fair and efficient legal system that enforces trade and intellectual property rights rules and laws. It also ensures the implementation of policies that focus on protecting these property rights to encourage creativity and innovation.

Education and human resources: the new global context, focused on knowledge, constitutes an obligation to improve the faculties of the population to adapt to new data. This is achieved by consolidating long-term investments in education. Otherwise, a well-educated and creative population is endowed with skills, which allow them to deal efficiently with knowledge in its creation, acquisition, adaptation, use and dissemination. The different levels of education, mainly primary, secondary, and tertiary education, particularly in the scientific and technical fields, contribute to the acquisition of knowledge that maximizes the ability of workers to assimilate foreign technologies for use in local production processes, especially for technology-importing developing countries.

Information and communication infrastructures: for the World Bank, information and communication infrastructures are composed of hardware, software, media (television and radio) and the networks that link them. Their role is to collect, store, transmit, and present information in various forms (voice, image, data, text...). In recent years, the requirements of the new global context and the rapid growth of information and communication technologies (ICT) make it necessary to modernize their infrastructure dedicated to promoting economic growth and sustainable development.

Innovation system: it is the set of interactions between the different institutions that form this network, including public and private companies, universities, research centers, non-governmental organizations, government and Think tanks. It aims to facilitate the production, acquisition, use and dissemination of knowledge to leverage the international knowledge base for local needs through interference between its actors. Thus, an effective and efficient innovation system ensures a favorable environment for R&D, which leads to creativity and innovation and consequently a positive impact on productivity and economic growth.

World Bank research generally associates the success of the knowledge economy with the prerequisites for its insertion. Therefore, efforts must be focused on the basic elements related to the main pillars. Nevertheless, taking into account only the bilateral exchanges between these entities independently of the others cannot constitute in itself the building of the knowledge-based economy, given the extent of the interdependence between its different pillars (Djeflat, 2007, 2008). Therefore, to better understand the scope of investment in these dimensions for the countries' economies, the World Bank has developed an indicator model that we will examine in the following section.

1.3.1.2. The Indicators of the Knowledge-Based Economy According to KAM

The KAM is an interactive and user-friendly benchmarking tool, allowing countries to know their strengths and weaknesses by comparing themselves to their competitors in the four pillars.

We refer to the latest version of the KAM (KAM 2012)[2]Which consists of 148 qualitative and structural variables for a sample of 146 countries divided into seven regions.These variables serve as proxies for the four pillars of the knowledge economy and measure each country's performance in this area. The KAM database is divided into seven groups such as:

- Overall economic performance
- Economic incentive and institutional regime, which includes:
- Economic regime
- Governance
- The innovation system
- Education and human resources

- Education
- Workforce
- Information and Communication Technology (ICT)

Working with 148 variables poses a real challenge, given a large number of variables. To address this, a simplified basic scorecard method was developed. It consists of only 12 variables (see Table 3) representing the different pillars, plus two other performance variables (the human development index and the annual growth rate of GDP), making a total of 14 variables. These variables provide insight into a country's readiness to enter a knowledge-based economy. These same data are used to construct the Knowledge Index (KI) and the Knowledge Economy Index (KEI), which we will see in more detail later. In the table below, the World Bank has provided a more comprehensive outline of the measurement indicators. However, these variables differ according to the units and scales of measurement adopted. For this reason, KAM has opted for the process of standardizing the data from 0 to 10 to ensure certain comparability.

Table 3. KAM's knowledge economy indicators

Pillar	Indicator
The economic and institutional regime	• Tariff and non-tariff barriers • Regulatory quality • The rule of law
Education and skills	• Adult literacy rate • Gross secondary enrollment rate • Gross tertiary enrollment rate
Innovation system	• Royalty payments and receipts, US $ per person • Technical journal articles per million people • Patents granted to nationals by the US Patent and trademark office per million people
Information infrastructure	• Telephones per 1000 people • Computers per 1000 people • Internet users per 1000 people

Source: The Knowledge Assessment Methodology (KAM) (www.worldbank.org/kam)

1.3.1.3. Normalization of variables

In general, the process of normalization allows for the adjustment of a data vector, which represents an incompatibility of measurement units between variables to make them comparable. Given that KAM is primarily a comparative analysis, it recognizes the need to bring all indicators to the same standard of measurement to calculate global indices of the knowledge economy and simplify graphic representations. Still, our benchmark is the KAM 2012. First, countries are ranked in descending order from "best" to "worst" using their actual data on each variable of the 148. Then, the data will be normalized according to the formula described below, on a scale of 0 to 10, against all countries in the comparison group. A value of 10 denotes the best performance, and 0 is given to the worst. For example, the top 10% of performers get a normalized score between 9 and 10, the second top 10% get a value between 8 and 9, so the distribution continues. Otherwise, the adopted 0-10 scale ranks each country's performance, relative to each variable, against the performance of the other countries in the sample concerned.

Several criteria for comparing and categorizing countries are adopted by KAM, including the income category criterion, the region criterion and the development criterion. Thus, a country can obtain different standardized scores depending on the comparison group chosen. In addition, using both actual (absolute) and normalized (relative) data gives a better picture of what is happening in a particular country or variable. To make it more straightforward, KAM presents us with the procedure for normalizing data through the following steps:

1. The data (u) are collected from the World Bank databases and international literature for the 148 variables in all 146 countries.
2. Country rankings are assigned based on the absolute values, which describe each of the 148 variables. Countries with the same performance are assigned the same rank. For example, rank 1 is given to a country that achieves the best performance for a given variable among the other countries in our sample, rank 2 for a country that achieves the second-best performance and so on.
3. For every country, the number of countries that rank below it (Nh) is calculated.
4. 4. The following formula is used to normalize the data for each country for each variable according to their rank and relative to the total number of countries in the sample (Nc) with available data:

Normalisé (u) = $10 * (1-N_h / N_c)$

5. The above formula assigns a normalized score on the 0-10 scale for each country.

1.3.1.4. The Knowledge Index (KI) and the Knowledge Economy Index (KEI)

Referring to the most recent version of the KAM (KAM 2012), two knowledge economy indices are developed, namely the Knowledge Index and the Knowledge Economy Index (See Figure 1).

1. The Knowledge Index (KI): It is an index that assesses the ability of a country to create, adopt and disseminate knowledge. It is an index constituted by the average of the normalized performance data of a country or a region on the critical variables of the knowledge economy related to the three pillars: the innovation system, education and human resources and information and communication technologies.
2. The Knowledge Economy Index (KEI): Proposed by the World Bank and defined as a composite indicator of several variables. It takes into account the importance of the environment for more efficient use of knowledge for economic development. It is calculated by averaging the normalized scores of a country's or region's performance in the four pillars of the knowledge economy.

In developing the KAM, the World Bank intended to simplify assessing the position of the countries in question in comparison with their neighbors, competitors or other countries regarding insertion in the knowledge-based economy. This method's ease of use, accessibility, and transparency has allowed researchers, policymakers, consultants, and government officials to exploit it and enhance concerted efforts in building this new economy. Abundant literature sees this knowledge revolution as a vector of economic growth, offering important opportunities to the countries involved. Thus, we will see below a broad overview of the theoretical and empirical literature on the performance of countries according to each of the four pillars of the knowledge economy.

Figure 1. The Knowledge Index (KI) and the Knowledge Economy Index (KEI)
Source: KAM, 2012

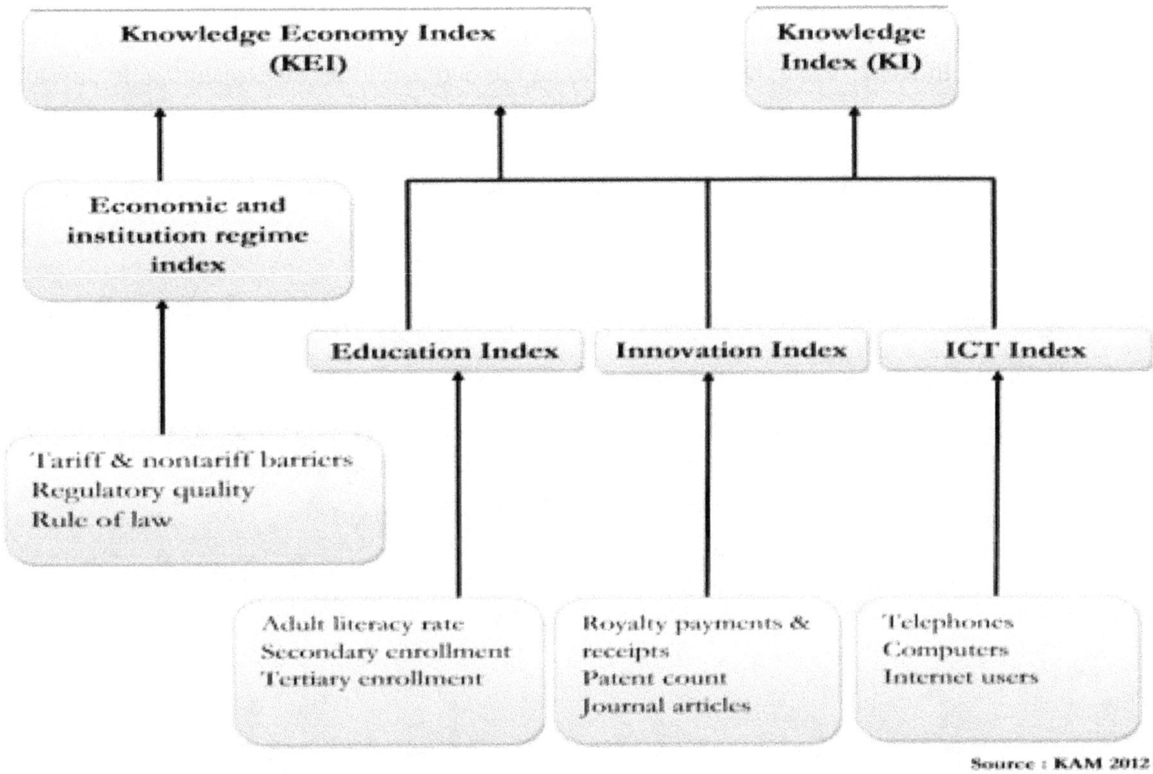

2. KNOWLEDGE ECONOMY AND ECONOMIC GROWTH

The heads of state and government of the European Union at the Lisbon European Council in 2000 set the goal of "*making Europe the most competitive and dynamic knowledge-based economy in the world, capable of sustainable economic growth with more and better jobs and greater social cohesion*"[3]. European economies link the building of a competitive knowledge society to achieving sustainable economic growth by implementing the necessary measures to strengthen the prerequisites for the transition to this new economy. But the question now arises why this new knowledge economy has been growing worldwide for years?

The research literature links this growing interest in knowledge to its central role as an engine of economic growth. In fact, according to the OECD (1996, p 3), "*The OECD economies are increasingly based on knowledge and information. Knowledge is now recognized as the driver of productivity and economic growth, leading to a new focus on the role of information, technology and learning in economic performance*".

The literature on endogenous growth has established a certain macroeconomic relationship between knowledge and economic growth through several mechanisms such as human capital (Nelson and Phelps, 1966, Lucas, 1988, Barro, 1991), innovation and R&D (Romer, 1986, 1990, Aghion and Howitt, 1992), technological infrastructure (Oliner and Sichel, 2000, Colecchia and Schreyer, 2003). Figure 2 illustrates how knowledge contributes to the economic progress of a country.

In light of the above, the objective of this section is to assess whether policies and investments in the knowledge economy are responsible for higher rates of economic growth. To this end, a substantial literature review on the relationship between growth, on the one hand, and investments (and diffusion) in information and communication technologies, the improvement of human resources, investments in innovation and R&D, and the establishment of an appropriate economic and institutional framework, on the other hand, will be highlighted to answer the above question. We will therefore continue with the study of each pillar about economic growth and the results obtained.

Figure 2. Knowledge and economic growth
Source: Gyekye and Oseifuah (2015, p 201)

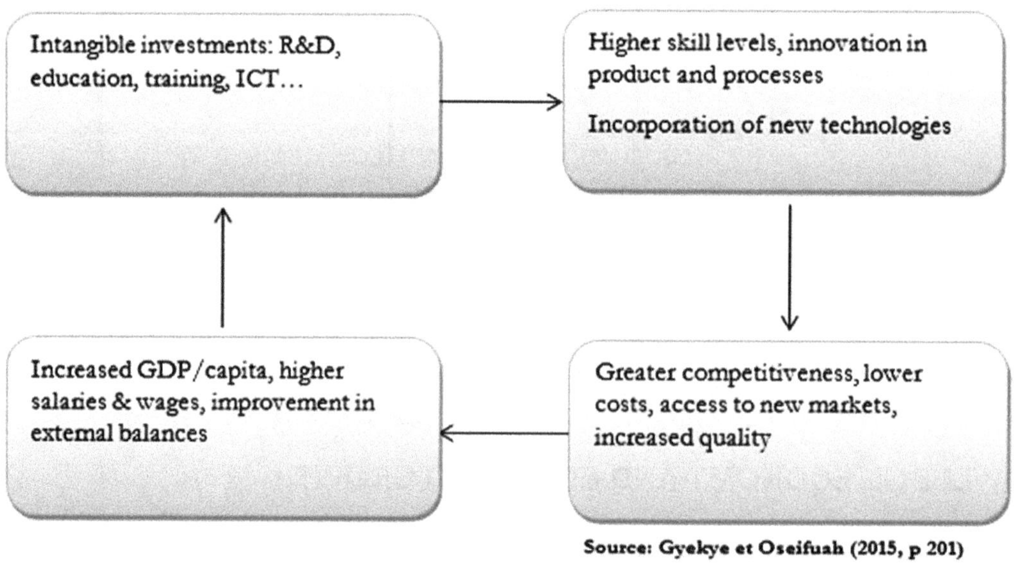

2.1. Information and Communication Technologies, Education, Innovation and Economic Growth: What Links?

2.1.1 Investment in Information and Communication Technologies and Economic Growth

The rise and diffusion of ICTs have led to a new paradigm of knowledge-based growth (Foray and Lundvall, 1996). As a result, abundant literature has been conducted to evaluate the contribution of ICT to economic growth for individual countries, such as the works initiated by Oliner and Sichel (1994, 2000) for the economy of the United States of America, Cette et al. (2002, 2004) and Audenis et al. (2005) for France, Antonopoulos and Sakellaris (2009) for Greece, Ben Youssef and M'Henni (2004) for Tunisia, Oulton (2002) for the United Kingdom. In addition, a series of works focused on international comparisons, considering groups of countries such as Schreyer (2000) for G7 economies, Colecchia and

Schreyer (2002, 2003), Nair et al. (2020) for OECD countries, Dutta and Otsuka (2004) for a sample of countries namely Australia, Japan South Korea, and Taiwan, Karagiannis (2007) for European Union countries, Ahmed and Ridzuan (2013) for a sample of Asian countries (Malaysia, Indonesia, Philippines, Singapore, and Thailand) plus 3 other countries (China, Japan, and South Korea), Gyekye and Oseifuah (2015), Tchamyou et al. (2019) for African countries.

We begin with the literature for individual country cases. Oliner and Sichel's (1994, 2000) work on the US economy has shown that the ICT production sectors have experienced enormous technological advances reflected in the gains in total factor productivity. Moreover, ICT use has given "*capital deepening*" in ICT equipment or capital/labor substitution. This capital intensity, combined with a dynamic ICT producing sector, is likely to boost productivity growth for the economy. The analyses of Cette et al. (2002, 2004) and Antonopoulos and Sakellaris (2009) have taken, respectively, the case of France and Greece. The result is that the contribution of ICT investments to potential growth and labor productivity has increased, benefiting the finance, insurance, service and real estate sectors and the wholesale and retail trade industries. Ben Youssef and M'Henni (2004) have shown, theoretically, the existence of transmission channels of ICT performance on growth, notably the multiplier effect of ICT investment, the deflator effect, and the capital deepening the total factor productivity effect and the quality effect. However, when applied to the growth of the Tunisian economy, the results found are quite different. The multiplier effect appears to be the most important during the period in question in Tunisia; the deflator effect is dependent on excessive trade protection of imports of ICT goods, contributing to limit the effects of these goods to growth. As for the substitution effect, given the low levels of investment in ICT, this effect is not as obvious, especially in non-ICT sectors. Similarly, the effects of total factor productivity and quality are not fully appreciable in the Tunisian economy.

Regarding international comparisons, for a sample of G7 countries, Schreyer (2000) showed that, in addition to the favorable effects of ICT capital goods on economic growth, they generated externalities that exceeded the direct returns to these technologies. Similarly, Dutta and Otsuka (2004) suggest that these externalities strongly contribute to the acceleration of R&D activities while a limited effect on growth is justified by introducing new technologies requiring a time lag to release its effects. Colecchia and Schreyer (2002, 2003) have shown that all nine OECD countries have experienced rapid growth in ICT investment, justified by a steady decline in the relative prices of IT equipment and software. As a result, the positive contribution to economic growth increased from 0.2% to 0.5% per year in the first half of the 1990s and from 0.3% to 0.9% in the second half of the decade. In the same line, Nair et al. (2020) confirm, for the OECD region between 1961 and 2018, that both R&D and ICT infrastructure development contribute to economic growth in the long run. Finally, Karagiannis (2007) split his sample of European Union countries into high-income and less wealthy countries. The first are the only ones to benefit from foreign R&D externalities, while for the second, the use of personal computers and the Internet positively and significantly influence growth.

Nevertheless, there is no unanimity on the extent of the effects of ICT on growth. Audenis et al. (2005) mention uncertainty about the importance of the impact of ICT on the French economy, both in the long term and in the short term. Bacache and Recuero Virto (2009) indicate that, although ICTs contribute positively and actively to economic growth in developed countries, the mechanisms of this contribution remain unclear, and the delay in the adoption of such technologies would slow down growth. Beyond developed countries, Gyekye and Oseifuah's (2015) study, for a group of Sub-Saharan African countries, reveals that these economies, except the southern African countries, South Africa and Botswana, are still lagging behind the rest of the world, although the penetration of telecommunication technologies has been significant. Similarly, the study by Tchamyou et al. (2019) confirms in part that ICT indicators do not significantly influence inequality and economic growth through tertiary school education and lifelong learning.

Most work agrees on the beneficial effects of ICT integration on economic growth. However, the creation and adoption of ICT impose a certain demand for a highly skilled workforce, with skills and training adapted to the new global context. A condition that verifies how much the education and research system must be maintained and strengthened.

2.1.2. Education and Economic Growth

The link between human capital, generally approximated by education, and long-term economic growth has been the subject of a great deal of work, especially with the advent of endogenous growth theory (Nelson and Phelps, 1966, Lucas, 1988, Barro, 1991, 2001, Mankiw, Romer and Weil, 1992). According to these models, the positive contribution of human capital on the labor productive efficiency and consequently on the growth of goods and services is confirmed (Lucas, 1988, Barro, 1991, Mankiw et al., 1992, Krueger and Lindahl, 2001, Hava and Erturgut, 2010, Kocourek and Nedomlelová, 2017, Armeanu et al., 2017, Liao et al., 2019). Although, this claim is widely questioned (Benhabib and Spiegel, 1994, Bils and Klenow, 2000, Pritchett, 2001, Marquez-Ramos and Mourelle, 2019).

Nelson and Phelps (1966) consider that education enables individuals to acquire the skills and knowledge necessary to satisfy their needs better and improve their absorption capacity. Moreover, the most efficient technologies are adopted quickly by economies rich in human capital, thus positively influencing growth. Lucas (1988) also highlights the importance of human capital as a determinant of economic growth and as a way for countries to escape the underdevelopment trap. He considers that "*learning by doing*" is another source of human capital accumulation. By examining a sample of 98 countries from 1960-1985, Barro (1991) shows that developing countries can converge towards the richest countries if they have a high level of human capital. In another study analyzed for a panel of 100 countries over the period 1965-1995, Barro (2001) argues that the effects of education differ by gender. Growth is positively related to the average number of years of study of adult males at the secondary and tertiary levels. However, it is insignificant for female adults. This result is justified by the fact that highly educated women are not adequately integrated into labor markets. Other than the quantity of education, as measured by the number of years of schooling, the author focused on the quality of education by referring to data on internationally comparable test scores in science, mathematics, and reading. He found a positive but insignificant coefficient for the quantity of education indicator, while the quality of education indicator had a positive and highly significant coefficient.

Mankiw et al. (1992) empirically tested the Solow growth model with and without the inclusion of the human capital variable and showed the importance of this variable for growth. Krueger and Lindahl (2001) and Léné (2005) highlighting the significant role of the initial level and accumulation of human capital on growth. Oketch (2006) and Liao et al. (2019) concluded that investment in human capital and physical capital are important determinants of growth and economic development. In the same vein, Lee and Kim (2009), Armeanu et al. (2017), and Kocourek and Nedomlelová (2017) concluded that strategies focused on improving higher education and technology appear to be more effective in generating growth for middle- and high-income countries. Havaa and Erturgut (2010) point out that quality education generates a more skilled workforce, reducing production and management costs. Countries with greater levels of education are more likely to innovate.

Beyond this compromise, some macro-economic approaches point to controversies on this issue, especially in developing countries. Benhabib and Spiegel (1994), Bils and Klenow (2000) and Pritchett (2001) point out that the misallocation of acquired cognitive skills, as well as an unfavorable institutional environment and the difference inefficiency in the transmission of knowledge, are at the origin of the recognized differences between countries in the contribution of education to growth. Castelló and Domenech (2002) have tried to construct new indicators for measuring inequality in human capital. The measures consist of calculating Gini coefficients and the distribution of education by quintiles for 108 countries over the five years from 1960 to 2000. The results provided showed low investment rates, coupled with high inequality in the distribution of education, consequently generating low-income growth rates. Castelló (2010) examined the mechanisms through which educational inequality transmits its effects on economic growth. The results obtained revealed that the greater the inequality in the distribution of education, the higher the fertility rate and the lower the life expectancy. This effect is most apparent in highly unequal societies with a poorly developed financial market, resulting in difficulties accessing credit for low-income and uneducated families to finance their children's schooling. This further influence human capital accumulation discourages investment and hinders growth.

Human capital should have specific skills and be knowledge-oriented to creativity and innovation in the new context, not imitation and reproduction. Thus, Mihaela and Titan (2014, p 1043) asked "*Why education? Why innovation? No State can exist without education. We cannot talk about culture and technology in a country with a low level of education or of the human development index. In everyday life, we can be inventive or creative, but at national level is not enough to be just talented. The talent, if isn't trained is lost. Extrapolating, I can say that a nation without education may not be an innovative country* ".

2.1.3 Innovation/R&D and Economic Growth

Investment in knowledge is seen as the fundamental basis for all innovation. In their models, proponents of endogenous growth theory have recognized technical progress and industrial innovation as determinants of long-term growth (Romer, 1986, 1990, Aghion and Howitt, 1992, Grossman and Helpman, 1994...). The most primitive thesis is that of Schumpeter (1942), who emphasized the major role of innovation in the economy's impetus under the entrepreneur's action, which he summarized by his formula of "*creative destruction*". It is a process by which innovative firms replace old ones, resistant to novelty and maintaining their routine practices, thus generating the permanent renewal of production structures and the obsolescence of old structures. This process provides firms with surplus profits and accelerates economic growth. On the other hand, in neoclassical growth models (Solow, 1956), technical progress is considered an exogenous component and economic growth are condemned, especially with the hypothesis of diminishing returns.

Nevertheless, the questioning of the neoclassical thesis gave rise to the theory of endogenous growth, which acknowledges its origin in the study of Romer (1986). He considers technical progress to be an endogenous factor. Thus, innovation is defined as an activity linked to the behavior and skills of economic agents, which increases the stock of knowledge and boosts economic growth.

In an extension of his basic model, Romer (1990) concludes that the ability of R&D activities to produce technical change, which is in favour of economic growth. Inspired by Schumpeterian creative destruction, Aghion and Howitt (1992) have formulated a model of innovation with an ambiguous aspect. On the one hand, it has the effect of enhancing productivity. On the other hand, in the context of the study of the interactions between market structure and innovation, the authors assume that the model of competition in which imitation is continuously increasing contributes to the deterioration of monopoly rents and consequently has a negative influence on the degree of innovation and economic growth. They predict that imperfect competition is more appropriate, and intellectual property protection through patents is more favorable. Beyond analyzing the direct impact of innovation on growth, positive externalities appear and considerably influence economic growth (Romer, 1986, 1990, Stokey, 1995). Innovation generates externalities that benefit other actors. The latter, from an imitation perspective, can improve their products without having to assume costs. Externalities arise from the exchange of know-how, the movement of personnel, patenting and interactions between actors (Griliches, 1998). On a macroeconomic scale, Coe and Helpman (1995) and Bayoumi et al. (1999) have shown that international trade considerably affects total factor productivity through knowledge transfers. The more open the economy, the greater the effects of international externalities. Maurseth and Verspagen (2002) and Bottazzi and Peri (2003) focused their analyses on European regions and found that innovation externalities are highly localized. In the sense that industries, which have a prevalence of knowledge externalities, tend to group in clusters. Mingyong et al. (2006) argue that long-term growth depends on improving the absorptive capacity of the host country and investing in human capital to take advantage of international technological externalities, the degree of openness of the economy and that FDI is a more important transmission channel than imports.

Nevertheless, some studies have shown the limits of innovation spillovers in stimulating growth. Cameron (1998) concluded that the innovation process generates significant externalities between firms, industries and countries. However, despite the magnitude of international externalities, they cannot account for all the productivity growth in an economy. The innovation efforts of domestic firms are most important and whose efforts spill over more easily to other domestic firms. More recently, other dimensions have been addressed, Yang Chih-Hai (2006) and Kacprzyk and Doryń (2017) argue that the increase in domestic patenting activities compared to international ones leads to increased economic growth. Hasan and Tucci (2010) and Fagiolo et al. (2020) showed that innovation's quantity and quality stimulate economic growth. Pradhan et al. (2019) found that both innovation diffusion and ICT penetration stimulate economic growth in the long run.

The theoretical and empirical literature about innovation and its relationship with economic growth has not failed to reveal the need to establish preconditions even before starting the innovation process. However, to exploit investments in new technologies, knowledge accumulation and R&D activities, it is imperative to guarantee the existence of a favorable economic and institutional framework that ensures the full benefit of the different pillars already analyzed and promotes economic growth. But through which mechanisms? This is what we will discuss in the next section.

2.2 Institutions and Economic Growth: An Ambiguous Relationship

For a long time, the question of institutions, particularly property rights and other aspects of economic and political institutions, has remained in the background of economic analysis. However, for more than thirty years, a considerable amount of work has been developed (North, 1981, 1990, 1994, Knack and Keefer, 1995, Sachs et al., 1995, Glaeser et al., 2004, Kaufmann et al., 2011 ...). This work has recently led to a renewed focus on the role of economic and political institutions in economic growth. This literature shows that these institutions positively influence economic growth.

North (1994, p 360) presents institutions as " *Institutions are the humanly devised constraints that structure human interaction. They are made up of formal constraints (e.g., rules, laws, constitutions), informal constraints (e.g.: norms of behavior, conventions, self-imposed codes of conduct), and their enforcement characteristics*". In this sense, they refer to the set of fundamental rules on which the legal system is based, forming the institutional environment in which institutional arrangements, particularly contracts, occur (Borner et al., 2004). These institutions are generally of two types: economic institutions and political institutions.

North (1990) confirms that institutions are considered the underlying determinant of the long-term economic performance of nations. The study by Hall and Jones (1999) notes that in the long run, a country's economic performance depends on the existence of better institutions and government policies, that govern the environment in which economic actors operate. Rodrik et al. (2004) used the instrumental variables approach to estimate a series of regressions linking income to measures of geography, economic integration, and institutions to recognize the role that institutions can play in the process of economic growth and development. Again, a positive causal relationship was detected. Finally, knack and Keefer (1995) examined the effects of property rights on economic growth. They used two indicators collected by private organizations to measure the security of property rights: The Business Environmental Risk Intelligence (BERI) and the International Country Risk Guide (ICRG). They find that property rights can explain 8 to 10 percent of the variation in growth rates between 1974 and 1989.

Also, Kaufmann et al. (2011) attempted to construct World Governance Indicators (WGI). These indicators consider six governance dimensions: Voice and Accountability, Political Stability and Absence of Violence/Terrorism, Government Effectiveness, Regulatory Quality, Rule of Law, and Control of Corruption. The latest updated version of their study covers 213 countries and territories for 1996, 1998, 2000 and from 2002 onwards for each year until 2020. To detect the effects of the economic regime on growth, Sachs et al. (1995) developed an indicator of trade openness for 80 developed and developing countries from 1960-1992. This indicator includes the main types of trade restrictions. They found that trade openness increases economic growth on average by 2.45 percentage points. Chen and Dahlman (2004) used a battery of indicators, including the index of trade openness to serve as an indicator of the type of economic regime and the index of the degree of protection of property rights that reflects the quality of institutions. The results suggest that economic openness and institutional quality play a large role in determining economic growth.

In a more developed analysis, Chen and Dahlman (2005) have pointed out that in a knowledge-based economy, the economic and institutional regime requires that economic agents have incentives for the efficient creation and use of knowledge. This must be based on transparent macroeconomic and regulatory policies. Borner et al. (2004) have tried to determine what good economic institutions are and establish and maintain them. This study found the importance of intellectual property rights through a series of regressions that showed a positive relationship with economic growth, using several variables including no threat of expropriation, low risk of state failure, or a low premium for black markets. Roberto (2017) found a negative effect of democracy and regime instability on growth, while a positive effect of legislative efficiency appears. In addition, spatial externalities seem to matter: being surrounded by countries with high levels of democracy boosts growth, while regime instability in neighboring countries has a negative effect.

Similarly, Setayesh and Daryaei (2017) found a positive and significant correlation between the rule of law and corruption control with economic growth. Wanjiru and Prime (2018) found that institutions influence long-term economic performance and that some institutions matter more than others. They suggest that institutions designed to regulate and legitimize markets and limit inefficiencies significantly affect productivity levels.

Some work has shown the limits of institutions in stimulating economic growth. For example, Glaeser et al. (2004) used the example of South and North Korea to argue against the primacy of institutions for economic growth but also to defend the importance of economic policies. They see human capital as the basic source of growth more than institutions.

After a broad review of the theoretical and empirical literature on the relationship in question, it was realized that few works have dealt with this relationship directly, but rather through mechanisms such as investment and diffusion of ICT, human capital accumulation, innovation capacity and the establishment of a favorable economic and institutional regime. The studies considered have varied between cases of developed and developing countries. Henceforth, our analysis will be more focused by addressing the situation of the knowledge economy in the countries of the Middle East and North Africa (MENA) region. To this end, we adopt the World Bank's provision for the KBE as explained above and attempt in what follows to assess the performance of MENA countries in the different pillars.

3. MENA COUNTRIES FACE THE CHALLENGE OF THE KNOWLEDGE-BASED ECONOMY (KBE)

Like any other region, the MENA region is influenced by the KBE wave that has affected most countries globally. Certainly, engagement in such an economy, of which knowledge is its decisive component, predisposes the availability of certain conditions referring to the pillars of the knowledge economy. The literature review allowed us to deduce the scarcity of works that have addressed this issue in the MENA region. This lack of studies was the primary motivation to dig into the state of the knowledge economy in this region and to evaluate the positioning of these countries in this new global context by using knowledge-related indicators offered by the literature.

With reference to the above-mentioned World Bank concept, the knowledge-based economy is pre-defined by its four pillars: education, innovation, ICT and the economic and institutional framework. For each pillar, a range of indicators is proposed to assess the performance of a given country in this pillar. To this end, our work will be divided into two parts. First, we will make a descriptive analysis of the components of the knowledge economy in the different countries of the MENA region. Several indicators allow us to establish the evolution of the state of development of the different pillars, particularly those related to knowledge such as innovation, information technology and education. Our ultimate objective in the first part of this section is to examine the place of MENA countries, in the knowledge economy. In other words, we will look at the reality of these different dimensions by focusing on the role of innovation, through a comparative study based on indicators used at the international level.

Second, we will estimate an endogenous growth model using dynamic panel data techniques. The aim is to conclude the effects of knowledge on economic growth for all MENA countries, by integrating qualitative and quantitative indicators related to the knowledge economy. In other words, we seek to provide some answers to the following question: Can knowledge be considered as an indispensable precondition for economic progress in a changing international context?

3.1. Positioning of MENA Countries in the Knowledge-Based Economy: A Descriptive Analysis

3.1.1. Evolution of Economic Growth

Before embarking on the analysis of the state of the knowledge-based economy in MENA countries, it is helpful to outline the evolution of economic growth in this region compared to other regions worldwide (figure 3). To measure the economic growth, we use GDP/capita variable, as adopted by many works (Lee and Kim, 2009, Andersson and Djeflat, 2013, Nour Samia, 2015...).

Figure 3. GDP per capita evolution (1968-2020)
Source: Conducted by the authors using World Bank Indicators (WBI)

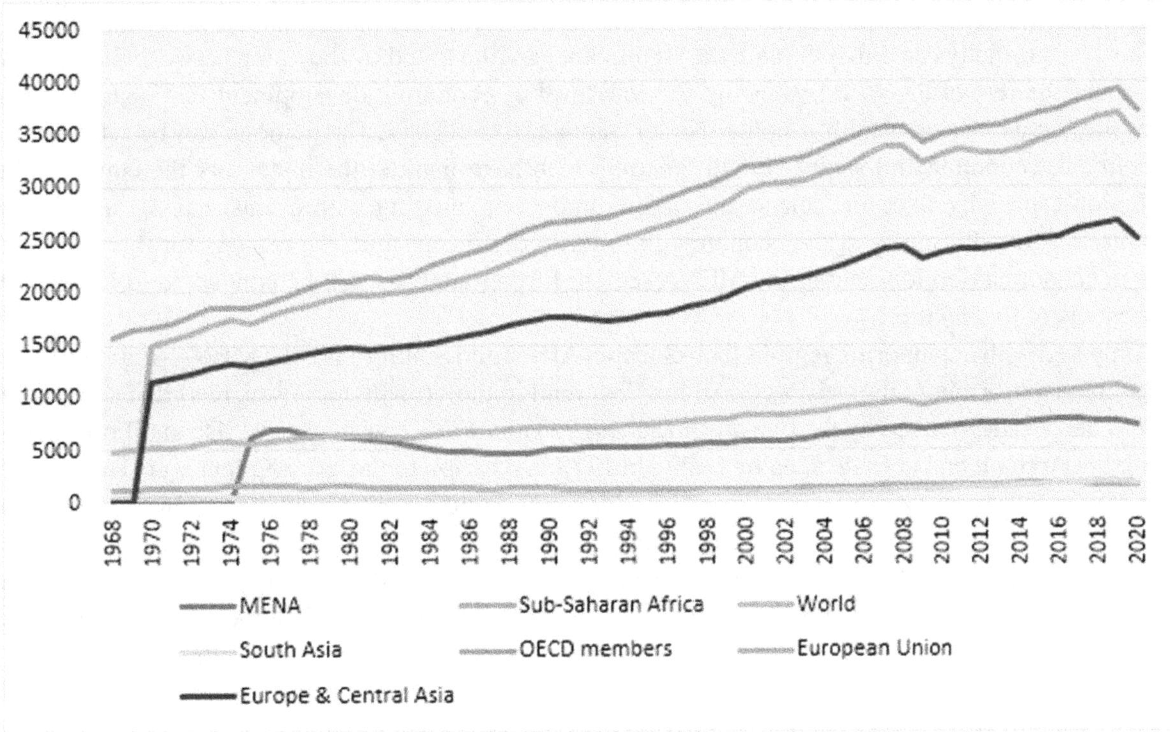

Source : Conducted by the authors using World Bank Indicators (WBI)

In the light of this graph, the evolution of GDP per capita in the MENA region over the 1968-2020 reveals a fluctuating growth rate. There are ups and downs, revealing the unsustainability of economic growth. The difference between the MENA countries as a whole and the other regions in question is striking. Growth progress is mixed ; on the one hand, MENA ranks ahead of sub-Saharan Africa and South Asia. On the other hand, economic activity is fragile, placing MENA below all of Europe and Central Asia, the European Union, and the OECD countries.

In the light of this graph, the evolution of GDP per capita in the MENA region over 1968-2020 reveals a fluctuating growth rate. There are ups and downs, revealing the unsustainability of economic growth.

The difference between the MENA countries as a whole and the other regions in question is clearly striking. In fact, growth progress is mixed ; on the one hand, MENA ranks ahead of sub-Saharan Africa and South Asia. On the other hand, economic activity is very weak, placing MENA below Europe and Central Asia, the European Union, and the OECD countries.

The MENA region comprises a heterogeneous set of countries, classified according to various classifications. A first distinction according to the availability of natural and human resources is made, such that the region is made up of resource-rich and labor-importing economies (Saudi Arabia, United Arab Emirates, Kuwait, Libya, Qatar, Oman, and Bahrain), resource-rich and labor-intensive economies (Algeria, Iran, Iraq, Syria, and Yemen), and resource-poor but labor-intensive economies (Egypt, Jordan, Morocco, Tunisia, Lebanon, and Djibouti) (World Bank, 2009). Another distinction made by the World Bank according to income level classifies high-income countries, which are mostly oil-producing (Bahrain, Israel, Kuwait, Malta, Oman, Qatar, Saudi Arabia, and the United Arab Emirates), and low- and middle-income countries (Algeria, Djibouti, Egypt, Iran, Iraq, Jordan, Lebanon, Libya, Morocco, Tunisia, Syria, and Yemen, West Bank & Gaza).

This heterogeneity can partly explain the significant gap illustrated by the graph between the MENA region and the rest of the world, showing the low level of economic development that characterizes it, despite the enormous wealth it holds (Nouer Samia, 2015). These fluctuations can be returned to the political, economic and social circumstances, which have marked the history of the countries in this region especially since the selected period of study was bursting with events, having significant repercussions on all aspects of the economy. In order to dig deeper into the reasons for this apparent delay in economic development in the MENA region, further analysis will be conducted to justify the components of this failure.

Compared with neighboring regions (sub-Saharan Africa and South Asia), the MENA Region's GDP per capita is performing relatively well. An upward trend in the growth curve was recorded during the 1970s. One decade, marked by the two oil shocks in 1973 and 1979, saw a massive rise in oil prices following the Arab oil embargo decided by OPEC in 1973 in reaction to the Yom Kippur war. The second wave of price increases occurred in 1979, mainly due to the Iranian revolution followed by the Iraq-Iran war of 1980-1988. This proves the increased dependence of growth variation on oil price changes, as Andersson and Djeflat (2013) mentioned, the level of growth achieved by the major Gulf Cooperation Council (GCC) countries is mainly from their huge oil and gas revenues. In fact, the oil countries in the MENA region significantly influence growth progress compared to the non-oil countries.

Despite the abundance of natural resources and the massive export revenues generated by the two oil shocks, the disparity in economic growth between the MENA region and the Western regions is considerable. The 1980s witnessed a relatively small slowdown in GDP/capita growth, followed by a fairly small recovery in the 1990s. In fact, in resource-poor countries the 1980s were characterized by economic imbalance and increasing external debt as a result of declining profits from tourism, the oil industry, persistent harsh climatic conditions (continuous drought), social tensions (Bread Riot in 1984), and the inability of public investment to contain the deteriorating situation, as is also the case for Algeria, Egypt, and Jordan (Hsaini 2007).

To cope with this economic stalemate, most MENA countries resorted to structural adjustment programs (SAPs), imposed by international financial institutions in the second half of the 1980s. The economic reform measures dictated by these programs consisted of reducing public spending on investment in favor of national and international private initiatives. However, private investment has failed to make up for this decline for several reasons related to poorly functioning competition in the markets, insufficient demand, a very restrictive macroeconomic policy, difficulties in allocating resources with underdeveloped financial systems, a tight monetary policy and an unfavorable business environment, especially since problems related to institutions, notably the inadequate protection of property rights and relations with the public administration and the judicial system, persist (Liouane, 2009).

Overall, SAPs have led to positive macroeconomic results such as lower inflation, lower budget deficits, and restoration of short-term solvency in the countries concerned. But the development process is still limited, with a poorly developed private sector and a dominant public sector. These economies remain on the bangs of the world economy, especially since the expected structural reforms have run up against a discouraging framework without achieving the planned objectives.

Towards the end of the 1980s and in a perspective of complete liberalization of developing economies, « *expanding trade and investment offers the best hope for generating the requisite growth and jobs. This effort requires moving decisively away from relying on the public sector and protected national economies as the main engine of growth-which did produce results in the past but has reached its limits-to relying on more open economies and a competitive private sector* » (World Bank, 2003, p xv). Therefore, free trade is partly the way out for the development of economic growth in the MENA region. In 1995, the Barcelona Process was launched at the initiative of the European Union, aiming at a Euro-Mediterranean Partnership (Euromed) between the countries of the Mediterranean basin (Algeria, Egypt, Jordan, Lebanon, Palestinian Authority, Syria, Morocco, Tunisia, Turkey, and Israel) and those of the European Union, aiming at the establishment of a free trade area by 2010 (Commission of the European Communities, CEC, 2008).

In order to consolidate multilateral relations about the political, economic and social dimensions, Euromed claims the expansion of trade between the various partners, encouraging the entry of foreign direct investment, freedom of exchange and transfer of earnings.. This trade integration was at the origin of a progressive dismantling of tariff barriers. Nevertheless, following this tariff dismantling, MENA countries were confronted with a decline in their customs revenues, considered important for public finances (Liouane, 2009).

Since 2000 and until today, the graph has shown that GDP per capita grew until it reached a peak in 2008 and then declined slightly in 2009, before resuming its slightly progressive trend until the outbreak of the Arab revolutions (Tunisia, Egypt, Yemen, Libya and Syria) in 2011. And since then, economic growth has suffered a continuous slowdown. The 2000s were initiated by the attacks of September 11, 2001, an event that affected the whole world followed by the invasion of Iraq in 2003. According to some specialists, from 2003 onwards, an acceleration the oil price was noted, reaching its peak in 2008, the date of the third oil shock. According to World Bank (2009), oil prices exceeded \$100 per barrel in early 2008, almost a 78 percent increase. In the MENA region, export revenues from oil and refined products rose from \$577 billion to \$632 billion, an increase of 11.6 percent.

The continued increase in hydrocarbon revenues has supported economic growth, although the level of growth achieved is still below the levels achieved by other developed regions. These revenues have financed domestic demand, which *"...remains the main source of growth in the region, but investment has increased significantly. The contribution of gross domestic investment to GDP growth nearly doubled in 2006, from 2.6 to 4.1 GDP growth points. In addition, private investment as a percentage of GDP has increased, indicating that growth is being driven more by the private sector"* (World Bank, 2007, p 3). FDI inflows reached \$45 billion in 2007, a slight decline from the \$52 billion recorded in 2006. The largest share of FDI was captured by Saudi Arabia, Egypt, and the United Arab Emirates (World Bank, 2009).

MENA countries experienced a significant increase in food prices during the 2000s, mainly due to higher fertilizer costs and a reduction in the amount of land devoted to food, the impact of which was felt differently in different countries. Those classified as low-income are the most vulnerable. In Yemen, for example, the increase in food prices exceeded 20% in 2007. The sharp rise in energy costs and increased in food prices had an inflationary effect in the MENA region, affecting fuel-dependent activities and food-importing countries respectively (World Bank, 2009). At the end of this decade, growth shows a recession in 2009, which can be justified by the global economic crisis of 2008 and its subsequent effects on the overall world economy.

The last phase of the study period selected is the years from 2010 to 2020. After the GDP/capita recession evident in 2009, the MENA region showed a recovery in 2010. Oil prices are upward, mainly due to the OPEC countries' reduction in oil production to limit global supply and set a price floor. Oil exporting countries are mainly benefiting from this increase, generating January 2010 revenues of about 605 billion dollars against 530 billion dollars in 2009. As for diversified economies, their goods exports are increasing, inflation gradually stabilized to a moderate level. Statistics showed that the global crisis moderately influenced the MENA region compared to other developing regions. GDP growth was 4.2 percent in 2008 and fell to 3.2 percent in 2009, a small decline compared with a 9.5 percentage point decline in growth in Europe and Central Asia (World Bank, 2010).

Low- and middle-income oil-exporting countries (Algeria, Iran, Syria, and Yemen) experienced a decline in hydrocarbon revenues in 2009, offset by increased activity in non-oil sectors in 2010. While the diversified economies (Tunisia, Morocco, Egypt, Jordan and Lebanon) experienced a decline in exports to European markets in 2009, and a reduction in tourism revenues and FDI flows from Europe due to the economic slowdown during the crisis. These are signs that the region will experience headwinds in 2010 and beyond (World Bank, 2010).

With the outbreak of the Arab revolutions in 2011, the MENA economies were affected by this wave, which hit Tunisia first, followed by Egypt, Yemen, Libya, and Syria. This event coincided with the Eurozone crisis according to Andersson and Djeflat (2013), which revealed the "gap" between southern European countries characterized by low productivity and high trade deficits, and northern European countries (e.g. Germany). According to the IMF (2013), the region's oil-exporting countries recorded a high growth rate of 5.7 percent on average in 2012, supported mainly by the expansion of oil production in the Gulf countries and the resumption of production in Libya. However, these results may be threatened by insecurity and possible regional geopolitical unrest.

Referring similarly to the IMF report (2013), oil-importing countries in the region averaged 2.7 percent growth in 2012. However, due to social tensions and political uncertainty, the level of investment is low, exports and tourist arrivals have declined due to the Eurozone crisis, energy and food prices are high globally. To alleviate social unrest, governments have resorted to increasing subsidies and salaries for the public sector. An imbalance has arisen between high public spending and low tax revenues, resulting in rising budget deficits averaging 8.4 percent of GDP, pushing up public debt.

Most MENA countries are in very difficult political, economic, and social situations caused by war and turmoil. Economic growth is still fragile (2.9% in 2014 ; 2.6% in 2015 ; 1,6% in 2017 ; 0,9% in 2018 ; 0,5% in 2019 ; -3,8% in 2020), even stagnant in 2014 in oil-importing countries and slightly up in oil-exporting countries. Growth forecasts for 2017 establish a rate of 3.5%. Investments are still low due to the unattractive climate, budget and external deficits persist, the unemployment rate is increasing, the security dimension is still fragile, and the risks of instability are significant (World Bank, 2016).

Like any other country in the world, the MENA region has been threatened by the COVID 19 health crisis, which has had negative repercussions on the entire world economy and particularly the countries of the region. According to the world bank statistics, the GDP regressed by 3.8% in 2020, a contraction of government revenues by 24%, which justifies the increase in public debt from 46% of GDP in 2019 to 54% in 2021 in the whole region and which can reach 93% in 2021 in oil importing countries (World Bank, 2021).

We have tried to provide a summary overview of the evolution of economic growth in the MENA region during 1968-2020. The general observation is that the level reached by this region is closely related to their huge oil and gas revenues. However, the paradox is that these countries, rich in natural and human resources, cannot achieve strong and sustainable growth that can catch up with developed countries. Some studies insist on the insufficiency of abundant natural resources to support growth (Andersson and Djeflat, 2013), while others even suggest that these resources may have the opposite effect on growth (Sachs and Warner, 1997, 2001). Hence the need for a new direction based on a new growth model, focused on technical progress, innovation and continuous learning, otherwise a knowledge-based economy (Aubert and Reiffers, 2003).

3.1.2. Status of the KBE in the MENA Region

We conduct a comparative study based on indicators used at the international level to place MENA countries in the knowledge economy. As an indication, we have selected 16 MENA countries[4] due to the lack of data availability for the rest of the countries.

3.1.2.1. Performance in Terms of ICT Indicators

The last few years have seen the development of the ICT market in the MENA region through the growth in the number of internet users and cell phone subscriptions. Figure 4 clearly shows the upward trend in the number of internet users in all countries in the region. In fact, Qatar and Bahrain have the highest number of internet users (% population) in 2020, followed by Kuwait and Saudi Arabia and Oman. However, some of these countries are still below the performance achieved by developed countries. According to the latest World Economic Forum (WEF) 2019 report, Qatar ranks 1st, Kuwait 2nd, Bahrain ranks 4th out of 141 economies covered by the Global Competitiveness Index (GCI), UAE ranks 5th. In addition, the North African zone, Morocco (75th), Egypt (98th), Tunisia (78th) and Algeria (83rd), against Iceland in 3rd place, Finland 7th place, Denmark 6th place.

Figure 4. Individuals using the Internet (% of population)[5]
Source: Conducted by the authors using World Bank Indicators (WBI)

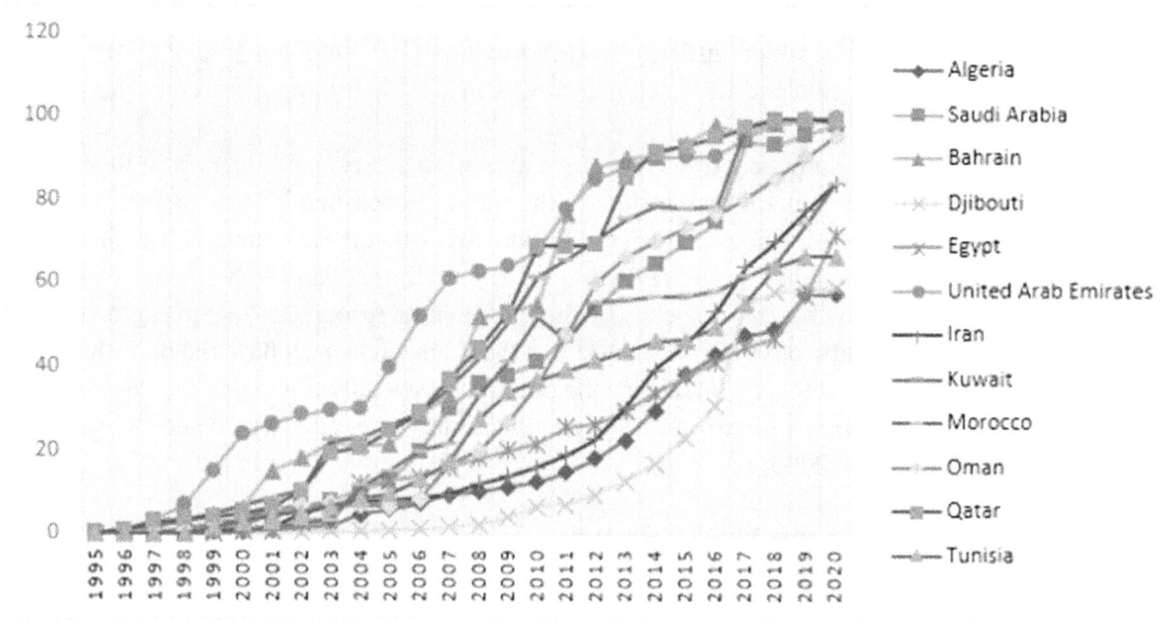

Source : Conducted by the authors using World Bank Indicators (WBI)

The number of cell phone subscriptions is much higher especially in the Gulf countries. The UAE is more advanced than the others with a value of 185.7 in 2020, followed by Jordan with 158.5 and Iran with 151.9. As for the other countries in the region, Figure 5 shows their rapid progress over1995-2020 but lags behind the GCC countries and developed countries. The WEF 2019 report presents the positions of 144 economies in terms of the indicator in question. The countries above occupy strong positions and are at the forefront of the KBE in this regard: UAE (2nd), Kuwait (6th), Qatar (19th). Other countries in the area, represent a delay compared to the rest of the world such as: Oman (34th), Bahrain (35th), Tunisia (47th), Morocco (52nd), Saudi Arabia (57th), Algeria (61st), Iran (85th) and Egypt (109th), in comparison to developed countries such as Hong Kong (1er), Monténégro (4eme), Thaïlande (5eme) et Costa Rica (7eme). Thus, it is visible that significant progress is being made in the region.

Figure 5. Mobile cellular subscriptions (per 100 people)[6]
Source: Conducted by the authors using World Bank Indicators (WBI)

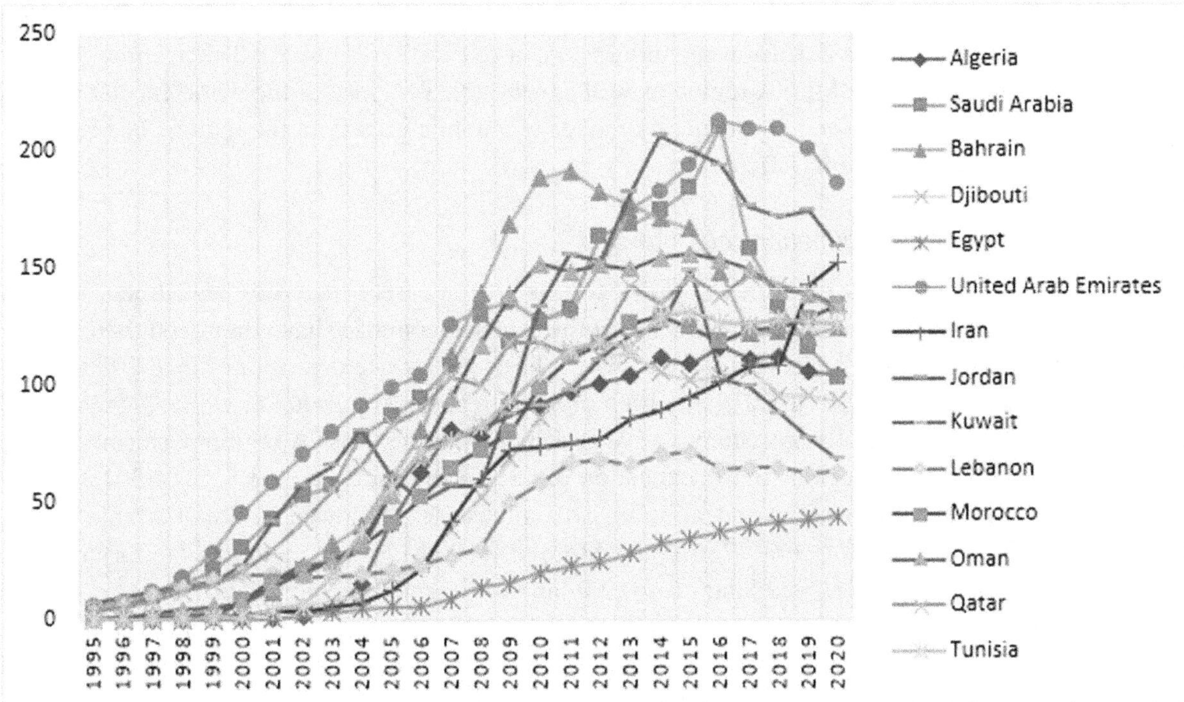

Source : Conducted by the authors using World Bank Indicators (WBI)

Figure 6. Individuals using the Internet (% of population)
Source: Conducted by the authors using World Bank Indicators (WBI)

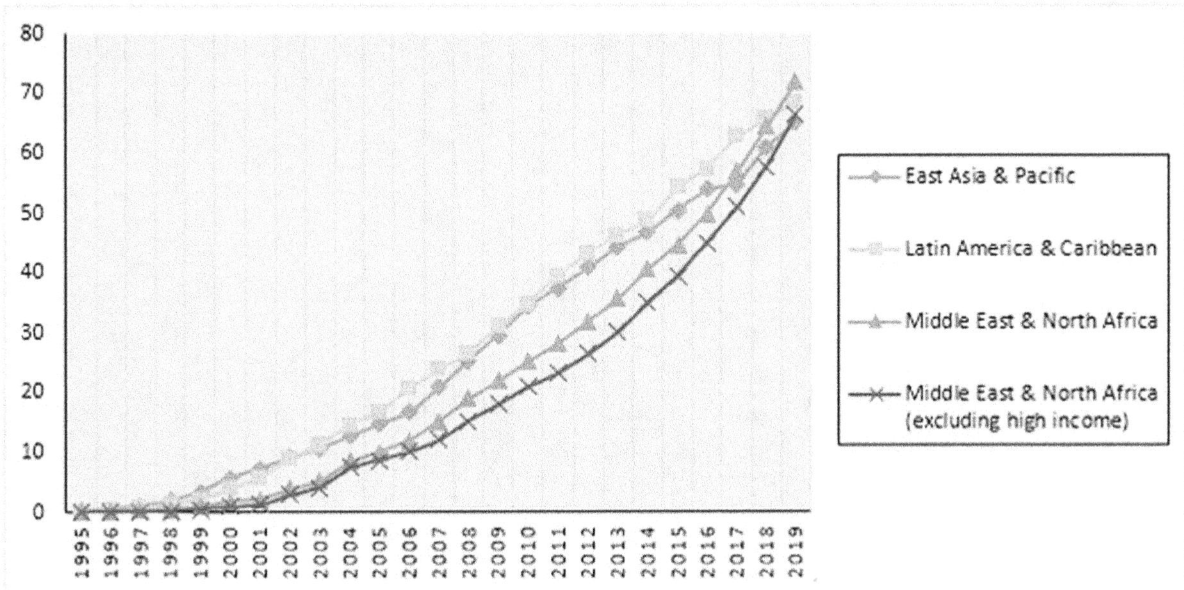

Although, statistics have shown the development of the information and telecommunication sector through the schemes undertaken either legally or through investments and expenditures made in the MENA region. The efforts made are insufficient and the region's countries are still lagging behind other regions such as Latin America & Caribbean and East Asia & Pacific (Figure 6). The accumulation of intra-country disparities in the MENA region as well as with other regions of the world further widens the North-South digital divide and consequently hinders economic growth in the region. The KBE requires deeper insertion into the ICT fields.

3.1.2.2. Performance on Education Indicators

The gap between the different countries in the region is also apparent regarding enrollment rates in higher education (Figure 7). The statistics show that the selected countries have improved their performance in this pillar since 1995 except for Qatar, which has seen its rate deteriorate since 2000 with a slight increase in 2015 and 2019. In 2019, the high rate was recorded by Bahreïn, while Qatar showed its lowest level of tertiary enrollment. Studies have concluded that the MENA region performs weakly and ranks behind developed regions in the education pillar. According to the WEF 2014-2015 report, Iran considered the best performer in education in 2012, ranks 50th, followed by Saudi Arabia (55th), Jordan (57th), Tunisia (73rd), Algeria (78th), and Morocco (100th). These countries are far ahead of Greece (1st), Korea (2nd), the United States (3rd), Finland (4th), and Singapore (5th).

Undoubtedly, MENA countries have been able to achieve significant improvements in education. We recognize several achievements, including compulsory schooling, equitable access to education, and the elimination of gender differentiation; secondary school enrollment increased threefold and tertiary enrollment increased fivefold between 1970 and 2003; the illiteracy rate was halved; and opportunities for formal education were more advanced (World Bank, 2007).

Figure 7. School enrollment, tertiary (% gross)[7]
Source: Conducted by the authors using World Bank Indicators (WBI)

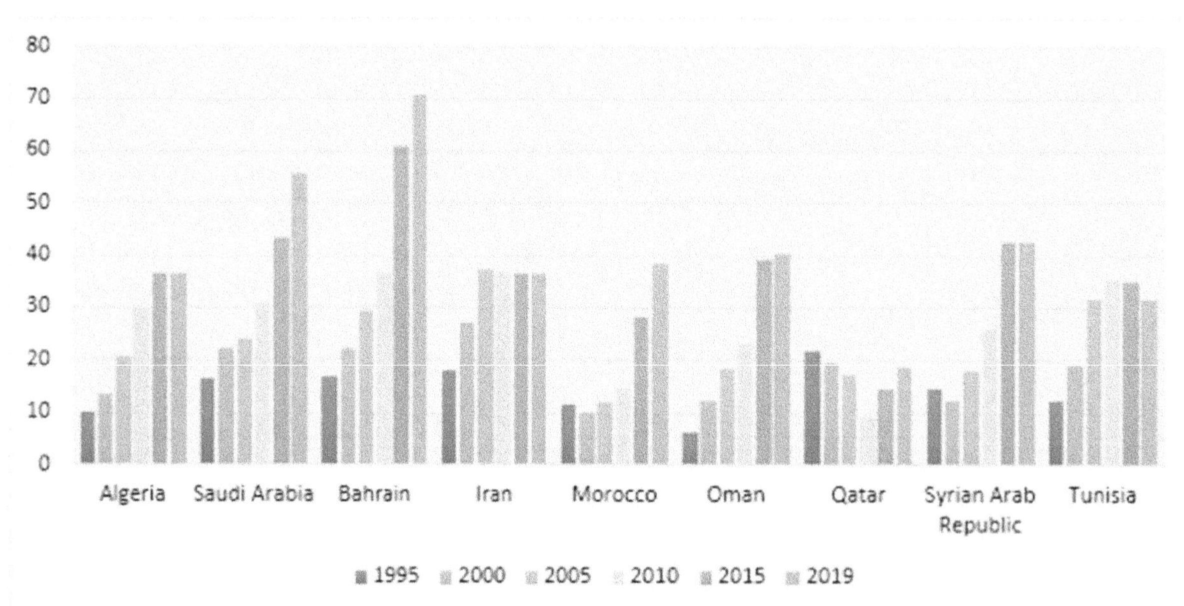

Source : Conducted by the authors using World Bank Indicators (WBI)

Nevertheless, the reforms undertaken are insufficient and the MENA region still lags behind several regions similar in economic development such as East Asia and Latin America in terms of years of schooling (MENA is more than one year behind both regions), illiteracy is twice as high as in the other two regions, the level of international tests is still below the levels achieved by middle-income countries, and this is due to the specialization of two-thirds of students in the social sciences and humanities as opposed to science and mathematics. In addition, the unemployment rate among graduates is high (World Bank, 2007).

Figure 8. School enrollment, tertiary (% gross)
Source: Conducted by the authors using World Bank Indicators (WBI)

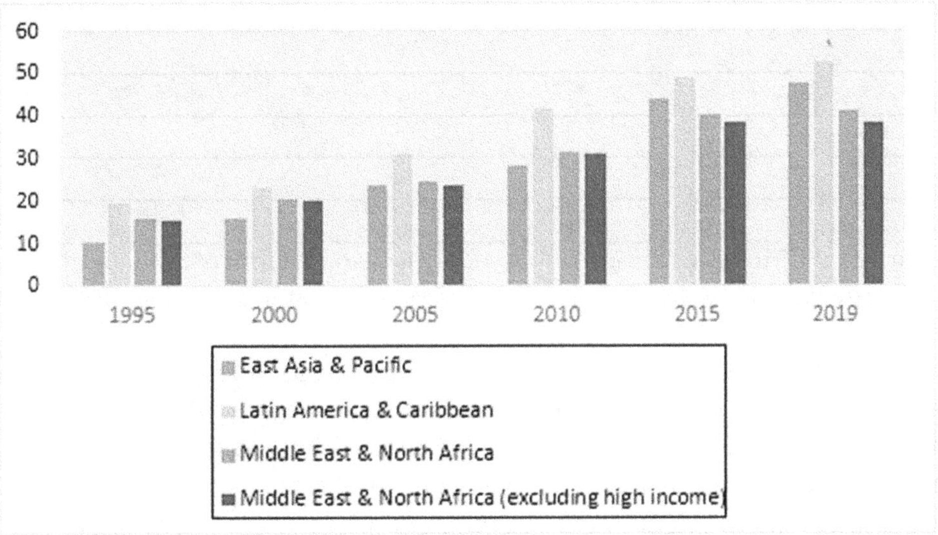

Perhaps MENA has succeed in the quantitative dimension but not necessarily in the qualitative dimension of education compared to developed countries. The education system in the region produces skills that are not adapted to the new global context. These shortcomings hinder integration into the knowledge-based economy, of which innovation is its main component and requires the complementarity of a skilled workforce and advanced technology. This requires a review of the strategies and reforms undertaken to ensure a better quality of education.

3.1.2.3. Performance in Terms of Innovation Indicators

For reasons of competitiveness, we have already shown the major importance of innovation in a knowledge-based context. Of course, prerequisites for innovation development should be put in place and exploited, notably R&D investments and the range of skills and educational abilities acquired. The outputs of these activities will be illustrated by the number of patent applications and scientific and technical journal articles published on a ten-year scale.

Figure 9. Patent applications[8]
Source: Conducted by the authors using World Bank Indicators (WBI)

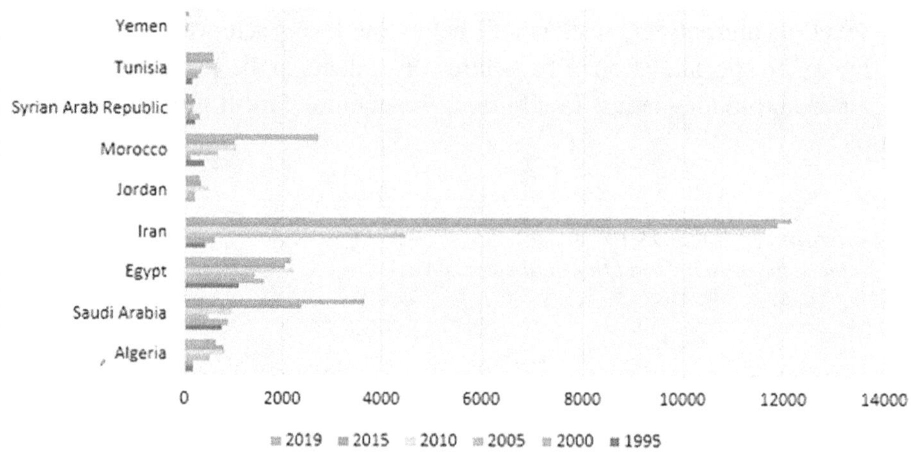

As shown in figure 8, MENA countries show a wide dispersion in terms of this indicator. Nevertheless, most of the selected countries show a relatively better improvement in patent applications from 1995 to 2019, except for Syria and Yemen, which show since 1995 too low values. This can be referred to the political difficulties and circumstances of the war that both countries are experiencing. Iran took the lead in 2019, the GCC countries do not appear in this ranking except for Saudi Arabia[9], whose patents are dominated by oil technologies, water and health (Andersson and Djeflat, 2013).

In comparative terms, North African countries are relatively successful in producing patents compared to the rest of the MENA countries, reflecting the level of innovation activity and the translation of knowledge into technological creation.

According to the European Patent Office, the period 2003-2011 was characterized by a very low number of patent applications filed under the Patent Cooperation Treaty (PCT) for the majority of MENA countries. These places MENA below OECD countries, East Asia and Pacific, North America, Europe and Central Asia, the European Union, Latin America and the Caribbean, and South Asia (Nour Samia, 2015).

Figure 10. Patent applications
Source: Conducted by the authors using World Bank Indicators (WBI)

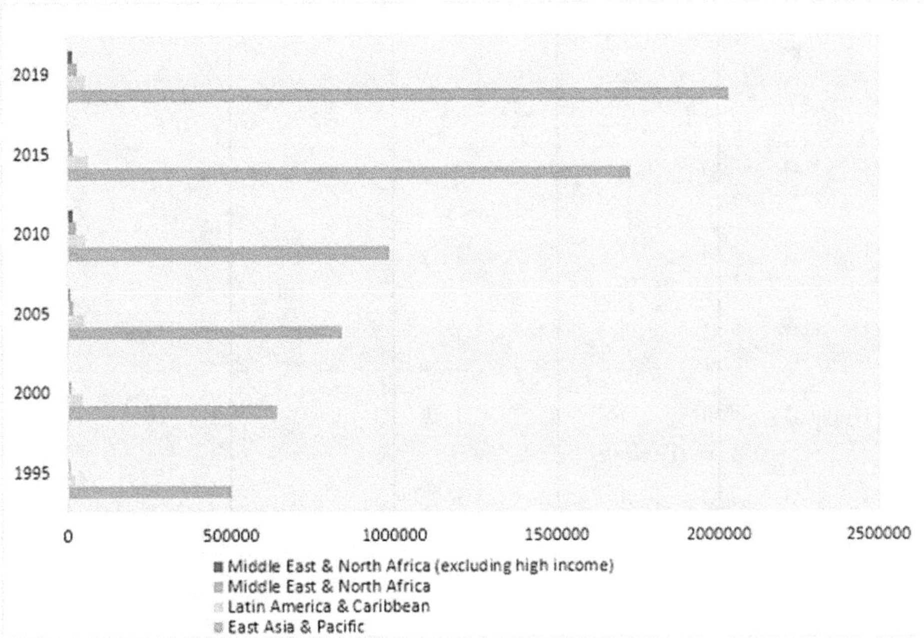

Although the MENA region has made considerable efforts to improve its patent output, it seems that it still lags behind the many regions in terms of R&D outputs. This lag can be attributed to the institutional and regulatory framework, which suffers from inadequate protection of property rights, poor private sector access to domestic credit, low liquidity of stock markets, lack of financing, and excessive costs of innovation activities. « *The other main weakness of the innovation system is the content of the education system. Despite improvements in the gross enrollment ratio, the education system has been unable to overcome illiteracy and to train enough engineers and scientists* » (Aubert et Reiffers, 2003, p 23).

Intra-country differences in the MENA region are also apparent in the number of scientific and technical papers published over selected years (Figure 9). Iran is ranked first among all countries with more than 48305 publications in 2018, followed by the North African countries (Egypt, Algeria, Tunisia and Morocco). The GCC countries have a low level of scientific production except for Saudi Arabia.

Figure 11. Scientific and technical journal articles
Source: Conducted by the authors using World Bank Indicators (WBI)

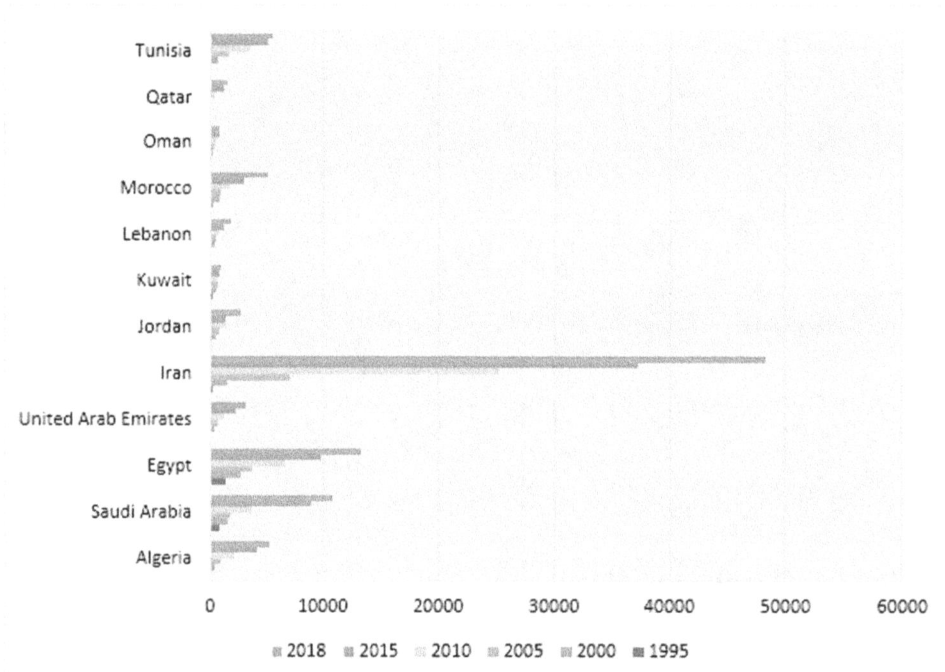

At the scale of the MENA region, in 2013, Iran contributed 36.8% of the total scientific output, Tunisia is ranked 5th behind Egypt and Saudi Arabia, but ahead of Algeria and Morocco which are ranked 6th and 7th respectively. Most countries in the region have seen the progression of their global shares with an average annual rate of 9.5% between 2003 and 2011 against 4.5%. Another advance is the quality of published scientific articles, measured by the average relative impact factor (ARIF).

3.1.2.4. The Performance in Terms of the Institutional Framework's Indicators

The theoretical studies cited above have shown the positive effects of the institutional framework on economic growth. The consolidation of the institutional dimensions creates a healthy climate, thus favoring investment with less risk and more profitability. The theory has proven that the pillars of the knowledge economy can only achieve a result if the institutional environment is favorable. We will try to show next the characteristics of institutions related to MENA countries, adopting the World Governance Indicators (WGI)[10]. It was developed by Kaufmann et al (2011), including voice and accountability, political stability, government effectiveness, regulatory quality, the rule of law, and corruption control.

We chose to compare the quality of governance for the year 2020, across countries in the region. Inspired by the ranking provided by Kaufmann et al (2005), which gathers these indicators into three groups: (1) the criteria by which governments are elected and/or voted out such as voice and accountability and political stability and absence of violence. (2) criteria of the performance and credibility of governments in implementing appropriate policies, such as government effectiveness and regulatory quality (3) criteria that demonstrate consideration and respect for institutions by citizens and the state, such as control of corruption and the rule of law.

Figure 12. Institutional Indicators
Source: Conducted by the authors using the World Governance Indicators (WGI)

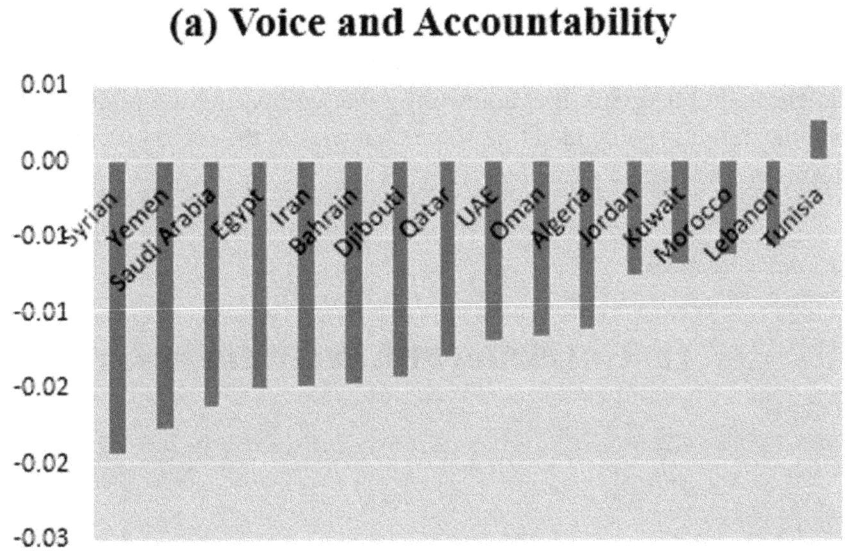

Figure (a) suggests that all countries in the region remain very weak in these democratic practices, where citizens are deprived of having a voice and accountability has no real place, except for Tunisia. In general, transparency within the MENA region is very limited, information asymmetry reigns, citizens are deprived of access to information on government practices, and freedom of expression is limited or nonexistent except for voices praising the government. Moreover, accountability mechanisms are weak, particularly in the MENA region, because of the monopoly of power in the hands of the executive (World Bank, 2003).

Figure 13. Institutional Indicators
Source: Conducted by the authors using the World Governance Indicators (WGI)

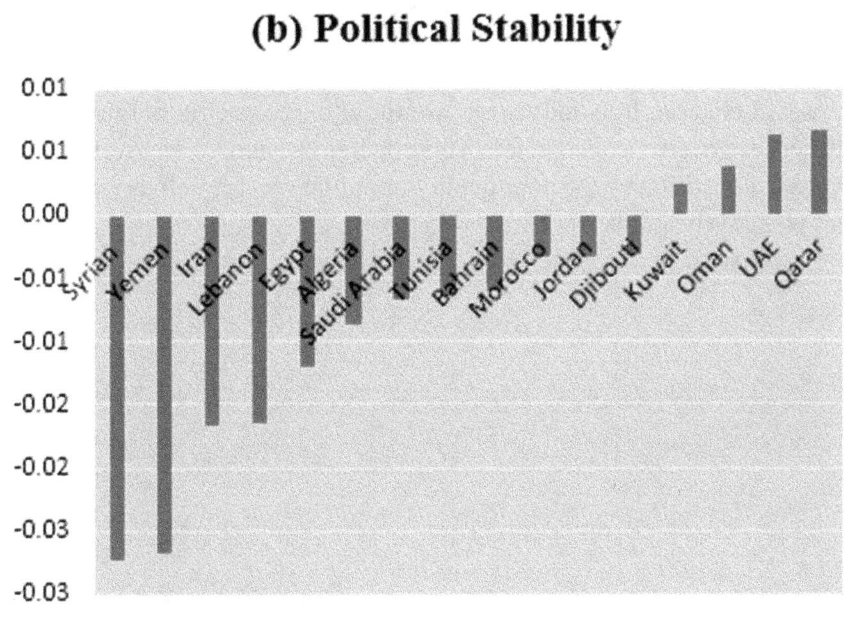

Figure (b) shows that most countries in the region have negative values, with Yemen and Syria being the worst in of political stability. This is justified by the war conditions these two countries have been experiencing since the outbreak of the Arab revolutions in 2011. However, some GCC countries including Oman, Koweït, Qatar and the UAE show positive values, revealing some political stability and the absence of violence and terrorism. It is noteworthy that comparing the political stability indicator with the previous indicator, it is concluded that some countries in the region perform better in terms of stability than in terms of democratic practices.

Figure 14. Institutional Indicators
Source: Conducted by the authors using the World Governance Indicators (WGI)

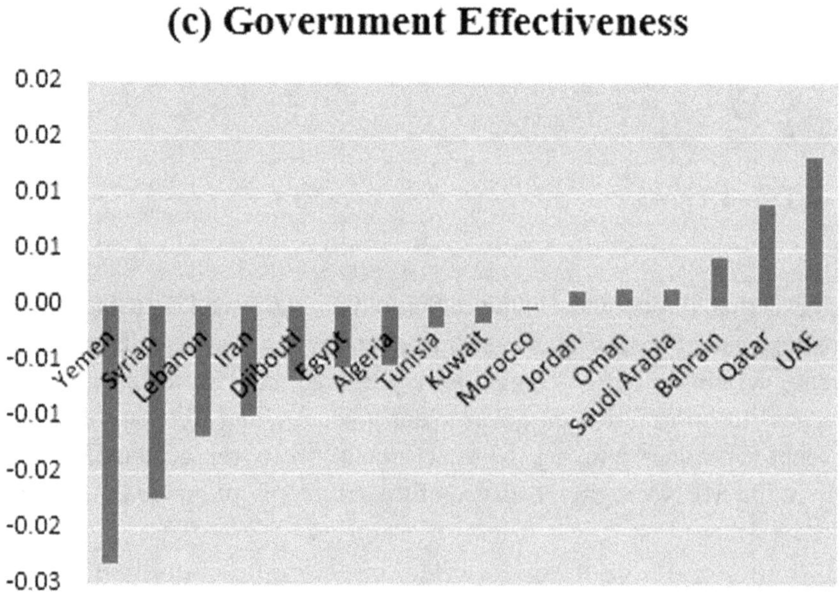

The analysis of figure (c) shows that monarchies perform better in government effectiveness than the fairly pluralistic countries, especially after the Arab revolutions. The indicator ranges from about -2.5 (for Yemen) to almost 1.5 (for the UAE). It is worth noting that the countries with the highest negative values, such as Yemen, Syria, Lebanon, Iran and Egypt, are those experiencing political unrest and conflict, which directly influences government conduct.. This apparent weakness in government performance in the MENA region can be justified by the poor quality of public service delivery, which is mainly due to the corruption that plagues the public sector.

Figure 15. Institutional Indicators
Source: Conducted by the authors using the World Governance Indicators (WGI)

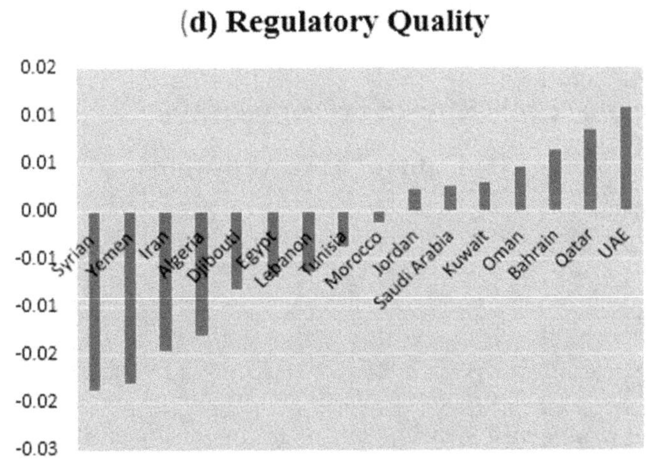

The best score in the figure (d) is for the UAE, at about (1.08), and Syria has the worst (-1.86). Compared to the previous indicator, we notice that the same countries in the region that have recorded a certain level of performance in terms of the quality of public services offered and the effective will to achieve the implemented policies, record a rather better result compared to the rest of the countries in the region. These countries are seeing some improvement in government enforcement of regulations that affect economic life.

Figure 16. Institutional Indicators
Source: Conducted by the authors using the World Governance Indicators (WGI)

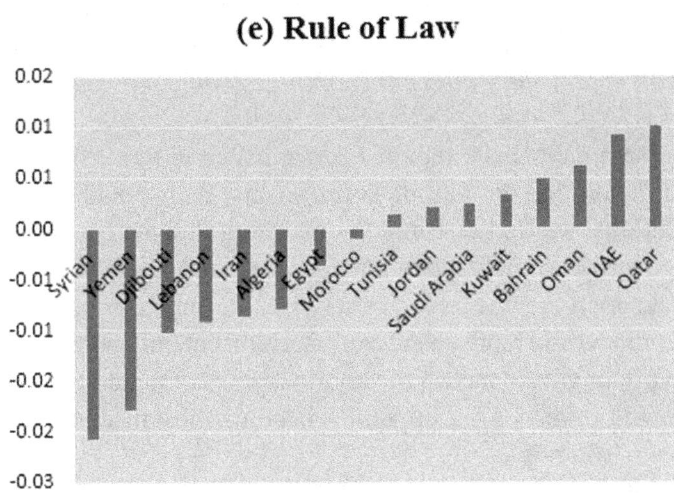

The GCC countries, are the best performers in realizing the role of the law in protecting individuals and their property from violence and looting. Ensuring the security of citizens is a public service, which confirms the performance of these same countries in the region on the indicator above of government effectiveness. Eight of the 16 selected MENA countries have negative scores, revealing a still weak performance in the enforcement of laws and rules and a fragile justice situation in the region.

Figure 17. Institutional Indicators
Source: Conducted by the authors using the World Governance Indicators (WGI)

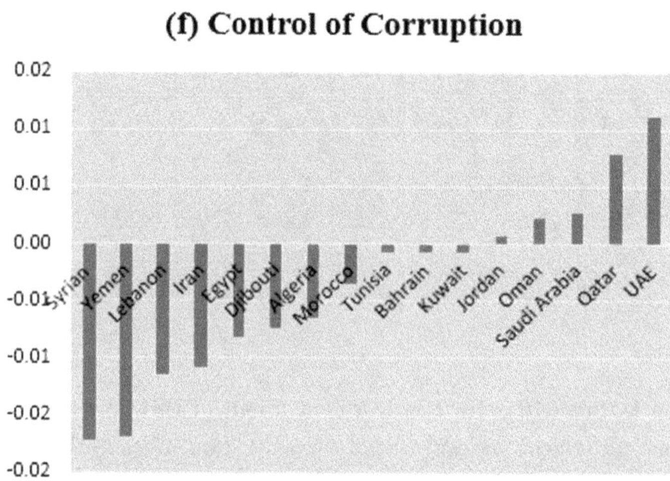

As can be seen from figure (f), the Gulf countries, except of Kuwait, have made efforts to fight corruption, which have resulted in low scores. But they are still ahead of the rest of the MENA countries, which show a weak performance in their fight against this abuse of power for private interests.

"One of the most common specific manifestations of poor governance is corruption, which takes the form of favoritism, nepotism or bribery. By denying the right to fair treatment, corruption denies inclusiveness; it stems from a lack of accountability, internal or external. Thus, it is a symptom of poor governance, even the elimination of corruption alone does not guarantee good governance" World Bank (2003, p 2).

After attempting to assess the MENA region's performance in terms of governance quality by examining the criteria that determine the fate of governments, their credibility, and their commitment to protecting state institutions, we find that middle- and high-income countries, particularly the Gulf countries, have a better governance quality than low-income countries. This confirms the global finding linking good governance to high-income levels. Otherwise, the huge incomes of these countries depend less on an enabling environment and more on the exploitation of abundant natural resources. Yet, despite the efforts made, the quality of governance in the region is low compared to other regions of the world. This unfavorable positioning reflects a lag in public accountability mechanisms and a corruption that corrodes and weakens state institutions.

This part of the descriptive analysis aims to assess the positioning of the MENA region in the new knowledge-based global context. This analysis has been carried out by comparing between the different countries of the region and other regions of the world, using indicators that present the four pillars of the knowledge-based economy. The most striking and inescapable feature is the efforts made by most of the countries in the region to meet the challenges in this continuously evolving context. These efforts include measures to develop the information and telecommunications sector, attempts to improve the education system and adapt it to global requirements, investments in R&D activities leading to a relative increase in scientific production and patents, and attempts to improve the quality of governance, which depends on the level of wealth of countries.

Nevertheless, these measures seem insufficient at almost all levels, as the region still lags behind the developed countries in the global ranking. The North-South digital divide is widening, the illiteracy rate is high, the quality of education is inadequate, the innovation system is weak due to flaws in the education system, and the business environment is repulsive. The question now is whether these dimensions will influence economic growth. A priori, the study of the evolution of growth in the MENA region has shown its high dependence on revenues generated from the exploitation of abundant natural resources. Yet these countries are unable to achieve strong growth compared to other developed regions. We therefore attempt to illustrate the inferences drawn from an econometric analysis to highlight the importance of knowledge in advancing economic growth.

3.2. The Impact of Knowledge on Economic Growth in the MENA Region: An Econometric Analysis

After examining the performance of MENA countries in the knowledge-based economy pillars individually, the objective is to try to position these economies relative to other regions in this new global context. In the following, we propose an aggregate analysis to determine the effects of knowledge on economic growth, through the different indicators of the knowledge economy. This is done through the estimation of an endogenous growth model, using the dynamic panel data technique. Our sample is composed of 16 MENA countries[11] (Algeria, Bahrain, Djibouti, Egypt, Iran, Jordan, Kuwait, Lebanon, Morocco, Oman, Qatar, Saudi Arabia, Syria, Tunisia, United Arab Emirates and Yemen).

3.2.1. Presentation of the Model Variables

The data are collected from the World Bank database "World Development Indicators" (WDI, 2015), they are available annually and we have selected the period 1995-2014. For the data related to the institutional regime, they were taken from the database "The Worldwide Governance Indicators" (WGI, 2015), they are available on the years 1996, 1998, 2000 and from 2002, the data are displayed every year until 2014. The model variables used will be described below in Table 4.

Table 4. Description of variables

Variables	Notation	Measure(s)	Author(s)	Source
The dependent variable				
Economic growth	Y	GDP/capita (current US$) expressed in log	Karagiannis (2007) Siddiquia&Ahmed (2013)	WDI (2015)
The independent variables				
The control variables				
Capital	K	Gross Fixed Capital Formation: GFCF (%GDP)		WDI (2015)
Labor	L	Total labor force		WDI (2015)
Inflation	I	Inflation, consumer prices (% annual)	Tchamyo (2015), Asongu (2013)	WDI (2015)
Domestic savings	S	Gross domestic savings (% GDP)	Siddiquia&Ahmed (2013) Carroll et Weil (1994),	WDI (2015)
The variables of the knowledge economy				
Education	EDU	EP, ES, ESU	Tchamyo (2015), Asongu (2013)	WDI (2015)
Enrollment in primary education Enrollment in secondary education Enrollment in higher education	EP ES ESU	Primary school enrollment (% gross) Secondary school enrollment (% gross) Tertiary enrollment (% gross)		
Information and Communication Technology	TIC	Internet, Mobile Phone, Fixed Phone	Karagiannis (2007), Tchamyo (2015) Asongu (2013)	WDI (2015)
Internet users Cell phone subscribers Fixed telephone lines	Internet Mobile Phone Fixed Phone	Internet users (per 100 inhabitants) Cell phone subscribers (per 100 people) Telephone lines (per 100 inhabitants)		
Innovation	INNOV	AST, Patent, Brand	Karagiannis (2007), Tchamyo (2015), Hasan et Tucci (2010) Asongu (2013)	WDI (2015)
Scientific and technical journal articles Patent applications Trademark applications	AST Patent Brand	Number of scientific and technical journal articles Resident patent applications + non-resident patent applications Total trademark applications		
Institutional regime	RINST	Corrup, ED, REG, SP, EFF-GOV, VR	Tchamyo (2015)	The Worldwide Governance Indicators (WGI, 2015)
Corruption control Rule of Law Regulatory quality Government Efficiency Voice and accountability Political stability	Corrup ED REG EFF-GOV VR SP	These variables are already defined above		
Economic incentives 1 (financial sphere)	ECO 1	Credit, Tx-Inter	Tchamyo (2015) Asongu (2013)	WDI (2015)
Credit Interest rate	Crédit Tx-Inter	Domestic credit provided by the banking sector (% of GDP) Interest rate differential (lending rate - deposit rate, %)		
Economic incentives 2 (commercial sphere)	ECO 2	OC, BT	Siddiquia&Ahmed (2013) Tchamyo (2015) Asongu (2013)	WDI (2015)
Trade openness Tariff barriers	OC BT	sum of exports and imports of goods and services (% GDP) Tariff rate, most favored nation, weighted average, all products (%)		

3.2.2. Methodology and Model Estimation

3.2.2.1. Principal Component Analysis

We have retained four pillars of the knowledge economy predefined by the method developed by the World Bank and called "Knowledge Assessment Methodology". Each dimension is measured by indicators, which can be correlated. In the absence of redundancy in the information provided by each dimension, we used principal component analysis (PCA). This statistical technique reduces a large number of correlated variables to a smaller number of non-correlated variables called principal components (PCs). These PCs explain the greatest proportion of variation in the original data (Cahuzac and Bontemps, 2008). The choice of principal components is determined by criteria derived from Kaiser (1974) and Jolliffe (2002), these two authors recommend principal components with an eigenvalue greater than one (1).

In order to reduce the number of variables, we aim to construct a composite index for each dimension of the knowledge economy. The construction of this synthetic indicator involves the following steps (Nardo et al, 2005): (a) the selection of relevant indicators, (b) Imputation of missing data (to fill in the missing data, we used the "XlStat" software and the estimation method used is called "NIPALS"), (c) Given that the units of measurement of the selected variables are different and to standardize them on the same scale, it is necessary to normalize these indicators by using the "Z-scores" method[12]. According to this technique, the normalization formula is as follows

$$V_n = \frac{X_{it} - \overline{X_{it}}}{\sigma_i^t}$$

With V_n: The normalized variable, X_{it} : The initial variable, $\overline{X_{it}}$: The mean of the initial variable, σ_i^t : The standard deviation of the initial variable. (d) Weighting the indicators, (e) Aggregation of the indicators: this is the final step in obtaining the composite index, which results from the weighted sum of the indicators.After carrying out these steps, we have the composite indices for the different dimensions of the knowledge economy. It should be noted that steps (d) and (e) being done by the SPSS.22 software.

3.2.2.2. Model Specification

Our econometric analysis focuses on 16 MENA countries over the period 1995-2014. It aims to examine the effects of the dimensions of the knowledge-based economy (education, information and communication technologies, innovation, and the economic and institutional framework) on economic growth. The dynamic form of the equation to be estimated is as follows:

$$Y_{it} - Y_{it-1} = \alpha_i + \theta Y_{it-1} + \beta X_{it} + \varepsilon_{it}$$

Where Y_{it} represents the logarithm of the Gross Domestic Product per capita of country i (i = 1....N) over period t (t = 1....T), X_{it} represents a vector of explanatory variables related to the knowledge economy, associated with the other variables that control for growth, α_i an individual specific effect and ε_{it} is the error term.

Our model considers the individual and time dimension, and the individual specific effect α_i which collects unobservable information not considered among the explanatory variables. The autocorrelation problem arises if the independent variables are correlated with the unobservable effects and the ordinary least squares (OLS) estimation will be biased. Thus to solve this problem, the model will be transformed into first differences to discard the individual effect.

Another problem detected generates biased coefficients, when country-specific unobservable effects embedded in the error term ε_{it} are correlated with the explanatory variables.

Thus, the authors (Arellano and Bond, 1991, Arellano and Bover, 1995, Caselli et al, 1996, Blundell and Bond, 1998, Bond et al., 2001) propose the Generalized Moment Method (GMM), which corrects for unobserved heterogeneity, omitted variable bias, measurement error and the endogeneity problem.

The interest of this method, for a growth model, is to solve the endogeneity bias for both the dependent and independent variables. This is done by using the instrumental variables generated by the lagged variables. In fact, the presence of the lagged endogenous variable declines the use of classical econometric techniques such as OLS because of biased and non-convergent estimators in the presence of the correlation between the lagged dependent variable Y_{it-1} and ε_{it} (the error terms are autoregressive).

Two tests must be verified for the dynamic panel GMM namely the Sargan/Hansen overidentification test, which determines the validity of the instruments. Indeed, the null hypothesis of this test assumes the validity of the instruments. That is to say, the lagged instrumental variables are uncorrelated with the residual. This test follows the $\chi 2$ (r-k) degrees of freedom, where r is the number of instruments and k is the number of parameters (estimated coefficients). The second test is the Arellano/Bond autocorrelation test, the null hypothesis represents the absence of second order autocorrelation AR(2) of the errors of the equation in difference.

3.2.2.3. The Contribution of the Knowledge Economy to Economic Growth in the MENA Region: Estimation Results and Interpretations

It should be noted that few studies have dealt with the case of MENA countries in a comprehensive way in the context of the knowledge economy. However, some studies have taken individual country cases, notably Algeria (Djeflat, 2007, 2008), Morocco (Driouchi and Djeflat, 2004), Jordan (Djeflat, 2003).

The descriptive statistics for the variables and the correlation matrix are presented in Appendix (tables 6 and 7).

The results of the dynamic panel models' regressions are summarized in Table 5. To appreciate the specific effects of knowledge, recognized as an indispensable source, on economic growth, we envisage interpreting the variables one by one according to their significance and their strong contributions in determining the level of growth. We outline our analysis by interpreting the control variables.

Table 5. Impact of the knowledge economy on economic growth

Variables	(1)	(2)	(3)	(4)	(5)	(6)	(7)
L.lnGDP/capita	0.834***	0.818***	0.694***	0.645***	0.657***	0.667***	0.654***
	(0.0138)	(0.0162)	(0.0243)	(0.0244)	(0.0257)	(0.0271)	(0.0286)
capital	-0.00283	-0.00247	-0.00826***	-0.00778***	-0.00733***	-0.00719***	-0.00887***
	(0.00185)	(0.00192)	(0.00198)	(0.00193)	(0.00199)	(0.00210)	(0.00229)
lnLabor	0.0207**	0.0154	-0.0255**	-0.171***	-0.167***	-0.0862***	-0.0652*
	(0.0104)	(0.0110)	(0.0120)	(0.0214)	(0.0220)	(0.0325)	(0.0349)
Inflation	-7.57e-06	9.18e-05	-0.000810	0.00302*	0.00403**	0.00207	0.00353
	(0.00179)	(0.00185)	(0.00172)	(0.00173)	(0.00185)	(0.00202)	(0.00218)
Savings	0.0114***	0.0112***	0.0143***	0.0155***	0.0144***	0.0141***	0.0138***
	(0.000928)	(0.000966)	(0.00102)	(0.000999)	(0.00118)	(0.00124)	(0.00128)
IndiceEDU		**0.0488****	**0.0400***	**0.0397***	**0.0508****	**0.0623*****	**0.0779*****
		(0.0226)	(0.0209)	(0.0203)	(0.0215)	(0.0229)	(0.0246)
IndiceTIC			**0.111*****	**0.110*****	**0.117*****	**0.0803*****	**0.0876*****
			(0.0170)	(0.0166)	(0.0173)	(0.0209)	(0.0218)
IndiceINNOV				**0.252*****	**0.233*****	**0.136*****	**0.167*****
				(0.0311)	(0.0333)	(0.0445)	(0.0480)
IndiceECO1					**0.0415****	0.0292	0.0127
					(0.0205)	(0.0218)	(0.0237)
IndiceECO2						**-0.0735*****	**-0.0727*****
						(0.0209)	(0.0215)
IndiceRINST							**0.0910****
							(0.0412)
Constant	0.837***	1.059***	2.769***	5.344***	5.192***	3.891***	3.727***
	(0.189)	(0.221)	(0.333)	(0.454)	(0.471)	(0.618)	(0.641)
Observations	236	236	236	236	236	236	236
Sargan test	[0.045]	[0.069]	[0.159]	[0.091]	[0.188]	[0.336]	[0.291]
AR(1)	[0.000]	[0.000]	[0.000]	[0.001]	[0.000]	[0.000]	[0.000]
AR(2)	[0.118]	[0.173]	[0.162]	[0.212]	[0.257]	[0.577]	[0.912]

Since GDP per capita is positively correlated with its lag variable, this result does not support the convergence theory hypothesis of Barro (1991), which holds that poor countries grow faster than rich countries. Our result justifies the absence of convergence in the MENA countries, so there is a tendency for initially rich countries to grow faster than poor ones over the period considered. Romer (1993) attributes the rapid speed of growth to technological advantages and their diffusion through productive structures. This lack of convergence could be explained by the lack of mobility of capital and labor between countries, the lack of technological transfer from the richer countries to the poorer ones and the lack of income redistribution from the richer to the poorer countries (Chavula, 2013). On the other hand, the high significance of the lagged variable for all seven regressions supports the use of the dynamic panel.

As for the control variables drawn from the literature, we retained the traditional growth factors, namely capital and labor. These factors negatively and significantly affect economic growth in most of the regressions. The theory argues that, in a knowledge-based economy, the traditional factors still exist as sources of growth, but they are not sufficient. Growth cannot be explained by factors of production alone ; there are even countries where these factors account for only a small part of economic growth.

Inflation has a negative impact on economic growth, with insignificant coefficients (regressions (1) and (3)), which may indicate that a policy aimed at controlling inflation allows GDP per capita to increase. Nevertheless, in the rest of the regressions, the coefficients on inflation are positive and significant for regressions (4) and (5). Note that inflation can be a growth stimulator in the context of the MENA countries, especially following large increases in oil prices. The theory has already been shown that GDP growth is closely linked to oil prices, in the MENA region. In addition, the coefficients of domestic savings are positive and highly significant, which confirms the importance of savings for growth through investment and capital accumulation (Carroll and Weil, 1994, Siddiqui and Ahmed, 2013).

As for the pillars of the knowledge economy, the results seem to confirm the existence of a positive and statistically significant correlation between education (IndexEDU) and economic growth for all regressions. For a long time, education has been considered as the main dimension in the creation of knowledge and the acquisition of skills, generating human capital that can influence the development process (Nelson and Phelps, 1966, Lucas, 1988, Barro, 1991, Mankiw et al, 1992, Krueger and Lindahl, 2001). In this sense, the MENA countries, aware of the importance of this pillar, have undertaken reforms to increase enrollment in the three levels of primary, secondary, and especially higher education. They have made some concrete progressNevertheless, these experiences have not escaped criticism, showing that the achievements are focused on the quantitative dimension at the expense of the quality of training and depriving graduates of a better insertion in the labor market.

As illustrated earlier by the graph and the estimation results, the MENA region has made efforts to improve the education system. However, these efforts remain insufficient for the implementation of a knowledge-based economy. Hence the need to revise the educational programs to produce skills that can adapt to the demands of the new global context. However, the expected results are confirmed by our model, the effect of human capital must be supported and complemented by the other dimensions of the knowledge economy to contribute to the general development of the economy of the countries in question.

Moreover, we find that the synthetic index of information and communication technologies (ICT Index) coefficients are positive and highly significant. Nelson and Phelps (1966) confirmed the importance of education in increasing the speed of diffusion of ICT, with a growth-enhancing effect. The most successful technologies are adopted quickly by rich economies in human capital, with a good absorption capacity. Several studies have confirmed this strong positive correlation (Oliner and Sichel, 1994, 2000, Jorgenson and Stiroh, 1995, 1999, Cette et al, 2002, 2004, Audenis et al, 2005, Ben Youssef and M'Henni, 2004, Antonopoulos and Sakellaris, 2009). Talking about the technological revolution reveals two aspects: the ICT user sector and the ICT producer sector. Since we are in the context of the MENA region, we limit ourselves to the first sector. The region has developed its ICT use and diffusion sector through legal measures and significant expenditures to invest in technological infrastructure (internet, fixed and cell phone lines), which is necessary to implement the KBE. But the ICT field in these countries suffers from the absence of technology-producing activities. Despite these weaknesses, ICT is an essential catalyst for the establishment of a knowledge-based economy.

The coefficient on the innovation variable (IndexINNOV) has a positive and significant expected sign. Thus, our results are well aligned with theoretical works (Romer, 1986, 1990, Aghion and Howitt,

1992, Grossman and Helpman, 1994, Coe and Helpman, 1995, Cameron, 1998, Bayoumi et al., 1999, Maurseth and Verspagen, 2002, Bottazzi and Peri, 2003). In fact, as part of its overall strategy to support economic growth in the MENA region, the World Bank has defined innovation as a pillar, which gives rise to a quantitative assessment of knowledge-based development measures. This is achieved through mutual support among various organizations in the economy, including companies, universities, research centers, and consultants, to increase knowledge capital.

From now on, the current global context drives the competitiveness of an economy and its growth prospects by its predisposition to innovate. This is where innovation gets its value and importance, recognized as a fundamental pillar of the knowledge-based economy. The dynamism of knowledge-intensive companies in research and development drives the implementation of the innovation process. However, these companies face various barriers that hinder their R&D and innovation activities throughout the process.

Despite the positive contribution of innovations to economic growth, it remains low when referring to its coefficient in MENA countries. This is justified by the study of Aubert and Reiffers (2003), who argue that the modernization of traditional sectors and the support for emerging industries remain insufficient, and that technological and managerial modernization suffers from the low volume of FDI. In addition, MENA countries have well-developed R&D institutes in some areas, but they are often constrained by rigid regulations, lack of budget autonomy, and lack of incentives to collaborate with industry. This perceived weakness, either through the evolution of the number of patents or scientific and technical articles, illustrated above by the graphs or by the results of the econometric estimation, justifies our subsequent analysis of the issue of innovation and the obstacles faced by firms.

Regarding the economic incentives pillar, which represents the economic conditions for the development of the knowledge-based economy, we chose in line with the theoretical literature (Asongu, 2013, Tchamyo, 2015) to split it into two components: a financial component (IndexECO1) and a trade component (IndexECO2). A positive and significant relationship is observed between the variable (IndexECO1) and GDP per capita. This result reveals the favorable impact of the granting of credit, especially to boost investments, which may contain investments directly related to the implementation of the knowledge economy.

As for the trade component, the link is negative and highly significant between the variable (IndexECO2) and GDP per capita. To conclude on the impact of openness on growth in MENA countries, the coefficients show unexpected results. These results suggest that despite the large flows of knowledge and technology to these countries due to openness and the abolition of tariff barriers, the economic framework seems unfavorable to the acquisition of this knowledge and technology (Chavula, 2013).

Moreover, when looking at the composite index of the institutional regime (IndexRINST) defined by the six dimensions of governance, anti-corruption, the rule of law, public efficiency and others, constructed by Kaufmann, its coefficient is found to be positive and statistically significant (North, 1981, 1990, 1994, Knack and Keefer, 1995, Sachs et al., 1995, Glaeser et al, 2004, Kaufmann et al, 2011...). This variable reflects the characteristics of MENA countries in terms of institutions and their quality. In other words, the quality of governance. Undoubtedly, good governance establishes a timely institutional framework for better economic growth. The region has been making efforts in this regard, especially with the World Bank's approach to establishing an economic and institutional system (lowering tariff barriers, respecting intellectual property, etc.) that provides incentives for the creation and dissemination of knowledge as well as changing the institutional environment that attracts foreign firms, since a more stable and efficient institutional and regulatory environment promotes positive effects on growth.

Although this result is consistent with the theoretical literature, it seems somewhat surprising for the MENA region, since the governance of these economies still contains weaknesses; economic compartmentalization, customs barriers, bureaucracy, lack of accountability, and corruption.

The results provided through our econometric modeling indicate repeatedly significant and positive effects of the knowledge economy pillars on economic growth. Thus, these results are expected in line with previous theoretical work, which confirms the finding of the importance of the contribution of knowledge in stimulating economic growth. It is noteworthy that the picture given by our regressions illustrates the interdependence of the four pillars in accordance with the words of Aubert and Reiffers (2003). They advocate that a knowledge economy strategy cannot rest on one pillar away from the other, but requires a systemic approach that integrates all the components that work together.

CONCLUSION

Several countries have understood that the knowledge economy is the engine of economic growth and insertion in such an economy is a required. Since the 2000s, MENA countries have implemented reforms to strengthen their integration in the new knowledge context. They have invested in all knowledge-related areas, including technology park programs to establish links between training, research, and industry, creating innovative companies, stimulating job creation, and rapidly disseminating knowledge.

Despite the efforts made, these development strategies are lacking in the MENA region compared to other developed regions. Based on our descriptive study and the studies undertaken by the World Bank, MENA is still lagging, despite significant improvements in Jordan, Morocco, Tunisia, Iran, and some Gulf Cooperation Council countries. Important investments in education but not enough quality, poorly developed innovation systems, progress in ICT but still scattered, and institutional environment still suffers from many weaknesses.

However, far from international comparisons, the measures taken to consolidate the pillars of the knowledge economy in the region's countries have produced highly significant results in terms of the internal effects of the knowledge dimensions on economic growth, in accordance with the theoretical literature. These results confirm a growing willingness on the part of the countries and a significant potential of the knowledge-based economy to serve as a sustainable growth stimulator.

Through our analysis, we have been able to place MENA countries relative to other regions. The comparative study has highlighted the reality of innovation via indicators used at the international level (patents and scientific production).

Of course, this study has some limitations. First limitation is that about the approach (of World Bank) used to measure the knowledge-based economy which represents some shortcomings (Canton, 2021; Piech, 2009; Strożek, 2014; Summad et al., 2018). KAM might underestimate the level of development of the knowledge economy when the products of innovation are services or the efficient and competitive production of low-tech products. Furthermore, it does not give a systematic process for the transition towards a knowledge economy and society given the contextual factors of a particular country including higher educational factors. Second limitation is that about the limited number of countries (from the MENA region) studied due to the availability of data. Third limitation is that about the heterogeneity of the sample of countries studied: oil-producing countries and other countries.

From above limitations, further research ought to be conducting in the following directions; (a) Differentiate, within the MENA region, between high-income countries and others (b) expand the sample of countries studied by integrating other regions, (c) develop more relevant indicators, available for assessment and accessible to databases.

REFERENCES

Aghion, P., & Howitt, P. (1992). A model of growth through creative destruction. *Journal of The Econometric Society*, *60*(2), 323–351.

Ahmed, E. M., & Ridzuan, R. (2013). The impact of ICT on East Asian economic growth: Panel estimation approach. *Journal of the Knowledge Economy*, *4*(4), 540–555.

Amable, B., & Askenazy, P. (2003). *Introduction à l'économie de la connaissance*. UNESCO.

Andersson, T., & Djeflat, A. (Eds.). (2012). *The real issues of the Middle East and the Arab Spring: Addressing research, innovation and entrepreneurship*. Springer Science & Business Media.

Antonopoulos, A., & Sakellaris, P. (2009). The contribution of Information and Communication Technology investments to Greek economic growth: An analytical growth accounting framework. *Information Economics and Policy*, *21*, 171–191.

Armeanu, D. Ş., Vintilă, G., & Gherghina, Ş. C. (2017). Empirical study towards the drivers of sustainable economic growth in EU-28 countries. *Sustainability*, *10*(1), 1–22.

Arrow, K. J. (1962). The Economic Implications of Learning by Doing. *The Review of Economic Studies*, *29*(3), 155–173.

Aubert, J. E., & Reiffers, J. L. (Eds.). (2003). *Knowledge economies in the Middle East and North Africa: Toward new development strategies*. World Bank Publications.

Audenis, C., Deroyon, J., & Fourcade, N. (2005). L'impact des Nouvelles Technologies de l'Information et de la Communication sur l'économie française. *Revue économique*, *56*(1), 99–125.

Barro, R. J. (1991). Economic growth in a cross section of countries. *The Quarterly Journal of Economics*, *106*(2), 407–443.

Barro, R. J. (2001). Human capital and growth. *The American Economic Review*, *91*(2), 12–17.

Bayoumi, T., Coe, D. T., & Helpman, E. (1999). R&D spillovers and global growth. *Journal of International Economics*, *47*(2), 399–428.

Ben Youssef, A., & M'Henni, H. (2004). Les effets des technologies de l'information et de la communication sur la croissance économique: Le cas de la Tunisie. *Revue Région et Développement*, *19*, 132–150.

Benhabib, J., & Spiegel, M. M. (1994). The role of human capital in economic development evidence from aggregate cross-country data. *Journal of Monetary Economics*, *34*(2), 143–173.

Bils, M., & Klenow, P. J. (2000). Does schooling cause growth? *The American Economic Review*, *90*(5), 1160–1183.

Borner, S., Bodmer, F., & Kobler, M. (2004). L'efficience institutionnelle et ses déterminants. *Le rôle des facteurs politiques dans la croissance économique.*

Bottazzi, L., & Peri, G. (2003). Innovation and spillovers in regions: Evidence from European patent data. *European Economic Review, 47*(4), 687-710.

Brousseau, É. (2001). E-economie qu'y a-t-il de nouveau ? *Annuaire des relations internationales.*

Cameron, G. (1998). *Innovation and Growth: a survey of the empirical evidence.* Nuffield College.

Canton, H. (2021). Economic Commission for Latin America and the Caribbean—ECLAC. In *The Europa Directory of International Organizations* (pp. 142-144). Routledge. doi:10.4324/9781003179900-19

Castelló, A., & Doménech, R. (2002). Human capital inequality and economic growth: Some new evidence. *Economic Journal (London), 112*(478), 187–200.

Castelló-Climent, A. (2010). Channels through which human capital inequality influences economic growth. *Journal of Human Capital, 4*(4), 394–450.

Cette, G., Mairesse, J., & Kocoglu, Y. (2002). Croissance économique et diffusion des TIC: le cas de la France sur longue période (1980-2000). *Revue française d'économie, 16*(3), 155-192.

Cette, G., Mairesse, J., & Kocoglu, Y. (2004). Diffusion des TIC et croissance potentielle. *Revue d'Économie Politique, 114*(1), 77–97.

Chen, D. H., & Dahlman, C. J. (2005). *The knowledge economy, the KAM methodology and World Bank operations.* World Bank Institute Working Paper, (37256).

Chen, D. H. C., & Dahlman, C. J. (2004). *Knowledge and development: a cross-section approach* (Vol. 3366). World Bank Publications.

Coe, D. T., & Helpman, E. (1995). International r&d spillovers. *European Economic Review, 39*(5), 859–887.

Colecchia, A., & Schreyer, P. (2002). ICT investment and economic growth in the 1990s: is the United States a unique case?: a comparative study of nine OECD countries. *Review of Economic Dynamics, 5*(2), 408–442.

Colecchia, A., & Schreyer, P. (2002). The contribution of information and communication technologies to economic growth in nine OECD countries. *OECD Economic Studies, 2002*(1), 153–171.

Commissariat Général du plan. (2001). *Séminaire économie de la connaissance.* Author.

Commission des communautés européennes. (2008). *Communication de la commission au parlement européen et au conseil: Le processus de Barcelone: Union pour la Méditerranée.* Author.

David, P. A., & Foray, D. (2002). Une introduction à l'économie et à la société du savoir. *Revue internationale des sciences sociales*, (1), 13-28.

Diallo, D. (2006). Les clusters innovants et leurs atouts: le cas des clusters numériques. *Vie sciences de l'entreprise*, (1), 9-24.

Djeflat, A. (2007). Rôle et place des TIC dans une économie fondée sur la connaissance. In Le Maghreb dans l'économie numérique. Institut de recherche sur le Maghreb contemporain. doi:10.4000/books.irmc.392

Djeflat, A. (2008). *L'Algérie et ldes défis de l'économie de la connaissance*. Academic Press.

Djeflat, A. (2012). *Les efforts du Maroc dans l'économie fondée sur la connaissance*. CMI Marseille, Rapport Septembre.

Dosi, G. (1988). Sources, procedures, and microeconomic effects of innovation. *Journal of Economic Literature*, 1120–1171.

Driouchi, A., Azelmad, E. M., & Anders, G. C. (2006). An econometric analysis of the role of knowledge in economic performance. *The Journal of Technology Transfer*, *31*(2), 241–255.

Drucker, P. (1968). From capitalism to knowledge society. In The knowledge economy. Butterworth.

Dutraive, V. (2008). Économie fondée sur la connaissance et théories récentes de la firme: Une lecture veblenienne. *Revue d'Economie Industrielle*, (124), 51–70.

Dutta, D., & Otsuka, K. (2004). *Knowledge Spillover from Information and Communication Technology: A Comparative Study of Australia*. Department of Economics.

Emmanuel, H. (2015). *Diagnostic du système national de recherche et d'innovation en Tunisie*. Rapport final, dans le cadre de Projet d'Appui au Système de Recherche et Innovation (PASRI).

Encoua, D., Foray, D., Hatchuel, A., & Mairesse, J. (2004). Les Enjeux économiques de l'innovation. Bilan du programme CNRS. *Revue d'économie publique, 114*(2), 133-168.

Fagiolo, G., Giachini, D., & Roventini, A. (2020). Innovation, finance, and economic growth: An agent-based approach. *Journal of Economic Interaction and Coordination*, *15*(3), 703–736.

Fonds Monétaire International. (2013). Perspectives économiques régionales: Moyen Orient et Afrique du Nord: Définir la voie à suivre. Washington, DC: FMI.

Foray, D. (2000). *L'économie de la connaissance*. La découverte.

Ganau, R. (2017). Institutions and economic growth in Africa: A spatial econometric approach. *Economics and Politics*, *34*(3), 425–444.

Glaeser, E. L., La Porta, R., Lopez-de-Silanes, F., & Shleifer, A. (2004). Do institutions cause growth? *Journal of Economic Growth*, *9*(3), 271–303.

Godin, B. (2006). The knowledge-based economy: Conceptual framework or buzzword? *The Journal of Technology Transfer*, *31*(1), 17–30.

Griliches, Z. (1998). Introduction. In R&D and productivity: The econometric evidence (pp. 1-14). University of Chicago Press.

Grossman, G. M., & Helpman, E. (1994). Endogenous innovation in the theory of growth. *The Journal of Economic Perspectives*, *8*(1), 23–44.

Gyekye, A. B., & Oseifuah, E. K. (2015). Knowledge and economic growth: a comparative analysis of three regional blocks in sub-Saharan Africa. *Environmental Economics*, *6*(4), 196-208.

Hall, R. E., & Jones, C. I. (1999). Why do some countries produce so much more output per worker than others? *The Quarterly Journal of Economics*, *114*(1), 83–116.

Harris, R. G. (2001). The knowledge-based economy: Intellectual origins and new economic perspectives. *International Journal of Management Reviews*, *3*(1), 21–40.

Hasan, I., & Tucci, C. L. (2010). The innovation–economic growth nexus: Global evidence. *Research Policy*, *39*(10), 1264–1276.

Hava, H. T., & Erturgut, R. (2010). An evaluation of education relations together with technology, employement and economic development components. *Procedia: Social and Behavioral Sciences*, *2*(2), 1771–1775.

Hsaini, A. (2007). *Le système national d'innovation et de recherche en Tunisie: Un essai de caractérisation et d'évaluation du rôle des centres techniques*. Université Pierre Mondes.

Jouyet, J. P., & Lévy, M. (2006). L'économie de l'immatériel, la croissance de demain. *Rapport de la Commission sur l'économie de l'immatériel. Rapport au Ministre de l'industrie*.

Kacprzyk, A., & Doryń, W. (2017). Innovation and economic growth in old and new member states of the European Union. *Economic research- Ekonomska Istrazivanja*, *30*(1), 1724–1742.

Karagiannis, S. (2007). The knowledge-based economy, convergence and economic growth: Evidence from the European Union. *Journal of Economic Asymmetries*, *4*(2), 65–85.

Kaufmann, D., Kraay, A., & Mastruzzi, M. (2005). *Governance matters IV: governance indicators for 1996-2004*. World bank policy research working paper series, (3630).

Kaufmann, D., Kraay, A., & Mastruzzi, M. (2011). The Worldwide Governance Indicators: Methodology and Analytical Issues1. *Hague Journal on the Rule of Law*, *3*(2), 220–246.

Kendrick, J. W. (1994). Total capital and economic growth. *Atlantic Economic Journal*, *22*(1), 1–18.

Knack, S., & Keefer, P. (1995). Institutions and economic performance: Cross-country tests using alternative institutional measures. *Economics and Politics*, *7*(3), 207–227.

Kocourek, A., & Nedomlelová, I. (2018). Three levels of education and the economic growth. *Applied Economics*, *50*(19), 2103–2116.

Korres, G. M., & Patsikas, S., & Polichronopoulos, G. (2002). A knowledge based economy, the socio-economic impact and the effects on regional growth. *Ecological Informatics*, *2*(1), 5–12.

Krueger, A. B., & Lindahl, M. (2001). Education for growth: Why and for whom? *Journal of Economic Literature*, *39*(4), 1101–1136.

Le Douaron, P. (2002). La formation tout au long de la vie. *Revue française d'administration publique*, (4), 573-580.

Lee, K., & Kim, B. Y. (2009). Both institutions and policies matter but differently for different income groups of countries: Determinants of long-run economic growth revisited. *World Development*, *37*(3), 533–549.

Léné, A. (2005). L'éducation, la formation et l'économie de la connaissance: Approches économiques. *Education et Sociétés*, (1), 91–103.

Liao, L., Du, M., Wang, B., & Yu, Y. (2019). The impact of educational investment on sustainable economic growth in Guangdong, China: A cointegration and causality analysis. *Sustainability*, *11*(3), 766.

Liouane, N. (2009). Ouverture et croissance économique dans les pays MENA, étude dynamique des effets des facteurs structurels et institutionnels. In *Le Maghreb face aux défis de l'ouverture en Méditerranée*. L'Harmattan.

Lucas, R. E. Jr. (1988). On the mechanics of economic development. *Journal of Monetary Economics*, *22*(1), 3–42.

Lundvall, B. Å., & Foray, D. (1996). The knowledge-based economy: from the economics of knowledge to the learning economy. Employment and Growth in the Knowledge-based Economy.

M'henni, H., Ben Othman, A., Ghozzi, C., Ben Salah, N., M'henni, S., & Trabelsi, M. (2007). *Le système national de recherche en Tunisie*. ESTIME Project Report.

Machlup, F. (1962). *The production and distribution of knowledge in the United States* (Vol. 278). Princeton university press.

Mankiw, N. G., Romer, D., & Weil, D. N. (1992). A contribution to the empirics of economic growth. *The Quarterly Journal of Economics*, *107*(2), 407–437.

Marquez-Ramos, L., & Mourelle, E. (2019). *Education and economic growth: an empirical analysis of nonlinearities*. Applied Economic Analysis.

Maurseth, P. B., & Verspagen, B. (2002). Knowledge spillovers in Europe: A patent citations analysis. *The Scandinavian Journal of Economics*, *104*(4), 531–545.

Mihaela, M., & Ţiţan, E. (2014). Education and innovation in the context of economies globalization. *Procedia Economics and Finance*, *15*, 1042–1046.

Mingyong, L., Shuijun, P., & Qun, B. (2006). Technology spillovers, absorptive capacity and economic growth. *China Economic Review*, *17*(3), 300–320.

Mondiale, B. (2003). Vers une meilleure gouvernance au Moyen-Orient et en Afrique du Nord. Améliorer l'inclusivité et la responsabilisation, Rapport sur le développement au Moyen-Orient et en Afrique du Nord.

Mondiale, B. (2008). Un parcours non encore achevé: la réforme de l'éducation au Moyen-Orient et en Afrique du Nord. Rapport sur le développement de la région MENA, Résumé analytique.

Mondiale, B. (2010). Moyen-Orient et Afrique du Nord: Perspectives économiques mondiales: Vents budgétaires contraires et reprise. Academic Press.

Mondiale, B. (2021). Vivre avec la dette: Comment les institutions peuvent tracer la voie de la reprise dans la région Moyen-Orient et Afrique du Nord, Bulletin d'information économique de la région MENA. Academic Press.

MRSTDC, (2006b). *R&D et innovation en Tunisie: Principaux indicateurs et positionnement international.* Technical report, Bureau des Etudes Prospectives de la Planification et des Statistiques, Ministère de la Recherche Scientifique, de la Technologie et du Développement des Compétences.

Nair, M., Pradhan, R. P., & Arvin, M. B. (2020). Endogenous dynamics between R&D, ICT and economic growth: Empirical evidence from the OECD countries. *Technology in Society*, *62*, 101315.

Nelson, R. R., & Phelps, E. S. (1966). Investment in humans, technological diffusion, and economic growth. *The American Economic Review*, *56*(1/2), 69–75.

North, D. (1990). Institutions, Institutional Change and Economic Performance. Cambridge University Press. doi:10.1017/CBO9780511808678

North, D. C. (1981). *Structure and change in economic history*. Norton.

North, D. C. (1994). Economic performance through time. *The American Economic Review*, *84*(3), 359–368.

Nour, S. S. O. M. (2015). Overview of knowledge economy in the Arab region. *Journal of the Knowledge Economy*, *6*(4), 870–904.

OCDE. (1995). *La mesure des activités scientifiques et technologiques, manuel sur la mesure des ressources humaines consacrées à la science et la technologie: Manuel de Canberra*. OCDE.

OCDE. (1996). *The knowledge-based economy*. OCDE.

OCDE. (2001). *Nouveaux indicateurs de la science et de la technologie*. STI Revue (N° 27).

OCDE. (2005). *Science, technologie et industrie: Tableau de bord de l'OCDE*. OCDE.

OCDE. (2018). *Science, technologie et industrie: Tableau de bord de l'OCDE 2017: La transformation numérique*. Éditions OCDE.

Oketch, M. O. (2006). Determinants of human capital formation and economic growth of African countries. *Economics of Education Review*, *25*(5), 554–564.

Oliner, S. D., & Sichel, D. E. (2000). The resurgence of growth in the late 1990s: Is information technology the story? *The Journal of Economic Perspectives*, *14*(4), 3–22.

Oliner, S. D., Sichel, D. E., Triplett, J. E., & Gordon, R. J. (1994). Computers and output growth revisited: How big is the puzzle? *Brookings Papers on Economic Activity*, *1994*(2), 273–334.

Paul, J. J., & Suleman, F. (2005). La production de connaissances dans la société de la connaissance: Quel rôle pour le système éducatif? *Education et Sociétés*, (1), 19–43.

Perez, C. (1983). Structural change and assimilation of new technologies in the economic and social systems. *Futures*, *15*(5), 357–375.

Piech, K. (2009). *Wiedza i innowacje w rozwoju gospodarczym: w kierunku pomiaru i współczesnej roli państwa*. Instytut Wiedzy i Innowacji.

Polanyi, M. (1966). *The tacit dimension*. Doubleday.

Powell, W. W., & Snellman, K. (2004). The knowledge economy. *Annual Review of Sociology*, *30*, 199–220.

Pradhan, R. P., Arvin, M. B., Nair, M., Bennett, S. E., & Hall, J. H. (2019). The information revolution, innovation diffusion and economic growth: An examination of causal links in European countries. *Quality & Quantity*, *53*(3), 1529–1563.

Pritchett, L. (2001). Where has all the education gone? *The World Bank Economic Review*, *15*(3), 367–391.

Rodrik, D., Subramanian, A., & Trebbi, F. (2004). Institutions rule: The primacy of institutions over geography and integration in economic development. *Journal of Economic Growth*, *9*(2), 131–165.

Romer, P. M. (1986). Increasing returns and long-run growth. *Journal of Political Economy*, *94*(5), 1002–1037.

Romer, P. M. (1990). Endogenous technological change. *Journal of Political Economy*, *98*(5, Part 2), S71–S102.

Sachs, J. D., & Warner, A. (1997). *Natural resource abundance and economic growth*. Academic Press.

Sachs, J. D., & Warner, A. M. (2001). The curse of natural resources. *European Economic Review*, *45*(4-6), 827–838.

Schreyer, P. (2000). *The contribution of information and communication technology to output growth: a study of the G7 countries*. Academic Press.

Schumpeter, J. A. (1942). Capitalism, socialism and democracy. Academic Press.

Setayesh, M. H., & Daryaei, A. A. (2017). Good governance, innovation, economic growth and the stock market turnover rate. *The Journal of International Trade & Economic Development*, *26*(7), 829–850.

Solow, R. M. (1956). A contribution to the theory of economic growth. *The Quarterly Journal of Economics*, *70*(1), 65–94.

Steinmueller, W. E. (2002). Knowledge-based economies and information and communication technologies. *International Social Science Journal*, *54*(171), 141–153.

Stokey, N. L. (1995). R&D and economic growth. *The Review of Economic Studies*, *62*(3), 469–489.

Strożek, P. (2014). A spatial analysis of the knowledge-based economy in Poland. *Comparative Economic Research*, *17*(4), 221–236.

Summad, E., Al-Kindi, M., Shamsuzzoha, A., Piya, S., & Ibrahim, M. K. (2018, January). A Framework to Assess a Knowledge-Based Economy: Special Focus to Higher Educational Institutions. In *Proceedings of the International Conference on Industrial Engineering and Operations Management Paris, France, July* (pp. 26-27). Academic Press.

Sundać, D., & Fatur Krmpotić, I. (2011). Knowledge economy factors and the development of knowledge-based economy. *Croatian Economic Survey*, (13), 105-141.

Tchamyou, V. S., Asongu, S. A., & Odhiambo, N. M. (2019). The role of ICT in modulating the effect of education and lifelong learning on income inequality and economic growth in Africa. *African Development Review*, *31*(3), 261–274.

Tocan, M. C. (2012). Knowledge based economy assessment. *Journal of Knowledge Management, Economics and Information Technology*, *2*(5), 1–13.

Wanjiru, R., & Prime, K. S. (2018). Institutions, economic growth and international competitiveness: a regional study. In *Contemporary Issues in International Business* (pp. 99–124). Palgrave Macmillan.

Winter, S. (1987). Knowledge and Competence as Strategic Assets. *The Competitive Challenge: Strategies for Industrial Innovation and Renewal*, 159-184.

World Bank. (2007). *Région Moyen-Orient et Afrique du Nord 2007: Développements récents et perspectives économiques: La création d'emplois en période de forte croissance*. World Bank.

World Bank. (2008). *Knowledge for development, the world bank Institute's program on building knowledge economies*. World Bank.

World Bank. (2009). *Middle East and North Africa Region 2008: Economic developments and prospects: Regional integration for global competitiveness*. World Bank.

World Bank. (2010). *Measuring knowledge in the world's economies: Knowledge assessment methodology and knowledge economy index*. World Bank.

World Bank. (2016). *Global economic prospects: Divergences and risks*. World Bank.

World Economic Forum. (2019. *The Global Competitiveness Report 2019*. Author.

Yang, C. H. (2006). Is innovation the story of Taiwan's economic growth? *Journal of Asian Economics*, *17*(5), 867–878.

ENDNOTES

1 Presidency Conclusions, Lisbon European Council, 23 and 24 March 2000.

2 For more details, consult this address: KAM - www.worldbank.org/kam.

3 Lisbon European Council, 23 and 24 March 2000, Presidency Conclusions.

4 The sample of MENA countries includes Algeria, Bahrain, Djibouti, Egypt, Iran, Jordan, Kuwait, Lebanon, Morocco, Oman, Qatar, Saudi Arabia, Syria, Tunisia, United Arab Emirates and Yemen.

5 Some countries in the sample were eliminated for lack of data, notably Syria, Lebanon, Jordan, and Yemen.

6 Some countries in the sample were eliminated for lack of data, notably Syria and Yemen.

7 Some MENA region countries are not mentioned in the graph due to a lack of data for United Arab Emirates, Egypt, Kuwait, Djibouti, Jordan, Yemen and Lebanon over the selected years.

8 Patent applications are determined by the sum of nonresident patent applications and resident patent applications.

9 GCC countries, such as the United Arab Emirates, Qatar, Kuwait, and Oman, are not included in Figure 8 due to the unavailability of data for all selected years.

10 The governance estimate ranges from approximately -2.5 (low governance performance) to 2.5 (high governance performance).

11 Israel is eliminated from the sample since in the area of knowledge, it stands out as having very high values compared to the rest of the countries in the region, leading to results that are difficult to interpret, due to the heterogeneity of the sample.

12 This method is commonly used, bringing all variables to a common scale with a mean of 0 and a standard deviation of 1.

APPENDIX

Table 6. Descriptive Statistics

Variable	Obs	Mean	Std. Dev.	Min	Max
LnGDP/capita	319	8.501803	1.366259	5.631102	11.4797
capital	289	22.88336	6.065338	7.869903	38.23645
Ln Labor	320	15.17957	1.978485	12.09488	20.88303
Inflation	271	5.838032	7.182683	-4.863278	55.08111
Savings	313	28.16073	19.2929	-15.06739	74.61317
Indice EDU	320	-1.25e-07	0.999999	-5.11103	2.66051
Indice TIC	320	-3.12e-07	1	-1.16752	2.77667
Indice INNOV	320	-3.12e-08	1	-.3094	6.52423
Indice ECO 1	320	-3.13e-07	0.999999	-3.26862	2.24655
Indice ECO 2	320	2.19e-07	1	-2.46861	2.10435
Indice RINST	320	3.12e-08	0.999999	-2.97301	2.30402

Table 7. Correlation matrix

	lnGDP/Capita	Capital	lnLabor	Inflation	Savings	Indice EDU	Indice TIC	Indice INNOV	Indice ECO1	Indice ECO2	Indice RINST
lnGDP/capita	1										
capital	-0,1029	1									
lnLabor	-0,4475	0,1515	1								
Inflation	-0,2870	0,1649	0,2643	1							
Savings	0,6339	0,1439	-0,0154	-0,0090	1						
IndiceEDU	0,6148	0,0275	-0,2320	-0,2042	0,2871	1					
IndiceTIC	0,7440	0,0790	-0,1922	-0,1099	0,4121	0,4642	1				
IndiceINNOV	-0,2383	0,1003	0,7246	0,0809	-0,0402	-0,0473	-0,0803	1			
IndiceECO1	-0,3076	-0,0226	0,1533	-0,0526	0,1382	-0,3441	-0,3679	0,1886	1		
IndiceECO2	-0,5594	0,1151	0,4912	0,2402	-0,1347	-0,3844	-0,5156	0,1389	0,1237	1	
IndiceRINST	0,5142	-0,1578	-0,5832	-0,3571	0,1140	0,3559	0,2589	-0,4743	-0,2147	-0,4003	1

Chapter 11
Digital Transformation Driven by Internet Data Center:
Case Studies on China

Poshan Yu
https://orcid.org/0000-0003-1069-3675
Soochow University, China & Australian Studies Centre, Shanghai University, China

Haiyue Gu
Shanghai University, China

Yue Zhao
Independent Researcher, China

Aashrika Ahuja
Independent Researcher, India

EXECUTIVE SUMMARY

With the acceleration of the digital transformation and technological upgradation of various industries, in the wake of application of new technologies such as 5G, artificial intelligence, and the internet of things, the demand for data storage, computing, transmission, and applications has greatly increased. Remote working, remote education, and e-commerce on account of the pandemic have led to a drastic increase in data consumption as well. The processing and analysis of massive data requires the construction of an information infrastructure—Internet Data Center (IDC). In the past few years, China's government has been dedicating itself to the task of constructing IDCs in some underdeveloped areas and establishing more detailed regulations. This chapter introduces some basic policies and implications behind this and a mathematical way to quantitatively analyse the investment efficiency of R&D resources in China's different regions. Several recommendations for the government and the society at large have also been outlined in this chapter for improvement in the whole ecosystem for IDCs in China.

DOI: 10.4018/978-1-7998-8417-0.ch011

1. INTRODUCTION

A data center serves as a hub of storing servers, network systems and subsystems, networking switches, routers, firewalls as well as all kind of information technology equipment for organizing, storing, processing and disseminating a large amount of data. Internet Data Center (IDC) is thus, a place that contains a large number of servers and auxiliary components. According to the rack scale, IDC can be divided into: super-large data centers, large data centers, medium data centers, micro data centers (computer rooms) and other types of data centers (Vance, 2008).

As the world economy continues to undergo a digital transformation mode, more and more industries are extracting valuable information by using structured or unstructured data resources such as the Internet of Things, Industrial Internet, and e-commerce. The processing and analysis of massive data requires construction of an information infrastructure—IDC. The scale and quality of information infrastructure construction will directly determine the speed and height of economic development in the current digital economy era. IDC is the underlying infrastructure of the smart economy and the construction of IDC is a necessary requirement for industrial digital transformation, which now has become a matter of international competitiveness (Cahen & Borini, 2020).

It is worth noting that, in recent years, China's policy has favored the construction of IDC in three- and four-tier cities such as Guizhou, rather than in one - and two-tier cities with higher economic levels and more high-tech industries, for example, Beijing and Shanghai.

This article mainly focuses on "triple helix" approach – coordinated efforts between academia, industry and government as a catalyst for transition and as a tool of fostering innovation (Wang, 2019). To explain that idea more clearly, a statistical method was applied to the data collected from 2006 to 2020 and this chapter briefly outlines the same. Section 2 talks about the current characteristics of IDC in China and other main developing countries, especially chalking out a contrast between the situation of developed and underdeveloped areas in China. Section 3 discusses about the role of the governments at all levels, including municipal, provincial and national. Section 4 answers an important question, about there being more focus on underdeveloped areas rather than in developed areas for this kind of technology. Section 5 uses some statistical methods to evaluate the input-output efficiency of China's R&D resources. Section 6 demonstrates the opportunities and challenges for construction of IDC in China. Lastly, section 7 provides a brief conclusion and discusses some possible recommendations for the IDC industry and the whole economy.

2. AN OVERVIEW OF IDCS IN DEVELOPING COUNTRIES

2.1 Characteristics of IDCS in China

2.1.1 Overall Situation

According to statistics from CCID Consulting (2020), there are currently approximately 74,000 IDCs in China, accounting for almost 23% of the total number of IDCs in the world. However, the proportion of large and super-large data centers in China still has a lot of room for development. In 2019, the number of super-large and large data centers accounted for 12.7%. Also, there are 320 data centers under construction. After completion, it is estimated that the number of super-large and large data centers will account for 36.1% of total number of IDC's (Wang, 2020). There is still a huge gap between China and developed countries such as the United States, where super-large data centers account for 40% of the global total count (CCID, 2020).

According to data released by Gartner (2020), from 2018 to 2020, the proportion of China's data center system expenditures to IT expenditures have increased on an yearly basis: In 2020, China's IT expenditure reached TO 2.84 trillion yuan, of which data center system expenditure was 250.8-billion-yuan, accounting for 8.85% of the total IT expenditure (Figure 1).

Figure 1.

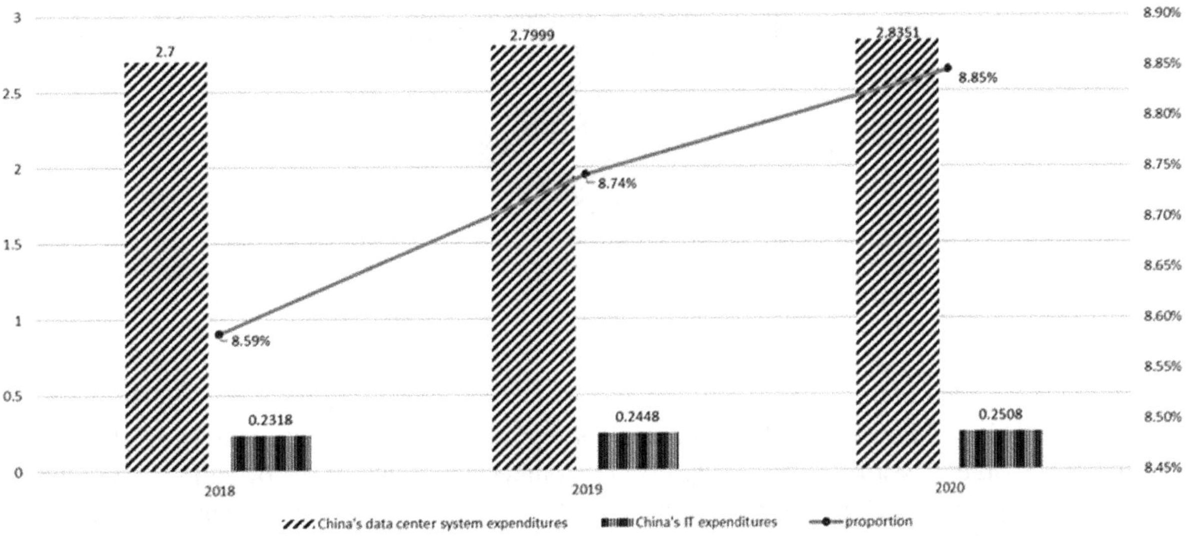

At present, China's data application is experiencing a transition from the consumer Internet of things to the industrial Internet of things. China has become one of the countries with the scope for most active, potential and optimal environment for big data applications to thrive in the whole world. However, China's IDC are plagued by problems such as imbalance between supply and demand. Some eastern regions have high application demand but are limited by high energy consumption cost and difficulties in building large-scale data centers (Jia, 2017); while some western regions are rich in renewable energy and have a suitable climate, but because of the high transmission cost, it is hard to effectively meet the eastern demand. This gap needs to be filled by a sustainable model in the long run that serves the purpose as well and at the same time enables effective utilization of resources at the same time.

2.1.2 Contrasting Differences Between Developed and Underdeveloped Areas

Data center manufacturers tend to invest in provinces (autonomous regions, municipalities) with high economic development, high population density, large data flow, and strong demand for industrial digital transformation. At present, there is still a high demand for data center construction in developed areas. According to China's Open Data Center Committee (CODCC), Beijing, Guangdong, and Jiangsu provinces rank in the top three in terms of number of IDC, with IDCs accounting for 14%, 13%, and 10% respectively (Figure 2).

Figure 2.

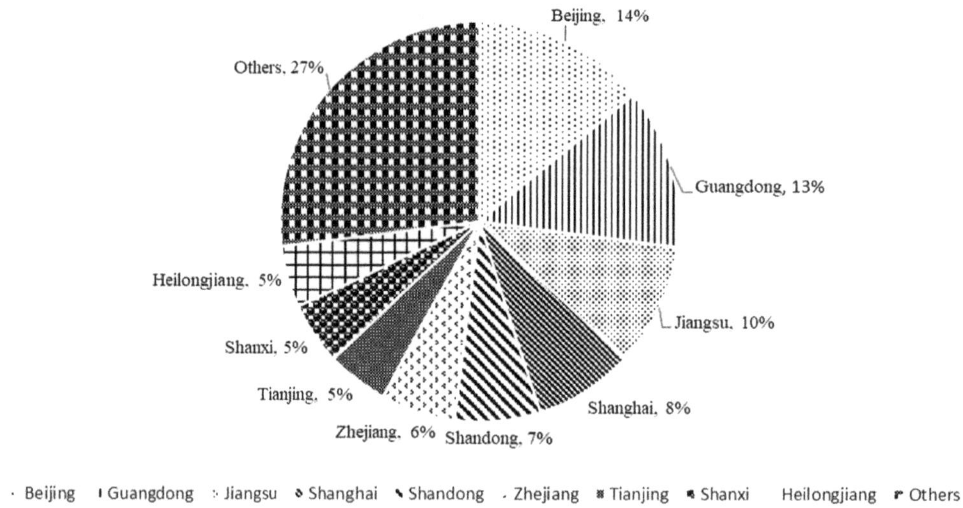

From the perspective of the regional distribution of IDC investment scale, the regions of North China, East China, and Central South are still the three major regional markets for data centers. In 2019, these three regional market investment scales (Figure 3) accounted for 79.6% of the overall scale (CODCC, 2021). At present, the core clusters for the development of China's IDC industry are in relatively developed areas such as Beijing, Shanghai, Guangdong, Jiangsu, and Zhejiang. These areas have an excellent foundation for the information industry, such as the continuous improvement of infrastructure, gradually expanding industrial scale, relatively complete industrial chain, and industry ready manpower (Xu, 2018).

Figure 3.

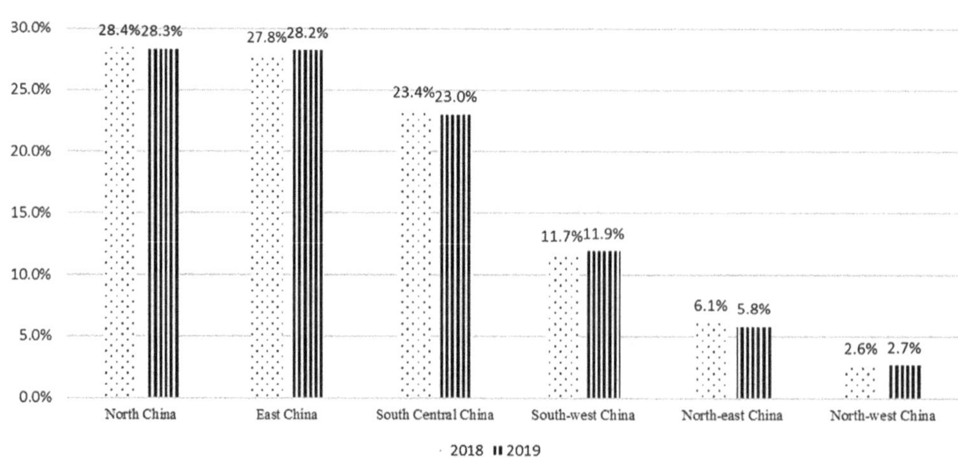

The rising demand for internet data centers is increasing global warming and exacerbating shortages of water resources. Reduction in consumption of electricity and efficient utilization of water resources are some of the most pressing issues that need attention if China wants to play a transformative role towards realization of UN Sustainable Development Goals Agenda towards 2030.

Understanding its role, the government in China has advocated the construction of green data centers. Green or sustainable data centers are a repository for storage, management and dissemination of data where all systems efficiently use energy thereby contributing to a reduction in carbon footprint. IDCs in Beijing, Shanghai, Shenzhen, and few other cities strictly limit the usage of power in a way to create effective (PUE) value standard, which is required to be lower than 1.4. PUE. PUE also referred to as power usage effectiveness is an indicator for evaluating the energy efficiency of data centers. PUE value closer to 1 indicates a higher energy efficiency level (Yuventi & Mehdizadeh, 2013, p. 64). Some IDC service providers have begun to deploy data centers in the northwest, southwest and other regions due to the advantages that these regions offer in terms of energy efficiency and energy supply, as well as preferential policy support from the government.

From the perspective of the distribution of the number of IDC racks in China, the developed regions have more number of IDC racks, due to significant economic growth, and concentration of large number of Internet and financial companies in those areas. According to Research Institute, iResearch Consulting (RIIC), from 2018 to 2019, the number of IDC racks (Figure 4) in Shanghai and surrounding areas ranked first in the country, accounting for 26% in 2019; followed by Beijing and surrounding areas (21%) and Guangzhou and surrounding areas (16%). The IDC racks in the central and western regions accounted for 34% in total (Figure 4), which shows that the IDCs in the central and western regions have developed rapidly (RIIC, 2020).

Figure 4.

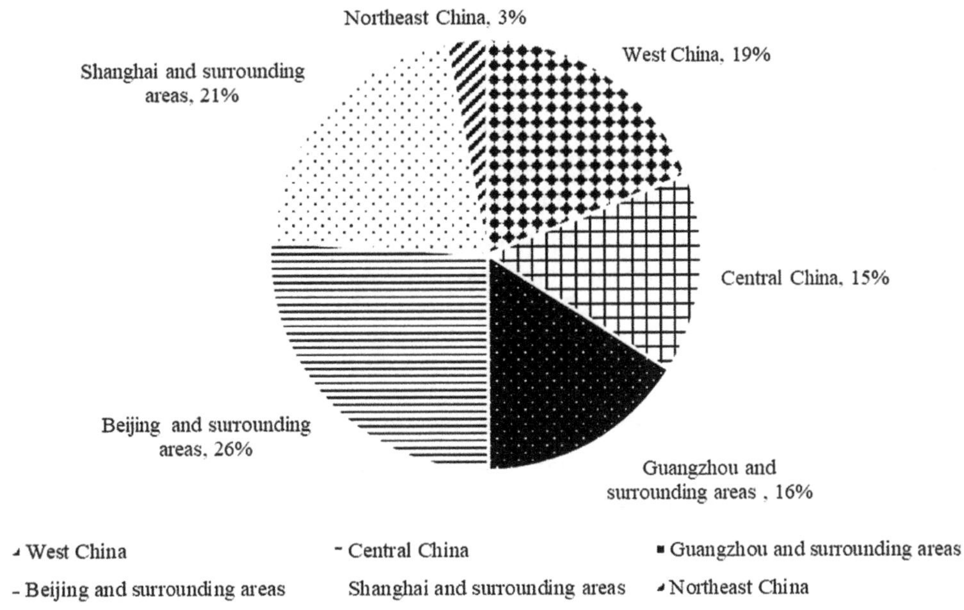

2.2 Emergence of IDCs In Other Developing Countries

As global data traffic continues to increase with each passing moment, effective management of data becomes a sine qua non for developing countries who fight to compete in the global data economy at a breakneck speed. Availability of IDC's in developing countries at this crucial juncture will enable developing countries to work on inclusivity by ensuring reliable and affordable connectivity among their population. Few case studies are discussed in this section to outline the progress in developing countries.

Thailand

As an investment promotion agency of the Thai government, the main responsibility of Thailand Office of the Board of Investment (BOI) is to promote investment in Thailand locally and globally along with providing services for Thai companies' overseas investment. BOI promulgated the "Seven-Year Investment Promotion Policy (2015-2021)" in December of 2014, including exemption of import tariffs on machinery, investment subsidies, financial incentives for innovation, and qualification to sign land lease agreements for up to 99 years (Fungtammasan, 2016), which paved the way for "Thailand 4.0". In 2016, the Thai government proposed the "Thailand 4.0" high-value-added economic growth model, which aimed to achieve a transition to a digital economy by introducing more innovative applications of high technology (Charoenrat & Harvie, 2017). Among them, the "Eastern Economic Corridor Plan" included the establishment of a "Thailand Digital Park" in Rayong Province, as well as promoting the expansion of IDCs. This plan makes Rayong Province, a region used to be famous for fishing and tropical fruits, to be high-tech center.

India

In India, State-level Data Centers (SDC) are considered to be an important aspect of the core infrastructure. In order to improve state-level electronic management and application of data, SDCs plan to establish IDCs in all states for purpose of building competent and safe IT infrastructure. By establishing state-level local area network and IDCs in rural areas, the state can realize the service from government to government (G2G), from government to citizen (G2C) and government to business (G2B) (Himanshu & Rahul, 2017). At the same time, through the implementation of the "Information Technology Investment Zone" plan, India provides preferential policies to promote the development of the regional software industry and the infrastructure for IDCs construction in the two and three tier cities (Himanshu & Rahul, 2017).

Russia

According to "2014-2020 Program", part of the "State Program of the Russian Federation for the Development of Science and Technology" (The Russian Government, 2013), Russia started to build optical fiber data transmission infrastructure in relatively remote areas since the year 2015. Those optical fiber lines have potential to become an important part of Russia's information technology infrastructure, so that Russia can promote national IDC platform construction.

3. THE ROLE OF GOVERNMENT

In recent years, China has paid a lot of attention to the development of IDCs, and government departments have made important arrangements to optimize the policy and environment for IDCs. The Ministry of Industry and Information Technology, the Development and Reform Commission, the Ministry of Land and Resources, and the National Energy Administration (Tang & Wang, 2018) have particularly played an important role. They have steadily promoted the development of IDCs mainly through market access, layout guidance, financial support, and industrial policies.

3.1 Policies

Table 1.

Title	Issuing Authority	Date Issued	Main Implications
National Data Center Application Development Guidelines	Ministry of Industry and Information Technology of the People's Republic China (MIIT)	3/4/2020	In order to alleviate the shortage of resources such as land, network, water, and electricity in big cities, and to promote the more rationalization of China's IDC industry layout, part of the data services are gradually transferred to the central and western regions.
Notice to Promote and Accelerate Development of Industrial IDCs	General Office of the Ministry of Industry and Information Technology	3/6/2020	1. Speed up the construction of new infrastructure. 2. Accelerate the improvement of the safety guarantee system. 3. Increase policy support.
Opinions on Promoting the High-quality Development of Infrastructure	Central Committee for Comprehensively Deepening Reform	3/21/2020	1. Support the construction of diversified applications and strengthen technology R&D and innovation. 2. Strengthen resource sharing and improve the efficiency of resource element allocation.
Industrial Internet Innovation and Development Action Plan (2021-2023)	MIIT	12/22/2020	1. Implement the innovative development strategy of the Industrial Internet. 2. Promote the integration and development of industrialization and informatization to a greater degree.
Guiding Opinions on Accelerating the Construction of a National Integrated IDC Collaborative Innovation System	National Development and Reform Commission (NDRC)	12/23/2020	1. By 2025, IDCs across the country will form an integrated infrastructure with a reasonable layout and a green infrastructure. 2. The east and west data centers will achieve a structural balance, and the PUE of large and super large data centers will drop below 1.3.
Notice on Promoting the Accelerated Development of Industrial Internet	MIIT	3/20/2021	1. Requiring to speed up the construction of the national industrial IDCs 2. Big data is gradually moving from the consumer field to the industrial field, from product marketing to the entire industrial chain.
Guiding Opinions on the Development of Industrial IDC	MIIT	5/13/2021	1. Further deepen the application of data. 2. Focus on deployment in terms of building an application ecosystem. 3. Pointing out the direction for advancing innovation in wider data applications.
National Integrated IDC Collaborative Innovation System Computing Power Hub Implementation Plan	NDRC	5/24/2021	1. In the future, national computing power network will be built in the underdeveloped areas. 2. China's IDC construction will be adjusted to promote the rational layout, balance of supply and demand, green intensiveness, and interconnection.

These policies show a trend of a transformation in IDCs from consumer Internet of things to industrial Internet of things. The three main policies are mentioned as hereunder:

3.1.1 Promotion and Acceleration in Development of Industrial IDCs (the "Notice")

As an important infrastructure for the industrial Internet of things, IDCs in China have ushered in a new development phase. The Ministry of Information and Technology of People's Republic of China has released a notice popularly known as "The Notice" for promotion and acceleration of industrial Internet. The "Notice" is expected to comprehensively enhance the industrial Internet's ability to support the real economy (MIIT, 2020). In the prevention and control of the COVID-19 epidemic, the national industrial IDCs have been giving full play to their data resources. Those IDCs also gather information with respect to the material requirements of more than 2,800 units for hospitals, enterprises, governments, and social organizations (Yu et al., 2020). At the same time, through real-time monitoring of the inventory and raw material requirements of upstream and downstream enterprises in the supply chain, this has enabled in realizing intelligent scheduling and efficient supply of materials. The national industrial IDCs also gather data from many industrial Internet companies to form a comprehensive monitoring of the resumption of work and production of more than 2.4 million small and medium-sized enterprises, providing strong data support for the overall planning of epidemic control (Tianye, personal communication, March 25, 2020).

The national industrial IDCs realize the unified deployment of production resources, which further strengthen the supply-side structural reform of China's manufacturing industry and play an instrumental role in resolving the problem of low-end overcapacity and high-end insufficiency.

The "Notice" proposes to formulate a new infrastructure to expedite the construction of IDCs (Tianye, personal communication, March 25, 2020).

The first suggestion is regarding the need for the government to build a complete industrial Internet data cooperation and sharing mechanism. Making good use of the infrastructure capabilities of the national industrial IDCs can accelerate the launch of a series of data applications such as the Industrial Internet Development Index assessment. The second proposal seeks to strengthen the industrial Internet data cooperation and sharing ecosystem. Efficient data cooperation and sharing among industries and enterprises must be encouraged. Further, the upstream and downstream of the industrial chain should be guided to jointly build a credible industrial Internet data space (Chen et al., 2020). Steady promotion of the construction of industrial Internet Data Sub-Centers (IDSC) is also a necessity. The sub-center is an important part of the big data center, as well as a service carrier. By adhering to the principle of "closest to industry", a number of industrial IDSCs should be built in areas with a good industrial foundation, which can further enhance the capacity of data collection in China's industrial economy and industrial Internet operations. It also has the ability of comprehensive monitoring and early warning for industrial Internet security threats. Thus, by promoting the use of the Industrial Internet to realize full capacity of various resources such as funds, technology, manpower, and policies, the development of the real economy can be further promoted to a greater extent (Lin, 2020, pp.8-12).

3.1.2 Industrial Internet Innovation and Development Action Plan (2021-2023) (the "Plan")

The next three years will be crucial for rapid growth of the Industrial Internet. By 2023, the construction and the industrial development ecosystem concerning IDCs will be further strengthened. The construction of the industrial Internet data center has significantly improved the overall industrial strength in People's Republic of China (Zhang & Zhao, 2020). As per Industrial Internet Action Plan released by Ministry of Information and Technology, for innovation and development of IDC's, there will be a rapid growth in terms of integrating of industrial Internet and 5G, the construction of industrial IDCs, and the construction of industrial Internet industry chains (Peijuan Li, personal communication, January 22, 2021).

This "Plan" promotes the integrated development of "5G + Industrial Internet". So, now 5G will open up the entire process of data collection, transmission, processing, and decision-making. Giving full play to the technology of cloud computing, artificial intelligence, and other technologies on the industrial Internet, it will further drive the industrial Internet to play its role in improving quality, reducing costs, and green safety in industrial production (Peijuan Li, personal communication, January 22, 2021). The industrial Internet is an important downstream application of 5G, in which the "Plan" will promote the coordinated development of 5G and industrial Internet from multiple perspectives such as operators, governments, and industrial enterprises (Yang, 2020).

Secondly, the "Plan" promotes the construction of more industrial IDCs. The demand for data centers is facing a switch from the consumer Internet to the industrial Internet. Industrial Internet scenarios represented by smart cities, smart transportation, and smart manufacturing will cause explosive growth in data volume and become an important driving factor for the growth of data centers.

The construction of big data sub-centers in various industries and the improvement of service capabilities will help the efficient circulation and integrated sharing of industry data. Further accelerating the digestion of data center resources will benefit the long-term development of the data center industry (MIIT, 2020).

Thirdly, the "Plan" focuses on changing the pattern of industrial software, industrial control systems and other core industrial software dominated by foreign giants in the past, which will help the development of domestic high-end industrial platforms and industrial software (Liu et al., 2020). Among them, it is mentioned that a number of key technologies in the fields of network security must achieve industrialization breakthroughs. By the end of the "Plan", a unified, integrated, and open industrial Internet standard system will be established (MIIT, 2020).

3.1.3 Guiding Opinions on the Development of Industrial IDC (the "Guiding Opinions")

Industrial Internet big data is the general term for the full life cycle of data of industrial products and services, including data generated and used by industrial enterprises in R&D, manufacturing, operation management, maintenance services and the data used in the industrial Internet platform. With the onset of the fourth industrial revolution, big data has gradually become the most significant strategic resource for industrial development (Huang, 2021, pp.28-31). In the next three to five years, with the development of 5G, industrial Internet, artificial intelligence, etc., industrial Internet big data will move from the initial stage of exploration to the development stage, and compete globally when the competition will become more intense.

The Ministry of Information and Technology of the People's Republic of China, released guiding opinions last year recommending ways of developing industrial Big Data.

The "Guiding Opinions" promote comprehensive data collection and high-quality aggregation, including promoting the openness of industrial equipment data interfaces and the compatibility of industrial communication protocols. Huang (2021) thinks that the purpose is to form a complete and connected high-quality data link to build the foundation for supporting enterprises to promote overall digital transformation in the dimension of the industrial chain.

In terms of sharing industrial data, the "Guiding Opinions" recommend the application of blockchain and other technologies in data circulation, starting from technical means, pricing mechanisms, transaction rules and other aspects to promote market-oriented configuration.

For a large number of industrial enterprises, data application is still at a low level (Jin et al., 2020). The "Guiding Opinions" organize industrial big data application pilot demonstration methods on the demand side; cultivate massive industrial APPs and their application ecology on the supply side. In this way, both supply and demand are contributing jointly to promote the comprehensive and in-depth application of industrial Internet big data.

4. CASE STUDY

This Chapter takes Guizhou Province as the representative of the underdeveloped regions. Guizhou Province once relied on Moutai, a distilled Chinese liquor, but nowadays, Guizhou is now known as the "Silicon Valley" of China's big data thanks to the rapid development of its IDC business.

4.1 Reviewing the Development History of IDC Construction in Guizhou

The IDC industry in Guizhou Province started its operations in 2013 and can be divided into the following three development stages.

4.1.1 2014-2015 — The Construction Period of IDC Industry Infrastructure

The main task at this stage was to initially build an IDC industry system. At that time, Guizhou Province was striving to complete the infrastructure construction of major large-scale IDCs by 2015 to improve big data collection and storage capacities (Feng, 2019). While completing the construction of the basic hardware environment, Guizhou Province increased its publicity efforts to attract various types of data resources to enter the big data project, which drove related industries to come together to form the basis for the large-scale development of the IDC industry.

4.1.2 2015-2017 — A Period of Concentrated and Rapid Development of IDC Industry

The main task at this stage was to improve the supporting industry system. At this stage, relying on the IDC industry system built in the previous stage, the development environment continuously strengthened IDC ecosystem further. At this stage, Guizhou Province was actively seeking national policy support, as well as support from scientific research institutions. It ended up attracting support from large enterprises in this stage (Sun, 2018, pp.20-22). The aim in this stage was to promote the high end and cluster development of the IDC industry in order to achieve the goal of building a leading domestic IDC industry base.

4.1.3 2017-2020 — A Breakthrough Period for the Development and Innovation of IDC Industry Guizhou Province

In this stage, put greater efforts in winning support of big data companies and the introduction of big data professionals. At this stage, it was necessary to focus on promoting, branding and increasing influence of IDC industry on the basis of innovation and breakthroughs, which would further consolidate the foundation of Guizhou Province in the domestic IDC ecosystem (Sun, 2018, pp.20-22).

4.2 Factors Considered in Choosing Location

When it comes to the question of choosing underdeveloped cities such as Guizhou instead of developed cities for strengthening Industrial IDC base, the same can be looked into from various perspectives as discussed and mentioned below:

4.2.1 Geographical Factors

The first and most important factor is the geographic location of the IDC. The factors that need to be analyzed include: the probability and frequency of natural disasters (floods, hurricanes, tornadoes, etc.) at the alternative site; environmental hazards (the extent of the data center's impact on the environment where it is located); and climatic factors (whether the climate of the site has natural cooling system). It is crucial to mention that, according to Jiang and Luo (2019), IDC is constructed in a way that there are many servers which dissipate a lot of heat, and in order to ensure the normal operation of the server, it needs to cool down. There are many cooling methods, but the cost of cooling also needs to be considered. So, the best way is to depend on the natural cooling system (MIIT, 2017, p. 9).

Guizhou Province is located near 26 degrees north latitude, with typical karst landforms. Thus, it has a stable geological structure and extremely low risk of earthquakes being destructive in nature (Sun, 2018, pp.20-22). Guizhou has a subtropical, warm and humid climate coupled with availability of sufficient water resources. This natural environment in Guizhou Province is conducive for construction of IDCs because the warm and humid monsoon climate can directly transport fresh air to IDC servers and reduce the energy consumption. Further, sufficient availability of water resources can provide reliable clean energy for the operation of IDCs and a stable geological structure guarantees the IDCs' security. At the same time, there is not much air pollution in Guizhou which ensures that there will not be any slowdown in cooling fans for the long term (He, 2019), and the scenario of corrosion of the circuit board too can be avoided.

4.2.2 Supply of Electricity

Electricity supply is one of the important factors as electricity and energy supply is the main component of operating the IDCs. The factors that need to be considered include:

1. availability of multiple mature grids in the alternative location;
2. low cost per kilowatt hour of power sources;

3. whether alternative locations have sufficient availability of renewable energy sources such as solar, wind, and air, which will help companies build a green IDC ecosystem (Yu et al., 2019). Moreover, electricity in Guizhou is abundant and cheap, which meets the requirements very easily.

4.2.3 ICT Factors

When selecting an IDC location, various factors need to be considered from the perspective of Information and Communication Technology (ICT).These factors include: the distance from the optical fiber backbone to the IDC location, which will help to measure the number of materials needed; the type of optical fiber, which will affect the transmission speed; the type of local communication service operator and the service mode it supports. Guizhou invested about 12 trillion yuan in construction of new communication digital facilities, which satisfies these above mentioned requirements (Guizhou Provincial Communications Administration, 2020).

4.2.4 Economic Factors

The development of an emerging industry has certain economic requirements. The quality of economic conditions directly determines the amount of capital that can be invested in emerging industries. As an industry in its nascent stage of development, IDC industry needs sufficient funds for its development. Favourable economic conditions promote the development of IDC industry in the following two aspects: Firstly, in the initial stages of development, sufficient funds are necessary for infrastructure construction, technological innovation and research, etc. and secondly, the sufficient funding sources can be used to adjust the industrial structure, guaranteeing the sound development of IDC industry in further stages (Pandit et al., 2018).

From an economic point of view, the implementation of the "Eastern Data and Western Calculation" project is an inevitable choice for maximizing national interests and optimizing technology and economy. The construction of IDCs is not only a technical issue, but also an important path to achieve industrial growth and balanced regional development. With the implementation of the "Eastern Data and Western Calculation" project, the flow of data will lead to expansion in the flow of funds, human resources, and technology, which will not only support the digital economy in China's East and West, but also inject new lease of life into the construction of digital China (Fang et al., 2017).

4.2.5 Human Resource and Technical Factors

The essence of entire IDC industry is to transform data resources into economically beneficial industries through a series of operations. In the entire process that involves operation, data collection, storage, cleaning, analysis, management, and display, capable manpower with sound professional knowledge and expertise is needed because in the absence of experienced professionals, technology will not be able to develop in the long term (Chen et al., 2019).

5. ANALYSIS OF CHINA'S EFFICIENCY OF INVESTMENT IN R&D RESOURCES

We have just discussed how there is a close relationship between the construction of IDCs and economic development. This part of the chapter will analyze the relationship between variables such as IDC investment, R&D expenditure, R&D practitioners, etc., which measure the level of R&D and economic development variables from a quantitative perspective. This part innovatively proposes to use Data Envelopment Analysis (DEA) as an efficiency evaluation method to measure the efficiency of resource allocation in China's R&D sector.

5.1 The Relationship Between Technological Progress and Economic Growth

Many researchers view introducing scientific and technological progress as the main variable into various economic growth models. They believe that the continuous upgradation in science and technology is one of the most important motivation for maintaining stable economic growth in the region. Moreover, the level of investment in science and technology of a country or region also determines the development trend of the country's economic growth module, upgradation in industrial structure, and other important issues related to the country's economic construction.

Schumpeter (1934) believes that successful innovation allows the original low-tech products to be replaced by high-tech products through the "creative destruction process". This type of technological progress is an important driving force for social and economic growth.

Romer (1986) believes that knowledge accumulation and technological progress are endogenous factors for the sustainable development of the regional economy, and the improvement in human capacity shows strong externalities, which is also positive for the formation of other production factors and the improvement of utilization efficiency. This kind of perspective is also referred by Lucas in 1988.

Solow (1956) pointed out, through the "Solow-Swan Economic Growth Model", that material capital, labor, and exogenous technological progress are the most important factors for the long-term stable growth of the regional economy.

5.2 Brief Introduction to DEA

As mentioned above, many technology-related variables can have a positive impact on national economic growth. As for China, the efficiency of investment into R&D resources over the years is a critical issue.

The method of "Data Envelopment Analysis" (DEA) can help us analyze the effectiveness of input and output variable between similar "Decision Making Units" (DMU) (Charnes, et al., 1978). It can also possibly analyze the overall input and output efficiency without considering the importance or weight coefficient of each input element (Wei, 2004).

The advantages of DEA (Wei, 2004) include: (1) Applicable to the efficient evaluation for the problem concerning multiple input and multiple output. (2) It enables only using the input and output data rather than processing other data. (3) There is no requirement for weights, and the optimal weights are only obtained from the actual input and output data of the decision-making unit, which has strong objectivity.

DEA basically includes two models: CCR (Charnes, et al., 1978) which is input oriented model with constant returns to scale and BCC (Banker et al., 1984) which is input oriented model with variable returns to scale. The names of these two models are made up of the initials of the last names of their inventors. Among them, the CCR model assumes that each DMU is under a constant return to scale (CRS), which is used to measure total efficiency. The BCC model assumes that each DMU is under a variable return to scale (VRS), which is used to measure pure technology and scale efficiency.

5.3 Analyzing the Input-Output Efficiency of China's R&D Resources Over Last 15 Years

This section uses the CCR model to conduct an analysis of the input-output efficiency of different types of R&D resources in China for a period of 15 years (2006-2020). Generally speaking, DEA efficiency variables include input variables and output variables. This section selects fixed capital investment (K), labor population (L), R&D expenditure (T1), patent application authorization number in R&D (T2), full-time equivalent of R&D researchers (T3) as input variables, and selects China's GDP increase (Y) as the output variable. The data is shown in Table 2.

Table 2.

Year	Y	T1	T2	T3	K	L
2006	32119.6	3003.1	268002	150.25	109998.2	76315
2007	50653.8	3710.2	351782	173.62	137323.9	76531
2008	49152.3	4616	411982	196.54	172828.4	77046
2009	29273.1	5802.1	581992	229.13	224598.8	77510
2010	63601.6	7062.6	814825	255.4	278121.9	78388
2011	75820.9	8687	960513	288.3	311021.9	78579
2012	50639.8	10298.4	1255138	324.7	374676	78894
2013	54383.2	11846.6	1313000	353.3	446294.1	79300
2014	50599.9	13015.63	1302687	371.06	512761	79690
2015	45295.1	14169.88	1718192	375.88	562000	80091
2016	57536.9	15676.75	1753763	387.81	606466	80694
2017	85640.8	17606.13	1836434	403.36	641238	80686
2018	87245.2	19677.93	2447460	438.14	645675	80525
2019	67234.1	22144	2591607	480.08	560874	81104
2020	29471	24426	3639000	509.19	527270	89438

Note: The unit of Y (the increase in GDP) is (100 million yuan), the unit of T1 (R&D expenditure) is (100 million yuan), the unit of T2 (patent application authorization number in R&D) is (pieces), the unit of T3 (full-time equivalent of R&D researchers) is (10,000 people per year), the unit of K (fixed capital investment) is (100 million yuan), and the unit of L (labor population) is (10,000 people).

Using "DEAP 2.1" to calculate and solve 15 efficiency evaluation models, the results are shown in Table 3.

Table 3.

DMUs	Score	Rank
2006	0.832	7
2007	1.000	1
2008	0.922	6
2009	0.486	14
2010	0.938	5
2011	1.000	1
2012	0.653	11
2013	0.686	9
2014	0.633	12
2015	0.552	13
2016	0.686	9
2017	1.000	1
2018	1.000	1
2019	0.789	8
2020	0.323	15

It can be seen from the table that the DEA scores of China's R&D investment efficiency in 2007, 2011, 2017, and 2018 are 1.000 (the DEA score represents the size of input-output efficiency), which means that China's R&D capital investment in those four years are relatively the most efficient. On the contrary, the other 11 different years of R&D capital investment DEA scores are all less than 1, which means in those 11 years, the input-output efficiency of R&D capital is not optimal. So, it is abundantly clear that China's R&D capital input-output efficiency has been quite low over past few years (2006-2020).

Taking 2020 as an example, the DEA score of China's R&D capital input-output efficiency is 0.323. This means that in 2020, to maintain the original output level as 2018, it only requires 32.3% of the amount of scientific and technological capital used in 2018. In other words, in 2020, 67.7% of the input elements including R&D capital did not make due contributions to China's economic growth. This can be explained by the impact to the entire technology industry chain caused by COVID-19 epidemic in 2020, so it was not possible for investments in R&D during that phase to efficiently contribute to economic growth.

The time period of 15 years from 2006 to 2020 is divided into three phases to calculate the average DEA score (2006-2011 being the first time period, 2012-2016 being the second time period, and 2017-2020 being the third time period). The average DEA score in the first time period is 0.863, the average DEA score in the second time period is 0.642, and the average DEA score in the third time period is 0.778. From the above-mentioned data, it can be seen that in the third phase (2017-2020), the efficiency of R&D capital investment has significantly improved as compared to that during the second phase (2012-2016). We can say that, had there been no epidemic in 2020, the DEA score in the third phase would have been much higher, that is, the efficiency of R&D capital investment would have significantly improved. The increase in DEA scores in the third phase can be explained by the fact that the Chinese government paid more attention to the development of high-tech industries in recent years, as a result of policy of "Intelligent Manufacturing in China".

DEA scores of the input-output efficiency of various types of R&D capital in China from 2006 to 2020 are shown in Figure 5.

Figure 5.

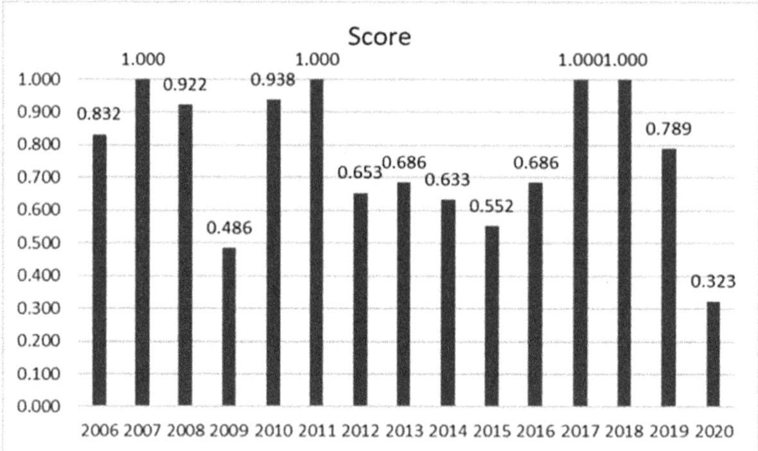

5.4 Analyzing Input-Output Efficiency of China's R&D Resources in Various Provinces in the Year 2019

5.4.1 Overall Technical Efficiency Analysis

This section selects fixed capital investment, labor force, R&D expenditures, number of patent application in R&D sector, full-time equivalent of R&D researchers as input variables, and the increase in regional GDP of each province in China over the previous year as output variable. Here, China's 31 provinces have

Table 4.

DMUs	Score	Rank	DMUs	Score	Rank
Beijing	1.000	1	Hubei	0.783	18
Tianjin	0.516	30	Hunan	0.856	14
Hebei	0.701	22	Guangdong	0.863	13
Shanxi	0.989	7	Guangxi	0.711	21
Inner Mongolia	0.969	8	Hainan	1.000	1
Liaoning	1.000	1	Chongqing	0.957	9
Jilin	0.413	31	Sichuan	0.799	16
Heilongjiang	0.567	29	Guizhou	0.758	19
Shanghai	0.881	12	Yunnan	1.000	1
Jiangsu	0.728	20	Xizang	1.000	1
Zhejiang	0.787	17	Shaanxi	0.809	15
Anhui	0.609	26	Gansu	0.901	11
Fujian	1.000	1	Qinghai	0.687	24
Jiangxi	0.606	27	Ningxia	0.610	25
Shandong	0.602	28	Xinjiang	0.942	10
Henan	0.697	23			

been selected as DMUs. In terms of year selection, in order to take into account, the latest situation of technological and economic development, as well as the adverse effects on the model analysis caused by the uncertain factors brought about by the 2020 epidemic, this section selects 2019 as the research object.

The details of the DEA overall technical efficiency scores based on the input-output efficiency of various types of R&D capital in China's provinces are shown in Table 4.

It can be seen from the table that in 2019, the maximum value of the overall technical efficiency of R&D investment in 31 provinces in China was 1.000, the minimum value was 0.413, and the average value was 0.798. In 2019, China had 6 provinces with an overall technical efficiency score of 1.000 for R&D capital investment efficiency (including Beijing, Liaoning, Hainan, Fujian, Yunnan, and Xizang).

In terms of the results of the model, the overall technical efficiency of four DMUs (Xizang, Yunnan, Inner Mongolia, and Xinjiang) showed obvious and abnormally high efficiency. This research speculates that although these underdeveloped regions have low investment, they are still in their infancy. The low base of investment in various aspects of R&D capital is likely to lead to relatively high input-output efficiency. Additionally, this situation may also be caused by the significant imbalance of technology investment in China's developed and underdeveloped regions, resulting in limitations in the accuracy of

Table 5.

DMUs	Score	Rank
Beijing	1.000	1
Liaoning	1.000	1
Fujian	1.000	1
Hainan	1.000	1
Shanxi	0.989	5
Chongqing	0.957	6
Gansu	0.901	7
Shanghai	0.881	8
Guangdong	0.863	9
Hunan	0.856	10
Shaanxi	0.809	11
Sichuan	0.799	12
Zhejiang	0.787	13
Hubei	0.783	14
Guizhou	0.758	15
Jiangsu	0.728	16
Guangxi	0.711	17
Hebei	0.701	18
Henan	0.697	19
Qinghai	0.687	20
Ningxia	0.610	21
Anhui	0.609	22
Jiangxi	0.606	23
Shandong	0.602	24
Heilongjiang	0.567	25
Tianjin	0.516	26
Jilin	0.413	27

source data. Therefore, simultaneous adaptation to both developed and underdeveloped regions cannot be achieved when using the BCC model. However, this model still has certain guiding significance for most other regions, especially developed regions.

Therefore, in order to ensure the accuracy of the follow-up analysis, this section adopts the method of manually adjusting the ranking, and removes those four underdeveloped areas that are obviously inconsistent with the actual situation. Table 5 shows results after adjusting.

The DEA score represents the efficiency of R&D capital investment in China's provinces, which means that in 2019, there were 4 provinces that had the most efficient capital investment in R&D sector. The DEA scores of the remaining 23 provinces were all less than 1, indicating that the efficiency of capital investment in R&D in these regions was relatively low.

At the same time, by looking at the distribution of scores, it can be said that there was a large gap in the input-output efficiency of R&D capital between various provinces in China.

Taking Jilin as an example, Jilin's DEA score was 0.413. The above data shows that while maintaining the same output level, only 41.3% of R&D capital investment is needed, which means that 58.7% of R&D capital investment in Jilin did not make a corresponding contribution to its economic development. In comparison, only 11.9% of its R&D capital investment in Shanghai did not contribute to economic growth.

It can be seen that in some provinces in China, the proportion of capital investment in R&D resources to economic growth is very inefficient, and most of these provinces are underdeveloped regions. In the next section, all the provinces are divided as the central, western, eastern and northeastern regions and then, compared by a scale efficiency analysis.

5.4.2 Scale Efficiency Analysis

According to the China Statistical Yearbook (2019), China is divided into four regions. The four regions are the eastern region, the northeast region, the western region, and the central region. The provinces and their scale efficiency is shown in Table 6 (IRS, DRS or a dash).

DMUs (Decision Making Units) associated with a dash are facing constant returns to scale; DMUs associated with IRS are facing increasing returns to scale, and DMUs associated with DRS are facing decreasing returns to scale. From the existing results, it is revealed that there are relatively more regions in the western region (underdeveloped regions) showing increasing returns to scale. This means the proportion of increase in input is less than that in output, which shows that the DMU has not reached the optimal scale and there is insufficient investment. If more capital in R&D resources is invested in these western regions, it will bring significant improvements to the local economy. At the same time, as mentioned above, with IDC and other high-tech industries entering the western region in recent years, the region now has developed with help of a stable climate, cheap electricity prices, and various government policies.

It is worth noting that some regions in the western region have recorded a state of decreasing returns to scale, which means that blindly and thoughtlessly increasing investment in R&D resources will bring about less increase in GDP, and at the same time, lead to wastage of resources. Therefore, under the current scale of investment in R&D, it is necessary to specify the goals and improve the accuracy of R&D investment; at the same time, it is also necessary to reduce wastage in resources effectively transforming the R&D investment into economic benefits.

Table 6.

Regions	DMUs	Scale efficiency
Northeast region	Liaoning	-
	Jiling	DRS
	Heilongjiang	IRS
Central region	Jiangxi	DRS
	Henan	DRS
	Anhui	DRS
	Shanxi	DRS
	Hubei	DRS
	Hunan	DRS
Eastern region	Shanghai	IRS
	Jiangsu	DRS
	Beijing	-
	Tianjing	IRS
	Hebei	DRS
	Shandong	DRS
	Zhejiang	DRS
	Fujian	-
	Hainan	DRS
	Guangdong	DRS
Western region	Guangxi	DRS
	Chongqing	DRS
	Sichuan	DRS
	Guizhou	DRS
	Yunnan	-
	Xizang	-
	Shaanxi	-
	Gansu	IRS
	Qinghai	IRS
	Ningxia	IRS
	Xinjiang	DRS
	Inner Mongolia	IRS

The reasons for the decreasing returns to scale in underdeveloped regions and preventive measures will be discussed in detail in the next section.

Although, the trend of IRS in DMUs in the western region (underdeveloped regions) is reasonable, the trend of DRS in the eastern DMUs (developed regions) such as Jiangsu, Guangdong and Zhejiang have been observed to be unreasonable. This trend is despite the fact that these eastern regions generally have more human, material, and financial resources. Such an abnormality can only be explained by the limitations of data mentioned like before. Due to the local conditions prevalent in China, it is possible that during the process of collating and collecting R&D-related data in some underdeveloped regions, some data are missing or distorted. So, after including these kinds of data into BCC model, results in few regions are inconsistent with the fact. Despite inconsistencies, it cannot be denied that the BCC model can still make reasonable judgments on the scale efficiency of DMUs in underdeveloped areas, and can provide some guidance for the process of R&D investment in these areas.

5.5 Limitations

This study has its own potential limitations, which will be discussed in this section. Firstly, in terms of data selection, when comparing to China's various provinces, only the cross-sectional data of 2019 was selected, rather than including historical data for several years. Secondly, for the variables representing R&D resources, only three variables are selected for analysis. Thirdly, as for the results of the model, the overall technical efficiency of four underdeveloped DMUs showed abnormally high efficiency, and there are also three developed DMUs showing results inconsistent with facts.

These inconsistencies are likely to be caused by the unequal distribution of R&D resources in China as a result of local prevailing conditions within the country. These inconsistencies have resulted into great inconvenience for the underdeveloped regions. Lack of specially compiled data, and many technology-related variables are missing or distorted as a result of which the BCC model is unable to show any concrete results.

However, the overall technical efficiency scores and scale efficiency in the remaining DMUs are basically consistent with the actual level of scientific and technological development in the region, so the results of this BCC model still have a certain guiding meaning. This limitation may be corrected after increasing the number of input-output indicators and increasing the time span of research.

When constructing and revamping the underdeveloped regions in the future, the authorities should pay more attention to data collection. At the same time, because the distribution of cities in China varies from tier 1 to tier 5, this huge gap can make the model hard to fit the overall situation. Therefore, when studying the efficiency of China's R&D investment in the future, an advanced model that is more modified and more suitable as per local conditions prevailing in China should be adopted.

6. OPPORTUNITIES AND CHALLENGES

As per the Granger Causality test, R&D is proved to be a trigger in the economy growth, which means, like mentioned before, IDC development can act as a catalyst for economic growth. So, in this section we will attempt to focus on opportunities and challenges.

6.1 Opportunities

With data becoming an important strategic resource, the scale of development of China's IDCs is also expanding. It predicts that from 2020 to 2022, the compound growth rate of China's IDC business market will be 27.8%, and the scale of big data center will reach 320 billion yuan in 2022 (IDC Circle, 2020).

The construction of the IDCs is expected to drive the coordinated development of many industries and realize effective industry linkages across various sectors. The industrial chain of IDCs mainly includes three links (Autio, 2017, pp.211-227). The upstream is the infrastructure construction link, including computer equipment, broadband, refrigeration equipment, power supply, etc.; the midstream is the IDC value-added link, including operators, cloud vendors and third-party service providers; the downstream is the application link of IDCs, covering various industries such as the Internet, manufacturing, finance, and medical care (Cahen et al., 2017). Therefore, the advancement of infrastructure in IDCs can have a ripple effect across many industries altogether.

Internet giants such as Tencent, Alibaba, and Kuaishou have recently invested heavily to accelerate the deployment of IDC projects. In Chongqing, the second phase of Tencent Western Cloud Computing IDC with a total investment of 4.5 billion yuan is about to start, which, after completion, will have the capacity of computing and storage as same as that of 200,000 servers (Sun, 2018, pp.20-22); in UlanQab, the Kuaishou Smart Cloud IDC project with an investment of 10 billion yuan is expected to go online at the end of 2022, and it will support the need of Kuaishou with respect to storage in the future with a scale of 300,000 servers (People's Government of Inner Mongolia Autonomous Region, 2020).

With the support of policies and investment of capital, the IDC industry is all set to take off to greater heights of development. An engineer of the China Industrial Internet Research Institute, has revealed that "a large amount of capital can directly consolidate the data value mining foundation for future construction of smart cities and industrial Internet, and it will inevitably increase the social impact of the IDC industry, helping build more diversified and inclusive ecosystem' (Tian Ye, personal communication, June 23, 2020).

Many policies issued after 2020 proposed methods such as the unified scheduling of IT resources, which are expected to significantly improve the service capacity and business requirements of the IDCs in central and western regions.

The trend of clustering in IDCs requires higher energy consumption and manpower resources. Further, many reports have revealed that Beijing-Tianjin-Hebei, the Yangtze River Delta, the Guangdong-Hong Kong-Macao Greater Bay Area, and Chengdu-Chongqing are listed as key areas that are expected to receive more energy and manpower resources (Chen, 2017, pp.32-34). This will be advantageous for many companies in related sectors and chances are that their development will be further strengthened. In addition, the problem of insufficient demand for large IDCs in non-first-tier cities is also on its way to resolution as a result of formation of a national integrated service system which will further increase the value of IDC.

At the same time, downstream demand on the data side is strengthening as well. The advancement of computing power resources and the acceleration of data circulation integration is expected to greatly reduce the cost of computing power and data usage, and further also expected to accelerate the development and innovation of downstream related big data application industries in the future, which will further benefit the IDC industry (Si, &Chen, 2020).

With the dual support from the government and investment in R&D, China's IDCs have developed rapidly, and the market size also has maintained rapid growth. The leading role of government in procurement of cloud services has become increasingly prominent, and many industries have adopted cloud IDCs to update their original systems to support business development (Tan et al., 2020). For example, the Zhejiang Provincial Water Resources Department outsourced the typhoon path real-time release system project to Alibaba Cloud. Few e-government systems in Gansu Province and Xinjiang Uygur Autonomous Region have migrated to third-party cloud servers; and the Guizhou Province New Rural Cooperative Project also uses the cloud provided by China Mobile, which has become one of the benchmarks for the medical information construction of the health care system (Tan et al., 2020).

The proposal of green and sustainable data policy will also benefit upstream industries such as refrigeration. Cooling power consumption accounts for more than 60% of the non-IT power consumption of data centers, so the introduction of advanced cooling equipment is one of the core of the ecosystem of green IDCs (Shi, 2020, pp.145-149). With further increase in PUE requirements, both the construction of new IDCs and the integration and transformation of old IDCs will significantly increase the demand for computer room air conditioners, and as a result, relevant upstream companies are expected to benefit to a great extent.

6.2 Challenges

However, with a rapid increase in the number of IDCs, it becomes crucial that they be connected, because if not done so within an appropriate time frame, the capacity of data processing will slow down. Another challenge is that large amount of government information is controlled by government agencies. Due to the requirements of confidentiality, a large part of the information related to the vital interests of the public and economic operations is difficult to disclose publicly, which restricts the re-excavation and utilization of the potential value of data. Further, due to certain limitations, China has not yet established a design for the sharing and application management of government information resources, which leads to the phenomenon of "information islands" (Chen et al., 2018). For example, a large amount of information cannot be converted into a machine-readable format; or due to lacking data sharing standards, changes in media and equipment procedures cannot be read, information systems within and between departments are not interconnected, resulting in poor information sharing, etc. Low accuracy and weak correlation of information resources seriously impacts the efficient use of data. This kind of challenge can be one of the reasons that leads to the low DEA scores in some regions in China as discussed in Section 5.

Additionally, the issues surrounding green and sustainable development of the IDCs cannot be ignored either. According to statistics, the current annual electricity consumption of various data centers in China has accounted for about 2% of the electricity consumption of the whole society, and the growth rate of electricity consumption has remained above 10% for many years (Liu et al., 2020). Electricity consumption is so high that some areas in the East have clearly classified data centers as high-energy-consumption industries that need to be restricted.

Although the Western region is rich in renewable energy resources, and has a suitable climate, it is limited by bottlenecks such as insufficient network bandwidth and high inter-provincial transmission costs. The region is entering a stage of structural surplus. The overall resource vacancy rate exceeds 50%, and the listing rate in some regions is even less than 10%. Compared with the 60%-80% listing rate in Beijing, Shanghai, Guangzhou and Shenzhen, there is a significant gap (Liu et al., 2020).

For example, although a certain city in Northeast China completed the construction of a digital government affairs platform and effectively improved administrative efficiency, government expenditures did not positively impact the whole society. That is, it did not focus on cultivating data application service companies in smart transportation, smart medical care, or smart education (Sun, 2020 In case, a city in an underdeveloped region hopes to build an IDC locally and use blockchain technology to establish a digital traceability system for local agricultural and animal husbandry products, so as to promote agricultural and animal product brands; the same will not be viable economically as renting servers will be a more rational alternative (Petti et al., 2019). Additionally, the cost of energy, manpower and other elements required to establish o IDCs in underdeveloped cities is not lower than that of the first-tier and second-tier cities. So it doesn't necessarily prove to be advantageous as well.

7. CONCLUSION AND RECOMMENDATION

Every IDC, from early phase of designing to construction, operation and maintenance, is a systematic project. Only by making good use of the respective roles of the government and the society, can there be promising development and construction of IDCs.

7.1 Government

The role of government needs to be strengthened in the overall planning of the new infrastructure, and promotion of coordination between the layout of the IDC clusters with the construction of communication networks. The national government should increase financial and scientific research support, and encourage research and development in IDC, energy saving and emission reduction (Jia et al., 2019). For example, supporting Huawei, ZTE and other data communication equipment suppliers to strengthen independent innovation of core technologies; developing basic products such as servers, switches, routers, and software; supporting cloud service providers such as Alibaba and Tencent to accelerate the development and application of cloud computing products, services and solutions; and accelerating the application of digital technologies such as 5G, big data, artificial intelligence, and quantum computing in the construction of IDCs.

There is an urgency for the government to not only strengthen the existing IDC ecosystem but also initiate and put in place a strong intellectual property protection regime. Data Center is vulnerable to data breaches and cyberattacks considering the breakneck speed with which digital economy and internet of things is permeating each sector and industry. Implementation of cybersecurity systems along with innovation as well as protecting IP by way of timely filing of patents, copyright, design can be an effective solution for making the ecosystem robust and strong in the long run. This can also make enforcement in case of any unforeseen damage a fruitful process once IP is protected.

The local government needs to cooperate with the implementation of the construction of the national integrated IDC, ensuring the supply of various elements such as energy, land, manpower, and capital. It also becomes necessary to promote the availability of data by providing free relative data download for governments, institutions, enterprises, the public, and researchers. Paying special attention to cultivation, the training and introduction of big data professionals and manpower can ensure effective development of IDC's in various regions.

7.2 Society

It becomes necessary to encourage public participation, by using formal or informal online platforms to provide the public with a window for opinion expression and decision support; as well as exploring crowdsourced urban governance models, such as an introduction of an app for public discovery and reporting of street pavement problems. This can enable the masses to participate in urban governance as well, and at the same time assist urban management department to find solution and accordingly repair things timely.

For enterprises that are deeply involved in the construction and use of IDCs, they need to dig deeper into the value of data, and create a batch of industry solutions with excellent performance, good application effects, and replicable promotion.

It is worth mentioning that telecom operators as well as innovators are an indispensable backbone in the wave of creation of new infrastructure for IDCs. There are mainly three telecom operators in China, namely China Mobile, China Unicom, and China Telecom. At present, China's economy is in the stage of accelerated digital transformation, which requires upgradation of IDCs. The three major telecom operators have accumulated user data for many years, such as user surfing behavior, user communication behavior, user consumption behavior and other structural data (Chen, 2018, pp.162). The expansion of big data industry by telecom operators can effectively connect individuals, industries and enterprises, thereby creating immense positive value for growth and development of all. During the epidemic, the three telecom operators launched services for personal inquiries. With the authorization of the user, based on the analysis of telecommunications big data in the country-wide IDCs, the users were provided with the service of "visiting the place within 14 days". This service could efficiently prove users' history regarding movements, and it is also helpful for the investigation of key groups and the implementation of precise prevention and control of epidemic.

In terms of the industry, IDCs for telecom operators are currently widely used in the financial and tourism industries. China Unicom Big Data and Ctrip Group jointly launched the "Unicom Smart Travel-Travel Product Booking Analysis Platform", which aims to provide management departments and related companies with customized and modular data platform services (Chen, 2018, pp.162). China Telecom cooperated with Citibank to integrate financial consumption data to help Citibank provide a series of big data practices of fintech product application services, such as expanding high-quality customer development and providing credit investigation to existing customers.

For the government, IDCs of telecom operators also contribute to the construction of smart government. In Tianshui, Gansu Province, China Telecom's big data analysis helped Tianshui issue 10 million yuan in consumer coupons to promote consumption replenishment and release consumption potential in Tianshui City (Tan et al., 2020). In Gui'an New District of Guizhou, relying on the China Mobile IDC, the entire new district can be divided into more than 400 grids (Tan et al., 2020). With big data mining and analysis, individual's residence time, time period, consumption ability, and behavior preference can be performed on each grid. As a result, it is clear that where it is suitable as a CBD, where should an industrial zone be planned, and where should be developed a logistics zone, which provides intelligent support for decision-making (Han, 2018, pp.31-32).

If the Chinese economy needs to sustain the pace of growth and development in the long run by driving the development and promotion of IDC's, it is crucial that same be done in a sustainable way so that many future generations can benefit from this ecosystem for many more years to come. Further, significance of putting in place a strong legal regime for implementation of data laws cannot be underscored at this point in time. Recognising the need to promote innovation and protect IP and strengthening the efforts in producing green and sustainable solutions are some of the ways in which digital transformation driven by Internet Data Centers can sustain in the long run.

REFERENCES

Autio, E. (2017). Strategic entrepreneurial internationalization: a normative framework. *Entrepreneurial Strategy, 11*, 211–227.

Banker, R. D., Charnes, A., & Cooper, W. W. (1984). Some models for estimating technical and scale inefficiencies in data envelopment analysis. *Management Science*, *30*(9), 1078–1092.

Cahen, F. R., Oliveira, M. M. Jr, & Borini, F. M. (2017). The internationalization of new technology-based firms from emerging markets. *International Journal of Technology Management*, *74*, 23–43.

Charnes, A., Cooper, W. W., & Rhodes, E. (1978). Measuring the Efficiency of Decision-Making Units. *European Journal of Operational Research*, *2*, 429–444.

Charoenrat, T., & Harvie, C. (2017). Thailand's SME Participation in ASEAN and East Asian Regional Economic Integration. *Journal of Southeast Asian Economies*, *34*(1), 148–174.

Chen, A.S. (2017). Analysis of the development status and trend of the Internet data center industry. *Wireless Internet Technology*, *16*, 32-34. doi:CNKI:SUN:WXHK.0.2017-16-015.

Chen, D.M., Wang, L.Z., & Chen, A.N. (2020). Digitalization and Strategic Management Theory—Review, Challenge and Prospect. *World of Management*, 5.

Chen, G.Q., Zeng, D.J., & Wei, Q. (2020). Decision-making paradigm transformation and enabling innovation in the Internet big data environment. *World of Management*, 2.

Chen, J., Yin, X., & Mei, L. (2018). Holistic innovation: an emerging innovation paradigm. *International Journal of Innovative Studies*, *2*(1), 1–13.

Chen, L., Shaheer, N., Yi, J., & Li, S. (2019). The international penetration of i-business firms: Network effects, liabilities of outsider ship and country clout. *Journal of International Business Studies*, *50*, 172–192.

Chen, X. (2018). Research on the application and development trend of 5G technology in the mobile Internet era. *China New Communications*, *22*, 162. doi:CNKI:SUN:TXWL.0.2018-22-130.

China's Open Data Center Committee. (n.d.). Retrieved June 1, 2021, from: https://dcp.odcc.org.cn/index.html

Christensen, C. M., Mcdonald, R., Altman, E., & Palmer, J. (2018). Disruptive innovation: An intellectual history and directions for future research. *Journal of Management Studies*, *55*(7), 1043–1078.

Consulting, C. C. I. D. (2020). *Status Quo and Prospects of the Development of China's Internet of Things Industry*. Author.

Fang, L., Lerner, J., & Wu, C. (2017). Intellectual property rights protection, ownership, and innovation: Evidence from China. *Review of Financial Studies*, *30*(7), 2446–2477.

Feng, W., Peter, W., & Yin, E. (2019). Enabling cost innovation by non-traditional organizational processes: The case of Chinese firms. *Technological Forecasting and Social Change*, *139*, 352–361.

Fungtammasan B. (2016). Industry-Oriented Graduate Programs in Thailand: A Review. *Asia Pacific Graduate Education,* 161-172.

Gartner. (2020). *Industrial IoT Platforms Reviews and Ratings Gartner 2020*. Author.

Guizhou Provincial Communications Administration. (2020). *Guizhou Province Internet Development Report*. Author.

Han, L. L. (2018). Benchmarking analysis of the core competitive products of the Internet data center-taking China Mobile as an example. *China Business Forum*, *11*, 31-32. doi:10.19699/j.cnki.issn2096-0298.2018.11.014

He, Z. (2019). The macro-structure of national digital governance. *E-Government*, 1.

Himanshu, S., & Rahul, P. (2017). E-Governance in India. *International Journal on Emerging Technologies*, *8*(1), 318–321.

Huang, S., & Wang, Y.R. (2021). A brief analysis of the status and development trend of the domestic industrial Internet industry. *Internet World*, *4*, 28-31. doi: CNKI:SUN:HLWT.0.2021-04-007

IDC Circle, . (2020). *2019-2020 China IDC Industry Development Research Report*. Author.

Jia, N., Huang, K. G., & Zhang, C. M. (2019). Public governance, corporate governance, and firm innovation: An examination of state-owned enterprises. *Academy of Management Journal*, *62*(1), 220–247.

Jia, Y. W. (2017). Research on the National Integrated National Internet Data Center System. *E-Government*, *06*, 31–36. doi:10.16582/j.cnki.dzzw.2017.06.005

Jiang, X.J., & Luo, L.B. (2019). Service Globalization in the Internet Era: New Engine, Acceleration and Competitiveness of Powers. *Chinese Social Sciences*, 2.

Jin, C., Robert, A. B., Li, J. X., Chang, C. H., & Gang, Z. (2020). Leading for constructive innovation: Preliminary evidence from China. *Journal of Engineering and Technology Management*, *57*, 101588.

Lin, Z.B. (2020). "New infrastructure" in the post-epidemic era has become a new growth point for China's economy. *Shanghai Information Technology*, *4*, 8-12. doi:CNKI:SUN:SHXX.0.2020-04-004

Liu, Y. H., Huang, X. T., & Shi, B. H. (2020). China's "New Infrastructure": Concepts, Status Quo and Problems. *Journal of Beijing University of Technology*, *06*, 1–12.

Liu, Y. Z., Sun, J. S., & Jiang, Y. C. (2020). The value discovery of big data: 4C model. *Management World*, 2.

Lucas, R. E. Jr. (1988). On The Mechanic of Economic Development. *Journal of Monetary Economics*, *22*(1), 40.

Ministry of Industry and Information Technology of the PRC. (2017). *Code for Design of Data Centers*. China Planning Press.

Ministry of Industry and Information Technology of the PRC. (2020). *Notice to Promote and Accelerate Development of Industrial IDCs (MIIT 2020 No. 8)*. Author.

National Bureau of Statistics of China. (2019). *China Statistical Yearbook*. Author.

Pandit, D., Joshi, M., Sahay, A., & Gupta, R. (2018). Disruptive innovation and dynamic capabilities in emerging economics: Evidence from the Indian automotive sector. *Technological Forecasting and Social Change*, *129*, 323–329.

People's Government of Inner Mongolia Autonomous Region. (2020). *Kuaishou invests tens of billions to build a data center in UlanQab*. Author.

Peter, J. W., Feng, W., Yin, E., & Lei, L. N. (2020). Is disruptive innovation in emerging economies different? Evidence from China. *Journal of Engineering and Technology Management*, *57*, 101590.

Petti, C., Tang, Y., & Margherita, A. (2019). Technological innovation vs technological backwardness patterns in latecomer firms: An absorptive capacity perspective. *Journal of Engineering and Technology Management*, *51*, 10–20.

Research Institute of iResearch Consulting. (2020). *2020 China Data Center Industry Research Report*. Author.

Romer, P. M. (1986). Increasing Returns and Long-Run Growth. *Journal of Political Economy*, *94*(5), 1002–1037.

Schumpeter, J. A. (1934). Harvard Economic Studies: Vol. 46. The Theory of Economic Development-An Inquiry into Profits, Capital, Credit, Interest, and the Business Cycle. Academic Press.

Shi, Z. Z. (2020). Research on the path of digital economy empowering high-quality development from the perspective of new infrastructure. *Open Management*, *12*, 145–149. doi:10.16517/j.cnki.cn12-1034/f.2020.12. 028

Si, S., & Chen, H. (2020). A literature review of disruptive innovation: what it is, how it works and where it goes. *The Journal of Engineering and Technology Management*. https://doi.org/. jengtecman.2020.101568 doi:10.1016/j

Solow Robert, M. (1956). A Contribution to the Theory of Economic Growth. *The Quarterly Journal of Economics*, *70*(3).

Sun, H. H. (2020). Research on the development trend of Internet + IDC under 5G commercial applications. *China Business Forum*, *8*, 117-118. doi:10.19699/j.cnki.issn2096-0298.2020.08.117

Sun, L. J. (2018). Research on the Development of Inner Mongolia's IDC Industry. University of Inner Mongolia, 20-22.

Tan, J., Wang, L., Zhang, H., & Li, W. (2020). Disruptive innovation and technology ecosystem: The evolution of the inter-cohesive public–private collaboration network in Chinese telecommunication industry. *Journal of Engineering and Technology Management*, *57*, 101573.

Tang, J. P., & Wang, Z. G. (2018). Practice and thinking on the training of big data talents. *Northern Economics*, *Z1*, 49–50.

The Russian Government. (2013). *On the Federal Targeted Program for Research and Development in Priority Areas of Development of the Russian Scientific and Technological Complex for 2014-2020*. Retrieved September 30, 2021, from: http://government.ru/en/docs/2129/

Vance, A. (2008, December 8). Dell Sees Double with Data Center in a Container. *The New York Times*.

Wang, W.L., Wang, Y.X, & Gao, Y.M. (2020). IDC based on the "new infrastructure" scenario: meaning, dilemma and approach. *Administrative Reform*, *10*, 68-74. doi:10.14150/j.cnki.1674-7453.2020.10.008

Wang, Y. Q. (2019). The legal connotation of public data and its standardized application path. *Digital Library Forum*, 8.

Wang, Z.X. (2020). Research on the construction of big data centers for the industrial Internet in the new era. *Technological Innovation and Application*, *15*, 71-72. doi: CNKI:SUN:CXYY.0.2020-15-028

Wei, Q. L. (2014). *Data Envelopment Analysis*. Beijing Science Press.

Xu, C. A. (2018). New Ideas for the Development of Internet Data Center Industry in Inner Mongolia. *China Construction Information Technology*, *1*, 54–57.

Yang, P. (2020). China's establishment of an integrated national Internet data center governance path setting. *Henan Social Sciences*, 4.

Yu, C., Ding, Y. C., & Wang, P. P. (2019). Research on the new infrastructure of future cities from the perspective of comprehensive regional development. *China Real Estate*, *20*, 53–60. doi:10.13562/j.china.real.estate.2019.20.016

Yu, S.Y., Wang, J.D., & Guo, Q.M. (2020). Challenges and Countermeasures Faced by China in Building a New Data Element Market System. *Henan Social Sciences*, 3.

Yuventi, J., & Mehdizadeh, R. (2013). A critical analysis of Power Usage Effectiveness and its use in communicating data center energy consumption. *Energy and Building*, *64*, 90–94.

Zhang, N., & Zhao, X. J. (2020). Understanding the blockchain-based government inter-departmental data sharing from collaborative consensus to smart contract. China Administration, 1.

Chapter 12
Green Technology for Industrial Development in Colombia

Danilo Piaggesi
https://orcid.org/0000-0003-4610-174X
Knowledge for Development (K4D), USA

Helena Landazuri
Knowledge for Development (K4D), USA

Bo Jia
Tsinghua University, China

EXECUTIVE SUMMARY

Colombia's economy is the fourth largest in Latin America. Though there has been significant growth in modern industries, most industries are still driven by agriculture and commodities. The main challenges Colombian industries face include becoming more energy-efficient, modernizing processes and organizational structures, and reducing their environmental impact. In the meantime, the Republic of Korea has made significant efforts to fuel its economy through innovation, and there is also a similarity in terms of both countries' interest and commitment to use ICT as a basis for their growth. This chapter presents a project that is a pilot test of adaptive transfer of "green" ICT technology innovation developed by specialized agencies/private sector in the Republic of Korea, to be applied to a host of Colombian industrial sectors volunteering to participate with the purpose of improving production through environmentally friendly technology.

INTRODUCTION

This chapter discusses the situation of Colombia's industrial sector in terms of its contribution to environmental sustainability, particularly in the areas of energy efficiency and green-house gas emissions. The chapter further discusses opportunities for collaboration with countries more technologically advanced than Colombia in this area, specifically with the Republic of Korea, and postulates that a bilateral agreement among the two countries would produce positive results.

DOI: 10.4018/978-1-7998-8417-0.ch012

The chapter does not intend to present a scientific analysis of the topic, but rather describe a proposed cooperation model for future application. In particular, the chapter postulates that environmental sustainability of the industrial sector through energy efficiency and reduced greenhouse gas emissions could be attained under the following circumstances: (i) policy convergence and overall similar economic and social contexts facilitate a commonality of purpose, which is crucial in every collaborative setting; (ii) widespread use of technology innovations to improve industrial products and processes; and (iii) "south-south" cooperation (among two developing countries) creates a more balanced exchange and better lends itself to win-win situations than "vertical" (developed to developing country) schemes.

CONCEPTUAL FRAMEWORK

Definitions

Environmental Sustainability is commonly defined as "the ability to maintain or improve standards of living without damaging or depleting natural resources for present and future generations" (United States Environmental Protection Agency, 2021). This concept applies to the present chapter to the extent that improvements in energy efficiency and lowering of greenhouse gases can contribute significantly to achieving a country's economic goals through industrial development that can be enacted with fewer costs and reduced environmental impact.

Energy Efficiency is referred to here as "energy efficiency refers to a method of reducing energy consumption by using less energy to attain the same amount of useful output" (Energeysage, 2019). In practical terms, energy efficiency eliminating or reducing energy waste. Energy efficiency brings a variety of benefits: reducing greenhouse gas emissions, reducing demand for energy imports, and lowering energy consume costs.

Greenhouse gases (GHG) are gases that trap heat in the atmosphere (carbon dioxide, methane, nitrous oxide, fluorinated gas, among others). GHG are emitted by man-made activities as well as by natural causes. Carbon dioxide is the primary GHG emitted through human activities. Large emissions of GHG lead to higher concentrations in the atmosphere, which in turn leads to the "greenhouse effect", or the trapping of the sun's warmth in the planet's lower atmosphere and therefore a rise in earth's biosphere temperature (United States Environmental Protection Agency, 2021).

Technology innovation refers to "new or improved product or process whose technological characteristics are significantly different from before" (Tilastokeskus, 2000[REMOVED HYPERLINK FIELD]). In the presentchapter, the term technology innovation is used to describe internet- or ICT-based changes in industrial processes and choice of raw materials that can result in greater industrial output while at the same time reducing its environmental impact.

Green ICT refers both, to the use of Information and Communications Technologies (ICT) to improve environmental sustainability of [industrial] products or processes, as well as the minimization of any negative impact of the IT operations themselves.

South-South cooperation is a term used to describe the "exchange of knowledge, resources and technology between developing countries.

Premises

This chapter presents a case based on three premises: (i) that energy efficiency and reduction in GHG emissions are important to enhance environmental sustainability; (ii) that technology innovation can contribute significantly to industrial integration of energy efficiency and reduced GHG emissions; and (iii) that south-south cooperation to facilitate the adoption of technology innovation for those purposes is a viable and effective way to generate such result.

COLOMBIA'S INDUSTRIAL SECTOR

Structure of the Industrial Sector

Colombia's economy is the fourth largest in Latin America as measured by GDP. The country's principal export is oil and derivatives (55% of its exports), followed by manufacturing industries, which make around 12% of Colombia's exports.

In Colombia, even though there has been significant growth in modern industries like shipbuilding, electronics, automobile, and tourism, most industries are still driven by agriculture and commodities. The main industries are textile, agribusiness (cut flowers, bananas, sugarcane, and coffee), beverages; other industries include mining (coal, gold, and emeralds), oil and petrochemicals, chemical products, metallurgy, cement, construction, iron and steel products, and metalworking, cardboard containers, and plastic resins. The industry sector represents 26.7% of the GDP and employs 19.3% of the workforce.

Environmental Sustainability in Colombian Industry Sector

Energy Efficiency

Energy supply in Colombia is heavily centralized around fossil fuel (coal and oil), which covers 77% of the supply, with the remaining 23% provided by hydroelectricity, natural gas and non-conventional sources of renewable energy (bagasse, biofuels and firewood). Energy consumption is increasing, mainly due to added demand from the manufacturing industry and the transport sector; the first accounts for an average 28% of energy consumption, and the second accounts for 35%. While renewable energy are a positive trend in terms of sustainability, hydroelectricity is more susceptible to changes in the natural environment associated to climate change.

Energy consumption has increased by close to 80% between 1975 and 2018, equivalent to an annual average growth rate of 1.81%. This growth is due mainly to an increase in energy consumption in the manufacturing industry with an annual average growth of 2.4%, and in the transportation sector, with 5.9%. (Global Transmission Report, 2020)

The environmental footprint of the manufacturing industry in Colombia is heavily affected by its reliance on fossil fuel sources. In 2018, the main energy sources utilized by industry were: natural gas (34.18%); coal (29.13%); bagasse (14.11%); electricity (19.02%), which means that fossil fuel sources supply 63.31% of the energy requirements of the manufacturing industry, with the water and air pollution impacts associated to the use of fossil fuels.

The sector's footprint could be reduced if the industry showed a high energy efficiency ratio. However, energy efficiency in the industry sector in Colombia, particularly in manufacturing industry, has been historically low, in spite of recent decades significant increase in investment. Such investments have focused on improving products and production lines; developing new products; adopting new management technologies; and training (Martínez, 2010). Even after these investments, several areas of improvement in terms of energy efficiency remain, including for example: optimization of electricity use for the driving force; optimization of combustion/boiler processes as well as in the cold chain; efficiency in illumination; introduction of energy management systems including cleaner production, cogeneration and autogeneration (Martínez and Piña, 2014).

Greenhouse Gases

While the manufacturing industry is directly responsible for only 4% of CO2 emissions to the atmosphere (USAID, 2017), agroindustry has a much larger indirect effect, inasmuch as the subsector livestock, cattle and met are directly related to the agriculture and land-use change and forestry sectors, and these account for a combined 40% of such emissions (USAID, 2017). Deforestation to open new pasture land, and direct emissions from cattle waste are important contributors of green house gases, besides having a significant impact on biodiversity and habitat conservation. Livestock production is also associated to impacts on water quality and water supply.

Another sector with strong environmental impacts is the leather goods sector, which utilizes highly contaminating chemicals, with effluents often released directly to the sewage system which in turn contaminate ground and surface water. There are also emissions released to the air, deteriorating local and regional air quality; the presence of strong odors associated to the industrial treatment of leather is a common complaint in areas where those industries are located.

The textiles and apparel industries, although responsible for lower levels of liquid effluents discharged in water systems and air pollutants discharged in the air, their impact is significant because of their wide-spread distribution among urban settlements, having therefore localized but intense impacts on the environment.

Among the non-commodities-related industries that are growing in Colombia, there is one sector of interest for the case being discussed here: electronics. This sector is interesting not only because of its direct environmental impacts as an energy-intensive, and heavy-metal-dependent sector, but also because it uses a disproportionate share of ICT products and services and therefore constitutes a good case for promoting the use of green technologies and minimizing the impact of ICT use itself.

Colombia's Industrial Development Challenges

Main challenges Colombian industries face include becoming more energy-efficient, modernizing processes and organizational structures, and reducing their environmental impact.

One crucial factor that affects the inability of Colombian industries to become more energy- efficient and less pollutant is technology obsolescence. Research conducted on energy use and digital technology applications undertaken by one of Colombia's prestigious universities –University of El Rosario–which has a Research Line on Technology Change and Strategic Innovation as part of its Business Administration Faculty, shows that one of the most serious problems faced by the Colombian productive sector is precisely technology obsolescence. This phenomenon affects prominently production processes, and has direct impacts on the environment, as well as on the productivity of each production factor.

Colombian industry development is also handicapped by deficiencies in human capital, specifically an insufficiently prepared labor force; only 0.3% of employees in Colombian industries have a Master's o PhD degree; yet, statistics show that it is this highly-educated segment the one with the greatest opportunities to put together an enterprise that will succeed, as this segment is overwhelmingly motivated by "opportunity" (90,5%) rather than "necessity", which tends to be the reason behind the great majority of new business openings, mostly headed by entrepreneurs who only finished high-school. Additionally, slower than desirable progress has been detected in engineering education, both in terms of teaching as well as in research, and the same is true for post-graduate education –master's and PhD, and there are opportunities to improve this situation through collaboration between Universities and industry (Celis and Acosta, 2016).

Main barriers for the development of opportunity-based enterprises are two:

1. Lack of access to innovative products and services that would allow the enterprise to differentiate its outputs from those of others; and
2. Lack of access to funding in the very early stages, particularly seed-money (National Development Plan 2018-2022).

In 2019 OECD's Development Centre in collaboration with the United Nations Economic Commission for Latin America and the Caribbean (ECLAC) generated a "Production Transformation Policy Review (PTPR)" for Colombia. The report points out that, although foreign investment in Colombia has increased considerably since 2016 –time of the peace deal–, the country's economy still relies too heavily on natural resources (about 80% of exports were based on primary production and mining). The report also noted that "despite a relatively long tradition of manufacturing, the sector is becoming less relevant and less competitive. Productivity has not increased enough for Colombia to catch up with more advanced economies. Economic opportunities continue to be limited to a few territories."

Facing and overcoming these challenges in a way that improves the environmental sustainability of the industrial sector is a high priority for the country and the subject of the project presented here.

COMMON INTERESTS AND OPPORTUNITIES FOR SYNERGIES IN A RELATIONSHIP BETWEEN COLOMBIA AND SOUTH KOREA

Policy Convergence

Republic of Korea

The Republic of Korea, after the Second World War, undertook a shift from an agrarian to an industrial economy, which intensified after the Korean War, resulting on a balance of 82% of its population living in urban areas. It has become a large industrial country, with some predictable consequences in terms of environmental sustainability. The country's mountainous, coastline and tropical and deciduous forests have not been adequately protected, and air quality in Seoul and surrounding province has deteriorated significantly (AZO Cleantech, 2015). The Republic of Korea has one of the worst air quality indexes of all advanced nations of the OECD, to a great extent resulting from emissions from industrial sites and power plants, while the rest originates in neighboring countries.

In July 2020, the Republic of Korea announced it commits USD61 billion to fund a "Green New Deal" by 2025, which is part of a wider national strategy to transform the economy away from carbon-dependency by boosting its renewable energy capacity, and creating new jobs at the same time (Renewables Now, 2020).

This strategy follows the line of previous efforts by the Republic of Korea to curb air pollution and improve air quality related to its internal processes. In the recent past, the Republic of Korea, through its Ministry of Knowledge Economy (MKE) which run between 2008 and 2013, and more recently the Ministry of Trade, Industry and Energy (MOTIE), is fostering the adoption of "green technologies" both in public and private sector operations, having established ambitious goals for the development and dissemination of green technology in different production areas. Given Korea's strong performance in the information and communication technology (ICT) sector, and in line with its green technology drive, Korea is a growing leader in the development of "green ICTs", a novel and promising application aimed at "encompassing environmentally sustainable information technology and the use of information technology to contribute to environment preservation" (Jung, 2016). "Green ICT" have a two-fold purpose: first, reduce the environmental footprint of industry and other productive sectors vital to the country´s economy through the application of information and communication technologies (ICT), and second, achieve this while avoiding the creation of an added source of contamination derived from the use of the ICT themselves.

The Republic of Korea's Green ICT policy is consistent with the country's past and current Intended Nationally Determined Contributions (INDC) Submission to the United Nations for 2030, where the country expressed its intention to reduce its greenhouse emissions by 37% from the business-as-usual level by 2030 across all economic sectors. Principal economic sectors where this reduction must come from include: industrial processes and product use, and agriculture and waste. Korea will make partial use of carbon credits from international market mechanisms to achieve its 2030 mitigation target. To instrument the policy, the government of Korea has pledged to use 2% of its gross domestic product annually to promote research and develop new green infrastructure.

Colombia

Colombia's environmental issues and policies are heavily influenced by difficult internal affairs related principally to drug trafficking and related guerrilla/peace processes. Directly related to those phenomena include deforestation and biodiversity loss, as well unsustainable land management practices that result in erosion and water contamination. Unrelated to such phenomena are environmental issues that stem from the growth of urban centers --encroachment into natural cover areas, air pollution and solid waste-- as well as industrial development that produces air, water and soil contamination often entailing chemical effluents, and industrial waste sometimes hazardous.

The combined effect of all these processes is generating Green House Gases (GHG) that worry not only the country itself but also the international community. Acting within the framework of the United Nations Framework Convention on Climate Change (UNFCCC), Colombia has voluntarily agreed to a 20% reduction of greenhouse gas emissions by 2030.

In 2018, Colombia issued an influential post-conflict strategy "Green Book 2030: Science and Innovation for Sustainable Development" with an emphasis on social justice and environmentally sustainable development through a transformative focus on science and innovation policy. To do this, there must be continuous investment in knowledge production strongly focused on the SDGs, make the university system more attuned to research impact, restructure the country's innovation systems, among others (TIP Consortium, 2018).

Central to Colombia's environmental policy is the transition to sustainable energy generation and consumption, which focuses on decentralization and digitalization of the energy network. To support this, the government is working on redefining energy systems, increasing the participation of new renewable sources and energy efficiency systems, and incorporating new technologies (Global Transmission Report, 2020).

Colombia's Ministry of Environment and Sustainable Development (MADS) guides the adoption of sustainability criteria applicable to the management of the productive and institutional sectors, promotes the incorporation of environmental management systems and fosters technological re-structuring and changes in consumption patterns to environmentally sustainable patterns. The Directorate of Sustainable Sector Development (DDSS) of MADS is responsible for proposing policies, strategies and regulations to fulfill those objectives.

Similarities and Differences Between the Cases of Colombia and Republic of Korea

There are both similarities and differences between the two countries; both first facilitate possible collaboration among them, the first as a source of common ground; the second as an opportunity to develop win/win situations.

Similarities among them, interestingly, revolve around the structure of the economy and the role the industry sector plays in it. There is also a similarity in terms of the countries interest and commitment to use ICT as a basis for their growth. These lines of similarity would facilitate the establishment of cooperation lines between the two. (See Table 1)

Table 1. Similarities between Colombia and R.of Korea: economic indicators for the industry and ICT sectors, 2019 and 2020

Indicators	Colombia	Rep. of Korea
Industry as % of GDP	26.27% (1)	33.0% (2)
Industry as % of labor force	20.02% (3)	25.0% (2)
Place as provider of IT services in its region	3rd (3)	3rd (4)

Source: ((1)(3)Statista,2020; (2)Nordea,2020; (4) U.S.News,2020))

Additionally, climate change is the central theme in both the Republic of Korea's and Colombia's environmental problems; achieving energy efficiency and reducing GHG emissions seat at the base of both countries' environmental strategies. Embracing "green" technologies would contribute both to energy efficiency and at the same time reduce harmful GHG emissions. The Republic of Korea has gained significant experience in the field of green technologies and is in a good position to share its findings with other countries.

There are of course great differences between the two countries when it comes to current knowledge-based industrial development, starting from the role of government to support it. (See Table 2)

Table 2. Differences between Colombia and the R.of Korea: investment in industry innovation

Area	Colombia	Rep. of Korea
Government investment in R&D	0.236% of GDP (2018) (1)	4.81% of GDP (2) USD 73.3 billion
Private sector investment in R&D	ND	USD 56 billion
Government sponsored R&D centers (#) supporting industry	12	25
Government funded innovation support systems	Green New Deal with ambitious goals for 2050	Green Book 2030: Science and Innovation for Sustainable Development
Government/University/Industry colaboration systems	Not mentioned in policy	Central to government policy

Source: ((1) Trading Economics, 2020; (2) World Bank, 2020))

The OECD's review of innovation policy has long suggested Colombia needs to improve its standing in relation to innovation in several areas of its productive sectors (OECD, 2014). Innovation has been identified as needed to raise productivity in manufacturing and agriculture, and also in service industries. To accomplish that, OECD has recommended further investment in ICT infrastructure, as well as adding new skill- and knowledge-intensive activities to add to the productivity and increase efficiency. Innovation-driven diversification has also been suggested as a means to increase value-added production, sustain employment growth and generate additional income.

In 2014, the OECD noticed progress in terms of Colombia's innovation policy, in particular, the introduction of innovation in the country's 2010-2014 National Development Plan, and an increase in resources devoted to science, technology and innovation (OECD, 2014). However, implementation of these plans has proven elusive. Government investment in R&D activities –which includes both capital and current expenditures in the four main sectors: Business enterprise, Government, Higher education and Private non-profit. R&D investment covers basic research, applied research, and experimental development; it peaked in 2014 when R&D constituted 0.31% of GDP, but went down to 0.23 in 2018. The current administration has pledged to increase R&D spending to 1.5% of GDP by 2022 (Wight, 2019). Low public investment in this area is reportedly tied to the fact that the manufacturing sector does not make sufficient use of such instruments to support its production (Inter-American Development Bank, 2011). While figures on private sector investment in R&D in Colombia are hard to come by, it is estimated that over 50% of the firms spend in R&D, compensating for the inefficient link with the public sector. Most Colombian industries out-source the bulk of their R&D. There is expectation that a newly established Ministry of Science will promote a more consistent approach (Wight, 2019).

In contrast, the Republic of Korea has made significant efforts to fuel its economy through innovation; the country's R&D spending is fifth largest among OECD members in 2018. R&D as a percentage of GDP was 4.81% in 2018 which, given the size of its economy, reaches the impressive figure of over 73 billion USD in 2018, an 8.8% increase over the previous year. The private sector is responsible for an also significant amount of investment in the R&D sector, having invested some USD65 billion in 2018, an increase of 9.4% over the year before (The Korea Herald, 2019).

Collaboration between government, industry and academia –a model known as "The Tripple Helix Approach" (Piaggesi, et al, 2013)— in the republic of Korea has empowered large industry-based R&D centers; the largest industrial groups (known locally as "chaebols") work with the government and local universities to increase R&D intensity focusing on applied knowledge in the petrochemicals, car manufacturing, shipbuilding and consumer electronics industries. Currently, companies are turning to new fields –biotechnology, artificial intelligence, cybersecurity--, backed by government funding and supported by the national technological infrastructure (Dayton, 2020).

Cooperation Mandates and Established Channels

In the Republic of Korea, the MOTIE and the Korean Ministry of Environment coordinate with the Ministry of Strategy and Finance to work in cooperation with the Korean International Development Agency (KOICA) to fulfill government directives to expand the international exposure of Korean-developed technology. KOICA, which has representation in Colombia, is in a position to fund pilot projects to facilitate development and transfer of Korean-originated and jointly-developed ICT innovation.

For the government of Colombia, the MADS has the function of developing sector management instruments through projects capable of channeling technical assistance to assist the adoption of sustainable growth strategies in the various economic sectors, including the use of science, technology and innovation as tools for improved competitiveness and development. In pursuing these goals, the MADS promotes Public-Private Partnerships (PPP) to facilitate the direct transfer of environmental management systems to its users. To undertake these activities, the MADS manages the channeling of international cooperation resources to complement the Ministry's investment in this area.

Policy directives and implementation strategies supported by the Republic of Korea could be of direct use to Colombia's efforts. The means by which the Republic of Korea tackles the implementation of such policies and strategies is potentially directly transferable to the case of Colombia for both, reduction in emissions and lowering of ICT impact.

Transferability of these strategies and tactics is explored in the project described below.

A PROJECT TO FOSTER SOUTH-SOUTH COOPERATION TOWARDS APPLICATION OF GREEN TECHNOLOGIES TO SELECTED INDUSTRIAL SECTORS IN COLOMBIA

Objective

The project is a pilot test of adaptive transfer of "green" ICT technology innovation developed by specialized agencies/private sector in the Republic of Korea, to be applied to a host of Colombian industrial sectors volunteering to participate with the purpose of improving production through environmentally friendly technology.

Two concepts are central to the design and implementation of the project: (i) technology innovation and ICT can be applied to select inputs, processes and products to improve environmental management and performance and reduce the environmental impact of economic activities by increasing automation, while at the same time improving efficiency; reducing redundancies; allowing real-time monitoring, among others; and (ii) potential environmental impacts of the use of ICT systems can be minimized by adopting measures like: virtualization to reduce emissions (cloud computing); maximizing energy efficiency using lower voltage systems; reducing electromagnetic pollution footprint; recycling hardware & chemical byproducts; improving efficiency of ICT operations by area cooling and optimization of space; among others.

The objective of the project is to demonstrate how green ICT developed by one country (Republic of Korea) and adapted to the particular circumstances of the beneficiary country (Colombia), can:

- Effectively reduce the selected sectors' environmental footprint;
- Generate organizational savings as well as sustainable business and employment opportunities;
- Contribute to reaching carbon-neutrality goals adopted by the beneficiary country;

Strategy

There are two principal decisions to make in order to implement the project:

1. Which industrial sectors in the beneficiary and donor countries would participate in the project; and
2. What types of technologies would be applied to participating companies.

As it concerns the *selection of sectors*, the project's strategy is to select those industrial sectors relevant to both participating countries, where technology innovation can have significant impact as demonstrated basically by the experience accumulated in the donor country. There are at least five industrial sectors where the Republic of Korea and Colombia share interest and investment and which could be good candidates to choose for the project: shipbuilding, electronics (Korea is the world's largest producer of semiconductors), car manufacturing, textiles and steel.

As it concerns the *type of technology* that would be applied, there are in turn two facets to it: technologies capable of improving efficiency and technologies capable of reducing environmental impact. In all five of these sectors the Republic of Korea has developed innovation technology capable of enhancing production white at the same time reducing the sector's environmental footprint (Nordea, 2020).

The choice of which of technologies to apply would be guided by the accumulated experience of the Republic of Korea. There, the intended reduction in industrial sectors´ footprint is accomplished basically by:

1. Gains in automation;
2. Lowering mobility needs;
3. Greater process efficiency; and
4. Fewer redundancies.

Low-environmental impact is achieved by:

1. Reductions in direct electro-magnetic and other emissions;
2. Maximum energy efficiency;

Lower hardware waste generation;

3. Chemicals recycling;
4. More efficient cooling and isolation systems; and
5. Optimization of work space design.

The actual choice of sectors and technologies would take place once the project negotiation with participating governments, specialized agencies and private sector participants starts. The list provided above is, in this sense, a suggestion to be confirmed or modified during the implementation phase of the project.

Organizational Structure

Three groups of participants are needed for the project to succeed:

1. Government agencies, both in the donor and beneficiary countries, in charge of industrial policy and incentives, education, technology innovation and ICT;
2. Public and private sector agencies specialized in technology development, including environmental management;
3. Universities and other instruction outlets. To these, private companies within the sectors selected for project implementation are added. This array of actors corresponds, grosso modo, to the KE architecture described earlier in this document; they describe the four pillars sustaining the KE: education (Universities and others); technology innovation (public and private research centers); ICT infrastructure (mostly government); and habilitating policies (government).

Government Agencies

For the government of the Republic of Korea, at least the following agencies would need to be engaged:

- Ministry of Trade, Industry and Energy (MOTIE, successor of the Ministry of Knowledge Economy), which regulates policy for the industry and energy sectors, and which has a Vice Minister in charge of: planning and coordination; industrial policy; industry and enterprise innovation; and energy and resources.
- Ministry of Science and ICT (MSIT), which under a 2nd Vice Minister, has an Office of ICT Policy, which has an ICT Policy Bureau that has mandate over: digital society planning; digital industry policy; and digital inclusion policy; as well as an ICT Industry Policy Bureau,which has mandate over: ICT industry policy; ICT and broadcasting technology policy; and ICT industry infrastructure.

For the Government of the Republic of Colombia at least two-Ministry level agencies would need to participate:

- The MADS, which has, among its functions: cooperating in the technical, scientific and technology fields; foster joint development of programs, activities and projects aimed at providing advise, performing research, education and extension in the fields of technology development and innovation associated to the area of environment, as well as others that would support technology development and innovation;

- The Ministry of Commerce, Industry and Tourism (MCIT), which has a Superintendency of Industry and Commerce that regulates fair business practices, promotes competitiveness and acts as the patent and registration office.

Specialized Agencies

In the Republic of Korea, there are two organizations specialized in fields pertinent to the project, who could either or jointly participate in the project as project coordinators or consultants: (i) Green Technology Center; and (ii) Korea Institute of Industrial Technology.

The Green Technology Center (GTC) was founded in Seoul in 2012 by the government of the Republic of Korea; the Center is a governmental organization that conducts high-quality research in the field of green technology R&D policies, with the purpose of counteracting climate change and the exhaustion of natural resources (KDFuelCell, 2013). The GTC works in three major areas: R&D policy and planning; networking and cooperation; and foresight for sustainable future (See Figure 1). Its mission is to act as a think-tank and become a successful communication channel between users and suppliers of green technology.

Figure 1. Role of the GTC
Source: Green Technology Center, 2020

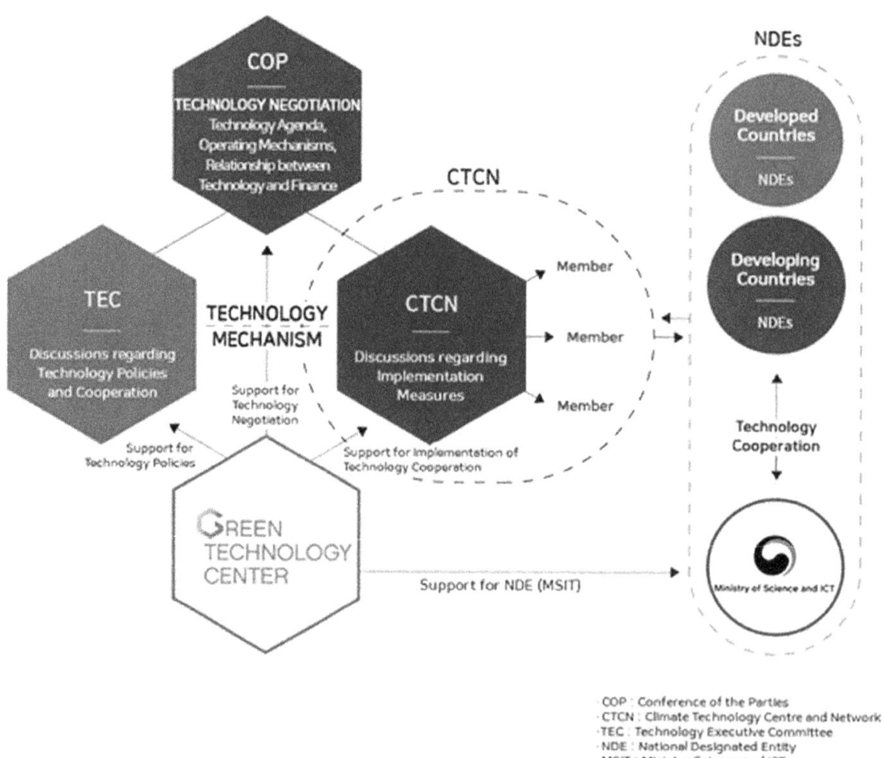

GTC has established cooperation agreements with several UN agencies (UNIDO, UNDP, UNESCAP) and works in tandem with the central government, in particular with the Ministry of Science and ICT (MSIT) to support the implementation of climate technology partnership projects; in that context, it conducts research on technology financing and marketing mechanisms for the development and transfer of technologies both nationally and internationally.

In particular, GTC works with developing countries to reduce international emissions by matching developing country technology needs with technology developed in the Republic of Korea. (See Figure 2)

Figure 2. International cooperation by the Korean GTC
Source: Green Technology Center, 2020

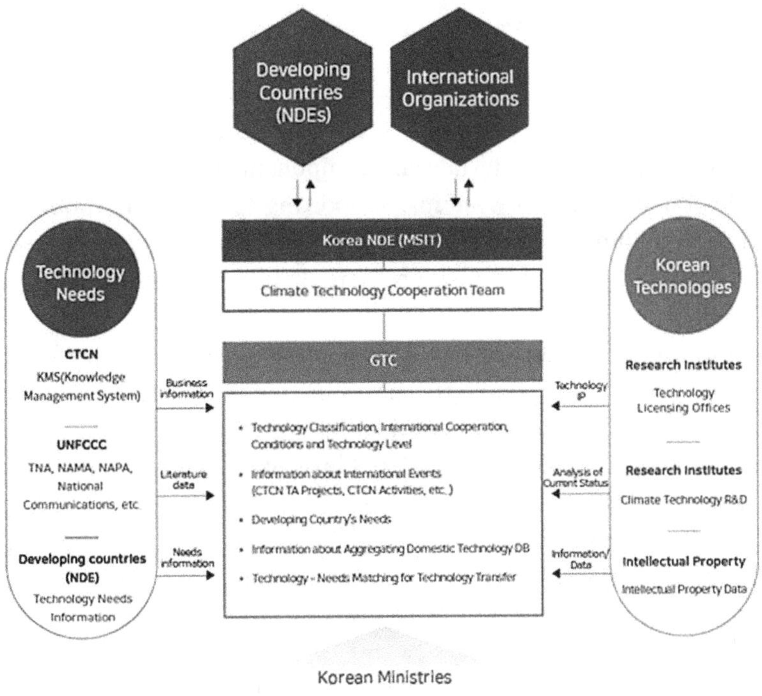

In performing these functions, the GTC's mandate is in close alignment with the intent and design of the project. While GTC does have established collaboration channels with KOICA, it has yet to set up projects in South America.

The Korea Institute of Industrial Technology (KITECH) was established by the Government of the Republic of Korea in 1989 as a governmental entity charged with supporting the industrial sector, in particular Small and Medium Enterprises (SME). Its mission is to contribute to the growth of the manufacturing industry through the development, application and commercialization of manufacturing technology. In doing this, the KITECH coordinates with and complements the work of academia, other R&D institutes and the industries themselves. (See Figure 3)

Figure 3. Role of KITECH
Source: KITECH, 2020

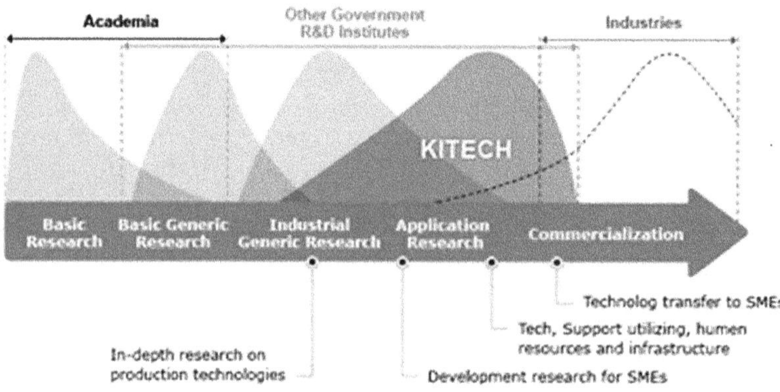

Among its areas of work, KITECH focuses on developing and expending manufacturing-based technologies to: improve the quality of materials and components in key industries (mostly metal-based industries); develop clean manufacturing systems, supporting low-cost, high-quality, energy-efficient, eco-friendly production; and complements this work by investing in industry convergence technology, looking to innovate existing industries and create new markets through convergence between technologies and industries.

In this sense KITECH constitutes an opportunity to link those industrial sectors where potential cooperation with Colombia exists with technologies developed in the Republic of Korea, whether readily available or newly tackled in the context of the project.

In Colombia, there are no wide-ranging specialized institutes such as the ones described for the Republic of Korea, but there are at least two organizations that could potentially participate in the project as they specialize in the various industrial sub-sectors which could be considered for inclusion: (i) Science and Technology Corporation for Naval, Maritime and Riverine Industry Development-COTECMAR; and (ii) Center for Technology Research and Development for Electric and Electronic Industries and ICT (CIDEI).

The Science and Technology Corporation for Naval, Maritime and Riverine Industry Development-COTECMAR is a non-for-profit corporation, associated to the Ministry of National Defense, registered as a private entity although it is funded by the central government. Its mission is to develop applied research to generate innovative solutions to the development of the maritime sector. COTECMAR responds to the "triple helix" approach mentioned earlier, as it works in tandem with the central government and universities.

The Center for Technology Research and Development for Electric and Electronic Industries and ICT (CIDEI) is a non-for-profit organization established in 2001 with seed capital from the Ministry of Science (COLCIENCIAS) and contributions from the private sector. Its mission if to contribute knowledge in the area of science, technology and innovation to improve the prospects of Colombia's productive sectors. To do this, CIDEI undertakes research projects to develop, integrate and transfer technology innovation in the fields of electricity, electronics and ICT, with the purpose of generating innovative industrial products; CIDEI also supports beneficiary industries in the adoption and management of such technologies, including providing advice and training as needed. CIDEI also works with Universities and other research centers, and has several international cooperation agreements.

Other Colombian organizations that could be interested in participating in the project include, for example the Business incubation and development corporation for technology-based companies (Cluster CREATIC) is a private sector initiative started by ICT companies wishing to promote the adoption of ICT and technology innovation in private enterprises in diverse sectors. There is also another organization with mandate in this field, although its geographical scope is limited; it is the Corporation Research and Technology Development Center for the Los Llanos region (CEINDETEC), which focuses in the areas of electronics and ICT, similarly to the Cluster CREATIC.

Specialized institutions from other countries could be invited to participate in the project. Among them, the Monterrey Institute of Technology in Mexico (ITM) would be a prime candidate. The Institute, established in 1943, is one of the most advanced R&D organizations in Latin America, with a research focus on the creation of wealth through innovation, technological development and knowledge administration. The objective of this research area is to design a systemic, techno-economic-social model supported by: information and communication technologies, modern innovation approaches, network-based economies, and economic principles of increasing value returns to create economic and social prosperity in emerging countries. Among the lines of research currently underway are: regional systems of innovation; clusters of innovation and competition; networks of techno-economical-social value; and impact of the impact of information technologies on economic growth in the social and environmental development of emerging Countries. The ITM has a faculty of some 300 international staff.

Finally, a non-for-profit organization based in the USA, would complete the group of participating agencies. The Knowledge for Development (K4D) is a non-for-profit non-governmental organization, which works to maximize the use of knowledge resources as a basis for development. Under its International Knowledge Economy Program (IKEP), K4D brokers project financing to support developing countries initiatives looking to apply the concept and instruments of the Knowledge Economy to specific development challenges. K4D is the project originator, in this case.

Universities and Other Education Centers

In the Republic of Korea, the University of Dongukk (UD), is proposed as lead academic institution to participate in the project. UD is a private institution established in 1906, and is one of Korea's top institutions of higher learning. UD has graduate schools in Image & Information Technology; Business Administration; Communication and Information; and Industrial Technology. Its distinguishing character is its openness to all cultures and faiths, and its intended purpose is to act as a bridge between East and West, and as such strives to make Korean culture and values known world-wide while at the same time opening opportunities for its students to learn of the world outside Korea.

In Colombia, University of El Rosario could be proposed as the local counterpart to UD. It was founded in 1653 and is the second oldest university in Latin America. Located in Bogota, Colombia, it is known as "The Cradle of the Republic". The institution remains very influential in Colombian culture and public life. At least 28 of Colombia's presidents have been students of this university. It has influenced and participated in very important transitional processes like the revolution for the independence from Spain and the drafting of the Political National Constitution of 1991. It is the only Colombian university accredited by the European Association of Universities; it is ranked as "Very Superior".

Project implementation foresses the participation of all agencies and organizations depicted in this summary, although the specific constitution of the team and allocation of responsibilities is subject to agreements that would be designed at the time of project implementation.
Roles adopted by each organization would follow a distribution that is suggested here:

1. Government organizations would be in charge of:
    a. supporting project implementation through approvals, sponsorships and funding if necessary;
    b. providing policy and regulatory guidance;
    c. negotiating cooperation agreements and external funding sources;
    d. sponsoring international exposure to project results and lessons learned.
2. Specialized agencies would be responsible for:
    a. project coordination;
    b. industry sector pre-selection and selection, after surveys and interviews at both ends of the spectrum;
    c. recruiting participating industrial outlets at both ends of the cooperation;
    d. drafting and negotiating all collaboration protocols and instruments needed for the operation of the project;
    e. selecting technology innovation products and processes in agreement with participating industries;
    f. leading decision-making regarding the potential need to adapt technology to specific needs of the beneficiaries;
    g. arranging the technology transfer instruments to materialize the cooperation;
    h. providing follow up, monitoring and evaluation;
    i. develop "best practice" studies and promote their analysis and presentation of project results in international fora. It is foreseen that the project originator (K4D) will provide initial impetus to launch the project and will establish the basic agreements among participants, as well as manage the funding requests to cover initial costs.
3. Universities would:
    a. provide theoretical backing to the choices of technology and transfer instruments;
    b. train project participants;
    c. providing feedback to the government on the workings of the policy directives that guide the project;
    d. implement the exchange programs through which the project experience will be multiplied and its benefits furthered.

In order to ensure the proper development of this agreement, Specific Covenants will be developed to tackle also specific subjects that involve the different participating organizations; such detailed agreements will describe the areas, fields, projects and activities that would be developed, and the specific conditions under which such activities would be undertaken.

Project Components

The following paragraphs describe the possible structure of project implementation, which would be later reformed as needed.

Component 1: Tailored Technical and Organizational Specifications

Under this component, the following activities are envisioned:

- Selection of thematic areas, economic sectors and participating organizations/industries in Colombia
- Survey on current environmental footprint of participating organizations/industries, and potential areas where significant improvements could be achieved by the application of green ICT instruments
- Selection of Korean R&D and Institutes:
  - specialized in ICT R&D for the generation of ICT innovative products and services; and
  - specialized in environmentally sustainable TIC and industrial applications
- Selection of Colombian R&D centers to participate in the pilot
- Joint --Colombian & Korean-- analysis of available ICT innovation products and services, and identification of further needs in terms of:
  - jointly developed new products and services; and/or
  - adaptation to existing innovation products and services
- Selection of green ICT palette, in conjunction with Korean and Colombian participants
- Construction of culturally sensitive, appropriate (adapted if necessary) ICT packaged into "knowledge modules" to be used in the green ICT knowledge transfer
- Tailored Pilots technical and organizational specifications design

Component 2: Selection of Participating Companies and Project Location

Under this component, the following activities are envisioned:

The project would focus its efforts on the industrial segment of the SMEs, a stronghold of Colombian development, which constitute 96.4% of all private sector enterprises and which concentrate 80.8% of employment sources (Colombia's Department of Statistics, 2019). It is in this sector where a reconversion of the technological makeup towards the use of Green ICT could have the greatest impact with the lowest cost and project results would have the greatest chance of being replicated and multiplied through the various lines of government financing available for the benefits of that particular industrial segment.

Among the SMEs, the project will seek –acting in coordination and agreement with governmental organizations and industry associations—to prioritize those industrial areas that make the greatest contribution in terms of emissions of green-house gases.

It would be advisable to choose a target site, or project focus geographical area. Current investment in scientific, technological and innovation activities in Colombia are highly concentrated in a few regions. First of all are the cities of Bogotá and Medellin, traditional industrial centers that, together, attract 70% of the country's investment in those areas. Other cities like Barranquilla and Cartagena in Colombia's Caribbean region, have achieved significant progress in industrialization; others worth mentioning include Pereira and Manizales, along the Coffee Corridor, as well as Cali, a large business center in the Valley of Cauca. The project's strategy will be to seek the participation of industrial companies who represent those areas with greater business development where private investment capabilities will be the highest, but will also include companies located in the regions where such investment is significantly lower, in an effort to maximize marginal benefit of the technology transfer.

Component 3: Pilot Application

Under this component, the following activities are envisioned:

- Application of ICT green technology knowledge-modules to participating Colombian organizations/industries:
    - application of Green ICT to improve environmental performance; and
    - application of strategies tailored to achieve zero net environmental impact from the application of ICT systems
- Development of best practice and methodology for replication
- Analysis of possible incentives to encourage the productive sector to invest in green ICT as a way to make their products more efficient and competitive in the market at the same time as reducing their environmental footprint.
- Brokerage of industry to industry innovation technology exchange events between Korean and Colombian industries
- Brokerage of Korean to Colombian R&D center collaboration and technology transfer
- Training of students and MADS personnel on environmental and Green Technology audit process
- Professional and student-teacher short-term exchange events among participating agencies and main project beneficiary (MADS)
- Promotion through awareness raising events

Component 4: Pilot Replication and Public Policy Implications

Under this component, the following activities are envisioned:

- Analysis of best practice data in an international context
- Analysis of potential public policy implications
- Proposition of policy (incentives and regulations) guidelines, goals and instruments to measure progress, and strategy to multiply effect
- Analysis of potential for carbon emissions market exchange, as Korea is the world's ninth largest polluter, with its carbon dioxide emissions rising more than 100% over the last two decades, while Colombia ranks low in emissions of GHG (0.37% of world total in 2004) even in the context of Latin America (lower than half of the region´s average).
- International events to discuss results and lessons-learned

Expected Outputs

Project implementation is expected to have a few significant results:

- Colombian policy on green technology and environmentally sustainable production will be informed by the learnings of a practical application exercise;
- Successful strategic guidelines and industry-specific practices will be replicable through direct participation and training of government and other agencies' staff participating in the project;

- Instruction on technology innovation applied to industry will receive support within participating universities, where trained instructors and students can widen the knowledge acquired through the project to delve into subjects like: green ICT design; industrial environmental and technology innovation auditing; public policy implications;
- Public policy and strategy to improve environmental sustainability in priority sectors would have been tested, and viable incentives to mitigate potential negative impacts would have been identified;
- Participating industries would have the opportunity to contribute to the attainment of MDG generating lower carbon emissions and promoting expansion of the model among their peers;
- Korean industries would have show-cased their best and most up-to-date green ICT, have benefitted from cross-fertilization with Latin American industrial and R&D partners, and have contributed to the furthering of Korean government policy in the area of green technology and international development aid;
- Participating Korean University and institutes would have helped implement Korea's Green ICT policy directive and the internationalization of Korean innovation expertise;
- Cross-fertilization between Korean and Latin American research, academic and industrial worlds would have enriched both in terms of testing innovation technology transfer in cross-cultural settings, and has opened doors for further collaboration;

Expected Benefits and Obstacles

Participating companies in Colombia would be the greatest beneficiaries of the project, as introduction of suggested technology application would improve production while generating good-will with the government in fulfillment of the nation's environmental and industrial policy.

On the side of the cooperating or donor country, technology generating companies would also benefit from placing their technology products and gaining additional notoriety as participants in an international development project.

In terms of obstacles, this effort at south-south cooperation may be limited by a few possible factors: lack of financing to start the process; dependence on central government support to use international cooperation agency funds; universities' slow decision making could difficult the adoption of an enterprise-oriented modus operandi.

Project Sustainability

Project sustainability is guaranteed by its own design, which follows closely the government of Colombia's objectives and strategic guidelines for 2020-2024, which includes the technological modernization of the SMEs' productive processes, and includes provisions for the creation of public financing programs to support ICT insertion into their productive structures and operations, as well as to support training entrepreneurs in ICT related subjects.

The project will provide advance financing to support the phases of conceptualization and pre-investment, which tend to be the most difficult to fund under governmental financing lines, as such lines tend to expect the proponent to come up with sufficient research on a solution for its needs as to allow clear-cut project assessment. While medium and large enterprises are often able to front the requisite funds to perform those preliminary investments, doing so is quite impossible for SMEs; which, in order to gain access to government funding routinely need to recur to other sources to finance such preliminary investment, sources that tend to imply processing time that may leave SMEs outside of the competitive process. The proposed project aims at facilitating a rapid insertion of the SMEs into the current of benefits, and plans to do so through practical pilots, focused on sub-sectors that are representative of the target sectors.

In practical terms, results from the pilots to be implemented by the project will identify new lines of investment, which in turn will become research, technology development and/or institutional strengthening projects which could apply for public and private investment lines. The companies participating in technology transfer sponsored by the project would be eligible for financing of fiscal incentives offered by the government to promote private investment in innovation-related activities.

In order to ensure that the investment made under the project will produce new work and financial lines for participating sectors, the project will invest in the analysis of project-sponsored best practices, on which future replication could be modeled. Also, the project will analyze and produce recommendations concerning the possibility of Colombian participants entering international carbon markets, based on possible reductions in carbon emissions brought about by the change in technology. Finally, the project will work with participating industries to identify internal financing lines which could be accessed to promote a deepening and multiplication of the project's positive impacts, following upon the lead provided by the growth targets set under Colombia's development plans.

After project completion, it is expected that the lines of cooperation that would have been established between Korean and Colombian industrial and R&D partners, as well as the collaboration that would have been started among governmental, specialized agencies and university partners will be incentive enough in ifself to ensure that they will continue well beyond the formal duration of the project.

Applied KE Architecture

This project complies with the elements identified as crucial to put in place knowledge-based economic growth:

- Education & skill development, including instruction for personnel to undertake technical assistance functions, and universities providing guidance to the process;
- Technology innovation in terms of green technology hardware and software;
- Modern and adequate ICT infrastructure
- Economic incentives and positive institutional regime, including an innovative institutional and entrepreneurial system;
- Social inclusion, to the extent that efforts will focus on smaller-sized industrial undertaking, capable of generating employment and income opportunities.

CONCLUDING REMARKS

While the project described here has not been implemented yet, the analysis of setting, policy directives, and operational circumstances, allows two preliminary conclusions: (i) that the proposed "south-south" cooperation would have a reasonable chance of success because it would be to both participants' advantage; and (ii) that its results would have greater opportunity to become durable and financially and socially sustainable than under a "vertical" model, where technology transfer is unilateral.

Furthermore, commonality of purpose in a collaborative arrangement as the one described here, by reinforcing the viability of achieving such socially relevant objectives while at the same time generating private sector benefits, would constitute a valid example for other countries in similar circumstances. A multiplier effect of this nature would be an important contribution to the international quest for environmental sustainability.

REFERENCES

Celis, J., & Acosta, O. (2016). Industrial Ph. D. Programs for the Strengthening of the Industry's Production of Innovation in Colombia. *Innovar (Universidad Nacional de Colombia)*, *26*(62), 129–146. doi:10.15446/innovar.v26n62.59393

CIDEI. (2020). *Homepage.* http://www.cidei.net

Cleantech, A. Z. O. (2015). *South Korea: Environmental Issues, Policies and Clean Technology.* https://www.azocleantech.com/article.aspx?ArticleID=552

Cluster, C. R. E. A. T. I. C. (2020). *Introduction.* https://minciencias.gov.co/content/corporacion-incubacion-y-fomento-empresas-base-tecnologica-corporacion-cluster-creatic

Colombia Government. (2018). *Green book 2030.* https://www.tipconsortium.net/wp-content/uploads/2018/09/GreenBook2030_25sept-002.pdf

Colombia Government. (2018). *National Development Plan 2018-2022.* https://www.dnp.gov.co/DNPN/Paginas/Plan-Nacional-de-Desarrollo.aspx#:~:text=El%20Plan%20Nacional%20de%20Desarrollo%20es%20un%20pacto%20por%20la,construir%20el%20futuro%20de%20Colombia

Colombia's Department of Statistics. (2019). *Geovisor Business Directory 2019.* https://geoportal.dane.gov.co/geovisores/economia/directorio-estadistico-de-empresas/?lt=4.456007353293281&lg=-73.2781601239999&z=5

Consortium, T. I. P. (2018). *Colombia embraces transformative innovation policy as national strategy for post-conflict development.* https://www.tipconsortium.net/news/colombia-embraces-new-innovation-theory-from-spru-as-national-strategy-for-post-conflict-development/

COTECMAR. (2020). *About Us.* https://www.cotecmar.com/en/about-us

Dayton, L. (2020). How South Korea made itself a global innovation leader. *Nature*, *581*(7809), S54–S56. doi:10.1038/d41586-020-01466-7

Ecuador Ministry of Public Health. (2020). *COVID-19 Situation.* https://www.salud.gob.ec/actualizacion-de-casos-de-coronavirus-en-ecuador/

Energeysage. (2019). *Energy efficiency 101: what is energy efficiency?* https://www.energysage.com/energy-efficiency/101/

Global Transmission Report. (2020). *Colombia: Focus on energy diversification and grid decentralisation.* https://www.globaltransmission.info/archive.php?id=38770

Green Technology Center. (2020). *Global Cooperation.* https://www.gtck.re.kr/frt/center/en/rnd/global_cooperation.do

Inter-American Development Bank. (2011). *Innovation, R&D investment and productivity in Colombian Firms (Working Paper IDB-WP-251).* Banco Interamericano de Desarrollo.

Jung, H. (2016). *Greener ICT, Greater Future. Green ICT and its transformation in Korea.* https://www.slideshare.net/nayahun2/green-ict-and-its-transformation-in-korea-green-startups

KDFuelCell. (2013). *Green Technology Center, Korea.* http://www.kdfuelcell.net/kdfuelcell/participants/gtc-k

KITECH. (2020). *Overview.* http://eng.kitech.re.kr/introduction/page2.php#b

Knowledge for Development. (2020). *Homepage.* https://www.k4d.org

Martínez, C. I. P. (2010). Investments and energy efficiency in Colombian manufacturing industries. *Energy & Environment, 21*(6), 545–562. doi:10.1260/0958-305X.21.6.545

Martínez, C. I. P., & Piña, W. H. A. (2014). Energy Efficiency in Colombia: Trends and Challenges. *International Journal of Energy Science, 4*(1), 31–34. doi:10.14355/ijes.2014.0401.08

Nordea. (2020). *The economic context of South Korea.* https://www.nordeatrade.com/fi/explore-new-market/south-korea/economical-context#:~:text=The%20main%20industries%20include%20textile,the%20active%20population%20in%202020

OECD. (2014). *OECD Review of Innovation Policy: Colombia Overall Assessment and Recommendation.* https://www.oecd.org/sti/inno/colombia-innovation-review-assessment-and-recommendations.pdf

OECD. (2019). *Production Transformation Policy Review of Colombia: Unleashing Productivity, OECD Development Pathways.* OECD.

Piaggesi, D., Axel, L., Andres, G., Martin, G., & David, D. (2013). *Center of Excellence for Technology Innovation in Favor of Persons with Disabilities –CETI-D. Concept Paper and Schematic Proposal.* Framericas.

Renewables Now. (2020). *South Korea commits USD 61bn to Green New Deal by 2025.* https://renewablesnow.com/news/south-korea-commits-usd-61bn-to-green-new-deal-by-2025-706741/#:~:text=July%2017%20(Renewables%20Now)%20%2D,post%2DCOVID%2D19%20era

Republic of Colombia. (2020). *Intended Nationally Determined Contribution.* https://www4.unfccc.int/sites/ndcstaging/PublishedDocuments/Colombia%20First/Colombia%20iNDC%20Unofficial%20translation%20Eng.pdf

Republic of Korea. (2020). *Intended Nationally Determined Contribution.* https://www4.unfccc.int/sites/ndcstaging/PublishedDocuments/Republic%20of%20Korea%20First/INDC%20Submission%20by%20the%20Republic%20of%20Korea%20on%20June%2030.pdf

Statista. (2020). *Colombia: Distribution of employment by economic sector from 2010 to 2020.* https://www.statista.com/statistics/369122/employment-by-economic-sector-in-colombia/#:~:text=The%20statistic%20shows%20the%20distribution,percent%20in%20the%20service%20sector

Statista. (2020). *Colombia: Share of economic sectors in the gross domestic product (GDP) from 2009 to 2019.* https://www.statista.com/statistics/369032/share-of-economic-sectors-in-the-gdp-in-colombia/#:~:text=Share%20of%20economic%20sectors%20in%20the%20GDP%20in%20Colombia%202019&text=In%202019%2C%20the%20share%20of,sector%20contributed%20about%2057.53%20percent

Statista. (2020). *Impact of the novel coronavirus (COVID-19) on gross domestic product (GDP) growth in selected countries in Latin America.* https://www.statista.com/statistics/1105099/impact-coronavirus-gdp-latin-america-country/

The Korea Herald. (2019). *Korea's R&D spending 5th largest among OECD members in 2018: ministry.* http://www.koreaherald.com/view.php?ud=20191218000777#:~:text=2019%20%2D%2016%3A25-,South%20Korea's%20research%20and%20development%20spending%20was%20the%20fifth%20largest,Ministry%20of%20Science%20and%20ICT

Tilastokeskus. (2000). *Technological innovation.* https://www.stat.fi/meta/kas/tekn_innovaatio_en.html

Trading Economics. (2020). *Colombia - Research And Development Expenditure (% Of GDP).* https://tradingeconomics.com/colombia/research-and-development-expenditure-percent-of-gdp-wb-data.html#:~:text=Research%20and%20development%20expenditure%20(%25%20of%20GDP)%20in%20Colombia%20was,compiled%20from%20officially%20recognized%20sources

United States Environmental Protection Agency. (2021). *Report on the Environment.* https://cfpub.epa.gov/roe/chapter/sustain/index.cfm

United States Environmental Protection Agency. (2021). *Overview of Greenhouse Gases* https://www.epa.gov/ghgemissions/overview-greenhouse-gases

U.S. News. (2020). *Top 10 Countries for Technological Expertise, Ranked by Perception.* https://www.usnews.com/news/best-countries/slideshows/top-10-countries-for-technological-expertise-ranked-by-perception

USAID. (2017). *Greenhouse Gas Emissions in Colombia.* https://www.climatelinks.org/sites/default/files/asset/document/2017_USAID_GHG%20Emissions%20Factsheet_Colombia.pdf

Wight, A. J. (2019). Colombia creates its first science ministry. *Nature*, *565*(7737), 273–275. doi:10.1038/d41586-019-00087-z PMID:30647420

Worldbank. (2020). *Research and development expenditure (% of GDP).* https://data.worldbank.org/indicator/GB.XPD.RSDV.GD.ZS?locations=KR

Chapter 13
Used Cooking Oil Campaign Experience in São Bernardo do Campo City:
Guinness World Record and Sustainable Development

José Carlos Gobbis Pagliuca
Prefeitura de São Bernardo do Campo, Brazil

Marta C. R. B. Suarez
Prefeitura de São Bernardo do Campo, Brazil

EXECUTIVE SUMMARY

Faced with the objective of carrying out environmental education campaigns and arousing the attention of Sao Bernardo do Campo´s residents to the correct disposal of used cooking oil, in 2019 a cooperation agreement between the Municipality of Sao Bernardo do Campo and the Triangulo Institute aiming at recycling used cooking oil was signed. The collection execution began with the installation of the used cooking oil voluntary delivery points. Before the installation, the awareness and training of the team involved in the receiving activity was carried out; in addition, it is important after the collection to pack, transport, and dispose of the oil.

I - SAO BERNARDO DO CAMPO, TERRITORY OF CONSERVATION AREAS AND WATER RESERVOIR

The municipality of Sao Bernardo do Campo (in the State of Sao Paulo, Brazil), with a population of around 850,000 is located in the Sao Paulo City metropolitan area. It is known for all the historical tradition of furniture industry and as the *city of the automobile*, it also holds more diversity than we imagine.

DOI: 10.4018/978-1-7998-8417-0.ch013

With a territory of 408.45 km^2 (157.70 sq mi), it has one of the largest Atlantic Forest reserves in Brazil, with 118.21 km^2 (45,64 sq mi) in urban areas, 214.42 km^2 (82,79 sq mi) in rural areas, in addition to having 75.82 km^2 (29,27 sq mi) belonging to the *Billings* Reservoir.

The environment in its territory is very significant, since 53.7% of its territory is considered as springs protection area. Close to *Serra do Mar* Mountain Range with original Atlantic Forest vegetation and, on the banks of the reservoir, low and sparse scrub.

The municipality has 43% of its territory covered by native forests that are present in parks and in smaller areas that we call vegetation fragments. These fragments are essential for the conservation of biodiversity in the region and occupy a significant area that, integrated to the *Serra do Mar* State Park, makes up part of the Sao Paulo Green Belt Biosphere Reserve and the Atlantic Forest Biosphere Reserve (EMPRESA BRASILEIRA DE PESQUISA AGROPECUÁRIA MINISTÉRIO DA AGRICULTURA, PECUÁRIA E ABASTECIMENTO, 2021).

Among all the environmental resources, so important for guaranteeing life and development, it is essential to highlight water, because without it we cannot survive. As mentioned before, in Sao Bernardo do Campo is located most of the *Billings* Reservoir, with 75.82 km^2 (29,27 sq mi) within the municipality, responsible for providing water for public supply in the municipalities of *Grande* ABC (composed by 7 municipalities with around 2.5 million people) and part of Sao Paulo City, transferring water to the *Guarapiranga* Reservoir and to the system of Upper Tiete River.

The *Billings* Dam, was built in the 1920s and it began its operations in 1926, to increase the capacity to produce electricity. Given the importance of the reservoir and the concern to protect it, in 2009 State Law no. 13,579, known as the Specific *Billings* Law, was passed. This law determines areas for environmental protection and aims to guarantee the existence of vegetation that protects the rivers and the dam from pollution, as well as providing areas that can be occupied by meeting reservoir conservation criteria.

The biggest reason for water quality degradation is caused by untreated sewage disposal, but it is not the only one. Industrial and domestic effluents are also sources of pollution if not treated and disposed correctly.

II- USED COOKING OIL DISCARD

According to *Oil World*, Brazil produces about 9 billion liters (2.4 billion gallons) of vegetable oils per year. Of this volume, about 1/3 are edible oils. Per capita consumption is around 20 liters (5.3 gallons) per year, which results in a production of 3 billion liters (0.8 billion gallons) of oil per year in the country.

If we take into account the amount of used vegetable oils collected in Brazil, we have less than 1% of the total produced, about 6.5 million liters (1.7 million gallons) of used oils. What about the rest? More than 200 million liters (53 million gallons) of used oil per month goes into rivers and lakes, compromising the environment of today and the future.

Today, oil is the major polluter of fresh and salt water in the densely populated regions of Brazil. Noting the generation of a significant amount of waste from used cooking oil, which when discarded inappropriately contaminates soil, water, and causes public health problems, due to environmental pollution (COMPANHIA AMBIENTAL DO ESTADO DE SÃO PAULO, 2021).

In other words, the oil discarded for example in the kitchen sink, ends up clogging the pipes and demanding chemical products for removal. If the sewage is not well treated, the oil can spread through rivers, settling on the surface and disrupting gas exchange, affecting the entire ecosystem. To give an idea, 1 liter (about 2 pints) of oil discarded in the environment can pollute 25,000 liters (6,600 gallons) of water! Water treatment costs also increase and the solution lies in awareness and oil recycling.

When inappropriately discarded on the soil, it can make it waterproof and ineffective for any type of crop and contribute to floods. The degradation of the oil itself generates methane gas, one of the gases that most aggravates the greenhouse effect (DISCONZI, 2014).

III -THE USED COOKING OIL CAMPAIGN

Faced with this problem and with the objective of carrying out environmental education campaigns, arousing the attention of Sao Bernardo do Campo´s residents to the correct disposal of used cooking oil, in 2019 a cooperation agreement was signed between the Municipality of Sao Bernardo do Campo and the *Triangulo* Institute, as published the 06/14/2019, aiming to destine used cooking oil for recycling (ABC do ABC, 2021).

The collection execution begins with the installation of the used cooking oil voluntary delivery points. Before the installation, the awareness and training of the team involved in the receiving activity is carried out. In addition, it is important after the collection to pack, transport and dispose the oil.

Residents voluntarily deliver the used cooking oil to the points of collection. The *Triangulo* Institute transports and recycles the oil delivered, transforming part into biodiesel and another part into ecological soap, made from discharged oil. In exchange citizens who deliver used cooking oil receive two soap bars for every two liters (0,5 gallons) of used cooking oil delivered.

According to the agreement between Sao Bernardo do Campo Municipality and *Triangulo* Institute, in addition to carrying out the collection and concern with storage, the main focus was to inform and insert the correct disposal of waste into the habits of the population. For this purpose, permanent campaigns were started to inform about the importance on how to separate properly the oil for recycling. The campaigns are part of the environmental education work (LUZZI, 2012), in which it is always explained how to separate used oil, without compromising health and the environment. Here is where the importance of Knowledge is evident: when people knew the damage being caused by domestic oil discharged inappropriately was doing to the environment, they changed their attitudes and switched to more environmentally friendly practices. Knowledge made the difference. In this sense, access to Knowledge in also linked to the concept of Citizenship (JACOBI, 2003).

In the campaign launch a competition was held awarding the first three schools that obtained the largest collection of used cooking oil. City public schools participated very actively. The whole infrastructure, collection points and a whole environmental education work with information and materials were installed.

The success of the first competition was so significant that soon after another one was held, this time with the participation of companies, social entities, in addition to public and private schools.

Even though the second competition took place soon after the first one, we managed to awaken in the citizenship the will to participate and in just one month we obtained a very expressive used cooking oil collection. On a single day of the campaign during the month of November 2019, we held "D-Day" with an invitation to the population -including the Municipality workers- to participate in the campaign of used cooking oil collection, and 11,088 litres (2,929 gallons) of used cooking oil was collected on this day. Below are the records in campaign material and photos.

In November 2019 alone, Sao Bernardo do Campo City collected 50,501.88 liters (13,341.19 gallons) of used cooking oil, which made the city a record holder in allocating its used cooking oil for recycling, being included in the *Guinness World Records* book.

During 2020, due to COVID-19, residents were not allowed to access many of the collection points throughout the city, such as schools, for example. For this reason, it was started to carry out the door-to-door collection, allowing people to continue the dispose used cooking oil for recycling. In this format, they get in touch with *Triangulo* Institute to remove the used cooking oil at the site and in exchange and as an incentive, they continue receiving ecological soap bars. Figure 13: Communication material - 2020

With the action in this new format, we were able to collect from January to December 2020, about 130,000 litres (34,328 gallons) of used cooking oil, which was destined for recycling.

Over the two years that the cooperation agreement between Sao Bernardo do Campo Municipality and *Triangulo* Institute has been in force, 309 collection points were opened, made up of schools (public and private), buildings, houses, public entities, bars, restaurants and neighborhood associations (SABESP, 2021).

IV - SUSTAINABLE DEVELOPMENT AND UN 2030 AGENDA SDGs

Through the campaign, the concept of sustainable development is clearly perceived, based on the three pillars of sustainability:

- Environmental: When used cooking oil is properly disposed, pollution, either water or soil, is avoided. Another point that deserves to be highlighted is that soap produced from oil is less aggressive to the environment, as it decomposes naturally and more easily as it has an organic origin.
- Economic: Income generation that enables self-sustainability of the collection network organized by *Triangulo* Institute, so that more and more people are mobilized (LEITE, 2003).
- Social: Through the social inclusion of young people from the local community. Recycling used cooking oil generates jobs for young people employed by *Triangulo* Institute, in addition to promoting a change in the habits of urban society, contributing to the sustainability of natural resources.

Taking into account the current concern that afflicts society with environmental issues and, particularly, the difficulty of finding alternatives to control the volume of waste that is thrown away in a disorderly manner, we find that this project is an opportunity to promote the strengthening of good practices, directly affecting the quality of life through a process of environmental sustainability.

In this case, we can see the importance of working in favor of nature neutralizing impacts of daily actions of man. In his world of social interaction, whether at home, at work, and more notably at school, in order of transforming human work into an instrument for controlling the harmful effects on life on the planet.

It is important to establish a working relationship and at the same time care for nature, so that even acting on natural elements does not cause negative and destructive impacts.

When disposing used cooking oil - which would be discarded - for recycling, we are minimizing the alarming damage that waste from this product, once released into the soil or sewer, causes the environment, giving it another direction that in addition to preventing damage to the environment, contributes to sustainable development and thus being fully in line with the UN's 2030 Agenda of the 17 Sustainable Development Goals (SDGs).

In 2015, in New York, representatives of the 193 UN Member States gathered and recognized that the eradication of poverty in all its forms and dimensions, including extreme poverty, is the greatest global challenge and an indispensable requirement for the sustainable development, committing to take bold and transformative steps to promote sustainable development over the next 15 years without leaving anyone behind.

The 2030 Agenda is an action plan for people, planet and prosperity that seeks to strengthen universal peace. The plan indicates 17 Sustainable Development Goals, the SDG 17, and 169 goals, to eradicate poverty and promote a decent life for all on the planet. These are clear objectives and goals for all countries to adopt according to their own priorities and to act in the spirit of a global partnership that guides the choices needed to improve people's lives, now and in the future (ORGANIZAÇÃO, 2021).

It is important to highlight that among the SDGs, we work directly on SDGs 11 and 12, highlighting:

11. Make cities and human settlements inclusive, safe, resilient and sustainable
11.6 By 2030, reduce the adverse per capita environmental impact of cities, including by paying special attention to air quality, municipal and other waste management.
12. Ensure sustainable consumption and production patterns
12.5 By 2030, substantially reduce waste generation through prevention, reduction, recycling, and reuse

We continue with the awareness that sustainable development is a process of change, in which the exploitation of resources, the targeting of investments, the orientation of technological development and institutional change are in harmony and reinforce the current and future potential to satisfy aspirations and human needs.

It is encouraging to see all the evolution of the collection and to note that with the action there was a change in the behavior of the citizens which, additionally, causes economic growth as well as environmental gains.

CAMPAIGN FEATURED NUMBERS

See Table 1.

Table 1.

Used cooking oil collected in 2020 (pounds)	257,833
Preserved water (gallons)	845,054,314
CO_2 reduction (kg/CO_2e.)	1,648,165
Recycled containers	26,754
Soap kits delivered	56,647

REFERENCES

ABC do ABC Fofocando em Você. (n.d.). https://www.abcdoabc.com.br/sao-bernardo/noticia/sao-bernardo-lanca-programa-reciclagem-oleo-cozinha-usado-82848

Brasil. (n.d.a). *Organização Das Nações Unidas – ONU*. https://brasil.un.org/pt-br/sdgs

Brasil. (n.d.b). *Companhia Ambiental do Estado de São Paulo*. Disponível em https://cetesb.sp.gov.br/sigor-mtr/sobre-o-sigor/

Brasil. (n.d.c). *Companhia de Saneamento Básico do Estado de São Paulo- SABESP*. Disponível em http://site.sabesp.com.br/site/interna/Default.aspx?secaoId=82

Brasil. (n.d.d). *Empresa Brasileira de Pesquisa Agropecuária Ministério da Agricultura, Pecuária e Abastecimento*. https://www.embrapa.br/busca-de-noticias/-/noticia/2307893/biodiesel-de-oleo-de-fritura-e-tema-do-conexao-ciencia

Disconzi. (2014). *Dissertação de Mestrado – Universidade Federal de Santa Maria/RS- 2014*. https://repositorio.ufsm.br/bitstream/handle/1/7639/DISCONZI%2C%20%20GRACIELA%20SCHMIDT.pdf?sequence=1&isAllowed=y

Jacobi, P. (2003). Educação ambiental, cidadanie e sustentabilidade. Cadernos de Pesquisa, 118.

Leite. (2003). *Logística Reversa Meio Ambiente e Competitividade*. Pearson Prentice Hall.

Luzzi. (2012). Educação em Meio Ambiente: Uma Relação Intrínseca. Manole.

Section 6

Urbanization and Transportation

Chapter 14
How E-buses Took off in Latin America to Save Lives, CO2 and Money

Manuel F. Olivera
C40 Cities, Bogota, Colombia

EXECUTIVE SUMMARY

Building confidence for zero emission buses has been the strategy to create demand in Latin America. A few cities have more e-buses than any other region in the world outside of China. It all started by testing hybrid and electric buses, sharing data, building innovative economic models, making site visits, and sharing results in workshops. It all occurred during the last 10 years. Institutions including development banks are now committed to assisting with the transition towards zero emission public transport in cities. A number of bus suppliers offer their technologies, most of them from China as Europe is still behind in the Latam e-bus market. Most barriers have already been broken, and confidence in the technology and the market has brought investors to the region. E-buses are key to reducing greenhouse emissions in the region, and the accelerated transition is helping cities with this challenge.

INTRODUCTION

In 2010, the Inter-American Development Bank (IADB) supported the first-of-its-kind project to test hybrid and electric buses in 4 cities in Latin America: Bogotá, Santiago de Chile, Rio de Janeiro, and São Paulo. It was carried out by C40 Cities and the Clinton Climate Initiative (CCI). The justification for such a project was the need to speed up the transition towards zero emission transport systems in order to reduce pollution and the greenhouse gas emissions (GHG) from the massive sectoral use of fossil fuels in public transport. In this sector old diesel buses were predominant, easy to maintain, mechanically well known by the bus operators, and good for business as they were cheap. However, these buses were not only very inefficient in terms of energy use but also the main source of deadly particle emission to the atmosphere: PM2.5. The hypothesis was simple: proving the availability of low or zero emissions

DOI: 10.4018/978-1-7998-8417-0.ch014

technologies to reduce fossil fuel consumption, therefore deadly particle and GHG emissions, would allow cities to transition towards zero emission transport.

However, proving the hypothesis was not enough to trigger the growth of the low or zero emission bus market. It was also essential to prove that: i) technologies were available and there were suppliers; ii) the technology was reliable; iii) buses, although more expensive, might end up costing less; iv) there were additional environmental and economic benefits that would be achieved, and v) bus operators and transport agencies in cities would be confident enough in the technologies to start the transition. All these subjects were, in essence, knowledge generation for decision makers.

However, it turned out that documenting and providing answers to the subjects mentioned above was far from enough to foster the transition towards low or zero emission transport. Several myths supported business as usual for bus operators and cities, such as: i) electric engines are not powerful enough to climb hills, ii) battery range was not enough to cope with the long journeys buses make every day, iii) batteries explode or burn, iv) batteries are not recyclable, v) buses are too expensive, vi) there are no electric buses in the market or the main bus suppliers are not prepared for them, and viii) buses are only built in China.

An important part of this chapter is the result of many meetings, site visits, discussions and field work undertaken by the author. These helped collect information that has been shared with stakeholders via projects like ZEBRA[1] in Latin America (Latam).

The chapter recaps the main facts that took place before two cities in Latam decided to jump into electromobility and highlights the economics behind the decisions. It also summarizes the most relevant elements regarding the knowledge that helped cities and transport operators make well-funded technological and economic decisions. Finally, it presents some facts and figures using the current state of the transition towards zero emission buses in the region.

The intention of this chapter is not to evaluate the co-benefits of the e-buses compared to the fossil buses as for example those derived from particle reduction, noise reduction and the like. It is focused on the economic and financial facts that are moving Latin America towards a zero-emission public transport fleet.

BACKGROUND

In August 2010, the Clinton Climate Initiative, C40's implementing agency at the time, signed a non-reimbursable technical cooperation with the IADB. This allowed C40 to test hybrid and electric buses in Bogotá, Santiago de Chile, Rio de Janeiro, and São Paulo, and to compare their performance and the life cycle economic cost or total ownership cost (TCO) against that of an equivalent bus that used diesel fuel.

This project, the first of its kind in the world, obtained the participation of several bus suppliers: BYD (electric - China), Eletra (hybrid - Brazil), Hankuk Fiber (electric - Korea), Mercedes Benz (diesel - Brazil), Volvo (diesel and hybrid – Sweden, Brazil), and Youngman (hybrid - China). All tests engaged bus operators in each of the cities and Bus Rapid Transit (BRT) authorities. Buses were imported from different places and an international consultancy team –International Sustainable Systems Research Center (ISSRC)– was hired to develop specific test protocols and to carry out the tests. Supervision of the field work was also contracted with international experts for each city.

Based on the performance results of the buses and with data provided by bus suppliers and bus operators, an economic analysis was carried out by Dalberg, a consulting firm that helped C40 carry out the first TCO in the world that compared the costs of diesel, hybrid, and electric buses. Results were published in April 2013 (C40, CCI & IADB, 2013).

The project took more time than expected as it faced many challenges: importing and exporting buses and chargers to and from different countries, releasing buses apprehended in customs, getting permits for temporary transit in cities, building charging infrastructure, importing testing equipment, not attracting any interest from electric utility companies in the project, paying back bus suppliers to cover the costs of moving buses internationally, among other activities. Getting economic data was one of the main challenges as little expertise was available for hybrid and electric buses, and in the case of diesel buses, operators were reluctant to disclose some of the data.

Several other studies followed C40's during the decade, some prepared by universities like Columbia (Aber, 2016), some by NGOs like the International Council on Clean Transportation (ICCT) (2018), and PNUMA (2017), and all reached similar results. Some independent consultants and others hired by the World Bank (2019, 2020) recently worked on the subject. Although most of the analyses that were carried out were positive, the World Bank's conclusions (2019) were discouraging as they arrived to figures of 30-40% higher annualized cost for electric buses over diesel ones and suggested delaying decisions for several years until cities and technologies were sufficiently prepared for the transition. However, in 2020 Steer (for the World Bank) concluded that the City of Santiago was on the right path when there were already several hundred buses running on the streets of the city.

Many studies support the transition towards zero emissions because electric vehicles are 3.5 to 7 times more efficient compared to the diesel vehicles in terms of energy consumption, as California Air Resources Board (2018) states, because they do not burn fossil fuels and therefore do not emit hazardous substances and particles to the atmosphere (which are causing millions of deaths per year, mainly in cities) and because in Latam transport is the main source of Greenhouse Gas emissions in cities. In fact, transport represents 30% of the energy consumed in the region (CEPAL, 2018) and is responsible for 36% of the GHG emissions too (Martínez, 2018); both of which are increasing. This means that in terms of energy efficiency, health, and GHG emissions, transport is a priority sector that requires intervention, particularly because most of the Latin American cities have power over public transport.

How fleets are taking over cities in Latin America can be seen in this web page: https://www.ebusradar.org/es/

Figure 1. E-bus Radar: e-buses deployment in Latam

LEARNING FROM EXPERIENCES

The case for the transition toward zero emission buses used to be a poorly known topic for most interested parties. Therefore, a lot of knowledge was required to open this black box and help make informed decisions. Despite the amount of expertise generated during the previous years, political reasons or economic interests to stop the transition towards zero emissions prevailed in some cases. For example, the Mayor of Bogotá only allowed TransMilenio S.A. to open a tender for 12m electric buses in 2019, only when the reality of thousands of e-buses deployed in some parts the word was overwhelming.

While cities were initially slow to implement electric transportation, several factors helped the private sector and transit authorities to make informed decisions in Latam, as will be seen in the next sections.

Years of Knowledge Generation and Sharing

Many activities have taken place throughout Latam regarding the generation and sharing of knowledge, quite often in connection with cities around the world.

Testing

Testing e-buses with the direct involvement of bus operators and the oversight of transit authorities was the first item on the agenda during the last 10 years. During that period knowledge was shared concerning bus specifications, costs, charging options, available battery technologies, and battery life cycle handling experiences (this last item was not thoroughly documented). The discussion mainly used sources from China, where the technology first took off in large scale.

After the testing program financed by the IADB, it was clear that more testing was required in the cities to keep building confidence, as skepticism was a constant. Bogotá took the results from the program seriously, to the point that it supported the procurement of 337 hybrid Volvo buses by operators in 2013. The procurement decision regarding hybrid buses was also based on having seen that technology in Mexico City, London, Shanghai, and Curitiba. Nevertheless, it had not moved towards zero emissions yet.

During the same year Bogotá also issued the decree 444 to set the path towards zero emissions. The city expected bus suppliers to put buses on the ground for testing purposes before making further decisions. Four years later, and after testing the evidence, Chile issued its National Strategy of Electromobility. In 2019, Colombia enacted Law 1964 and its National Strategy of Electromobility, and in 2020 Bogotá's Council issued the Climate Emergency law one of which mandates makes it compulsory for Bogotá to stop buying fossil buses from January 1st, 2022 (Concejo de Bogotá, 2020).

Several e-bus producers were invited by C40 to showcase their buses in Latam: Volvo, Zhongtong, Eletra, Zonda, Foton, Yutong, Higer, Proterra, Hankuk Fiber, New Flyer, and BYD. The latter accepted the challenge to build and deploy buses of different sizes (12m (2013), 18m (2015), and more recently (2020) a 27m electric bus) and to publicly share the results of the tests. In 2017, Yutong gave a 12m bus to an operator in Santiago to test it and draw conclusions.

Bogotá was the first city that saw BYD buses built to comply with the requirements of the city`s BRT system (12m in 2011, 18m in 2015, and 27m in 2020) on the streets. In Santiago, BYD sent another bus in 2013 after the testing program, but since it was designed for flat geographies, it did not perform well in some of the hilly routes along the city. In 2016 two more buses served in limited areas in the city center and finally Metbus, a RED operator,[2] included those buses in its fleet for commercial service. Through a local dealer, Yutong put a 12m bus in the hands of Vule, another RED operator in Santiago in 2017. Medellín received a 9m and an 18m BYD bus; Quito tested a 12m and an 18m bus from the same brand. In Brazil, several cities and their operators tested a few electric BYD buses and Campinas decided to buy the first 10 in 2015 as a testing fleet. Other Latam cities also received buses for testing purposes (Panamá City, Costa Rica, Guayaquil, Mexico City, Buenos Aires, etc.). More recently, following the example of Santiago, Mexico City signed an agreement with Engie, a French energy utility company, to test an 18m Yutong bus, and it has been running since 2020. As the results were good 9 more buses were recently added to the fleet.[3]

Lots of testing has taken place in the Latam and the results are more than enough to confirm the good performance of the buses and thus to make confident technical decisions. It is shown later in this chapter that decisions also make sense from an economic perspective.

Obviously, there are commercial interests from proponents, whatever the technology is offered, when a city carries out a procurement process, and for this reason it is absolutely important that transparent data and information is secured to help cities make sound decisions.

Site Visits

If testing has been relevant for showcasing and building confidence on electrical buses, site visits have made the difference, as will be shown below.

The program mentioned above, supported by the IADB, organized a large visit in 2012 for some bus operators, transit authorities, bus manufacturers, and research institutions to Mexico City, London,

Gothenburg, Stockholm, Shenzhen, and Shanghai. Bus operators and transit authorities that participated on the tour discussed their experiences with their peers and hosts. China proved to be the most advanced country in electromobility.

Many other site visits have taken place in Madrid, London, Berlin, and cities in Italy, among others. Visits were organized by cities, projects like C40-CFF, the IADB, GIZ, other NGOs, or were carried out by operators themselves. The results of the visits were variable. Some helped Bogotá to request buses to test, to procure hybrid buses and to issue the mentioned decree 444 (2013), which established the technological pathway for the city. Operators from Santiago, based on their own site visits, made the decision to procure 100 buses. Mexican city officials decided to move at a very slow pace compared to other cities until recently, when Metrobus (the BRT agency) decided to change gears towards zero emissions. Some operators in Medellín compiled all reasons to not go ahead with the transition and are now behind the region's progress towards zero emission public transportation.

Workshops, Webinars, Cases

Skepticism around the technology and the economics of the transition towards zero emissions has prevailed for almost a decade. On several occasions C40 has presented the program's results plus the knowledge gathered so far, and with the support of its transport networks the organization began to advocate for zero emission transport. Several workshops took place around the word and representatives of cities like Santiago, Bogotá, Mexico, São Paulo, and Rio de Janeiro were invited to share their views, to discuss other experiences and present their strategies to move towards electromobility or zero emission transit.

The first business roundtable in the world to foster the procurement of hybrid and electric buses was held in Bogotá in 2013. It was organized by the City Hall, Invest in Bogotá, the City's Chamber of Commerce and C40. No zero-emission bus was bought immediately by operators during this event as there was no clever business model to foster deals, CAPEX was still an issue, and several other factors were part of the ongoing barriers (factual or fictitious) that were blocking decisions. However, months later, Bogotá opened the door for hybrid buses and some operators procured 337 hybrid buses to start reducing all emissions. C40 considers these buses to be a transitional technology towards zero emissions.

Besides the IADB and C40, no other international organization was really fostering zero emission buses in Latam to eliminate all emissions to the atmosphere. Even after the Paris Agreement was signed in 2015, it took a couple of years for institutions such as WRI, ICCT, ITPD, the World Bank, GIZ, and many others to "get on the bus". Since then, lots of workshops have occurred in Mexico City, Santiago, São Paulo, Salvador de Bahia, Medellín, etc., and many reports have been published with interesting data highlighting the relevance of the technology.

In another effort to create confidence and share knowledge among cities, operators, investors, and bus manufacturers, C40 and ICCT structured a project in 2019 called ZEBRA —Zero Emission Bus Rapid-deployment Accelerator—and received financial support from P4G.[4] Officials from a network of 35 Latam Cities have been exchanging information and discussing subjects that are helping to make decisions on zero emission buses. Recent ZEBRA virtual workshops gathered 270 participants by the end of 2020 and 146 in 2021, which include city officials, e-bus manufacturers, investors, and press. These figures show how the interest has grown among cities in Latam where a market of only five C40 cities moves around 25,000 buses that need replacing before 2030.

ZEBRA is also showcasing experiences with e-buses at a fast pace, so all interested parties know the basic data about available experiences. The most important experience in Latam regarding the direct involvement of the private sector is the one in Santiago de Chile. An example of this case study was prepared by ZEBRA in June 2020 (ZEBRA, 2020). In terms of involvement of the public sector regarding tenders, the most relevant experience is Bogotá, with a case study that is under preparation.

Private Sector Gets Confident and Triggers E-bus Businesses

It was the private sector in Chile that, overcoming years of uncertainty and facing apparent unbreakable barriers, triggered the market for e-buses. Enel X decided to invest in buses in Chile, partnering with a bus operator, Metbus, that visited various colleagues in China and Europe.[5] This offered a lesson to all stakeholders around the world.

Based on the experience gathered by Metbus by testing, in real conditions, two electric buses that were brought to Santiago, Enel X and Metbus decided to close a deal to start with a 100 e-buses fleet. This agreement took place under the contract that Metbus holds, as a BRT operator of RED, with the Minister of Transport of Chile.

Overall, the conditions established by the government in support of the private initiative required changes in the contract with Metbus. The agreed subjects included:

- E-buses were permitted instead of diesel buses, but no additional remuneration for the e-buses, compared to what used to be paid for the equivalent diesel bus, was accepted -all CAPEX and OPEX costs were included.
- Electricity for charging purposes had to be green -wind or solar sourced.
- Since the current concession contract was expiring well before its original 10-year agreement, the conditions approved by the government included transferring the leasing contract to the operator awarded with the service area that Metbus currently had under concession, or just keeping the contract as it was in case Metbus continued to be the concessionaire after service areas were tendered.
- The operator was obliged to render data regarding maintenance and operational costs.
- Remuneration to Enel X was granted by the government in case Metbus was not able to comply with its commitments towards Enel X. This last item was perhaps the most important of all for the investor.

Metbus and Enel X included in their pact:

- A 10-year leasing agreement of the buses that would be transferred to a new bus operator in case Metbus did not win the respective tender for the same operation area.
- Metbus would oversee the basic maintenance while learning and taking over the knowledge provided for maintenance purposes by BYD —the e-bus supplier in this case— regarding batteries, electronics related to the functioning of the bus and the power train.
- Enel X, as the capital investor and e-bus owner, would guarantee that BYD would in turn warrant the performance of the e-buses and, most importantly, that the batteries (same brand of the bus) would have no less of 70% of their capacity for at least 4,000 charging cycles.

Table 1 presents some facts and figures related to the signed agreement between Metbus and Enel-X, and the performance that the fleet has shown so far. Data reinforces how good this business is for the private sector, which explains why more investors throughout the continent are attracted by it.

Table 1. Fact and figures related to Enel X and Metbus agreement

Operator	Metbus
Investor	Enel, bus owner
Type of business model	Leasing of buses to Metbus
Contract length	10 years
Bus brand and size	BYD, 12 meters, air conditioning and heating
Cost estimate per bus	$295,000 + VAT (19%)
Initial procurement	100 buses
Current fleet (2021)	436
Batteries and guarantee	4 packs per bus, 276 kWh total capacity, guaranteed for 70% of its original capacity after 4,000 cycles
Chargers	1 per 2 buses
Charging type and time	AC, 80 kW and 3-4 hours
Energy source	Certified clean energy
Energy cost	+/- $0.06/kW, long term contract with 40% discount
Cost relation diesel/electric	$0.42/km vs. $0.12/km or 71% savings
Energy performance	+/- 1 kW/km
Availability index	99.6%

(Data Source: some data is coming from personal communication of the author with Metbus, Enel and BYD. See also ZEBRA (2020) and Taborelli (2021)).

Vule and SPT, two bus operators and concessionaires of RED in Santiago, closed a deal with Engie for the leasing of 75 buses and 25 Yutong e-buses respectively, after testing one Yutong bus. They followed the path of Metbus, with which they share some stockholders. The main differences in the closed agreements among Engie and those operators were related to i) 12 years leasing and ii) 8 years guarantee of 80% of charge capacity of the batteries and 10 years for 70% charge capacity, with batteries supplied by CATL, a large Chinese battery company.

A corollary and a question can follow the above facts: E-buses make business sense for the private sector, which is not there to lose money, so how can they not make sense for the public sector, which can rely on the long-term financial capacity of investors to avoid compromising the city's cash flow in the short term?

Business Models: Making Them Attractive

The transition towards zero emissions in transport has faced several barriers; the one that appeared insurmountable was the cost of the e-buses: *they are far too expensive*. It turns out that the essence of the deals is based on what C40 proved in 2012: regardless of the high capital cost of the bus, the total cost of ownership (TCO) within the economic life span of the bus ranges from similar to much lower than the equivalent in diesel or natural gas.

The discussion around capital cost of e-buses is based on the old business model of fossil buses in which vehicles were owned by the operator and paid back in full by the city within 3-5 years. Moving away from the capital cost and payback period alone has allowed for new business models.

For this evolution it is relevant to understand that the profit for the operators was not only made by owning and exploiting a bus, but also by the allowance to the bus owner by the transit authorities to sell the asset at a "market" value even after the bus life span was completed. Thus, the operators were able to recover several times the initial capital, aside from making earnings over 10-20 years.

Also, it was and perhaps still is a usual practice in some deals in which operator (buyer) and bus supplier agree underpricing the fossil bus for the operator to charge the authority the full cost shown in a public price list.

Additionally, the profit for the operator is related to the maintenance costs: since operators knew very well how to maintain fossil buses, they used to overcharge the contracting authorities to receive higher remuneration for this item too.

In summary, more important than good quality public service to the citizens, the business for some operators became a financial one: management of a good and granted long cash flow, with a large part coming from cities and citizens. This explains why it is meaningless for a conventional operator to save money due to a very efficient equipment like an e-bus, hence the resistance to transition toward zero emission buses.

Bogotá and Santiago have evolved for good in their contracting modes: Now they separate bus ownership from operation, so the operator just operates and maintains buses under costs defined by the e-bus supplier to the city through their offer. Bus suppliers are required to deliver a machine guaranteed to have a good performance. Good quality of the service rendered to the citizens is now a reachable objective.

Total Ownership Cost (TCO) became the driving model for transit authorities to procure e-buses. Considering that e-buses last 15 years compared to the usual 10 of the fossil buses, the contracts could last longer, allowing a better and steadier capital return to potential investors. Also, the model allows distributing the capital cost during the length of the contract in even instalments, reducing the burden of high disbursements during the initial 2-5 years -as it used to be in old business models- to cover buses costs, and even with the additional financial toll incurred in a long-term payment, the model allows to understand how fossil buses are more expensive than e-buses. Having the TCO figures clear in terms of CAPEX and OPEX, transit authorities can separate operation from procurement for more transparent tenders.

In their tenders, Santiago and Bogotá first proceeded to separate ownership from operation through different schemes. Santiago kept both fully separated also contracting independently the electric infrastructure and depots provision. Bus suppliers offering different technologies —fossil or electric— were invited to compete on price; the winners stand-by with their proposals until bus operators are selected and choose the preferred technology from the chosen supplier. Operators take the risk of the bus performance, not the government. Their contract, if they select fossil buses, would last 5 years and could be extended for 5 more, based on their performance. If the operators awarded select electric buses, their contract would last 7 years with a potential extension of 7 more. This of course is an incentive to choose e-buses, which are included in Santiago's business model. Currently, the tender for operation is managed as a road concession and should be awarded during 2021.

In the tender for 100% electric buses in 2019, Bogotá forced bus suppliers to couple with an operator and winners earned 15-year contracts throughout which all costs will be paid monthly (fixed and variable costs). In 2020, Bogotá opened a tender for all technologies to compete. The door was opened for operators to make independent proposals, which was unfeasible in practical terms because operating costs were defined by the bus suppliers in their bids, and some operators had financial limitations when trying to comply with the requirements of the tender. Nevertheless, this tender had several interesting elements as a business case:

- Finance capacity required by transit authorities to e-buses bidders was more than 50% higher than for fossil techs, arguably because e-buses are much more expensive than fossil ones. In theory, this guarantee proves that the bus suppliers have the economic ability to produce all buses offered.
- The amount of the guarantee to cover the seriousness of the proposal (legally required in Colombia to avoid bidders quitting during the evaluation of proposals) was also 50% higher for e-buses than for fossil techs.
- The total remuneration ceiling per e-bus per year foreseen in the budget established by TransMilenio was 23% lower than the one for fossil buses.
- The contract for e-buses was 15 years, while the fossil buses would last 10.
- Remuneration (CAPEX and OPEX) was spread as evenly as possible throughout the length of the contract.
- Offers could compete with endurance guarantees for the buses so e-bus bids were given a maximum of 1 point in the final ranking over fossil buses.
- Up to 43 points were given to the technical offers with 100% e-buses.
- Score given to the economic offers was much more important than the one given to the technical component — 36/10— so it was impossible to win just with a good technical proposal.

As a result of this tender, 1002 e-buses were awarded as no bidders presented fossil bus proposals. Two main capital funds were involved: Vitol with Transfondo, while BYD was the only e-bus supplier prepared to comply with all the requirements set by TransMilenio in the tender documents. Admittedly, BYD has been learning how to participate in tenders in Colombia for around 10 years through expensive trial and error and yet other e-bus suppliers are still trying to understand how to comply and compete.

It is important to note that both Chile and Colombia are attracting investors (capital funds), more than local banks, to finance the transition towards zero emission buses.

One of the possible reasons for the lack of fossil bus bidders in the 2019-2020 tender in Bogota is the change in the long-term remuneration scheme based on TCO. In this regard, the author compared the total remuneration to contractors of e-buses and CNG buses of tenders awarded in 2019 and in 2020 which prices were adjusted to 2019 for a fair comparison (exchange rate, producers price index and consumer price index).

Considering only 12m e-buses and using as reference the cheapest CNG contract as a 100% of TCO, monthly remuneration of three e-bus contracts in 2019 are between 4-8% lower (not considering in any case land as in some contracts depot was existing and already paid for). Compared to the most expensive CNG buses contract, e-buses are between 9 and 14% less expensive. Regarding 2020 e-bus contracts, compared to the less expensive remuneration contracted for CNG buses, the difference in remuneration ranges between 1 and 7% less for e-buses. The same comparison with the most expensive CNG contract results in a range of -7% to -13% difference in favor of the e-buses. (See table 2 and Figure 2).

Table 2. Comparison of remuneration between e-buses and fossil buses in Bogota

	Comparison of remuneration per bus, costs adjusted to 2019								
	Contracts e-buses 2019			Contracts CNG 2019		Contracts e-buses 2020			
Depot / contract name	FONTIBON I	USME I	FONTIBON II	SUBA CENTRO IV	USME III	Fontibon III	Fontibon V	Fontibon IV	USME
Remuneration compared to cheapest CNG buse	92%	95%	96%	100%	106%	99%	96%	98%	93%
Cost of an e-bus vs. cheapest CNG bus (100%)	-8%	-5%	-4%	0%	6%	-1%	-4%	-2%	-7%
Cost of an e-bus vs. most expensive CNG bus	-14%	-11%	-9%	-6%	0%	-7%	-9%	-8%	-13%

Source: Calculations made by the author based data in contracts signed by Transmilenio, Bogota

Figure 2. Savings in remuneration for Bogota
Source: Calculations and graphic made by the author

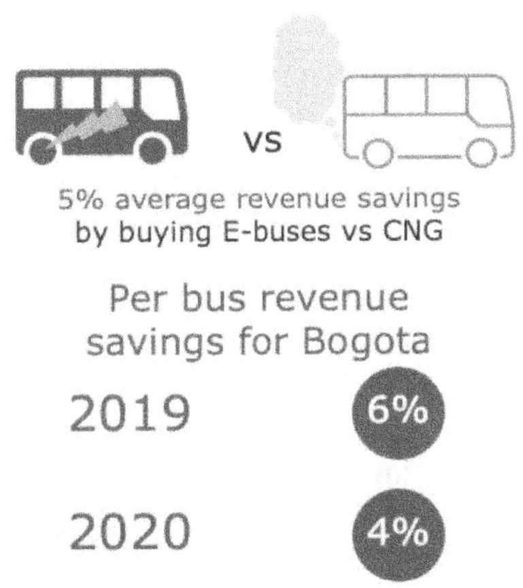

Arriving to the above figures showed that the volatility of the USD$/COL$ exchange rate and somehow inflation, play a relevant role in the final pricing of a bus, which is considered in the risk analysis investors make —only bus bodies are built in Colombia. TCO basis, e-buses are competitive against fossil buses despite e-buses costing more than 50% more than a fossil bus. This explains why no fossil bus producer bid for Bogota´s tender in 2020.

This exercise carried out by C40 based on data from real contracts helped the Council of Bogotá to make decisions regarding the requirement imposed on the city to stop procuring more fossil buses.

This kind of analysis based on real life contracts is not easy to build as contracts are difficult to obtain or data is kept confidential. This is the case of Chile regarding the current operators. There are other interesting TCO analysis made by ZEBRA, for a conventional bus operator willing transition by itself toward zero emissions, and for San Paulo and Santiago, soon to be not published, again with a positive TCO for zero emission buses.

Graph 2 is an example of a TCO for a conventional (independent and private) bus operator Medellin, kind of operator found in many cities in Latam. This case used real data from the operator regarding its diesel fleet (passengers before the pandemic, during and finally an estimated average for the post pandemic), from an e-bus supplier (e-bus price) and from a Metro Medellin feeder company that has the type of buses of interest for the new operator -already running in the city (operational costs). The result is positive for any number of buses.

Figure 3. TCO case for a proactive bus operator in Medellin, Colombia
Source: Adapted by the author from calculations made by ZEBRA in 2020-2021 for the bus operator with its own data for diesel buses

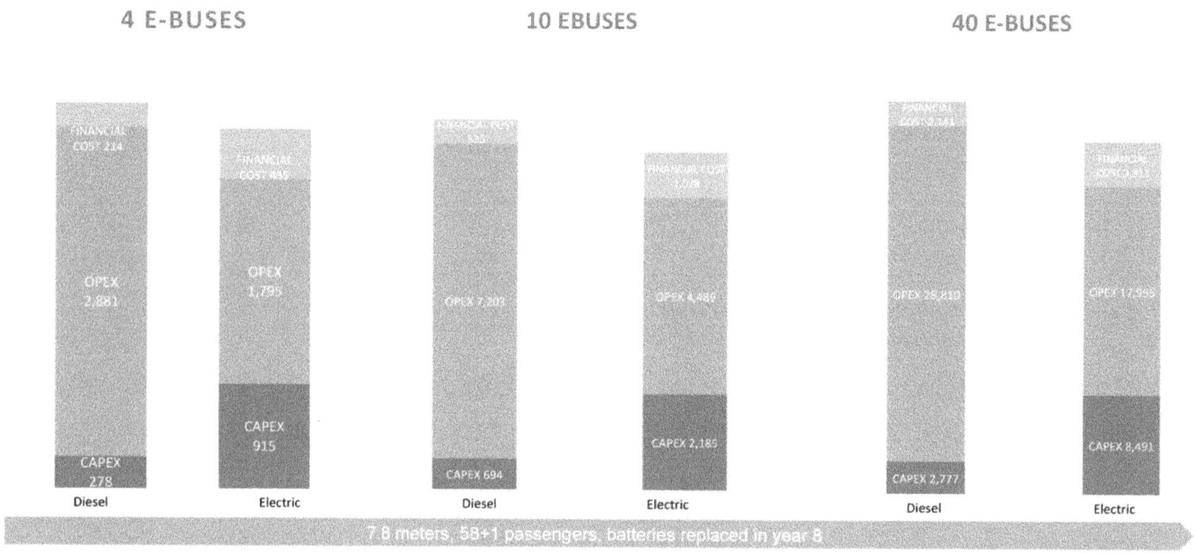

The company interested in the transition was so enthusiastic about the results that requested However, a low-cost credit line available in Medellin and during 2021 no bank has been willing to lend the money even for the first 4 buses and with real guarantee from the company upfront. This operator wants to own buses as has been its usual aim during many decades just increase assets, but if this operator were more open to a leasing model or to a partnership with an investor the buses would had been already ordered.[6]

Breaking Barriers

All kinds of arguments have been used to stop or at least delay the transition towards zero emissions in public transport. Some of those remain as myths that reflect, in some cases, the interest of businesses related to the fossil fuel industry and, in others, lack of knowledge. Table 3 is a summary of those myths confronted with factual-based knowledge.

Table 3. Some usual myths found in the discussion around the transition towards zero emissions in public transport

Myth	Facts
Too expensive compared to diesel or natural gas	There is no dispute about the higher up-front cost of an e-bus, but decisions based on TCO or life cycle costs have proved initially in 2012 (Hybrid and Electric Bus Test Program), then in 2019 (Santiago) and finally in 2020 (Bogota) to have been similar or lower compared to fossil buses.
Only China produces e-buses	China is the largest producer of e-buses, but Europe has been the second largest producer for several years.
There will be no e-bus production in Latam	One Chinese company started producing e-buses (2015) and batteries (2020) in Brazil. At least one Swedish bus company has a factory in Brazil that can be quickly adapted to produce e-buses too.
Only one company produces buses for the Latam standard	No company in the world has commercial production of e-buses with high floors with the Latam standards for BRTs. Buses are produced on demand. At least 5 Chinese companies are prepared to produce under those standards and, with some adaptation to the plant, a Swedish bus company is prepared as well.
Nobody in Latam knows how e-buses function	E-buses tests took place throughout Latam involving operators and they are now operating hundreds of e-buses (Santiago, Bogota, Guayaquil, Sao Paulo, Medellin, Cali, Guadalajara, Montevideo, Campinas, etc.).
There is only one supplier	12m buses and smaller sizes are already supplied by 5 Chinese companies in Latam; for large capacity buses (18m, 27m) there are two with prototypes already in Latam. At least 10 European companies are producing different sizes of e-buses with European standards.
Technology is nonexistent	In commercial terms and not counting trolley buses, E-buses first took off in China and knowledge about them started flowing in North America and then in Latam more than 10 years ago. In fact, they arrived after hybrid buses had already been on the market for a decade.
Technology is not proved	Thousands of E-buses with batteries have been running on the streets for more than 10 years already.
Technology is obsolete	Batteries have been improving for more than 20 years and keep improving permanently. All technologies become obsolete as fast as research and development advances, but decisions cannot stop expecting future technologies. Additionally, there is always the possibility of upgrading one or two e-buses with new techs in batteries after their cycle is over, as e-buses have proven that they last longer than fossil buses which, in turn, are so obsolete that several countries like UK are now setting a policy to ban diesel bus production (UK Department of Transport, 2021).
There are no policies	There are countries such as Colombia and Chile with clear policies regarding the transition. Also, some cities have local policies in place, like Bogotá (regarding electric mobility) or São Paulo (to take fossil fuel emissions to zero).
Transition needs several years of planning	Experiences have shown that E-buses usually are needed to replace fossil buses so little basic planning is required provided decision makers have good information about the e-bus deployment, mostly related to slopes and traffic -tech requirements-, energy supply capacity and infrastructure, training for maintenance and good driving practices.
Batteries are too heavy; therefore, the buses or vehicles are too heavy too.	Yes, the electrical batteries make the vehicles heavier, but due to the higher efficiency of electric motors compared to internal combustion ones, e-bus efficiency is still in the range of 73% and 81% higher in terms of energy consumption compared to diesel buses (C40, CCI & IADB, 2013).
As e-buses are heavier than fossil buses, e-buses emit more non exhaust particles than fossil buses	Non exhaust emissions are produced basically by the wearing out of tyres, breaks and road surface (OECD, 2020). Data shared with the author by Sucinc (2021) a bus operator in Guayaquil that owns and runs 20 e-buses since 2019, shows that every 100,000 km e-buses and fossil buses use one set of tyres, and fossil buses need two sets break wearable parts while e-buses need no change of these parts.[7] These real-life figures contradict the estimations made by the same author OECD (2020).
Batteries give buses low range	The increase in energy density in batteries is currently giving e-buses longer ranges compared to what they had 10 years ago. Additionally, experience shows that e-buses can be recharged several times a day, which gives them longer range, larger life span to the batteries and a smaller need for battery packs. Hence, the discussion is not about range but about operational logistics, as e-buses should be handled with appropriate operational criteria that are different from those for fossil fuel buses.
Batteries are not recyclable	As the chemistry of the batteries evolves, a marginal number of hazardous components are included in batteries and 95% of materials used are recyclable (Overhouse, 2020). Most components of the batteries have value, such as nickel, cobalt, copper, aluminum, graphite and of course lithium (percentages of these components change according to technologies used). However, as it has been ruled in some countries regarding hazardous materials, batteries producers or importers should be responsible for recycling, or disposing them -at the country of origin- after a second or a third life of the battery has been ended. That is, at least two decades.
Batteries are full of hazardous materials	In fact, most electric vehicles batteries contain cobalt, nickel, copper, and lithium in very low amounts. All these elements can be handled safely.
Batteries have a high risk of explosion	This used to be the case with home batteries. Vehicle batteries based on lithium have been built with high levels of protection against explosion, even when there is an outside fire. Gasoline cars are, on the contrary, moving bombs.

Continued on following page

Table 3. Continued

Myth	Facts
Batteries have no guarantees	All e-bus suppliers guarantee the batteries that their buses carry. For now, there are two companies that produce their own batteries: BYD and Mercedes Benz (for its Citaro). The main e-bus brands in the market use the CATL brand. All batteries have a guarantee based on a minimum charge capacity, usually 70% of the original 100% charge, either in terms of cycles or in terms of years of use.
There is no charging infrastructure	Charging infrastructure for public transport is linked to the needs of the operation, so there is no reason to imagine any shortage of electric charging points.
Bus suppliers overcharge batteries to cope with rage	Although you can see that kind of statements in poor consulting reports, batteries cannot be overcharged unless you change the whole protection of the charging system which generates i) fast reduction of charging capacity and therefore exposure to guarantee application to the battery, and ii) explosion risk of the batteries and the elements of the charger.
Chargers are not compatible to the local voltage	High voltage chargers always require a transformer that requires to be built as they are not available on a shelf. That equipment, although not very expensive, are tailored to the needs.
No electricity, no charging	Electric power cuts are much less frequent than permanent electric flow. However, as in all projects, a backup plan is usually considered for occasional power cuts. These backups are either fossil fuel plants or battery packages in containers, the latter becoming a second life for batteries.
Thousands of jobs are going to be lost	Current fleets of buses and cars need maintenance in the long run (10-20 years). New jobs will be created with the production and maintenance requirement of new e-bus fleets.
There will be an ever-lasting technology dependence with the bus supplier	The relationship will be related to long term guarantees mainly for the batteries, so this connection becomes the best option for the e-bus operator.
There is no representation of e-bus companies in Latam	As demand grows in Latam, several companies have either installed their offices or signed contracts with companies representing the brand. Therefore, in most Latam countries it is possible to discuss business with different e-bus brands.
Electric buses are too heavy and destroy roads	All vehicles wear out roads, some more than others. Regulations of weight in all countries set the limit of the weight of the vehicles, usually considering weight allowance per axle. All e-buses need to comply with those regulations like any other vehicle.
Electric buses do not climb hills	Like any lift, depending on the number of passengers it is required to move, and the slope conditions, bus suppliers install the proper motor to cope with the force required.
Banks do not lend money for e-buses	This used to be the case because of lack of knowledge. Although some banks are reluctant to lend money capital funds are ready to get involved in this business. More importantly, insurance companies are now involved.

(Source: the table was built by the author based on his own research, public knowledge, and references were included when required).

E-bus Production

Producing e-buses in the region is a relevant solution to reach some price stabilization, generate green jobs and foster the green economy of the transport sector in the countries. However, the demand is crucial. C40 continually explains that if there is no demand there will be no supply of e-buses, as has been proven in Santiago, Bogotá, and other cities. Despite the large numbers regarding the potential demand in the region (around 25,000 buses that need replacement before 2030 in five cities, although overall fleets sum more than 40,000 buses, most of them in Brazil, Mexico and Colombia), some countries still have no policy to accelerate the transition towards zero emission buses for public transport. Brazil's case is especially interesting as explained next.

The bus industry in Brazil is protected with a 35% import duty that makes it impossible for any imported bus to compete with fossil buses produced in the country. To face this, BYD decided to build an e-bus factory in Campinas, investing around $48 million (Energías Renovables, 2015) in a 100 buses/year plant (several sizes). Since batteries form between 30 and 40% of the total cost of an e-bus, the import duty on batteries was still heavy in relation to the total price of the vehicle; hence, the company also decided to invest $2.7 million in a battery factory in Manaus (BYD, 2020). Production started in 2020.

Given those restrictions on imports, C40 encourages e-bus manufacturers to invest and produce in Brazil or at least in a Mercosur country, where import duties, if any, can be very low. Companies such as Sunwin, Foton and Higher have been studying the possibility of investing in Brazil, but the country's reluctance to swiftly move towards zero emission transport, and therefore to stimulate its large market towards that technology, keeps companies hesitating about investing or partnering to produce e-buses.

In terms of market signals, only the city of São Paulo issued a local law in 2018 setting a zero allowance for CO_2 emissions from fossil fuels by 2038, expecting a 50% reduction by 2028, which means that all fleets need to transition at once to zero emissions.[8] The Covid-19 pandemic has delayed decisions from the transit authorities.

Curiously, some officials in Brazil used to say that there was no e-bus production in the region, therefore they could not make zero emission technologies to cities or bus operators compulsory. Now that there is a factory, those officials say that there is only one brand in the market, which they cannot support alone. This has been a strategy to delay decisions despite the fact that business models have proven that it is profitable for the cities and mainly for the environment to transition towards zero emission buses.

Financial Breakthrough: From Banks to Investors

Expecting to keep business as usual, bus operators claim that they cannot get loans to buy buses. Colombia's transport system entered a deep financial crisis because of a poor structure behind the contracts of what used to be called Integrated Transport System, the collective bus fleets. Banks became reluctant to lend more money claiming they were already too exposed within the sector, despite the fact that Bancoldex, the Colombian Development Bank, had allocated concessional credit lines to finance new projects, including one specific line with Clean Technology Fund resources that were not fully used.

BNDS, the development bank of Brazil, has had a concessional credit line since 2005 and electric bus manufacturers need to get approval for their vehicles from the bank before any interested client can have access to the credit line. Conditions are as follows: 1% interest rate per year, which is 1.5% and 2.5% less than for hybrid and fossil buses respectively, and up to 10 years payback period (Banco Nacional do Desenvolvimento [BNDS] 2005). Only until 2020 the first financeable busses were approved.

Almost all countries in Latam have concessional credit lines for public transport, Chile is one of the exceptions where the market started to move without any incentive. In Chile, even VAT must be fully paid, while in Colombia VAT is 5% for electric buses and can be excluded after several months of a procedure before the National Environmental Licenses Authority (ANLA for its acronym in Spanish).[9]

What became impressive in the evolution of the e-bus businesses that occurred in Latam was that banks were no longer needed to finance buses. Investors began to bring fresh capital and took the financial risks in several projects. Table 4 presents a summary of investors involved in some projects of Latam's projects.

Table 4. Investors involved in e-buses businesses in Latam

Project (operator)	Investors	e-Buses
Santiago de Chile (Metbus)	Enel X	100 BYD
Santiago de Chile (Vule and SPT)	Engie	100 Yutong
Santiago de Chile (Metbus)	Enel X and AMP	336 BYD
Cali (Blanco y Negro)	Celsia with ARC	26 Sunwin
Bogotá – public tender	Celsia	120 BYD
Bogotá – public tender	Enel X with AMP Capital	401 BYD
Bogotá – public tender	Transfondo and Vitol	195 BYD
Santiago de Chile (Transdev)	NEoT	25 King Long
Santiago de Chile (STP)	Copec Voltex	215 Foton

(Source: Table built by the author based on his own research and public knowledge).

Aside from the investors mentioned in Table 4, ZEBRA has unveiled the interest of several other potential investors or capital funds like Ascendal, Ashmore, EDP, John Laing, and Siemens Financial Services; funds like Vitol or AMP have a large appetite for 2000 e-buses or more in Latam in 2021-2022. In fact, Vitol, in partnership with BYD, is willing to create a green transport fund with up to USD$2.5 billion.

This investors' interest in e-buses in Latam is clearly solving one of the main barriers that used to exist in the transition towards zero emission public transport buses: the lack of financial availability. Funds involved are happy to bring money to the region for long term projects like those for e-buses. Now the challenge is: where are those projects?

The answer has several elements. Beyond the lack of policies or political interest, which is an issue in some cases, almost all public transport systems depend on subsidies. This means that either the local or the national governments cover the deficit. The Covid-19 pandemic made the situation of the public transport worse by cutting the system's income from passenger fees up to ⅔, while strongly reducing the city's revenues from taxes and similar sources.[10]

The above-mentioned situation led cities to reduce the ambition of the procurement of e-buses. This was the case in Bogotá, where the expectation in early 2020 was to tender 2,024 buses but the final procurement was only for 1,295, because TransMilenio, the BRT agency, could not grant funds to pay contractors back in the long run for more buses. A similar case happened in Guadalajara, where the expectation was to procure 112 units in July 2020 and they finally leased 38 in March 2021, and in Quito, where around 70 e-buses were planned to be procured, but it was not possible to open any tender.

The case of São Paulo is different, although also affected by the pandemic. There are 32 contracts in the hands of 21 bus operators for 15 years (SPTrans, 2019);[11] contractors need to transform the old fleets they have (around 16,000 buses) to zero emission fleets to comply with the local law regarding zero emissions, but the transit authority, with some reason, is delaying the decision based on the economic difficulties of the bus operators and the city.

Bankable projects, and guarantees for investors´ payback, are required. Several initiatives or institutions have supported some cities in Latam with project preparation, such as C40-CFF, ZEBRA, IFC, CAF, IADB, and recently the Gap Fund and the Green Climate Fund. Nevertheless, there are very few bankable projects available. And on the side of guarantees, a matter on which multilateral banks should have the necessary expertise, the work done is marginal.

In summary, two sides of the same coin appear to block the involvement of investors: on the one hand, the lack of bankable projects and, on the other, a solution for the lack of guarantees from cities to pay back investors.

The Battery Paradigm

Although it seems obvious, sometimes it is forgotten that storage is the key to make the best use of any energy source: fossil fuels have their storage capacity underground; water requires dams to store potential energy; hydrogen is best stored in water and in natural gas and, when freed from oxygen, in tanks; batteries are the key storage element for solar and wind energy to be properly used. Therefore, batteries are the key component of electric vehicles if they are to run without connection to the grid, as opposed to trolleybuses.

After more than a century of battery development, a breakthrough took place in the 1980s: the safe use of lithium made recharging possible. Research and development took off heavily, pulled by the cellphone industry mainly and then by the car and bus industries, all in search for more energy per kg of storage and extended battery life.

Hydrogen is the ideal source of energy because of its enormous energy by mass (39,500 Wh/kg) (Battery University, 2020). All fossil fuels are also 50-70 times more efficient than batteries in terms of energy by mass storage. Except for Panasonic batteries made for Tesla's Model 3, which has reached 260Wh/kg (Reuters 2020), most batteries made for cars, buses and trucks in the market are still approaching 200 Wh/kg, while diesel fuel packs 12,700 Wh/kg and gasoline 12,200 Wh/kg, all of which are still far below hydrogen.

The discussion about hydrogen is confronting "green" from water and "blue" from natural gas mainly. In terms of climate change and environmental impact the scale is quite against the blue. Aside from the pros and cons discussion (see for instance Howarth, 2021) where the fossil fuel industry is also involved for its obvious interest, the experience in public transport and availability of real data, despite decades of research, is not helping to run economic and financial models in the way this chapter does regarding the fossil buses and the e-buses.

In relation to the economics of batteries, the production price has created a barrier to electromobility even though in terms of USD$/kWh costs have dropped 87% from 2010 to 2019, reaching $156/kWh, according to Bloomberg NEF (BNEF) (2020). Nevertheless, vehicles are still at least 50% more expensive than the equivalent in diesel or gasoline. The same research found that density of batteries is rising by 4-5% per year.

It is interesting that the top six battery producers for vehicles are based in Korea, China and Japan. The next four, although with no recent data on market share available, are also located in the same region. China holds 38.3% of the world's market, while Korea has taken almost 31% of the pie. Table 5 details the battery producers, their market share and country of origin.

Table 5. Battery producers by market share and country

Ranking	Company	Country	World Market Share
1	CATL	China	31.5
2	LG Energy Solutions	Korea	20.5
3	Panasonic	Japan	16.7
4	BYD	China	6.8
5	Samsung SDI	Korea	5.3
6	SK Innovation	Korea	5.1
7	AESC	Japan	N/I
8	Gouxuan	China	N/I
9	PEVE	Japan	N/I
10	CALB	China	N/I

(Data Sources: 1-6: Kyun-don (2021). 7-10: Palandrani (2020))

E-buses Market

Asian companies not only dominate the battery production in Latam, but their bus companies have begun to take over the same market. However, having the largest share in the battery business is not enough explanation for why European bus brands are not present with any e-bus product in Latam, even though three European companies dominate the diesel bus market: Mercedes Benz, Volvo, and Scania, all of which have production facilities in Brazil and some in Mexico.

The main European brands are focused on the European market and are still competing against Chinese brands. Currently, BYD (alone or with Alexander Denis) and Solaris are leading the deployment of e-buses with 50% of the e-bus business (29%-20% respectively). Then Volvo (10%) Yutong (7.3%), VDL (6.2%) and Iveco, Ebusco, Mercedes, Caetano, Alstom, Optare, Irizar, MAN and others share 26.5% of the market (Sustainable Bus, 2020). It is hard to explain why none of those companies have Latam on their radar.

One possible reason for this might be that those companies are willing to produce e-buses with European batteries and they are behind the R&D capacity of their Asian competitors. If this is the case, green hydrogen technology might find its place in Europe before e-buses with European batteries are able to cope with their internal market, not to mention the foreign one.

CONCLUSION

It took 7 years of tests, site visits, workshops, research and discussions, for the public and private sectors to become confident about e-buses for the transition towards zero emission in public transport in Latam. A couple of buses tested by operators, plus a business model based on TCO, opened the door for the first deal among private companies, which ensured the first 100 and then delivered more than 650 e-buses in Santiago. In Bogota, a few tests allowed operators to start with 377 hybrid buses and then, thanks to a TCO model, the city has 1485 e-buses procured.

Partnerships among electric utility companies, bus operators and bus suppliers broke the vicious circle created by fossil fuel interests: lack of information, fear of the technology, risk aversion, lack of guaranties, lack of finance, lack of policies, and the like. Then capital funds found their niche to invest, as was the case of the public tenders in Bogota, where they assured around USD$350 million for 15 years.

Thanks to that first step, the Latin American Region has the largest e-bus fleet in the world, outside of China, in a few cities. And the process seems unstoppable, although reduced in speed because of the Covid-19 pandemic. Still, the challenge is to replace 25,000 fossil buses by 2030 and to double the figure by 2040.

The intake of e-buses in the Latin American market by a few cities has proved that, despite the higher capital cost, e-buses are competitive with fossil buses.

A fast transition towards zero emission buses in Latam cities will also cut fast the contribution of the public transport to emissions from tailpipes reducing environmental and health burdens the citizens.

Several capital funds, aside from electric utility companies, are interested in large and long-term e-bus projects. What is missing are projects that are properly structured and bankable, with appropriate guarantees to secure a return on the investments. Investors are not interested in old business models where bus operators own buses; on the contrary they are willing to bet on business models in which they can structure creative proposals based on the total cost of ownership and second use of batteries.

Real maintenance data from fossil buses compared to e-buses is showing that non-exhaust particle emissions are lower in the case of e-buses.

Despite the fact that the cost per kWh in batteries has dropped by 87% between 2010 and 2019, and the density of energy in the batteries has increased 4-5% per year, battery cost makes vehicles much more expensive than the equivalent in fossil fuels. However, TCO makes business feasible when cashflow or remuneration to investors is expanded for more than 10 years.

Most batteries and therefore e-buses are coming from China to Latam, even though production is already in place in Brazil. What is unclear is why well-established European bus companies in Latam have had this market outside their radar. It seems that those companies prefer to focus on the future of green hydrogen rather than partnering with Asian companies to build and deploy buses in Europe or Latam.

REFERENCES

C40, CCI, & IADB. (2013). *Low carbon technologies can transform Latin America's bus fleets: Lessons from the C40-CCI Hybrid & Electric Bus Test Program: Hybrid and electric technologies are a viable solution to reduce carbon emissions in the world's megacities.* IADB.

Aber, J. (2016). *Electric Bus Analysis for New York City Transit.* Columbia University.

Banco Nacional do Desenvolvimento. (2005). *BNDES cria novas condições para compra de ônibus no Brasil e exportação de carros* [BNDES creates new conditions for buying buses in Brazil and exporting cars]. https://www.bndes.gov.br/wps/portal/site/home/imprensa/noticias/conteudo/20050923_not245_05

Battery University. (2020). *Compare battery energy with fossil fuel and other resources. BU-1007: Net Calorific Value.* https://batteryuniversity.com/learn/article/bu_1007_net_calorific_value

Bloomberg, N. E. F. (2020). *Electric Vehicle Outlook 2020.* https://about.bnef.com/electric-vehicle-outlook/

BYD. (2020). *BYD Starts Operations at its Lithium Iron Phosphate Battery Factory in Brazil.* https://www.byd.com/en/news/2020-09-01/BYD-Starts-Operations-at-its-Lithium-Iron-Phosphate-Battery-Factory-in-Brazil

California Air Resources Board. (2018). *Battery Electric Truck and Bus Energy Efficiency Compared to Conventional Diesel Vehicles.* https://ww2.arb.ca.gov/sites/default/files/2018-11/180124hdbevefficiency.pdf

CEPAL. (2018). *Economics of Climate Change in Latin America and the Caribbean: A Graphic View.* United Nations.

Concejo de Bogotá. (2020). *Acuerdo 790 de 2020 Por el cual se declara la emergencia climática en Bogotá D.C., se reconoce esta emergencia como un asunto prioritario de gestión pública, se definen lineamientos para la adaptación, mitigación y resiliencia frente al cambio climático y se dictan otras disposiciones* [Agreement 790 from 2020. Whereby a climate emergency is declared in Bogotá D.C., this emergency is recognized as a priority issue of public management, guidelines are defined for adaptation, mitigation and resilience to climate change and other provisions are issued]. https://www.alcaldiabogota.gov.co/sisjur/normas/Norma1.jsp?i=103745&dt=S

Energías Renovables. (2015, July 16). *Campinas: Diez buses eléctricos para la flota de transporte público* [Campinas: Ten electric buses for public transport fleet]. Energías Renovables. https://www.energias-renovables.com/movilidad/campinas-diez-buses-electricos-para-la-flota-20150716" \h

HowarthR. (2021). https://www.theguardian.com/environment/2021/aug/12/uk-replace-fossil-gas-blue-hydrogen-backfire-emissions

International Council on Clean Transportation. (2018). *International Evaluation of Public Policies for Electromobility in Urban Fleets.* BROMOB-e.

Kyun-don. (2021, May 13). *Korea accounts for 31% of global EV battery market in Q1.* The Korea Herald. http://www.koreaherald.com/view.php?ud=20210512000946

La República. (2021, January 20). *Enel X ganó contrato para dotar de buses eléctricos y estaciones de carga a Bogotá* [Enel X won the contract to provide Bogotá with electric buses and charging stations]. https://www.larepublica.co/globoeconomia/enel-x-gana-contrato-para-dotar-de-buses-electricos-y-estaciones-de-carga-a-bogota-3113459

Martínez, H. (2018). *El desafío del sector transporte en el contexto del cumplimiento de las contribuciones determinadas a nivel nacional de América Latina.* CEPAL.

OECD. (2020). *Non-exhaust Particulate Emissions from Road Transport. An Ignored Environmental Policy Challenge.* https://www.oecd.org/env/highlights-non-exhaust-particulate-emissions-from-road-transport.pdf

Overhouse, D. (2020, November 30). *The Race to Crack Battery Recycling—Before It's Too Late.* Wired. https://www.wired.com/story/the-race-to-crack-battery-recycling-before-its-too-late/

Palandrani, P. (2020, December 9). *Four Companies Leading the Rise of Lithium & Battery Technology.* https://www.globalxetfs.com/four-companies-leading-the-rise-of-lithium-battery-technology/

PNUMA. (2017). *Movilidad Eléctrica: Oportunidades para Latinoamérica.* https://movelatam.org/Movilidad%20electrica_%20Oportunidades%20para%20AL.pdf

Reuters. (2020). *Tesla's Musk hints of battery capacity jump ahead of industry event.* https://www.reuters.com/article/us-tesla-batteries-idUSKBN25L0MC

SPTrans. (2019). *Prefeitura assina contratos da licitação do transporte público por ônibus.* https://www.sptrans.com.br/noticias/prefeitura-assina-contratos-da-licitacao-do-transporte-publico-por-onibus/

Sucinc S.A. (2021). *Repuestos cambiados en buses eléctricos vs combustión - Ecuador 31-05-21* [Spare parts changed in electric vs. combustion buses]. Unpublished.

Sustainable Bus. (2020). *The pandemic doesn't stop the European e-bus market: +22% in 2020.* https://www.sustainable-bus.com/news/europe-electric-bus-market-2020-covid/

Taborelli, M. (2021). *MetBus concentró estrategia en la carga de buses eléctricos para mejorar competitividad y va por más en Chile.* Portal Movilidad. https://portalmovilidad.com/metbus-concentro-estrategia-en-la-carga-de-buses-electricos-para-mejorar-competitividad-y-va-por-mas-en-chile/

UK Department of Transport. (2021). *Bus Back Better.* https://www.gov.uk/government/publications/bus-back-better

World Bank. (2019). *Green Your Bus Ride: Clean Buses in Latin America – Summary Report.* World Bank Group. https://documents.worldbank.org/curated/en/410331548180859451/Green-Your-Bus-Ride-Clean-Buses-in-Latin-America-Summary-Report

World Bank. (2020). *Lessons from Chile's Experience with E-mobility: The Integration of E-Buses in Santiago.* World Bank. https://openknowledge.worldbank.org/handle/10986/34435

ZEBRA. (2020). *From Pilots to Scale: Lessons from the Electric Bus Deployments in Santiago de Chile.* https://www.c40knowledgehub.org/s/article/From-Pilots-to-Scale-Lessons-from-Electric-Bus-Deployments-in-Santiago-de-Chile?language=en_US

KEY TERMS AND DEFINITIONS

Battery: An electric system able to generate electricity via chemical reactions or to store electricity coming from external sources.

Battery Cycle: The process of recharging a battery until it reaches 100% of its storage capacity.

Battery Density: The amount of Watt hours (Wh) that can be held in a certain volume. It can also be expressed in terms of gravimetric density or Watt hours per kilogram (Wh/kg).

BRT: Bus rapid transit.

C40-CFF: The Cities Finance Facility of C40 Cities.

CAF: The Latin American Development Bank.

CAPEX: Capital expenditures is the money a company needs to procure, upgrade, or maintain physical assets and includes the financial cost of the money.

CNG: Compressed natural gas.

E-Bus: A large electric vehicle used to carry passengers by road whose energy source is electricity provided directly from the electric grid, from a storage equipment like a battery or from fuel cells.

Fossil Bus: Any large ground passenger transportation vehicle that has an engine that functions with fossil fuels.

GHG: Greenhouse gas.

GIZ: Deutsche Gesellschaft für Internationale Zusammenarbeit, the German society for international cooperation.

Hybrid Bus: Any large ground passenger transportation vehicle that operates with an internal combustion engine and electricity stored in batteries.

IADB: Inter-American Development Bank.

ICCT: International Council on Clean Transportation.

IFC: International Finance Corporation – World Bank Group.

Investor: An organization interested in putting money in projects looking for profits in a certain period.

ITPD: Institute for Transportation and Development Policy.

NGOs: Non-governmental organizations.

OPEX: Is the set of all expenses in which a company incurs in to keep the business running and includes administration, maintenance taxes and the like.

R&D: Research and development.

TCO of a Bus: Total Cost of Ownership is the sum of the capital cost of an asset, including financial costs, and the operations costs that include fix and variable costs to keep the asset running.

VAT: Value added tax.

WRI: World Resources Institute.

Zero Emission Bus: A large ground passenger transportation vehicle that has no tailpipe outflows.

ZEBRA: Zero Emissions Bus Rapid-Deployment Accelerator, a program of ICCT and C40 Cities.

ENDNOTES

1 ZEBRA: https://p4gpartnerships.org/pioneering-green-partnerships/all-p4g-partnerships/zero-emission-bus-rapid-deployment-accelerator

2 RED, formerly Transantiago, is the mobility metropolitan network that integrates the BRT, the metro, and the train in the metro area of Santiago de Chile. It reports to its board, DPTM, that in turns reports to the Ministry of Transport and Telecommunications of Chile.

3 Engie was very enthusiastic when it began to invest in electric buses as it did in Santiago de Chile in 2018 and it got involved in Mexico City with a testing project of up to 20 articulated e-buses, 10 in place in 2021. Then they began to prepare a business strategy for Colombia and suddenly, in mid-2020, the corporation decided to get out of the e-buses business. They kept the projects they have in Chile and Mexico selling all assets to a new investor structured in Mexico as VEMO (https://mundoempresarial.com.mx/?p=41791).

4 https://p4gpartnerships.org/

5 Enel's e-buses business is managed by Enel X, a subsidiary, after little interest shown for years in this business, particularly in Colombia. In 2010 Enel's CEO in Colombia rejected the invitation that C40 made to the company to participate in the Hybrid and Electric Bus Test Program, arguing that electric vehicles will not be in the country before a decade. Enel also delayed the implementation

of the e-taxi pilot in Bogotá and finally got involved pushed by the acting Mayor in 2011. In 2014, Enel proposed to the City Hall a PPP on trolleybuses and when the new administration arrived in 2015 the idea never took off. Because of this expensive failure (apparently, they spent $20 million preparing the proposal) Enel decided to join the testing activities of the e-buses that were already in Bogotá and finally began to be part of the transition process towards electromobility, first as a contractor of TransMilenio to deploy 222 charging stations and then as investor who won the right to deploy 401 buses with their chargers in the 2020-2021 tender in Bogotá (La República, 2021).

6 Another conventional operator let ZEBRA run a TCO and it is also negotiating a loan with a commercial bank.

7 Sucinc uses Mercedes 0500 diesel buses and BYD H9G 100% electric buses.

8 Law No. 16,802, January 17, 2018, Câmara Municipal de São Paulo.

9 http://portal.anla.gov.co/exclusion-del-iva-adquisicion-elementos-maquinaria-y-equipos-requeridos-sistemas-control-y-monitoreo

10 This information results from many conversations with transit authorities in the region and news.

11 Although the contracts were initially signed for 20 years there was a legal ruling that cut the duration to 15.

Chapter 15
Local Perspectives of Sustainable Urbanism:
Solutions Based on the Spanish Legislation Model

María Jesús Garcia García García
University of Valencia, Spain

EXECUTIVE SUMMARY

The protective actions of restoration, especially when they affect urban spaces formally declared as areas of restoration, must have an urban reflection and be projected and reflected in the corresponding planning and management techniques. Planning legislation provides the instruments (plans) and the proper techniques to make urban planning adjusted to the parameters of the restoration performing actions that seek to promote the rational use of the natural and cultural resources, in particular the territory, the soil, and the urban and architectural heritage that are the support, the object, and the scene of the quality of life.

SETTING THE STAGE

After a few years of uncontrolled urban development in Spain, the public authorities seem once again interested in urban restoration policies. The urban planning model based on uncontrolled urban growth seems to have come to an end, more because of economic problems than because of the pernicious effects of all kinds that it has generated. In this cyclical alternation of public policies, it seems that the time has come again to return to the virtues of urban restoration. However, it is not the first time that the public authorities show their interest in it. The successive housing plans that have been approved both at the regional and state levels have opted for restoration, financing and subsidizing actions in this regard, and during the nineties there were several local administrations that created restoration offices determined to promote these actions. However, currently the interest in restoration is no longer limited only to the norms on development, of individual scope and little economic importance, but splashes

DOI: 10.4018/978-1-7998-8417-0.ch015

the urban legislation, to propose a model of urban restoration with the participation of public powers, but also of the private sector to channel the activity of a sector that has been badly damaged as a result of the urban model of recent years. It is about turning urban restoration into a profitable urban activity. Restoration policies seem to be resurfacing not so much because of their virtues or because of their adaptation to constitutional objectives, as because of the exhaustion of an urban model of unsustainable development. From these premises, the following questions are analyzed.

The term restoration is synonymous with re-enabling or restoring to a property the conditions of use that it has lost. When we refer to urban restoration we are talking about a set of both public and private actions that fall on both the urbanized and built-up heritage of cities and that are aimed at restoring the conditions of use and utility to the properties or spaces (Kennedy C, Cuddihy J, Engel-Yan J, 2020). These are actions that are supported by the built heritage, mainly destined for a residential purpose, but also the urbanized heritage and the urban spaces deteriorated in their elements due to the passage of time, lacking the necessary public endowments., which have lost their original functionality and are in an advanced state of physical deterioration with the economic and social implications derived from these processes. Very fundamentally the spaces that are affected are the historic centers of the cities, although urban restoration is not sticks exclusively to this context, but manifests itself in t more general terms, such as a need to rehabilitate degraded urban spaces and to preserve the properties that should be the object of preservation. Urban restoration affects the deteriorated or degraded heritage of cities and tries to recover these elements, but it also has a broader purpose, to the extent that it is crossed by social and economic objectives. Thus, the restoration processes are intended to maintain the existing population in these areas, avoiding their eviction, and at the same time they intend to economically and functionally revitalize these spaces by implanting in them activities and services, public and commercial uses, etc. that are demanded by society and that they endow them with a new functionality. Thus, urban restoration is transcended by numerous economic, sociological, etc. factors that are articulated on the premise of the physical and material recovery of urban spaces and the elements that make them up.

The Constitution links the right to decent housing and the right to an adequate environment with the regulation of land uses. But it also advocates the rational use of natural resources. Urban planning must be oriented towards restoration to comply with the constitutional precept, given that restoration does not consume land and allows to take advantage and use, reuse the existing heritage (Freytag T, Gössling S, Mössner S, 2019).

In short, and as established in the statement of reasons of state Law 7/2015, October 30th, which approves the revised text of the Land Law, restoration seeks to promote the rational use of the natural and cultural resources, in particular the territory, the soil and the urban and architectural heritage that are the support, the object and the scene of the quality of life.

Likewise, the same legal text also states in its explanatory statement that "the urban land— the city already made-also has an environmental value, as a collective cultural creation that is the object of a permanent recreation, so its characteristics must be an expression of its nature and its management must favor its restoration and encourage its use".

All this shows an interest in the restoration of the consolidated urban fabric, for the city already made. Urban restoration as restoration of urban spaces requires urban treatment. Urban planning can not only deal with the growth and expansion of population centers, but also with the action on the interior of cities to adapt them to the new demands of higher quality of life in an urban context that allows the enjoyment of adequate housing with adequate spaces and equipment.

Recent Spanish legislation, both at the state and regional levels, has affected the treatment of restoration, establishing some provisions that tend to favor these actions. In addition to the techniques and instruments it makes available for restoration, it allows the resources obtained by the Administration derived from urban management to be used to finance these actions.

Thus, Spain's Urbanism Law 7/2015, October 30th, extends the purposes of the municipal land heritage (Webster C, Lai LWC, 2003), allowing the alienation of the land of the same to be used for restoration operations. This is evident in article 86 of this Law, which establishes that the income obtained by the Administration as a result of the alienation of land will be used for the conservation and extension of the municipal land heritage or by specific agreement of the competent body for the following purposes:

- Obtaining and executing local endowments on consolidated urban land.
- Actions of public initiative of urban renewal, interior reform or restoration of housing.
- Relocation and return expenses
- Purchase and, where appropriate, restoration of buildings for protected housing or public facilities.

And these same provisions are extended by the urban planning legislation to the extent that there is the replacement of the use that corresponds to the Administration by its economic equivalent that can be used for the same purposes.

The restoration actions are also contemplated by the urban regulations on the occasion of the regulation of the reserve of land for the construction of protected housing (Law 8/2013, June 26th). According to this regulation, the General Urban Plans and in accordance with them the development planning instruments must establish in sectors or units of unconsolidated or apt-for-development urban land whose characteristic use is residential, land reserves for the construction of protected housing. However, according to the same article, when it is not possible to establish these reservations, they may be replaced by restoration actions outside the scope of action.

In any case, a certain skepticism about the possibility that through the generality of these precepts the expected results will be obtained cannot be overemphasized. It is not the first time that the standards take urban restoration as a reference, however the experience of recent years shows that the economic benefits of uncontrolled urban growth have won over to restoration. Restoration policies therefore seem to resurface not because of their virtues or their adaptation to constitutional precepts, but because of the exhaustion of an urban development model that no longer gives more of itself.

In any case, the current interest of Spanish public authorities in this option is undeniable, which gives rise to their intervention from very different points of view, both regulatory and management. In this sense it can be said that the various forms of administrative activity are projected in a more complete way on the restoration activity, although it can be said that urban restoration is primarily urban restoration (Wolman A, 1965).

Thus, to the extent that the restoration consists of actions on the public spaces of urbanization or redevelopment we are talking about a public function that can be managed both directly and indirectly (Chance T, 2009)). In contrast to urban renewal or urbanization of land apt-for-development, where the economic benefits are substantial and stimulate private investment and indirect management systems, in the case of restoration, the absence of profitability retracts private subjects from carrying out these actions, resulting in the need for greater investment by the public sector that thus supplements the inhibition of the private sector.

In other cases, the restoration actions are carried out by the administration, but the Administration, based on the interest they have, intervenes by encouraging these activities or checking their compliance with the law.

Hence the need to delimit the competences in the field of restoration to specify which public administrations are competent to act in the matter and what their level of intervention must be.

CASE DESCRIPTION

Because of the importance of the actions being carried out, two types of restoration can be distinguished: isolated restoration and integrated restoration. The first is the one that considers the object on which it falls in its own individuality, without major implications or connections with the surrounding elements. On the contrary, integrated restoration is one that considers the element on which it is projected included in a larger space in which it is integrated. Integrated restoration is the restoration of urban spaces. It does not dispense with the restoration of individual elements, but those are taken into consideration insofar as they are included in an urban context that interests to revitalize and their effects transcend the individual element on which they fall to be projected on the physical space that contains it.

The distinction mentioned is of fundamental importance because it affects the transcendence of the actions that are going to be developed, and the breadth of them, conditioning the techniques used and the legal instruments put at the service of restoration. In this context, the use of digital technologies to facilitate the planning and execution of restoration projects is of capital importance.

It is the restoration of buildings and homes intended primarily for residential use that aims to provide housing with the necessary living conditions for that residential use and is carried out by the owners or holders of some right over the property on which it acts.

In this type of restoration, the public activity usually consists of financing and promotion activities based on economic incentives, the main exponent of which is usually the provision of subsidies.

It can be distinguished between restoration actions that seek to achieve a structural and constructive adaptation of those others that are aimed at achieving a functional adaptation. By structural adaptation works are understood all those that provide the house with constructive security conditions, so that its stability, resistance, firmness and solidity is guaranteed. This is to ensure that the property meets sufficient guarantees of security and stability.

With regard to those works of restoration aimed at achieving the functional suitability, it should be noted that the criterion that guides the performance of the same is based on the achievement of habitability, integrating in this concept, according to the Law 8/2013, June 26th the improvement of the conditions of access of people with disabilities, the existence and proper functioning of health services, electrical installations, sanitation and plumbing, heating, smoke extraction and ventilation, actions related to thermal and acoustic insulation and those that promote energy saving systems. As can be seen, this is an ecological and sustainable restoration (Batty M, 2013).

The restoration is usually voluntary in these cases and is limited by the duty of conservation of the owner and the declaration of ruin that are configured as duties consubstantial with the property right.

In urban spaces restoration involves a set of actions that involve the protection, conservation, restoration and improvement of its urban fabric, through the enhancement and more appropriate use of the urbanized and built heritage contained in its perimeter.

In these areas, restoration actions go beyond the purely material or physical perspective, so that they also have a social or economic dimension of recovering degraded environments. Thus, for example, it is a question of maintaining the existing population, improving their living conditions and especially the quality of housing and the promotion of economic activities compatible with the aforementioned objectives. the State Housing Plan states that protected restoration actions must ensure social diversity and rehousing of the resident population. The Law of the Community of Madrid on degraded urban spaces (Allen C, Clouth, 2012) also includes restoration actions proposals to revive the activity in the degraded area, with special reference to the maintenance of existing functions and, in particular, trade and crafts and the creation of new ones, taking into account the socio-economic, cultural and technical structure of the area.

In short, the restoration of these spaces aspires to the achievement of a plurality of social and community purposes (improvement or recovery of urban complexes or rural areas, of economic and social activities and the living conditions of their residents) but always on the budget of an action on urban spaces and the elements that compose them.

Normally the restoration processes will be carried out on urban land consolidated by the building located in the historic center of the cities. However, areas or neighborhoods that are undergoing a process of deterioration or degradation may also undergo restoration. We can talk about suburbs or slums, outskirts of cities not coinciding with the historic Center and where the limits to restoration will not be as intense as in the historic centers.

This configuration of the urban space as an object of restoration requires in any case an urban instrument (urban planning) that delimits the affected space and that foresees these actions in the framework of urban planning, which leads us to consider the restoration from an urban perspective

CURRENT CHALLENGES FACING THE ORGANIZATION

The term restoration is primarily coined by the state and regional regulations that address the financing of public housing and urban planning policies. But to the extent that it affects urban spaces and configures urban planning, it has an urban vocation that must be contemplated by this sectoral legislation.

The protective actions of restoration, especially when they affect urban spaces formally declared as areas of restoration, must have an urban reflection and be projected and reflected in the corresponding planning and management techniques.

Planning legislation provides the instruments (plans) and the proper techniques to make an urban planning adjusted to the parameters of the restoration performing actions that tend to increase the endowments, to the estate or redevelopment of urban spaces and even the construction of houses subjected or not to a regime of protection to the public (Donatiello JE, 2015).

The restoration has a clear urban vocation, and that urban vocation is made effective through planning. The plans, transferred by the budgets of the restoration, affect the urban spaces, the city already consolidated, and order it in the indicated sense. The development of restoration actions through urban planning through planning has the following effects:

- It allows to configure urban planning in advance based on a plurality of actions that do not appear disconnected from each other, but integrated within the framework of general forecasts that is only possible to establish if there is an urban figure that anticipates these contents.

- The planning contemplates the rehabilitated element not in its own individuality but in the framework of a broader urban context that interests to rehabilitate, so that its effects go beyond the individual plane to produce broader effects.
- Determines the result of the provision and promotion activity that will tend to develop within the framework of the coordinates laid down by the plan.
- It is able to integrate the different sectoral rules that affect the same urban space and combine the different declarations and legal regimes to which they are subject with the urban planning of the same. Thus regulations on restoration, areas of integrated restoration for promotion purposes, regulations on historical heritage, declaration of cultural interest, etc.
- The plans establish the distinction between consolidated and unconsolidated urban land, which determines the form of execution of the restoration actions, the subjects involved in it and the duties of the affected owners.

Contrary to what it might seem, a planning that starts from rehabilitating premises is not characterized by the extreme maintenance of the existing patrimonial elements, but also admits alterations of the same (demolition, substitutions), as long as these actions are informed by rehabilitating purposes. Urban planning can contribute to promote the restoration and conservation of buildings basically in two ways:

- Not creating urban expectations higher than those already existing.
- Establishing a duty to rehabilitate.

It should be borne in mind that degraded urban spaces have traditionally been considered from the urban perspective, mainly through internal reform operations, although it is not until relatively recent dates when urban legislation and urban plans adopt the perspective of restoration and are transcended by their objectives.

There is no single typology of urban planning with the capacity to influence the restoration, but there can be several urban figures that adapt to these objectives (Adhya A, Plowright P, Stevens J 2011). In any case, it should be noted that urban restoration actions require detailed planning that can be provided by different plans.

For example, general plans if they contain a detailed arrangement. Law 8/2013, June 26th provides that the general plan may delimit one or several traditional historical centers where the urban planning does not allow the indiscriminate replacement of buildings and requires that their conservation, implementation, reform or renovation harmonize with the historical typology.

In the absence of such a detailed arrangement, the approval of the relevant special plan will be required (Moroni S, 2015). The special plans of interior reform have been the figure of planning that has usually affected the urban fabric already consolidated, that is, in the city already made to undertake operations of interior reform (Roggema R, 2012a). But its content has not always been transcended by the purposes of restoration. On the contrary, sometimes such planning has served to carry out renovation operations that are totally opposed to those of restoration (Alfasi N, Portugali J 2007).

In any case, and transcended by these purposes and objectives, the special interior reform plans are well adapted to the actions of urban restoration. Thus, among the objectives of the aforementioned plans are: decongestion or renewal of urban land use, creation of urban development and community equipment, sanitation of unhealthy neighborhoods, resolution of traffic or aesthetic problems and improvement of the urban environment or public services or other similar purposes (Cohen J, Stewart I, 1994)).

All these purposes coincide to a large extent with the objective scope of restoration, but at the same time the breadth of the expression other similar purposes, allow the objectives of these plans to be extended to other purposes related to it.

The approval of special plans for the protection of cultural heritage is unavoidable in those cases in which the affected urban space has been declared a site of cultural interest. Article 59 of the Law 8/2013, June 26th establishes that the declaration of set of cultural interest will determine the obligation of the city council to draft a number of special plans for the protection and, where appropriate, sanitation and renovation of the affected area (Sharifi A, 2016), in accordance with the provisions of the cultural heritage legislation.

This type of plan clearly shows its capacity to integrate the different rules and legal regimes that coexist in the same urban space (De Roo G, Hillier J, van Wezemael J, 2020). Aragonese legislation is a good example. Aragonese Cultural Heritage states that the special plan will establish for all public uses the priority order of its installation in buildings and spaces that are suitable for them. This same planning will determine the areas of restoration. Urban renovations will be possible but only if they involve an improvement with the territorial and urban environment. At the same time the planning will establish the limits to the restoration in accordance with the cultural legislation. The replacement of buildings is therefore considered exceptional and may only be carried out when it contributes to the general conservation of the complex. In any case, the urban alignments will be maintained.

On some occasions urban spaces subject to restoration are the subject of a formal declaration by the administration, giving rise to the concept of restoration area. It is in these cases when the link between restoration and urban planning is most clearly seen.

This expression refers to a space legally delimited by an administrative declaration on which the various restoration actions are planned and affected. The legal delimitation to which we refer is carried out through an administrative act that establishes the presence in the area subject to the declaration of the necessary requirements to confer such character.

The declaration of restoration area is a complement to urban planning. Through them, the aim is to complement the urban perspective from which degraded urban spaces have traditionally been contemplated, and allow the coordination of the activity of the different public administrations, especially with regard to the financing of actions carried out in these urban contexts.

Keep in mind that the statement of area of restoration involves the determination by the Administration of certain physical circumstances that are present in the urban space, but does not by itself the capacity to implement the interventions planning to need to undergo spatial domains on which it acts, interventions that have come previously determined for the plan.

The restoration areas therefore constitute the space on which the restoration actions previously defined by the planning are projected, hence the importance of having the appropriate determinations in this regard prior to the declaration. Article 55 of the State Housing Plan (RD 801/2005, of 1 July) is clear in this regard, since it states that the protected restoration actions must "conform to the regulations of the current urban planning that is applicable...».

SOLUTIONS AND RECOMMENDATIONS

The urban restoration presents the peculiarity that it affects spaces on which there is consolidated building where there is an urban development already materialized on which the urban planning is projected.

For its part, planning can establish a subjective use different from the materialized use. In this way, it should be noted that for a plan to have a content adjusted to the parameters of restoration in the sense that it promotes the maintenance of constructions and buildings, it is necessary that its determinations maintain the balance between the use already materialized and the use susceptible of appropriation that results from the planning. Thus two magnitudes appear on whose balance will depend the decisions of individuals when it comes to the verification or not of restoration actions. They are ultimately entrusted with the verification or not of voluntary restoration interventions

The rupture of the equation between both magnitudes can be given by two circumstances:

1. By the need to proceed with the legal duty to cede the land in which the corresponding use is located to the city council as a result of the realization of restoration actions. Situation already seen in the previous section
2. As a result of a modification of the planning that involves the alteration of the uses and intensities foreseen in the previous arrangement. Indeed, the modification of the planning can lead to an imbalance between the use susceptible of appropriation and the materialized and patrimonialized use in those cases in which the urban planning alters the uses or intensities foreseen in the previous planning. To favor the conservation of the properties, the planning must avoid creating expectations higher than those already existing (increases in use) and must tolerate certain situations previously defined based on the previous management when the materialized use exceeds the objective use foreseen by the plan. This provision is contained in Article 102.2 of Spanish urban planning legislation. Thus in the isolated operations of restoration whenever the buildings are conserved, if it gives the circumstance that the edificability materialized historically exceeds the objective use, such edificability will be taken as a reference of subjective use.

Indeed, the alteration of the use susceptible of appropriation with respect to the already patrimonialized and materialized is a factor of considerable importance for the decision to verify restoration actions.

In urban land consolidated by the urbanization, subject to isolated actions, the appropriate use refers to the plot. And if the materialized use is higher than the objective use marked by the planning, the materialized use will be taken as a reference of the subjective use, as long as the building is preserved and it is not in a situation of out of order

This provision favors the conservation and restoration of buildings, especially once the legal duty of conservation and restoration has ceased, since it allows to maintain the materialized use as long as the property in question is maintained (Shafiea FA, Dasimah O, Karuppannanb S 2013).

Also the urbanism state Law 7/2015, October 30th establishes special treatment to the unique properties of the cultural heritage. The general Plan may provide that the destination of the unique properties of cultural heritage and protected by the planning applications in hospitality and commercial to not consume the area corresponding to the execution unit or sector.

On the other hand, this legislation allows, within the framework of the provisions of the state legislation, that the urban development that has to be transferred to the city council can be replaced by its economic equivalent (transitional provision second b) of the Land Law).

3. Other urban duties inherent in restoration: the duty of conservation and the duty of restoration (Roggema R, 2015))

The duties of conservation and restoration oblige owners to maintain their properties in conditions of safety, health and safety. accessibility and adornment, and to keep the goods in a condition to serve for their use to the extent of the legal duty of conservation.

These duties of conservation and restoration are established in the basic legislation, specifically article 9 of the T. R. of the Land Law, establishes them within the duties and burdens that make up the essential content of the property right.

For its part, article 31 of the same Law states that failure to comply with the duties of building or restoration will entitle for expropriation for failure to fulfill the social function of the property or for the application of the regime of forced sale or replacement.

The duty of conservation reaches and is enforceable to the owner up to the limit provided for in the urban legislation. However, it must be borne in mind that the limit of the duty of conservation is not established in the basic state legislation, unlike what happened in the previous regulation, so that the autonomous regulations will establish the aforementioned limits.

Planning legislation autonomic based on these forecasts state ends up shaping the content of these duties, establishing in the majority of cases, a regime more benevolent to the conservation of the property as set forth in the regulations of state (first in the Revised Text of the Land Law of 1992 and later, after the declaration of unconstitutionality of article 247 of the mentioned legal text, for in article 183 of the Revised Text of the Land Law of 1976), where the declaration of ruin entailed as a legal consequence the demolition of the property. In this sense, the regional legislation has had an impact both in the regulation of the scenarios that may lead to the declaration of ruin (yet very linked to economic criteria), as in the legal consequences of that declaration, that allow the owner to preserve or demolish, through the intervention of the Administration to which they are recognized ability to alter the physical state of ruin.

A good example of these statements is Spanish urban planning legislation that distinguishes between the limit of the duty of conservation of the owner and the limit of the duty of conservation of the property.

The limit of the legal duty of conservation for the owner is constituted by an economic magnitude and is reached when the conservation work exceeds half the value of the buildings, excluding the soil under section 186.2 of the urban legislation. The economic limit of the duty of conservation that is demanded to the owner is constituted by the 50 percent of the value of the buildings excluding the soil. Or what is the same, the only thing that can be imposed on the owner is a conservation that does not exceed 50 percent of the value of the property.

However, the assessment of this limit does not automatically determine the declaration of ruin and subsequent demolition, but once the same has been established, the owner can choose between requesting subsidies or aid to the administration in the part that exceeds the previous limit, or requesting the declaration of ruin of the buildings. It must be borne in mind that the limit of 50% of the value of the building that marks the cessation of the duty of conservation coincides with the first assumption of ruin, physical ruin. On the other hand, the assumptions of technical ruin can also be traced back to economic criteria.

In short and always before the declaration of ruin, it allows the owners to choose either to request the formal declaration of ruin or for the conservation of the property with the limit to their charge of 50 percent of the value of the building, paying the administration the remaining part.

The declaration of ruin marks the limit of the duty of conservation of the property. The binomial ruin demolition is maintained so that declared the ruin proceeds the demolition of the property, but to declare the ruin it is necessary to take into consideration two circumstances: material, physical or factual and formal, consisting in the assessment by the Administration of such circumstances.

For this reason, the declaration of ruin is subject to the will of the Administration, since the factual situation of ruin in a property, the Administration can prevent the declaration of it through the alteration of the physical state of the property by initiating the necessary conservation works to eliminate the state of ruin and all the possible effects derived from it. The owner must pay the amount of the works corresponding to half of the value of the buildings, excluding the land. Again, the owner is subject to a limit of 50 percent of the value of the building, and the Administration must pay for the works in the amount that exceeds that percentage. This demonstrates the involvement of the Administration in the duty of conservation.

REFERENCES

Adhya, A, Plowright, P, & Stevens, J. (2011). Defining sustainable urbanism: towards a responsive urban design. In *Proceedings of the conference on sustainability and the built environment*. King Saud University.

Alfasi, N., & Portugali, J. (2007). Planning rules for a self-planned city. *Planning Theory*, *6*(2), 164–182. doi:10.1177/1473095207077587

Allen,, C., & Clouth,, S. (2012). *A guidebook to the green economy*. UNDESA.

Batty,, M. (2013). *A new science of cities*. MIT Press.

Birkmann, J., Garschagen, M., Kraas, F., & Quang, N. (2010). Adaptive urban governance: New challenges for the second generation of urban adaptation strategies to climate change. *Sustainability Science*, *5*(2), 185–206. doi:10.100711625-010-0111-3

Chance, T. (2009). Towards sustainable residential communities; the Beddington zero energy development (BedZED) and beyond. *Environment and Urbanization*, *21*(2), 527–544. doi:10.1177/0956247809339007

Cohen,, J., & Stewart,, I. (1994). *The collapse of chaos: discovering simplicity in a complex world*. Penguin Group Ltd.

De Roo,, G., Hillier,, J., & van Wezemael,, J. (2020). *Complexity and planning: systems, assemblages and simulations*. Ashgate Publishing.

Donatiello, J. E. (2015). The world's population: An encyclopedia of critical issues, crises, and ever-growing countries. *Reference and User Services Quarterly*, *54*(4), 85. doi:10.5860/rusq.54n4.85b

Drury, F. (2019). Enchanting photos of the abandoned village taken over by hippies living in fairytale houses in the Spanish mountains. *MailOnline*. http://www.dailymail.co.uk/news/article-3139295/Enchanting-photos-abandoned-village-taken-Spanish-hippies-living-fairytale-houses-mountains.html

Freytag,, T., Gössling,, S., & Mössner,, S. (2019). Living the green city: Freiburg's Solarsiedlung between narratives and practices of sustainable urban development. *Local Environment*, *19*(6), 644–659.

Girardet,, H. (1996). *The GAIA atlas of cities: new directions for sustainable urban living*. Gaia Books Limited.

Habitat III. (2016). *Revised zero draft of the new urban agenda*. https://www.habitat3.org/zerodraft

Kennedy,, C., Cuddihy,, J., & Engel-Yan,, J. (2020). The changing metabolism of cities. *Journal of Industrial Ecology*, *11*(2), 43–59.

Kennedy,, C., Pincetl,, S., & Bunje,, P. (2010). The study of urban metabolism and its applications to urban planning and design. *Environmental Pollution*, *159*(8–9), 1965–1973. PMID:21084139

Kreimer,, A., Arnold,, M., & Carlin,, A. (2003). *Building safer cities: the future of disaster risk*. The International Bank for Reconstruction and Development/The World Bank.

Moroni, S. (2015). Complexity and the inherent limits of explanation and prediction: Urban codes for self-organising systems. *Planning Theory*, *14*(3), 248–267. doi:10.1177/1473095214521104

Roggema, R. (2012a). *Swarm planning: the development of a spatial planning methodology to deal with climate adaptation* (PhD thesis). Delft University of Technology.

Roggema,, R. (2012b). *Shifting paradigms. The design charrette: ways to envision sustainable futures*. Springer.

Roggema, R. (2014). Towards enhanced resilience in city design: A proposition. *Land (Basel)*, *3*(2), 460–481. doi:10.3390/land3020460

Roggema, R. (2015). Three urbanisms in one city: Accommodating the paces of change. *Journal of Environmental Protection*, *6*(09), 946–956. doi:10.4236/jep.2015.69084

Searns,, R.M. (1995). The evolution of greenways as an adaptive urban landscape form. *Landscape and Urban Planning*, *33*(1), 65–80.

Shafiea,, F.A., Dasimah,, O., & Karuppannanb,, S. (2013). Urban metabolism: a research methodology in urban planning and environmental assessment. *Proceedings of the 1st international conference on research methodology for built environment and engineering*.

Sharifi, A. (2016). From garden city to eco-urbanism: The quest for sustainable neighborhood development. *Sustainable Cities and Society*, *20*, 1–16. doi:10.1016/j.scs.2015.09.002

Webster,, C., & Lai,, L.W.C. (2003). *Property rights, planning and markets*. Edward Elgar.

Wolman,, A. (1965). The metabolism of cities. *Scientific American*, *213*(3), 179–190. PMID:14338520

World Commission on Environment and Development. (1987). *Our common future*. Oxford University Press.

Compilation of References

ABC do ABC Fofocando em Você. (n.d.). https://www.abcdoabc.com.br/sao-bernardo/noticia/sao-bernardo-lanca-programa-reciclagem-oleo-cozinha-usado-82848

Aber, J. (2016). *Electric Bus Analysis for New York City Transit*. Columbia University.

Adhya, A, Plowright, P, & Stevens, J. (2011). Defining sustainable urbanism: towards a responsive urban design. In *Proceedings of the conference on sustainability and the built environment*. King Saud University.

Aghion, P., & Howitt, P. (1992). A model of growth through creative destruction. *Journal of The Econometric Society, 60*(2), 323–351.

Ahmed, E. M., & Ridzuan, R. (2013). The impact of ICT on East Asian economic growth: Panel estimation approach. *Journal of the Knowledge Economy, 4*(4), 540–555.

Alfasi, N., & Portugali, J. (2007). Planning rules for a self-planned city. *Planning Theory, 6*(2), 164–182. doi:10.1177/1473095207077587

Allen,, C., & Clouth,, S. (2012). *A guidebook to the green economy*. UNDESA.

Alonso, C., Berg, A., Kothari, S., Papageorgiou, C., & Rehman, S. (2020). Will the AI revolution cause a great divergence? *IMF Working Papers, 2020*(184). doi:10.5089/9781513556505.001

Al-Riyami, A. Z., Louw, V. J., Indrikovs, A. J., Nedelcu, E., Bakhtary, S., Eichbaum, Q. G., & Smit Sibinga, C. Th. (2021) Global Survey of Transfusion Medicine Curricula in Medical Schools – Challenges and Opportunities. *Transfusion, 61*, 617-26.

Amable, B., & Askenazy, P. (2003). *Introduction à l'économie de la connaissance*. UNESCO.

Andersson, T., & Djeflat, A. (Eds.). (2012). *The real issues of the Middle East and the Arab Spring: Addressing research, innovation and entrepreneurship*. Springer Science & Business Media.

Antonopoulos, A., & Sakellaris, P. (2009). The contribution of Information and Communication Technology investments to Greek economic growth: An analytical growth accounting framework. *Information Economics and Policy, 21*, 171–191.

Araujo, O. (2010). *SWOT Analysis (Strengths, Weaknesses, Opportunities, Threats) or (Strengths, Weaknesses, Opportunities and Threats)*. Available at: http://www.dearaujo.ecn.br/cgi-bin/asp/analiseSwot.asp

Armeanu, D. Ş., Vintilă, G., & Gherghina, Ş. C. (2017). Empirical study towards the drivers of sustainable economic growth in EU-28 countries. *Sustainability, 10*(1), 1–22.

Arrow, K. J. (1962). The Economic Implications of Learning by Doing. *The Review of Economic Studies, 29*(3), 155–173.

AtkinsonA. B.MorelliS. (2014, March 8). Chartbook of economic inequality. SSRN. doi:10.2139/ssrn.2422269

Aubert, J. E., & Reiffers, J. L. (Eds.). (2003). *Knowledge economies in the Middle East and North Africa: Toward new development strategies*. World Bank Publications.

Audenis, C., Deroyon, J., & Fourcade, N. (2005). L'impact des Nouvelles Technologies de l'Information et de la Communication sur l'économie française. *Revue économique*, *56*(1), 99–125.

Autio, E. (2017). Strategic entrepreneurial internationalization: a normative framework. *Entrepreneurial Strategy, 11*, 211–227.

Autor, D., Katz, L., & Kearney, M. (2008). Trends in U.S. Wage Inequality: Revising the Revisionists. *The Review of Economics and Statistics*, *90*(2), 300–323. doi:10.1162/rest.90.2.300

Bagheri, M. (2012, September). The Challenge of Slums: Socio-Economic Disparities. *International Journal of Social Science and Humanity*, *2*(5).

Banco Nacional do Desenvolvimento. (2005). *BNDES cria novas condições para compra de ônibus no Brasil e exportação de carros* [BNDES creates new conditions for buying buses in Brazil and exporting cars]. https://www.bndes.gov.br/wps/portal/site/home/imprensa/noticias/conteudo/20050923_not245_05

Banker, R. D., Charnes, A., & Cooper, W. W. (1984). Some models for estimating technical and scale inefficiencies in data envelopment analysis. *Management Science*, *30*(9), 1078–1092.

Baron & Basalama. (2021). *The Century Foundation World Report: "The Case of the Hadhramaut: Can Local Efforts Transcend Wartime Divides in Yemen?"* Academic Press.

Barro, R. J. (1991). Economic growth in a cross section of countries. *The Quarterly Journal of Economics*, *106*(2), 407–443.

Barro, R. J. (2001). Human capital and growth. *The American Economic Review*, *91*(2), 12–17.

Battery University. (2020). *Compare battery energy with fossil fuel and other resources. BU-1007: Net Calorific Value*. https://batteryuniversity.com/learn/article/bu_1007_net_calorific_value

Batty,, M. (2013). *A new science of cities*. MIT Press.

Baumeister, R. F., & Leary, M. R. (1997). Writing Narrative Literature Reviews. *Review of General Psychology*, *1*(3), 311–320. doi:10.1037/1089-2680.1.3.311

Bayoumi, T., Coe, D. T., & Helpman, E. (1999). R&D spillovers and global growth. *Journal of International Economics*, *47*(2), 399–428.

Ben Youssef, A., & M'Henni, H. (2004). Les effets des technologies de l'information et de la communication sur la croissance économique: Le cas de la Tunisie. *Revue Région et Développement*, *19*, 132–150.

Benhabib, J., & Spiegel, M. M. (1994). The role of human capital in economic development evidence from aggregate cross-country data. *Journal of Monetary Economics*, *34*(2), 143–173.

Bernardez, M. (2017, September 17). *Apps for positive social impact: From Uber™ to Neighbors™*. Retrieved from LinkedIn: https://www.linkedin.com/pulse/apps-positive-social-impact-from-uber-neighbors-mariano-bernardez/

Bernardez, M., & Perelrozen, M. (2019). Nanoeconomia del Barrio 31. *Performance Improvement Journal*, 12-18.

Bernardez, M. (2021). Social Innovation strategies to transform slums into successful neighborhoods in Latin America. In J. A. Rolle, J. Kisato, & C. Kebaya (Eds.), *A handbook on the future of work and entrepreneurship for the underserved* (pp. 30–61). Centre for Business & Economic Research.

Bernardez, M., Arias Vallarino, C., Krivatsy, A., & Kaufman, R. (2012). City Doctors: A systemic approach to transform Colon City, Panama. *Performance Improvement Quarterly*, *4*(4), 41–60. doi:10.1002/piq.20125

Besler, S. (2009). The effectiveness of the decision-making process and strategic consensus. *Journal of Public Administration,* 89 - 108. https://app.trdizin.gov.tr/publication/paper/detail/T1RFMk1qSXk=

Bils, M., & Klenow, P. J. (2000). Does schooling cause growth? *The American Economic Review*, *90*(5), 1160–1183.

Birkmann, J., Garschagen, M., Kraas, F., & Quang, N. (2010). Adaptive urban governance: New challenges for the second generation of urban adaptation strategies to climate change. *Sustainability Science*, *5*(2), 185–206. doi:10.100711625-010-0111-3

Bloomberg, N. E. F. (2020). *Electric Vehicle Outlook 2020.* https://about.bnef.com/electric-vehicle-outlook/

Borner, S., Bodmer, F., & Kobler, M. (2004). L'efficience institutionnelle et ses déterminants. *Le rôle des facteurs politiques dans la croissance économique.*

Bottazzi, L., & Peri, G. (2003). Innovation and spillovers in regions: Evidence from European patent data. *European Economic Review, 47*(4), 687-710.

Brasil. (n.d.a). *Organização Das Nações Unidas – ONU.* https://brasil.un.org/pt-br/sdgs

Brasil. (n.d.b). *Companhia Ambiental do Estado de São Paulo.* Disponível em https://cetesb.sp.gov.br/sigor-mtr/sobre-o-sigor/

Brasil. (n.d.c). *Companhia de Saneamento Básico do Estado de São Paulo- SABESP.* Disponível em http://site.sabesp.com.br/site/interna/Default.aspx?secaoId=82

Brasil. (n.d.d). *Empresa Brasileira de Pesquisa Agropecuária Ministério da Agricultura, Pecuária e Abastecimento.* https://www.embrapa.br/busca-de-noticias/-/noticia/2307893/biodiesel-de-oleo-de-fritura-e-tema-do-conexao-ciencia

Brazilian Institute of Geography and Statistics. (2013). *Brazilian Census.* http://basededados.sedpcd.sp.gov.br/dadoscensitarios.php

Brooks, D. (2000). *Bobos in paradise: The new upper class and how they got there.* Simon & Schuster.

Brousseau, É. (2001). E-economie qu'y a-t-il de nouveau ? *Annuaire des relations internationales.*

Brunette, W., Vigil, M., Pervaiz, F., & Levari, S. (2015). *Optimizing Mobile Application Communication for Challenged Network Environments.* Academic Press.

Bukowitz, W. R., & Williams, R. L. (2002). *Knowledge Management Manual.* Bookman.

BYD. (2020). *BYD Starts Operations at its Lithium Iron Phosphate Battery Factory in Brazil.* https://www.byd.com/en/news/2020-09-01/BYD-Starts-Operations-at-its-Lithium-Iron-Phosphate-Battery-Factory-in-Brazil

C40, CCI, & IADB. (2013). *Low carbon technologies can transform Latin America's bus fleets: Lessons from the C40-CCI Hybrid & Electric Bus Test Program: Hybrid and electric technologies are a viable solution to reduce carbon emissions in the world's megacities.* IADB.

Cahen, F. R., Oliveira, M. M. Jr, & Borini, F. M. (2017). The internationalization of new technology-based firms from emerging markets. *International Journal of Technology Management*, *74*, 23–43.

Calidadsalud. (2020). *Private health establishments participating in the provision of services.* http://www.calidadsalud.gob.ec/wp-content/uploads/2020/10/22-10-Privados.pdf

California Air Resources Board. (2018). *Battery Electric Truck and Bus Energy Efficiency Compared to Conventional Diesel Vehicles*. https://ww2.arb.ca.gov/sites/default/files/2018-11/180124hdbevefficiency.pdf

Cameron, G. (1998). *Innovation and Growth: a survey of the empirical evidence*. Nuffield College.

Canton, H. (2021). Economic Commission for Latin America and the Caribbean—ECLAC. In *The Europa Directory of International Organizations* (pp. 142-144). Routledge. doi:10.4324/9781003179900-19

Cassapo, M. F. (2011). *What We Understand Exactly by Tacit Knowledge and Explicit Knowledge.* Available in: www.sgbc.org.br

Castelló, A., & Doménech, R. (2002). Human capital inequality and economic growth: Some new evidence. *Economic Journal (London)*, *112*(478), 187–200.

Castelló-Climent, A. (2010). Channels through which human capital inequality influences economic growth. *Journal of Human Capital*, *4*(4), 394–450.

Castells, M. (2005). A Sociedade em Rede: do Conhecimento à Política. In *A Sociedade em Rede: do Conhecimento à Política*. Universidade Federal de Santa Catarina. Retrieved 06/09/21. https://egov.ufsc.br/portal/sites/default/files/a_sociedade_em_rede_-_do_conhecimento_a_acao_politica.pdf

Castells, M. (1996). *The Rise of the network society, the Information age: Economy, society and culture, 1*. MacMillan.

Cavendish, W. (2000). Empirical regularities in the poverty-environment relationship of rural households: Evidence from Zimbabwe. *World Development*, *28*(11), 1979–2003. doi:10.1016/S0305-750X(00)00066-8

Celis, J., & Acosta, O. (2016). Industrial Ph. D. Programs for the Strengthening of the Industry's Production of Innovation in Colombia. *Innovar (Universidad Nacional de Colombia)*, *26*(62), 129–146. doi:10.15446/innovar.v26n62.59393

CEPAL. (2018). *Economics of Climate Change in Latin America and the Caribbean: A Graphic View*. United Nations.

Cette, G., Mairesse, J., & Kocoglu, Y. (2002). Croissance économique et diffusion des TIC: le cas de la France sur longue période (1980-2000). *Revue française d'économie, 16*(3), 155-192.

Cette, G., Mairesse, J., & Kocoglu, Y. (2004). Diffusion des TIC et croissance potentielle. *Revue d'Économie Politique*, *114*(1), 77–97.

Chance, T. (2009). Towards sustainable residential communities; the Beddington zero energy development (BedZED) and beyond. *Environment and Urbanization*, *21*(2), 527–544. doi:10.1177/0956247809339007

Charnes, A., Cooper, W. W., & Rhodes, E. (1978). Measuring the Efficiency of Decision-Making Units. *European Journal of Operational Research*, *2*, 429–444.

Charoenrat, T., & Harvie, C. (2017). Thailand's SME Participation in ASEAN and East Asian Regional Economic Integration. *Journal of Southeast Asian Economies*, *34*(1), 148–174.

Chen & Dahlman. (2006). *The Knowledge Economy*. The KAM Methodology and World Bank Operations World Bank Institute.

Chen, A.S. (2017). Analysis of the development status and trend of the Internet data center industry. *Wireless Internet Technology*, *16*, 32-34. doi:CNKI:SUN:WXHK.0.2017-16-015.

Chen, D. H. C., & Dahlman, C. J. (2006). The Knowledge Economy, the KAM Methodology and World Bank Operations. World Bank Institute.

Chen, D. H., & Dahlman, C. J. (2005). *The knowledge economy, the KAM methodology and World Bank operations.* World Bank Institute Working Paper, (37256).

Chen, D.M., Wang, L.Z., & Chen, A.N. (2020). Digitalization and Strategic Management Theory—Review, Challenge and Prospect. *World of Management*, 5.

Chen, G.Q., Zeng, D.J., & Wei, Q. (2020). Decision-making paradigm transformation and enabling innovation in the Internet big data environment. *World of Management*, 2.

Chen, J., Yin, X., & Mei, L. (2018). Holistic innovation: an emerging innovation paradigm. *International Journal of Innovative Studies*, *2*(1), 1–13.

Chen, X. (2018). Research on the application and development trend of 5G technology in the mobile Internet era. *China New Communications*, *22*, 162. doi:CNKI:SUN:TXWL.0.2018-22-130.

Chen, D. H. C., & Dahlman, C. J. (2004). *Knowledge and development: a cross-section approach* (Vol. 3366). World Bank Publications.

Chen, L., Shaheer, N., Yi, J., & Li, S. (2019). The international penetration of i-business firms: Network effects, liabilities of outsider ship and country clout. *Journal of International Business Studies*, *50*, 172–192.

China's Open Data Center Committee. (n.d.). Retrieved June 1, 2021, from: https://dcp.odcc.org.cn/index.html

Choo, C. W. (2006). *The Knowledge Organization: How Organizations Use Information to Create Knowledge, Build Knowledge, and Make Decisions* (2nd ed.). Sao Paulo: Senac São Paulo.

Christensen, C. M., Mcdonald, R., Altman, E., & Palmer, J. (2018). Disruptive innovation: An intellectual history and directions for future research. *Journal of Management Studies*, *55*(7), 1043–1078.

CIDEI. (2020). *Homepage.* http://www.cidei.net

Cingano, F. (2014). *Trends in income inequality and its impact on economic growth.* OECD Social, Employment and Migration Working Papers, No. 163, OECD Publishing. doi:10.1787/1815199X

Cleantech, A. Z. O. (2015). *South Korea: Environmental Issues, Policies and Clean Technology.* https://www.azocleantech.com/article.aspx?ArticleID=552

Cluster, C. R. E. A. T. I. C. (2020). *Introduction.* https://minciencias.gov.co/content/corporacion-incubacion-y-fomento-empresas-base-tecnologica-corporacion-cluster-creatic

Coe, D. T., & Helpman, E. (1995). International r&d spillovers. *European Economic Review*, *39*(5), 859–887.

Cohen,, J., & Stewart,, I. (1994). *The collapse of chaos: discovering simplicity in a complex world.* Penguin Group Ltd.

Colecchia, A., & Schreyer, P. (2002). ICT investment and economic growth in the 1990s: is the United States a unique case?: a comparative study of nine OECD countries. *Review of Economic Dynamics*, *5*(2), 408–442.

Colecchia, A., & Schreyer, P. (2002). The contribution of information and communication technologies to economic growth in nine OECD countries. *OECD Economic Studies*, *2002*(1), 153–171.

Collison, C., & Parcell, G. (2001). *Learning to Fly.* Capstone.

Colombia Government. (2018). *Green book 2030.* https://www.tipconsortium.net/wp-content/uploads/2018/09/GreenBook2030_25sept-002.pdf

Colombia Government. (2018). *National Development Plan 2018-2022.* https://www.dnp.gov.co/DNPN/Paginas/Plan-Nacional-de-Desarrollo.aspx#:~:text=El%20Plan%20Nacional%20de%20Desarrollo%20es%20un%20pacto%20por%20la,construir%20el%20futuro%20de%20Colombia

Colombia's Department of Statistics. (2019). *Geovisor Business Directory 2019.* https://geoportal.dane.gov.co/geovisores/economia/directorio-estadistico-de-empresas/?lt=4.456007353293281&lg=-73.2781601239999&z=5

Commissariat Général du plan. (2001). *Séminaire économie de la connaissance.* Author.

Commission des communautés européennes. (2008). *Communication de la commission au parlement européen et au conseil: Le processus de Barcelone: Union pour la Méditerranée.* Author.

Concejo de Bogotá. (2020). *Acuerdo 790 de 2020 Por el cual se declara la emergencia climática en Bogotá D.C., se reconoce esta emergencia como un asunto prioritario de gestión pública, se definen lineamientos para la adaptación, mitigación y resiliencia frente al cambio climático y se dictan otras disposiciones* [Agreement 790 from 2020. Whereby a climate emergency is declared in Bogotá D.C., this emergency is recognized as a priority issue of public management, guidelines are defined for adaptation, mitigation and resilience to climate change and other provisions are issued]. https://www.alcaldiabogota.gov.co/sisjur/normas/Norma1.jsp?i=103745&dt=S

Consortium, T. I. P. (2018). *Colombia embraces transformative innovation policy as national strategy for post-conflict development.* https://www.tipconsortium.net/news/colombia-embraces-new-innovation-theory-from-spru-as-national-strategy-for-post-conflict-development/

Consulting, C. C. I. D. (2020). *Status Quo and Prospects of the Development of China's Internet of Things Industry.* Author.

Cooperapas. (2021). *Cooperativa dos Produtores Rurais e de Água Limpa da Região Sul de São Paulo.* Retrieved 06/09/21. https://www.instagram.com/Cooperapas/?fbclid=IwAR1VtnVdgaYAH7f8kQ7euOvlNHEeCB4LkTWble00mtduKPrNAnEYyFqo1BI

CoronavirusEcuador. (2020). *Official information on the pandemic affecting Ecuador.* https://www.coronavirusecuador.com/

COTECMAR. (2020). *About Us.* https://www.cotecmar.com/en/about-us

Dai, X. C. (2001). *The role of the project management office in achieving project success* (Doctoral thesis). The George Washington University.

Daugherty, P., & Wilson, J. (2018). *Human + machine: Reimagining work in the age of AI.* Harvard Business Review Press.

Davenport, T. H., & Prusak, L. (1998). *Business Knowledge How Organizations Manage Their Intellectual Capital.* Campus.

David, P. A., & Foray, D. (2002). Une introduction à l'économie et à la société du savoir. *Revue internationale des sciences sociales*, (1), 13-28.

Dayton, L. (2020). How South Korea made itself a global innovation leader. *Nature, 581*(7809), S54–S56. doi:10.1038/d41586-020-01466-7

De Roo,, G., Hillier,, J., & van Wezemael,, J. (2020). *Complexity and planning: systems, assemblages and simulations.* Ashgate Publishing.

Diallo, D. (2006). Les clusters innovants et leurs atouts: le cas des clusters numériques. *Vie sciences de l'entreprise*, (1), 9-24.

Dillahunt, T. (n.d.). *Technology for underserved communities; personal fabrication.* Association for Computing Machinery. http://www.tawannadillahunt.com/wp-content/uploads/2012/12/abridgedacmqueuearticle.pdf

Dinsmore, P. C. (1999). *Winning in business with enterprise Project management*. Amazon Books.

Disconzi. (2014). *Dissertação de Mestrado – Universidade Federal de Santa Maria/RS- 2014*. https://repositorio.ufsm.br/bitstream/handle/1/7639/DISCONZI%2C%20%20GRACIELA%20SCHMIDT.pdf?sequence=1&isAllowed=y

Distro. (2012). *Travel to Eat: Myrrh and Frankincense*. https://traveltoeat.com/myrrh-and-frankincense-1/

Djeflat, A. (2007). Rôle et place des TIC dans une économie fondée sur la connaissance. In Le Maghreb dans l'économie numérique. Institut de recherche sur le Maghreb contemporain. doi:10.4000/books.irmc.392

Djeflat, A. (2008). *L'Algérie et ldes défis de l'économie de la connaissance*. Academic Press.

Djeflat, A. (2012). *Les efforts du Maroc dans l'économie fondée sur la connaissance*. CMI Marseille, Rapport Septembre.

Donatiello, J. E. (2015). The world's population: An encyclopedia of critical issues, crises, and ever-growing countries. *Reference and User Services Quarterly, 54*(4), 85. doi:10.5860/rusq.54n4.85b

Dosi, G. (1988). Sources, procedures, and microeconomic effects of innovation. *Journal of Economic Literature*, 1120–1171.

Driouchi, A., Azelmad, E. M., & Anders, G. C. (2006). An econometric analysis of the role of knowledge in economic performance. *The Journal of Technology Transfer, 31*(2), 241–255.

Drucker, P. (1968). From capitalism to knowledge society. In The knowledge economy. Butterworth.

Drucker, P. F. (1998). *Managing in Times of Great Change*. Pioneer.

Drury, F. (2019). Enchanting photos of the abandoned village taken over by hippies living in fairytale houses in the Spanish mountains. *MailOnline*. http://www.dailymail.co.uk/news/article-3139295/Enchanting-photos-abandoned-village-taken-Spanish-hippies-living-fairytale-houses-mountains.html

Dutraive, V. (2008). Économie fondée sur la connaissance et théories récentes de la firme: Une lecture veblenienne. *Revue d'Economie Industrielle*, (124), 51–70.

Dutta, D., & Otsuka, K. (2004). *Knowledge Spillover from Information and Communication Technology: A Comparative Study of Australia*. Department of Economics.

Dweck, C. (2006). *Mindset, The New Psychology of Success*. Ballantine Books.

Ecuador Ministry of Public Health. (2020). *COVID-19 Situation*. https://www.salud.gob.ec/actualizacion-de-casos-de-coronavirus-en-ecuador/

EdTech[Hub] & eLearning Africa. (2020). *The Effect of Covid-19 on Education in Africa and its Implications for the Use of Technology. A survey of the experience and opinions of educators and technology specialists*. doi:10.5281/zenodo.4019774

Edward, P., & Sumner, A. (2013). *The future of global poverty in a multi-speed World: New estimates of scale and location, 2010–2030*. Center for Global Development.

Ellen MacArthur Foundation. (2021). *Economia circular do alimento em São Paulo*. Retrieved 06/09/21. https://youtu.be/hsxrPxFwWMA

Emmanuel, H. (2015). *Diagnostic du système national de recherche et d'innovation en Tunisie*. Rapport final, dans le cadre de Projet d'Appui au Système de Recherche et Innovation (PASRI).

Encoua, D., Foray, D., Hatchuel, A., & Mairesse, J. (2004). Les Enjeux économiques de l'innovation. Bilan du programme CNRS. *Revue d'économie publique, 114*(2), 133-168.

Energeysage. (2019). *Energy efficiency 101: what is energy efficiency?* https://www.energysage.com/energy-efficiency/101/

Energías Renovables. (2015, July 16). *Campinas: Diez buses eléctricos para la flota de transporte público* [Campinas: Ten electric buses for public transport fleet]. Energías Renovables. https://www.energias-renovables.com/movilidad/campinas-diez-buses-electricos-para-la-flota-20150716" \h

Estado de São Paulo Newspaper, O. (2021). *Agricultores orgânicos de Parelheiros: eles vivem de cultivar a terra na cidade de São Paulo*. Retrieved 06/09/21. https://sustentabilidade.estadao.com.br/noticias/geral,produtores-organicos-de-parelheiros-eles-tentam-encurtar-o-caminho-da-roca-para-o-centro,70003729084

Fagiolo, G., Giachini, D., & Roventini, A. (2020). Innovation, finance, and economic growth: An agent-based approach. *Journal of Economic Interaction and Coordination*, *15*(3), 703–736.

Fang, L., Lerner, J., & Wu, C. (2017). Intellectual property rights protection, ownership, and innovation: Evidence from China. *Review of Financial Studies*, *30*(7), 2446–2477.

Feng, W., Peter, W., & Yin, E. (2019). Enabling cost innovation by non-traditional organizational processes: The case of Chinese firms. *Technological Forecasting and Social Change*, *139*, 352–361.

Flowers, S. P. (2005). *Knowledge Management: Competitive strategies for the creation and mobilization of knowledge in the company: discover how to leverage and multiply intellectual capital and knowledge of the organization*. Qualitymark.

Fonds Monétaire International. (2013). Perspectives économiques régionales: Moyen Orient et Afrique du Nord: Définir la voie à suivre. Washington, DC: FMI.

Foray, D. (2000). *L'économie de la connaissance*. La découverte.

Freytag,, T., Gössling,, S., & Mössner,, S. (2019). Living the green city: Freiburg's Solarsiedlung between narratives and practices of sustainable urban development. *Local Environment*, *19*(6), 644–659.

Friends of the Hadhramaut. (n.d.). http://hadhramaut.co.uk/

Fungtammasan B. (2016). Industry-Oriented Graduate Programs in Thailand: A Review. *Asia Pacific Graduate Education,* 161-172.

Ganau, R. (2017). Institutions and economic growth in Africa: A spatial econometric approach. *Economics and Politics*, *34*(3), 425–444.

Gartner. (2020). *Industrial IoT Platforms Reviews and Ratings Gartner 2020*. Author.

Giffi, G., Dollar, B., Gangula, B., & Rodriguez, D. (2015). Help Wanted. American manufacturing competitiveness and the looming skills gap. *Deloitte Review*, *16*, 97–113.

Girardet,, H. (1996). *The GAIA atlas of cities: new directions for sustainable urban living*. Gaia Books Limited.

Glaeser, E. L., La Porta, R., Lopez-de-Silanes, F., & Shleifer, A. (2004). Do institutions cause growth? *Journal of Economic Growth*, *9*(3), 271–303.

Global Transmission Report. (2020). *Colombia: Focus on energy diversification and grid decentralisation*. https://www.globaltransmission.info/archive.php?id=38770

Godin, B. (2006). The knowledge-based economy: Conceptual framework or buzzword? *The Journal of Technology Transfer*, *31*(1), 17–30.

Graziano da Silva, J. (2002). *O novo rural brasileiro*. Instituto de Economia, Universidade Estadual de Campinas (Unicamp). https://www.eco.unicamp.br/images/publicacoes/Livros/pesquisa/O-novo-rural-Brasileiro.pdf

Green Technology Center. (2020). *Global Cooperation.* https://www.gtck.re.kr/frt/center/en/rnd/global_cooperation.do

Greenhalgh, T. (n.d.). Five biases of new technologies. *British Journal of General Practice, 63*(613), 425.

Greenhalgh, T. (2012). The organization vision for telehealth and telecare: Discourse analysis. *BMJ Open, London, 2*, 1–14.

Grero, M. L. (2018). *Mismatch between the education system and the job market in Sri Lanka with special reference to soft skills* [Unpublished doctoral dissertation]. AIMS College.

Griliches, Z. (1998). Introduction. In R&D and productivity: The econometric evidence (pp. 1-14). University of Chicago Press.

Grossman, G. M., & Helpman, E. (1994). Endogenous innovation in the theory of growth. *The Journal of Economic Perspectives, 8*(1), 23–44.

Guille, D. (2008). O que distingue a economia do conhecimento? Implicações para a educação. *Cadernos de Pesquisa, 38*(135), 611–636. doi:10.1590/S0100-15742008000300004

Guizhou Provincial Communications Administration. (2020). *Guizhou Province Internet Development Report*. Author.

Gyekye, A. B., & Oseifuah, E. K. (2015). Knowledge and economic growth: a comparative analysis of three regional blocks in sub-Saharan Africa. *Environmental Economics, 6*(4), 196-208.

Habitat III. (2016). *Revised zero draft of the new urban agenda.* https://www.habitat3.org/zerodraft

Hall, R. E., & Jones, C. I. (1999). Why do some countries produce so much more output per worker than others? *The Quarterly Journal of Economics, 114*(1), 83–116.

Han, L. L. (2018). Benchmarking analysis of the core competitive products of the Internet data center-taking China Mobile as an example. *China Business Forum, 11*, 31-32. doi:10.19699/j.cnki.issn2096-0298.2018.11.014

Hanushek & Woessmann. (2015). *The Knowledge Capital of Nations: Education and the Economics of Growth*. MIT Press.

Harpan & Draghici. (2014). Debate on the Multilevel Model of the Human Capital Measurement. *Procedia: Social and Behavioral Sciences*, 170–177.

Harris, R. G. (2001). The knowledge-based economy: Intellectual origins and new economic perspectives. *International Journal of Management Reviews, 3*(1), 21–40.

Hasan, I., & Tucci, C. L. (2010). The innovation–economic growth nexus: Global evidence. *Research Policy, 39*(10), 1264–1276.

Hava, H. T., & Erturgut, R. (2010). An evaluation of education relations together with technology, employement and economic development components. *Procedia: Social and Behavioral Sciences, 2*(2), 1771–1775.

Hayes, A. (2021). Knowledge Economy. *Investopedia*. Accessible at https://www.investopedia.com/terms/k/knowledge-economy.asp#:~:text=The%20knowledge%20economy%20is%20a,is%20based%20on%20intellectual%20capital.&text=In%20a%20knowledge%20economy%2C%20a,workers'%20knowledge%20or%20intellectual%20property

He, Z. (2019). The macro-structure of national digital governance. *E-Government*, 1.

Hersch, J. (2017). Sex discrimination in the labor market. *Foundations and Trends in Microeconomics, 2*(4), 281–361. https://scholarship.law.vanderbilt.edu/faculty-publications/668

Himanshu, S., & Rahul, P. (2017). E-Governance in India. *International Journal on Emerging Technologies, 8*(1), 318–321.

HowarthR. (2021). https://www.theguardian.com/environment/2021/aug/12/uk-replace-fossil-gas-blue-hydrogen-backfire-emissions

Hsaini, A. (2007). *Le système national d'innovation et de recherche en Tunisie: Un essai de caractérisation et d'évaluation du rôle des centres techniques.* Université Pierre Mondes.

Huang, S., & Wang, Y.R. (2021). A brief analysis of the status and development trend of the domestic industrial Internet industry. *Internet World*, *4*, 28-31. doi: CNKI:SUN:HLWT.0.2021-04-007

IBGE. (2012). *2010 Census: number of Catholics falls and number of Protestants, Spiritists and persons without religion records increase.* https://censo2010.ibge.gov.br/en/noticias-censo?view=noticia&id=1&idnoticia=2170&t=censo-2010-numero-catolicos-cai-aumenta-evangelicos-espiritas-sem-religiao#:~:text=In%202010%2C%20the%20employed%20population,23.7%20million)%20were%20not%20employed

IDC Circle, . (2020). *2019-2020 China IDC Industry Development Research Report.* Author.

ILO. (2018), https://www.ilo.org/weso-greening/documents/WESO_Greening_EN_web2.pdf

Imka. (2021). *Yemen's 10 universities "My Top Schools".* Academic Press.

INEC-RAS. (2018). *Actividades y Recursos de Salud.* https://www.ecuadorencifras.gob.ec/actividades-y-recursos-de-salud/

INSPER. (2020). *Projeto Campo-Favela.* Retrieved 06/09/21. https://www.insper.edu.br/noticias/crowdfunding-projeto-campo-favela/

Inter-American Development Bank. (2011). *Innovation, R&D investment and productivity in Colombian Firms (Working Paper IDB-WP-251).* Banco Interamericano de Desarrollo.

Inter-American Development Bank. (2021). *Innopolis Urban Innovation 2020 Contest: resultados da competição.* Retrieved 06/09/21. https://convocatorias.iadb.org/pt/rede-de-cidades/innopolis-concurso-inova%C3%A7ao-urbana-2020

International Council on Clean Transportation. (2018). *International Evaluation of Public Policies for Electromobility in Urban Fleets.* BROMOB-e.

International Organization of Migration (IOM) Yemen. Ma'rib Response. (2021). https://www.iom.int/sitreps/yemen-marib-response-28-april-15-may-2021

Iturralde, P. (2015). *Privatización de la salud en Ecuador Estudio de la interacción pública con clínicas y hospitales privados.* Quito: Plataforma por el Derecho a la Salud/CDES.

Jacobi, P. (2003). Educação ambiental, cidadanie e sustentabilidade. Cadernos de Pesquisa, 118.

Jia, N., Huang, K. G., & Zhang, C. M. (2019). Public governance, corporate governance, and firm innovation: An examination of state-owned enterprises. *Academy of Management Journal*, *62*(1), 220–247.

Jiang, X.J., & Luo, L.B. (2019). Service Globalization in the Internet Era: New Engine, Acceleration and Competitiveness of Powers. *Chinese Social Sciences*, 2.

Jia, Y. W. (2017). Research on the National Integrated National Internet Data Center System. *E-Government*, *06*, 31–36. doi:10.16582/j.cnki.dzzw.2017.06.005

Jin, C., Robert, A. B., Li, J. X., Chang, C. H., & Gang, Z. (2020). Leading for constructive innovation: Preliminary evidence from China. *Journal of Engineering and Technology Management*, *57*, 101588.

Jouyet, J. P., & Lévy, M. (2006). L'économie de l'immatériel, la croissance de demain. *Rapport de la Commission sur l'économie de l'immatériel. Rapport au Ministre de l'industrie.*

Jung, H. (2016). *Greener ICT, Greater Future. Green ICT and its transformation in Korea.* https://www.slideshare.net/nayahun2/green-ict-and-its-transformation-in-korea-green-startups

Kacprzyk, A., & Doryń, W. (2017). Innovation and economic growth in old and new member states of the European Union. *Economic research- Ekonomska Istrazivanja, 30*(1), 1724–1742.

Kaluzny, A. D. (n.d.). Diffusion of innovative health care services in the United States: a study in hospitals. *Medical Care, 8*(6), 274.

Kanaane & Formigari. (2010). Manual of training and development of human potential (2nd ed.). São Paulo: Atlas.

Karagiannis, S. (2007). The knowledge-based economy, convergence and economic growth: Evidence from the European Union. *Journal of Economic Asymmetries, 4*(2), 65–85.

Kaufmann, D., Kraay, A., & Mastruzzi, M. (2005). *Governance matters IV: governance indicators for 1996-2004.* World bank policy research working paper series, (3630).

Kaufmann, D., Kraay, A., & Mastruzzi, M. (2011). The Worldwide Governance Indicators: Methodology and Analytical Issues1. *Hague Journal on the Rule of Law, 3*(2), 220–246.

KDFuelCell. (2013). *Green Technology Center, Korea.* http://www.kdfuelcell.net/kdfuelcell/participants/gtc-k

Kemp, S. (2018). *2018 Global Digital Report.* We Are Social.com.

Kendrick, J. W. (1994). Total capital and economic growth. *Atlantic Economic Journal, 22*(1), 1–18.

Kennedy,, C., Cuddihy,, J., & Engel-Yan,, J. (2020). The changing metabolism of cities. *Journal of Industrial Ecology, 11*(2), 43–59.

Kennedy,, C., Pincetl,, S., & Bunje,, P. (2010). The study of urban metabolism and its applications to urban planning and design. *Environmental Pollution, 159*(8–9), 1965–1973. PMID:21084139

Kerzner, H. (2002). *Project Management Best Practices.* Bookman.

Kimenyi & Moyo. (2011). *Leapfrogging Development Through Technology Adoption.* Brookings Institution.

KITECH. (2020). *Overview.* http://eng.kitech.re.kr/introduction/page2.php#b

Knack, S., & Keefer, P. (1995). Institutions and economic performance: Cross-country tests using alternative institutional measures. *Economics and Politics, 7*(3), 207–227.

Knowledge for Development. (2020). *Homepage.* https://www.k4d.org

Kocourek, A., & Nedomlelová, I. (2018). Three levels of education and the economic growth. *Applied Economics, 50*(19), 2103–2116.

Korres, G. M., & Patsikas, S., & Polichronopoulos, G. (2002). A knowledge based economy, the socio-economic impact and the effects on regional growth. *Ecological Informatics, 2*(1), 5–12.

Kreimer,, A., Arnold,, M., & Carlin,, A. (2003). *Building safer cities: the future of disaster risk.* The International Bank for Reconstruction and Development/The World Bank.

Krueger, A. B., & Lindahl, M. (2001). Education for growth: Why and for whom? *Journal of Economic Literature, 39*(4), 1101–1136.

Kyun-don. (2021, May 13). *Korea accounts for 31% of global EV battery market in Q1*. The Korea Herald. http://www.koreaherald.com/view.php?ud=20210512000946

La República. (2021, January 20). *Enel X ganó contrato para dotar de buses eléctricos y estaciones de carga a Bogotá* [Enel X won the contract to provide Bogotá with electric buses and charging stations]. https://www.larepublica.co/globoeconomia/enel-x-gana-contrato-para-dotar-de-buses-electricos-y-estaciones-de-carga-a-bogota-3113459

Le Douaron, P. (2002). La formation tout au long de la vie. *Revue française d'administration publique*, (4), 573-580.

Lee, K., & Kim, B. Y. (2009). Both institutions and policies matter but differently for different income groups of countries: Determinants of long-run economic growth revisited. *World Development*, *37*(3), 533–549.

Leite. (2003). *Logística Reversa Meio Ambiente e Competitividade*. Pearson Prentice Hall.

Léné, A. (2005). L'éducation, la formation et l'économie de la connaissance: Approches économiques. *Education et Sociétés*, (1), 91–103.

Liao, L., Du, M., Wang, B., & Yu, Y. (2019). The impact of educational investment on sustainable economic growth in Guangdong, China: A cointegration and causality analysis. *Sustainability*, *11*(3), 766.

Lin, Z.B. (2020). "New infrastructure" in the post-epidemic era has become a new growth point for China's economy. *Shanghai Information Technology*, *4*, 8-12. doi:CNKI:SUN:SHXX.0.2020-04-004

Liouane, N. (2009). Ouverture et croissance économique dans les pays MENA, étude dynamique des effets des facteurs structurels et institutionnels. In *Le Maghreb face aux défis de l'ouverture en Méditerranée*. L'Harmattan.

Liu, Y. H., Huang, X. T., & Shi, B. H. (2020). China's "New Infrastructure": Concepts, Status Quo and Problems. *Journal of Beijing University of Technology*, *06*, 1–12.

Liu, Y. Z., Sun, J. S., & Jiang, Y. C. (2020). The value discovery of big data: 4C model. *Management World*, 2.

Lucas, R. E. Jr. (1988). On The Mechanic of Economic Development. *Journal of Monetary Economics*, *22*(1), 40.

Lucas, R. E. Jr. (1988). On the mechanics of economic development. *Journal of Monetary Economics*, *22*(1), 3–42.

Lundvall, B. Å., & Foray, D. (1996). The knowledge-based economy: from the economics of knowledge to the learning economy. Employment and Growth in the Knowledge-based Economy.

Luzzi. (2012). Educação em Meio Ambiente: Uma Relação Intrínseca. Manole.

M'henni, H., Ben Othman, A., Ghozzi, C., Ben Salah, N., M'henni, S., & Trabelsi, M. (2007). *Le système national de recherche en Tunisie*. ESTIME Project Report.

Machlup, F. (1962). *The production and distribution of knowledge in the United States* (Vol. 278). Princeton university press.

Mankiw, N. G., Romer, D., & Weil, D. N. (1992). A contribution to the empirics of economic growth. *The Quarterly Journal of Economics*, *107*(2), 407–437.

Marquez-Ramos, L., & Mourelle, E. (2019). *Education and economic growth: an empirical analysis of nonlinearities*. Applied Economic Analysis.

Martínez, C. I. P. (2010). Investments and energy efficiency in Colombian manufacturing industries. *Energy & Environment*, *21*(6), 545–562. doi:10.1260/0958-305X.21.6.545

Martínez, C. I. P., & Piña, W. H. A. (2014). Energy Efficiency in Colombia: Trends and Challenges. *International Journal of Energy Science*, *4*(1), 31–34. doi:10.14355/ijes.2014.0401.08

Martínez, H. (2018). *El desafío del sector transporte en el contexto del cumplimiento de las contribuciones determinadas a nivel nacional de América Latina*. CEPAL.

Maurseth, P. B., & Verspagen, B. (2002). Knowledge spillovers in Europe: A patent citations analysis. *The Scandinavian Journal of Economics*, *104*(4), 531–545.

McKinsey & Company. (2019, August 13). *The economic impact of closing the racial wealth gap*. https://www.mckinsey.com/industries/public-and-social-sector/our-insights/the-economic-impact-of-closing-the-racial-wealth-gap

Melo, L. E. V. (2003). *Knowledge Management: Concepts and Applications*. Erica.

Mihaela, M., & Ţiţan, E. (2014). Education and innovation in the context of economies globalization. *Procedia Economics and Finance*, *15*, 1042–1046.

Mingyong, L., Shuijun, P., & Qun, B. (2006). Technology spillovers, absorptive capacity and economic growth. *China Economic Review*, *17*(3), 300–320.

Ministry of Industry and Information Technology of the PRC. (2017). *Code for Design of Data Centers*. China Planning Press.

Ministry of Industry and Information Technology of the PRC. (2020). *Notice to Promote and Accelerate Development of Industrial IDCs (MIIT 2020 No. 8)*. Author.

Ministry of Public Health of Ecuador. (2021). *Situation of COVID 19*. https://www.salud.gob.ec/el-ministerio-de-salud-publica-del-ecuador-msp-informa-situacion-coronavirus/

Miranda, Z. A. I. (2002a). *A incorporação de áreas rurais às cidades: estudo de caso sobre Campinas* (Doctoral thesis). Universidade Estadual de Campinas (Unicamp), São Paulo, Brazil. Retrieved 06/09/21. http://www.repositorio.unicamp.br/handle/REPOSIP/286485

Miranda, Z. A. I. (2002b). As terras que a cidade engoliu. In: *Livro Verde: desafios para a gestão da Região Metropolitana de Campinas*. Instituto de Economia, Universidade Estadual de Campinas (Unicamp), São Paulo, Brazil. Retrieved 06/09/21. https://www.eco.unicamp.br/colecao-geral/livro-verde-desafios-para-a-gestao-da-regiao-metropolitana-de-campinas

Mondiale, B. (2003). Vers une meilleure gouvernance au Moyen-Orient et en Afrique du Nord. Améliorer l'inclusivité et la responsabilisation, Rapport sur le développement au Moyen-Orient et en Afrique du Nord.

Mondiale, B. (2008). Un parcours non encore achevé: la réforme de l'éducation au Moyen-Orient et en Afrique du Nord. Rapport sur le développement de la région MENA, Résumé analytique.

Mondiale, B. (2010). Moyen-Orient et Afrique du Nord: Perspectives économiques mondiales: Vents budgétaires contraires et reprise. Academic Press.

Mondiale, B. (2021). Vivre avec la dette: Comment les institutions peuvent tracer la voie de la reprise dans la région Moyen-Orient et Afrique du Nord, Bulletin d'information économique de la région MENA. Academic Press.

Moroni, S. (2015). Complexity and the inherent limits of explanation and prediction: Urban codes for self-organising systems. *Planning Theory*, *14*(3), 248–267. doi:10.1177/1473095214521104

MRSTDC, (2006b). *R&D et innovation en Tunisie: Principaux indicateurs et positionnement international.* Technical report, Bureau des Etudes Prospectives de la Planification et des Statistiques, Ministère de la Recherche Scientifique, de la Technologie et du Développement des Compétences.

Nair, M., Pradhan, R. P., & Arvin, M. B. (2020). Endogenous dynamics between R&D, ICT and economic growth: Empirical evidence from the OECD countries. *Technology in Society*, *62*, 101315.

National Bureau of Statistics of China. (2019). *China Statistical Yearbook*. Author.

Nelson, R. R., & Phelps, E. S. (1966). Investment in humans, technological diffusion, and economic growth. *The American Economic Review*, *56*(1/2), 69–75.

Nonaka, I., & Takeuchi, H. (1997). *Creation of Knowledge in the Company How Japanese Companies Generate the Dynamics of Innovation*. Campus.

Nordea. (2020). *The economic context of South Korea*. https://www.nordeatrade.com/fi/explore-new-market/south-korea/economical-context#:~:text=The%20main%20industries%20include%20textile,the%20active%20population%20in%20 2020

North, D. (1990). Institutions, Institutional Change and Economic Performance. Cambridge University Press. doi:10.1017/CBO9780511808678

North, D. C. (1981). *Structure and change in economic history*. Norton.

North, D. C. (1994). Economic performance through time. *The American Economic Review*, *84*(3), 359–368.

Nour, S. S. O. M. (2015). Overview of knowledge economy in the Arab region. *Journal of the Knowledge Economy*, *6*(4), 870–904.

OCDE. (1995). *La mesure des activités scientifiques et technologiques, manuel sur la mesure des ressources humaines consacrées à la science et la technologie: Manuel de Canberra*. OCDE.

OCDE. (1996). *The knowledge-based economy*. OCDE.

OCDE. (2001). *Nouveaux indicateurs de la science et de la technologie*. STI Revue (N° 27).

OCDE. (2005). *Science, technologie et industrie: Tableau de bord de l'OCDE*. OCDE.

OCDE. (2018). *Science, technologie et industrie: Tableau de bord de l'OCDE 2017: La transformation numérique*. Éditions OCDE.

OECD. (2014). *OECD Review of Innovation Policy: Colombia Overall Assessment and Recommendation*. https://www.oecd.org/sti/inno/colombia-innovation-review-assessment-and-recommendations.pdf

OECD. (2019). *Production Transformation Policy Review of Colombia: Unleashing Productivity, OECD Development Pathways*. OECD.

OECD. (2020). *Non-exhaust Particulate Emissions from Road Transport. An Ignored Environmental Policy Challenge*. https://www.oecd.org/env/highlights-non-exhaust-particulate-emissions-from-road-transport.pdf

OECD/European Union. (2015). *The missing entrepreneurs 2015: Policies for self-employment and entrepreneurship*. OECD Publishing; doi:10.1787/71b7a9bb-

OECD/European Union. (2018). *Meeting of the OECD Council at Ministerial Level*. OECD Publishing. https://www.oecd.org/mcm/2018/documents/C-MIN-2018-5-EN.pdf

Oketch, M. O. (2006). Determinants of human capital formation and economic growth of African countries. *Economics of Education Review*, *25*(5), 554–564.

Oliner, S. D., & Sichel, D. E. (2000). The resurgence of growth in the late 1990s: Is information technology the story? *The Journal of Economic Perspectives*, *14*(4), 3–22.

Oliner, S. D., Sichel, D. E., Triplett, J. E., & Gordon, R. J. (1994). Computers and output growth revisited: How big is the puzzle? *Brookings Papers on Economic Activity*, *1994*(2), 273–334.

Out of Hadhramaut. (2006). https://hadhramouts.blogspot.com/2006/01/know-hadhramaut.html#:~:text=There%20are%20no%20recent%20population%20census%20of%20Hadhramout%3B,very%20fertile%20Wady%20Hadhramout%20and%20along%20the%20Coast

Overhouse, D. (2020, November 30). *The Race to Crack Battery Recycling—Before It's Too Late*. Wired. https://www.wired.com/story/the-race-to-crack-battery-recycling-before-its-too-late/

Palandrani, P. (2020, December 9). *Four Companies Leading the Rise of Lithium & Battery Technology*. https://www.globalxetfs.com/four-companies-leading-the-rise-of-lithium-battery-technology/

Pan American Health Organization. (2021). *Teleconsultations during a pandemic*. https://iris.paho.org/handle/10665.2/52006

Pandit, D., Joshi, M., Sahay, A., & Gupta, R. (2018). Disruptive innovation and dynamic capabilities in emerging economics: Evidence from the Indian automotive sector. *Technological Forecasting and Social Change*, *129*, 323–329.

Paul, J. J., & Suleman, F. (2005). La production de connaissances dans la société de la connaissance: Quel rôle pour le système éducatif? *Education et Sociétés*, (1), 19–43.

People's Government of Inner Mongolia Autonomous Region. (2020). *Kuaishou invests tens of billions to build a data center in UlanQab*. Author.

Perez, C. (1983). Structural change and assimilation of new technologies in the economic and social systems. *Futures*, *15*(5), 357–375.

Peter Senge, M. (1998). *The fifth discipline: art and practice of the organization that learns*. Sao Paulo Beste Seller.

Peter, J. W., Feng, W., Yin, E., & Lei, L. N. (2020). Is disruptive innovation in emerging economies different? Evidence from China. *Journal of Engineering and Technology Management*, *57*, 101590.

Peters. (2008). Education and the Knowledge Economy. Academic Press.

Petti, C., Tang, Y., & Margherita, A. (2019). Technological innovation vs technological backwardness patterns in latecomer firms: An absorptive capacity perspective. *Journal of Engineering and Technology Management*, *51*, 10–20.

Pew Research Center. (2020, January 9). *Most Americans say there is too much economic inequality in the U.S., but fewer than half call it a top priority* [Press release]. https://www.pewresearch.org/social-trends/wp-content/uploads/sites/3/2020/01/PSDT_01.09.20_economic-inequailty_FULL.pdf

Philanthropies, B. (2016). *City of São Paulo Selected as the 2016 Grand Prize Winner in Bloomberg Philanthropies' Latin American and Caribbean Mayors Challenge*. Retrieved 06/09/21. https://www.bloomberg.org/press/city-sao-paulo-selected-2016-grand-prize-winner-bloomberg-philanthropies-latin-american-caribbean-mayors-challenge/

Piaggesi, D., Axel, L., Andres, G., Martin, G., & David, D. (2013). *Center of Excellence for Technology Innovation in Favor of Persons with Disabilities –CETI-D. Concept Paper and Schematic Proposal*. Framericas.

Piech, K. (2009). *Wiedza i innowacje w rozwoju gospodarczym: w kierunku pomiaru i współczesnej roli państwa*. Instytut Wiedzy i Innowacji.

Pierce, W., Schroeder, D., & Suchecki, R. (2021). *Telehealth in Latin America: Progress, challenges, and opportunities in the face of COVID-19.* Telehealth and Medicine Today.

PMBOK® Guide Project Management Body of Knowledge. (2021). *Project Management Institute, Global Standards* (7th ed.). Newton Square, PA: PMI.

PNUMA. (2017). *Movilidad Eléctrica: Oportunidades para Latinoamérica.* https://movelatam.org/Movilidad%20electrica_%20Oportunidades%20para%20AL.pdf

Polanyi, M. (1966). *The tacit dimension.* Doubleday.

Powell, W. W., & Snellman, K. (2004). The knowledge economy. *Annual Review of Sociology, 30,* 199–220.

Pradhan, R. P., Arvin, M. B., Nair, M., Bennett, S. E., & Hall, J. H. (2019). The information revolution, innovation diffusion and economic growth: An examination of causal links in European countries. *Quality & Quantity, 53*(3), 1529–1563.

Pritchett, L. (2001). Where has all the education gone? *The World Bank Economic Review, 15*(3), 367–391.

Probst, G. (2002). *Knowledge Management - The building elements of success.* Bookman.

Rambiritch, V., Vermeulen, M., Bell, H., Knox, P., Nedelcu, E., Al-Riyami, A. Z., & Callum, J. (2021). Transfusion medicine and blood banking education and training for blood establishment laboratory staff: A review of selected countries in Africa. *Transfusion,* 1-10. doi:10.1111/trf.16372

Rambiritch, V., & Smith-Tolken, A. (2019). The imperative of teaching professionalism to biomedical technologists. *AJHPE, 11*(4), 139–144. doi:10.7196/AJHPE.2019.v11i4.1101

Renewables Now. (2020). *South Korea commits USD 61bn to Green New Deal by 2025.* https://renewablesnow.com/news/south-korea-commits-usd-61bn-to-green-new-deal-by-2025-706741/#:~:text=July%2017%20(Renewables%20Now)%20%2D,post%2DCOVID%2D19%20era

Republic of Colombia. (2020). *Intended Nationally Determined Contribution.* https://www4.unfccc.int/sites/ndcstaging/PublishedDocuments/Colombia%20First/Colombia%20iNDC%20Unofficial%20translation%20Eng.pdf

Republic of Korea. (2020). *Intended Nationally Determined Contribution.* https://www4.unfccc.int/sites/ndcstaging/PublishedDocuments/Republic%20of%20Korea%20First/INDC%20Submission%20by%20the%20Republic%20of%20Korea%20on%20June%2030.pdf

Research Institute of iResearch Consulting. (2020). *2020 China Data Center Industry Research Report.* Author.

Reuters. (2020). *Ecuador prepares for COVID-19 vaccination campaign with private sector.* https://www.reuters.com/business/healthcare-pharmaceuticals/ecuador-prepares-covid-19-vaccination-campaign-with-private-sector-2020-12-16/

Reuters. (2020). *Tesla's Musk hints of battery capacity jump ahead of industry event.* https://www.reuters.com/article/us-tesla-batteries-idUSKBN25L0MC

Rodrik, D., Subramanian, A., & Trebbi, F. (2004). Institutions rule: The primacy of institutions over geography and integration in economic development. *Journal of Economic Growth, 9*(2), 131–165.

Roggema, R. (2012a). *Swarm planning: the development of a spatial planning methodology to deal with climate adaptation* (PhD thesis). Delft University of Technology.

Roggema,, R. (2012b). *Shifting paradigms. The design charrette: ways to envision sustainable futures.* Springer.

Roggema, R. (2014). Towards enhanced resilience in city design: A proposition. *Land (Basel), 3*(2), 460–481. doi:10.3390/land3020460

Roggema, R. (2015). Three urbanisms in one city: Accommodating the paces of change. *Journal of Environmental Protection*, *6*(09), 946–956. doi:10.4236/jep.2015.69084

Rolle, J., & Kisato, J. (2019). The future of work and entrepreneurship for the underserved. *The Business & Management Review*, *10*(2), 224–234.

Romer, P. M. (1986). Increasing returns and long-run growth. *Journal of Political Economy*, *94*(5), 1002–1037.

Romer, P. M. (1986). Increasing Returns and Long-Run Growth. *Journal of Political Economy*, *94*(5), 1002–1037.

Romer, P. M. (1990). Endogenous technological change. *Journal of Political Economy*, *98*(5, Part 2), S71–S102.

Sachs, J. D., & Warner, A. (1997). *Natural resource abundance and economic growth*. Academic Press.

Sachs, J. D., & Warner, A. M. (2001). The curse of natural resources. *European Economic Review*, *45*(4-6), 827–838.

Salge, T. O. (2012). The temporal trajectories of innovative search: Insights from public hospital services: Insights from Public Hospital Services. *Research Policy*, *41*(4), 720-733.

Samal, P. K., Palni, L. M. S., & Agrawal, D. K. (2003). Ecology, ecological poverty and sustainable development in Central Himalayan region of India. *International Journal of Sustainable Development and World Ecology*, *10*(2), 157–168. doi:10.1080/13504500309469794

Santos, A. R. (2001). *Knowledge Management: An Experience for Business Success*. Champagnat University.

São Paulo State Government. (2021). *Conexão Mata Atlântica*. Retrieved 06/09/21 https://www.infraestruturameioambiente.sp.gov.br/conexao/

São, P. C. H. (2014). *Plano Diretor Estratégico 2014*. Retrieved 06/09/21. https://gestaourbana.prefeitura.sp.gov.br/marco-regulatorio/plano-diretor/arquivos/

São, P. C. H. (2016). *Connect the Dots Project*. Retrieved 06/09/21. https://sampamaisrural.prefeitura.sp.gov.br/uploads/post/file/21/1415b14e-b1f0-4265-9cfd-e3e2b50b5ed5.pdf

São, P. C. H. (2019a). *Projeto Produtor receptivo de escolas*. Retrieved 06/09/21. https://www.youtube.com/watch?v=QS8q4PRc43o&t=41s

São, P. C. H. (2019b). *Prefeitura de São Paulo e USP vão estabelecer parceria para o desenvolvimento sustentável da zona rural sul da cidade*. Retrieved 06/09/21. https://www.prefeitura.sp.gov.br/cidade/secretarias/licenciamento/noticias/?p=289284

São, P. C. H. (2020a). *Ligue os Pontos: Relatório da Fase 1*. Retrieved 06/09/21. https://gestaourbana.prefeitura.sp.gov.br/wp-content/uploads/2019/01/RELAT%C3%93RIO_SITE_PTBR.pdf

São, P. C. H. (2020b). *Ligue os Pontos: Relatório da Fase 2*. Retrieved 06/09/21. https://ligueospontos.prefeitura.sp.gov.br/wp-content/uploads/2020/12/LoP_Relatorio2.pdf

São, P. C. H. (2020c). *Os agricultores guarani e a atual produção agrícola na Terra Indígena Tenondé Porã, Município de São Paulo*. Retrieved 06/09/21. https://sampamaisrural.prefeitura.sp.gov.br/uploads/post/file/38/05144f1a-44a8-4495-b5d1-a5f5b69ce86c.pdf

São, P. C. H. (2020d). *Imigrantes e refugiados preparam marmitas saudáveis com alimentos de produtores rurais de Parelheiros*. Retrieved 06/09/21. https://ligueospontos.prefeitura.sp.gov.br/imigrantes-e-refugiados-preparam-marmitas-saudaveis-com-alimentos-de-produtores-rurais-de-parelheiros/#:~:text=O%20Projeto%20Ligue%20os%20Pontos,conex%C3%A3o%20dessa%20cadeia%20de%20produ%C3%A7%C3%A3o.&text=O%20Projeto%20apoia%20a%20log%C3%ADstica,Hotec%2C%20regi%C3%A3o%20central%20da%20cidade

São, P. C. H. (2020e). *Informe Urbano nº 45: Quem são os produtores agrícolas da Zona Sul de São Paulo?* Retrieved 06/09/21. https://www.prefeitura.sp.gov.br/cidade/secretarias/upload/desenvolvimento_urbano/arquivos/45_IU_PRODUTORES-AGRICOLAS_2020_final.pdf

São, P. C. H. (2020f). *Transcrição da 152ª Reunião Plenária Ordinária do Conselho do Fundo Especial do Meio Ambiente (CONFEMA), realizada em 26 de Junho de 2020*. Retrieved 06/09/21. https://www.prefeitura.sp.gov.br/cidade/secretarias/upload/meio_ambiente/ATA%20DA%20152%2026%20DE%20JUNHO%20DE%202020.pdf

São, P. C. H. (2020g). *Plano Municipal de Pagamento por Serviços Ambientais (PMSA)*. Retrieved 06/09/21. https://ligueospontos.prefeitura.sp.gov.br/wp-content/uploads/2020/08/PMSA-web.pdf

São, P. C. H. (2021a). *GeoSampa*. Retrieved 06/09/21. https://gestaourbana.prefeitura.sp.gov.br/noticias/geosampa-prefeitura-disponibiliza-a-visualizacao-de-lotes-no-mapa-digital/

São, P. C. H. (2021b). *Sampa+Rural: sobre*. Retrieved 06/09/21. https://sampamaisrural.prefeitura.sp.gov.br/sobre

São, P. C. H. (2021c). *SisRural*. Retrieved 06/09/21. https://ligueospontos.prefeitura.sp.gov.br/agricultura-familiar/sisrural/

São, P. C. H. (2021d). *Ligue os Pontos*. Retrieved 06/09/21. https://ligueospontos.prefeitura.sp.gov.br/

São, P. C. H. (2021e). *Agenda Municipal 2030 para o Desenvolvimento Sustentável*. https://www.capital.sp.gov.br/noticia/prefeitura-publica-agenda-municipal-2030-para-o-desenvolvimento-sustentavel-da-onu

São, P. C. H. (2021f). *Adesampa: TEIA Parelheiros*. Retrieved 06/09/21. http://adesampa.com.br/teia/work/teia-parelheiros/

São, P. C. H. (2021g). *Comunidade que Sustenta Agricultura (CSA vídeo)*. Retrieved 06/09/21. https://www.youtube.com/watch?v=2XnCUW_Suu0&t=7s

São, P. C. H. (2021h). *Comunidade que Sustenta Agricultura (CSA site)*. Retrieved 06/09/21 https://sampamaisrural.prefeitura.sp.gov.br/explorar?term=comunidade%20que%20sustenta%20agricultura

Schreyer, P. (2000). *The contribution of information and communication technology to output growth: a study of the G7 countries*. Academic Press.

Schumpeter, J. A. (1934). Harvard Economic Studies: Vol. 46. The Theory of Economic Development-An Inquiry into Profits, Capital, Credit, Interest, and the Business Cycle. Academic Press.

Schumpeter, J. A. (1942). Capitalism, socialism and democracy. Academic Press.

Searns,, R.M. (1995). The evolution of greenways as an adaptive urban landscape form. *Landscape and Urban Planning*, *33*(1), 65–80.

Setayesh, M. H., & Daryaei, A. A. (2017). Good governance, innovation, economic growth and the stock market turnover rate. *The Journal of International Trade & Economic Development*, *26*(7), 829–850.

Shafiea,, F.A., Dasimah,, O., & Karuppannanb,, S. (2013). Urban metabolism: a research methodology in urban planning and environmental assessment. *Proceedings of the 1st international conference on research methodology for built environment and engineering*.

Sharifi, A. (2016). From garden city to eco-urbanism: The quest for sustainable neighborhood development. *Sustainable Cities and Society, 20,* 1–16. doi:10.1016/j.scs.2015.09.002

Shi, Z. Z. (2020). Research on the path of digital economy empowering high-quality development from the perspective of new infrastructure. *Open Management, 12,* 145–149. doi:10.16517/j.cnki.cn12-1034/f.2020.12. 028

Si, S., & Chen, H. (2020). A literature review of disruptive innovation: what it is, how it works and where it goes. *The Journal of Engineering and Technology Management.* https://doi.org/. jengtecman.2020.101568 doi:10.1016/j

Silva, S.L. (2004). Knowledge management: A critical vision guided by the approach of knowledge creation. *Information Science, 33*(2).

Silva, R. V. (2004). *Company Management in the Age of Knowledge.* Serinews.

Smit Sibinga, C. T., & van Galen, J. P. (2020). The Blood Supply – A special manufacturing process.Manufacturing Systems: Recent Progress, 165-186.

Smit Sibinga, C.T., Louw, V. J., Nedelcu, E., Al-Riyami, A. Z., Bakhtary, S., Johnson, S. T., Rambiritch, V., Seoraj, V., Callum, J., Berg, K., Vermeulen, M., Barrett, C. A., & Eichbaum, Q. G. (2021). Modelling Global Transfusion Medicine Education. *Transfusion, 61*(10), 3040–3049. doi:10.1111/trf.16641 PMID:34469008

Snyder, H. (2019). Literature review as a research methodology: An overview and guidelines. *Journal of Business Research, 104,* 333–339. doi:10.1016/j.jbusres.2019.07.039

Solow Robert, M. (1956). A Contribution to the Theory of Economic Growth. *The Quarterly Journal of Economics, 70*(3).

Solow, R. M. (1956). A contribution to the theory of economic growth. *The Quarterly Journal of Economics, 70*(1), 65–94.

SPTrans. (2019). *Prefeitura assina contratos da licitação do transporte público por ônibus.* https://www.sptrans.com.br/noticias/prefeitura-assina-contratos-da-licitacao-do-transporte-publico-por-onibus/

Statista. (2020). *Colombia: Distribution of employment by economic sector from 2010 to 2020.* https://www.statista.com/statistics/369122/employment-by-economic-sector-in-colombia/#:~:text=The%20statistic%20shows%20the%20distribution,percent%20in%20the%20service%20sector

Statista. (2020). *Colombia: Share of economic sectors in the gross domestic product (GDP) from 2009 to 2019.* https://www.statista.com/statistics/369032/share-of-economic-sectors-in-the-gdp-in-colombia/#:~:text=Share%20of%20economic%20sectors%20in%20the%20GDP%20in%20Colombia%202019&text=In%202019%2C%20the%20share%20of,sector%20contributed%20about%2057.53%20percent

Statista. (2020). *Impact of the novel coronavirus (COVID-19) on gross domestic product (GDP) growth in selected countries in Latin America.* https://www.statista.com/statistics/1105099/impact-coronavirus-gdp-latin-america-country/

Steinmueller, W. E. (2002). Knowledge-based economies and information and communication technologies. *International Social Science Journal, 54*(171), 141–153.

Stewart, T. A. (1998). Intellectual capital: The new competitive advantage of companies. Rio de Janeiro: 11. Ed. Campus.

Stokey, N. L. (1995). R&D and economic growth. *The Review of Economic Studies, 62*(3), 469–489.

Strożek, P. (2014). A spatial analysis of the knowledge-based economy in Poland. *Comparative Economic Research, 17*(4), 221–236.

Sucinc S.A. (2021). *Repuestos cambiados en buses eléctricos vs combustión - Ecuador 31-05-21* [Spare parts changed in electric vs. combustion buses]. Unpublished.

Summad, E., Al-Kindi, M., Shamsuzzoha, A., Piya, S., & Ibrahim, M. K. (2018, January). A Framework to Assess a Knowledge-Based Economy: Special Focus to Higher Educational Institutions. In *Proceedings of the International Conference on Industrial Engineering and Operations Management Paris, France, July* (pp. 26-27). Academic Press.

Sun, H. H. (2020). Research on the development trend of Internet + IDC under 5G commercial applications. *China Business Forum*, *8*, 117-118. doi:10.19699/j.cnki.issn2096-0298.2020.08.117

Sun, L. J. (2018). Research on the Development of Inner Mongolia's IDC Industry. University of Inner Mongolia, 20-22.

Sundać, D., & Fatur Krmpotić, I. (2011). Knowledge economy factors and the development of knowledge-based economy. *Croatian Economic Survey*, (13), 105-141.

Sustainable Bus. (2020). *The pandemic doesn't stop the European e-bus market: +22% in 2020.* https://www.sustainable-bus.com/news/europe-electric-bus-market-2020-covid/

Taborelli, M. (2021). *MetBus concentró estrategia en la carga de buses eléctricos para mejorar competitividad y va por más en Chile.* Portal Movilidad. https://portalmovilidad.com/metbus-concentro-estrategia-en-la-carga-de-buses-electricos-para-mejorar-competitividad-y-va-por-mas-en-chile/

Tang, J. P., & Wang, Z. G. (2018). Practice and thinking on the training of big data talents. *Northern Economics*, *Z1*, 49–50.

Tan, J., Wang, L., Zhang, H., & Li, W. (2020). Disruptive innovation and technology ecosystem: The evolution of the inter-cohesive public–private collaboration network in Chinese telecommunication industry. *Journal of Engineering and Technology Management*, *57*, 101573.

Tchamyou, V. S., Asongu, S. A., & Odhiambo, N. M. (2019). The role of ICT in modulating the effect of education and lifelong learning on income inequality and economic growth in Africa. *African Development Review*, *31*(3), 261–274.

The Economist Magazine. (2021, Mar. 27). Bangladesh turns 50. *The Economist Magazine*.

The Korea Herald. (2019). *Korea's R&D spending 5th largest among OECD members in 2018: ministry.* http://www.koreaherald.com/view.php?ud=20191218000777#:~:text=2019%20%2D%2016%3A25-,South%20Korea's%20research%20and%20development%20spending%20was%20the%20fifth%20largest,Ministry%20of%20Science%20and%20ICT

The Russian Government. (2013). *On the Federal Targeted Program for Research and Development in Priority Areas of Development of the Russian Scientific and Technological Complex for 2014-2020.* Retrieved September 30, 2021, from: http://government.ru/en/docs/2129/

Thomas, W. I., & Thomas, D. S. (1928). *The Child in America*. Alfred Knopf.

Tilastokeskus. (2000). *Technological innovation.* https://www.stat.fi/meta/kas/tekn_innovaatio_en.html

Tocan, M. C. (2012). Knowledge based economy assessment. *Journal of Knowledge Management, Economics and Information Technology*, *2*(5), 1–13.

Trading Economics. (2020). *Colombia - Research And Development Expenditure (% Of GDP).* https://tradingeconomics.com/colombia/research-and-development-expenditure-percent-of-gdp-wb-data.html#:~:text=Research%20and%20development%20expenditure%20(%25%20of%20GDP)%20in%20Colombia%20was,compiled%20from%20officially%20recognized%20sources

Treff, L., & Battistella, Lr. (2013). *Innovation in Project Management in Public Administration.* Brasport.

U.S. News. (2020). *Top 10 Countries for Technological Expertise, Ranked by Perception.* https://www.usnews.com/news/best-countries/slideshows/top-10-countries-for-technological-expertise-ranked-by-perception

UK Department of Transport. (2021). *Bus Back Better.* https://www.gov.uk/government/publications/bus-back-better

UN. (2021). *Humanitarian Overview*. UN.

UNDP. (2018). *2018 Statistical Update: Human Development Indices and Indicators*. Accessible at http://hdr.undp.org/en/content/human-development-indices-indicators-2018-statistical-update

UNDP. (2020). *Human Development Index*. Accessible at Wikipedia https://en.wikipedia.org/wiki/Human_Development_Index#:~:text=The%20Human%20Development%20Index%20(HDI,four%20tiers%20of%20human%20development

UNDP. (2020). *In Ecuador, COVID-19 could cause 11 percent dive in GDP this year.* https://www.undp.org/content/undp/en/home/news-centre/news/2020/Ecuador_COVID-19_cause_11_percent_dive_GDP.html#:~:text=The%20COVID%2D19%20PDNA%20for,term%20total%20US%242.7%20billion

UNDP. (2020). *Socio Economic Assessment COVID-19 PDNA. March-May 2020.* https://www.undp.org/content/dam/undp/library/covid19/Ecuador-Eval-Soc-Econ_EN.pdf

United Nation World Food Program. (2019). *Fórum Regional das Cidades Latino-Americanas Signatárias do Pacto de Milão reúne especialistas para debater políticas de alimentação urbana*. Retrieved 06/09/21 https://www.fao.org/brasil/noticias/detail-events/pt/c/1196064/

United Nations Department of Economic and Social Affairs. (2020). *World social report 2020: Inequality in a rapidly changing world.* https://www.un.org/development/desa/dspd/wp-content/uploads/sites/22/2020/01/World-Social-Report-2020-FullReport.pdf

United Nations. (2008). *Convention on the Rights of Persons with Disabilities and Optional Protocol.* https://www.un.org/disabilities/documents/convention/convoptprot-e.pdf

United States Environmental Protection Agency. (2021). *Overview of Greenhouse Gases* https://www.epa.gov/ghgemissions/overview-greenhouse-gases

United States Environmental Protection Agency. (2021). *Report on the Environment.* https://cfpub.epa.gov/roe/chapter/sustain/index.cfm

UN-OHRLLS. (2020). *LDCs in Facts and Figures, 2018. 'Utoikamanu, F. UN Chronicle*. Closing the Technology Gap in Least Developed Countries.

USAID. (2017). *Greenhouse Gas Emissions in Colombia.* https://www.climatelinks.org/sites/default/files/asset/document/2017_USAID_GHG%20Emissions%20Factsheet_Colombia.pdf

Van Winkle, B., Carpenter, N., & Moscucci, M. (2021). Why aren't our digital solutions working for everyone? *AMA Journal of Ethics*, *19*(11), 1116–1124. doi:10.1001/journalofethics.2017.19.11.stas2-1711 PMID:29168683

Vance, A. (2008, December 8). Dell Sees Double with Data Center in a Container. *The New York Times*.

VanDen Berg. (2017). *Economic Growth and Development* (3rd ed.). World Scientific Publishing.

Vargas, F. G. (2015). *Pagar por serviços ambientais.* Centro de Estudos da Sustentabilidade. https://pagina22.com.br/2015/02/27/pagamento-por-servicos-ambientais-impoe-desafios/

Vargas, R., & Nir, M. (2014). *Building Highly Effective Teams*. Brasport.

VERIS Ecuador. (2020). www.veris.com.ec

Vivo, C. (2020). *Refugiados preparam marmitas saudáveis com alimentos de Parelheiros*. Retrieved 06/09/21. https://ciclovivo.com.br/covid19/refugiados-marmitas-parelheiros/

Wang, W.L., Wang, Y.X, & Gao, Y.M. (2020). IDC based on the "new infrastructure" scenario: meaning, dilemma and approach. *Administrative Reform, 10*, 68-74. doi:10.14150/j.cnki.1674-7453.2020.10.008

Wang, Y. Q. (2019). The legal connotation of public data and its standardized application path. *Digital Library Forum*, 8.

Wang, Z.X. (2020). Research on the construction of big data centers for the industrial Internet in the new era. *Technological Innovation and Application, 15*, 71-72. doi: CNKI:SUN:CXYY.0.2020-15-028

Wanjiru, R., & Prime, K. S. (2018). Institutions, economic growth and international competitiveness: a regional study. In *Contemporary Issues in International Business* (pp. 99–124). Palgrave Macmillan.

Webster,, C., & Lai,, L.W.C. (2003). *Property rights, planning and markets*. Edward Elgar.

Wei, Q. L. (2014). *Data Envelopment Analysis*. Beijing Science Press.

Welcome in Colony Association. (2021). *Acolhida em Parelheiro*. Retrieved 06/09/21 https://acolhida.com.br/viajar-para/sao-paulo/acolhendo-em-parelheiros/

WHA. (1975). *Resolution 28.72 Blood Safety and Availability*. Accessible at https://www.who.int/bloodsafety/en/WHA28.72.pdf

WHO (2021a). *Guidance on Centralization of Blood Donation Testing and Processing*. Licence: CC BY-NC-SDA 3.0 IGO.

WHO, OECD & World Bank. (2020). *3rd Joint IMF-OECD-World Bank Conference on Structural Reforms*. https://www.oecd.org/economy/reform/joint-imf-wb-oecd-conf-structural-reform-2020/

WHO. (1988). *GBSI/GPA/2E Global Blood Safety Initiative background paper*. World Health Organization.

WHO. (2015). *Quality Management Training for Blood Transfusion Services*. Accessible at https://www.who.int/blood-safety/publications/qmp_toolkit/en/

WHO. (2017). *Global Status Report on Blood Safety and Availability 2016*. Accessible at http://apps.who.int/iris/bitstream/handle/10665/254987/9789241565431-eng.pdf;jsessionid=1349FE91E41956276C864FB396ABF158?sequence=1

WHO. (2020). *Blood Safety and Availability. Key Facts*. Access at https://www.who.int/news-room/fact-sheets/detail/blood-safety-and-availability

WHO. (2021b). *Safe Blood and Blood Products: Distance Learning Materials*. Accessible at https://apps.who.int/iris/handle/10665/61622

WHO. (2021c). *Global Patient Safety Action Plan 2021-2030. Towards eliminating avoidable harm in health care*. Accessible at https://www.who.int/docs/default-source/patient-safety/global-patient-safety-action-plan-2021-2030_third-draft_january-2021_web.pdf?sfvrsn=948f15d5_17

Wiedmann, T. O., Schandl, H., Lenzen, M., Moran, D., Suh, S., West, J., & Kanemoto, K. (2015). The material footprint of nations. *Proceedings of the National Academy of Sciences of the United States of America, 112*(20), 6271–6276. doi:10.1073/pnas.1220362110 PMID:24003158

Wight, A. J. (2019). Colombia creates its first science ministry. *Nature, 565*(7737), 273–275. doi:10.1038/d41586-019-00087-z PMID:30647420

Wikipedia. (n.d.a). *Hadhramaut, Hadhrami Diaspora*. https://en.wikipedia.org/wiki/Hadhramaut

Wikipedia. (n.d.b). *Hadhramaut, History, Modern*. https://en.wikipedia.org/wiki/Hadhramaut

Wikipedia. (n.d.c). *Hadhrami Insurgency*. https://en.wikipedia.org/wiki/Hadramaut_insurgency

Winter, S. (1987). Knowledge and Competence as Strategic Assets. *The Competitive Challenge: Strategies for Industrial Innovation and Renewal*, 159-184.

Wolman,, A. (1965). The metabolism of cities. *Scientific American, 213*(3), 179–190. PMID:14338520

World Bank Group. (2019). *Kenya Digital Economy Assessment. Summary Report.* World Bank.

World Bank. (2007). *Région Moyen-Orient et Afrique du Nord 2007: Développements récents et perspectives économiques: La création d'emplois en période de forte croissance.* World Bank.

World Bank. (2008). *Knowledge for development, the world bank Institute's program on building knowledge economies.* World Bank.

World Bank. (2009). *Middle East and North Africa Region 2008: Economic developments and prospects: Regional integration for global competitiveness.* World Bank.

World Bank. (2010). *Measuring knowledge in the world's economies: Knowledge assessment methodology and knowledge economy index.* World Bank.

World Bank. (2016). *Global economic prospects: Divergences and risks.* World Bank.

World Bank. (2019). *Green Your Bus Ride: Clean Buses in Latin America – Summary Report.* World Bank Group. https://documents.worldbank.org/curated/en/410331548180859451/Green-Your-Bus-Ride-Clean-Buses-in-Latin-America-Summary-Report

World Bank. (2020). *Lessons from Chile's Experience with E-mobility: The Integration of E-Buses in Santiago.* World Bank. https://openknowledge.worldbank.org/handle/10986/34435

World Bank. (2021). *EdStats Database.* Author.

World Commission on Environment and Development. (1987). *Our common future.* Oxford University Press.

World Economic and Social Survey. (2018). Department of Economic and Social Affairs of the United Nations Secretariat (UN/DESA).

World Economic Forum. (2019. *The Global Competitiveness Report 2019.* Author.

World Employment and Social Outlook Trends. (2020). *ILO.* https://www.ilo.org/wcmsp5/groups/public/---dgreports/---dcomm/---publ/documents/publication/wcms_734455.pdf

World Health Organization. (n.d.). Available in: https://www.who.int/classifications/icf/en/index.html

World Inequality Lab. (2020). *2020 Report update.* https://wid.world/fr/news-article/global-inequality-data-2020-update

World Resource Institute. (2021). *Cities for Forest.* Retrieved 06/09/21 https://www.wri.org/our-work/project/cities4forests

Worldbank. (2020). *Research and development expenditure (% of GDP).* https://data.worldbank.org/indicator/GB.XPD.RSDV.GD.ZS?locations=KR

Worldometer. (2020). *COVID-19 Coronavirus pandemic.* https://www.worldometers.info/coronavirus/

Xu, C. A. (2018). New Ideas for the Development of Internet Data Center Industry in Inner Mongolia. *China Construction Information Technology, 1*, 54–57.

Yang, P. (2020). China's establishment of an integrated national Internet data center governance path setting. *Henan Social Sciences*, 4.

Yang, C. H. (2006). Is innovation the story of Taiwan's economic growth? *Journal of Asian Economics*, *17*(5), 867–878.

Yin, R. K. (2011). Case Study – planning and methods (2nd ed.). Porto Alegre: Bookman.

Yu, S.Y., Wang, J.D., & Guo, Q.M. (2020). Challenges and Countermeasures Faced by China in Building a New Data Element Market System. *Henan Social Sciences*, 3.

Yu, C., Ding, Y. C., & Wang, P. P. (2019). Research on the new infrastructure of future cities from the perspective of comprehensive regional development. *China Real Estate*, *20*, 53–60. doi:10.13562/j.china.real.estate.2019.20.016

Yuventi, J., & Mehdizadeh, R. (2013). A critical analysis of Power Usage Effectiveness and its use in communicating data center energy consumption. *Energy and Building*, *64*, 90–94.

ZEBRA. (2020). *From Pilots to Scale: Lessons from the Electric Bus Deployments in Santiago de Chile*. https://www.c40knowledgehub.org/s/article/From-Pilots-to-Scale-Lessons-from-Electric-Bus-Deployments-in-Santiago-de-Chile?language=en_US

Zhang, N., & Zhao, X. J. (2020). Understanding the blockchain-based government inter-departmental data sharing from collaborative consensus to smart contract. China Administration, 1.

Zhenmin. (2019). Frontier Technologies: A window for Leapfrogging. *UN Chronicle*.

About the Contributors

Danilo Piaggesi is Managing Director of the "Knowledge for Development" (K4D), an N.G.O. in a special consultative status with the U.N. K4D focuses on Knowledge Society, ICT, and innovation for development. He was Knowledge Economy Coordinator in the Vice Presidency and Division Chief of the ICT4D Division, of the Inter-American Development Bank (IADB). He worked for the U.N. FAO in Africa and Latin America in technology transfer for development. He worked for Telespazio, in the Strategic Alliances and International Activities Division. He consulted for the European Union, in ICT. He consulted again for the U.N. FAO in the establishment of an International Digital Council, and for Ernst & Young in the evaluation of the D4D strategy of Belgium. He is a Geophysicist from the University1 of Rome, and an Executive International Business Certificate from Georgetown University/John Cabot University, in Washington D.C . He contributed to several IGI publications on trends, issues and challenges surrounding the governance of ICT in a globalized, knowledge-based world. Furthermore, he is board member of ACPI, Academic Conferences & Publishing International Organization based in London. Physicist by training, with specialization in Geo-Physics from the University of Rome, focusing on the application of satellite technology to development planning at FAO (1981-1991) and Telecom/Telespazio (1991-1998). Led the establishment as Division Chief of the Inter American Development Bank's line of business in applications of Information and Communication Technologies to development investment (1998-2011). Currently involved in furthering the use of Knowledge Economy concepts and architecture in development projects at K4D foundation (2011 to present).

Helena Landazuri is a sustainable development and environmental management specialist with degrees in natural resource policy and planning from Cornell University and environmental science from Clark University. Senior environmental specialist at Inter American Development Bank in Washington DC (1990-2016); head of operations at K4D (2017-present).

Bo Jia specialized in digital innovation and global governance. Worked in the field of digital agriculture as Capacity Building Specialist at FAO. Currently pursuing a Dual Degree Master of Public Policy for Sustainable Development Goals in Tsinghua University and Geneva University.

* * *

Yetmgeta Eyayou Abdella has over 20 years of experience in blood banking, transfusion medicine and public health in the WHO African and Eastern Mediterranean regions. He received his MD and MPH from Addis Ababa University (Ethiopia) and his visiting scholar certificate in blood banking and transfusion medicine from Emory University (US). He has worked for Centres for Disease Control and Prevention (CDC) and the World Health Organization (WHO) at country, regional and global levels. Currently, he is a medical officer for Blood and other Products of Human Origin at the WHO Regional Office for the Eastern Mediterranean based in Cairo, Egypt.

Aashrika Ahuja is an experienced corporate and intellectual property rights lawyer, advisor, researcher, writer and author. With an experience of 8 years in the field of law, she is now well conversant with various aspects of the profession .She has handled legal matters in diverse fields including Civil, Criminal, Intellectual Property Rights, Sexual Harassment against Women and Children, Cyber laws, is a licensed Attorney and is eligible to appear and practice before various courts in India. She is well versed with corporate governance and with strong entrepreneurship skills, has successfully advised as well as worked with various corporates, organizations and institutions. She has an experience of working and handling clients all across the globe. She has a keen interest in research and writing and has authored research paper in the prestigious International Journal for Scientific and Engineering Research. While handling drafting, review of various kinds of legal Agreements, Contracts and other legal documents, she also provides legal opinion on diverse matters relating to Intellectual Property Rights. She is passionate about realizing and working towards United Nations 2030 Agenda for Sustainable Development Goals and with her strong advocacy skills has been actively working in the development field to leave no one behind.

Najeh Aissaoui is a professor at the Higher School of Economics and Business of Tunis (ESSEC), University of Tunis, holder of a doctorate in economics (University of Sfax), and associate researcher at the LARIME laboratory. Her research interests focus on innovation, digital economy, inequalities in development economics, entrepreneurship and sustainable development.

Sultana al-Qu'aiti was born in London. After graduating in French from Punjab University, Lahore and later Reading University UK, she spent a year at Montpellier University and trained to become a French teacher. When she married Sultan Ghalib al-Qu'aiti of Hadhramaut, she moved to Jeddah where she taught English at expatriate and Saudi schools. She has 3 children and 7 grandchildren. In 1997, she co-founded Friends of Hadhramaut, a UK registered charity and in 2007 was awarded a MBE by HM the Queen in recognition of services to the people of Hadhramaut.

Olfa Boussetta is a professor at the Higher School of Economics and Business of Tunis (ESSEC), University of Tunis, holder of a doctorate in economics (University of Tunis El Manar), and associate researcher at the PS2D laboratory. Her research interests focus on Knowledge Economy, Industrial Economy, Technological Innovation, R&D, ICT, National Innovation System, public strategy, governance, Economic growth.

Giulia D'Amico has expertise in technology, education, social transformative projects and government relations, with a special focus on emerging and developing countries. For over a decade she has been developing products, programs and youth policies for LEGO, MIT Media-lab One Laptop Per Child (OLPC), the Italian Government working closely with international institutions. As CEO of OLPC, she led the growth of the program expanding it in over 85 countries across the world. Her work with the United Nations agencies focuses on developing public-private partnerships frameworks to support Governments and local stakeholders in innovating their school systems and fostering employability to their young populations. Giulia is Italian by origin, have lived in various geographies and she is an advocate for youth empowerment promoting social inclusion through innovation.

Gu Haiyue (Helen) is an ELT lecturer at SILC Business School, Shanghai University and the Deputy Director of Australian Studies Centre, Shanghai University. She has been actively involved in various academic events of Australian Studies in China, and has cooperated with fellow researchers to edit the serial of New Developments in Australian Studies in China from 2008 to 2013. Her research interests include tourism economy, startups, education policies, transnational education, and value studies.

Zoraide Itapura de Miranda is an agronomist, graduated at São Paulo State University, with doctorate and post-doctorate degree at University of Campinas, São Paulo. Technical Advisor of the President of São Paulo Urbanism (2019/2021) and Housing Metropolitan Company (2017/2019) of São Paulo City Hall. Manager, Coordinator and Technical Advisor of the São Paulo State Government Metropolitan Planning Company (2012/2017). Researcher at Unicamp (2010/2012). Professor at Senac University Center (2006/2010) and Paraiba Valley University - Univap (2003/2006).

Fabian Koss worked for 24 years at the Inter-American Development Bank (IDB), as a senior specialist and team leader. In 1995, he was appointed youth liaison and was responsible for organizing the IDB- Youth forum, which was the first time that a multi-lateral bank brought together young leaders from around the world to discuss development issues. Fabian was one of the founders of the Inter-American working group on youth development, a consortium of international donor agencies, which increased resource support and promoted learning around effective youth development programs in the hemisphere. He led and developed various programs & international partnerships with the public & private sectors. He was instrumental in creating the partnership, which united CDI Brazil, Microsoft, and StarMedia together with the IDB to launch the CDI Americas Initiative to help bridge the “digital divide” in Latin America. Fabian facilitated the creation of awareness-building campaigns with major international media networks to promote the active participation of young people in the development process. He was responsible for forging the partnership with the IDB and MTV Latin America. This strategic alliance with MTV produced numerous projects, which highlighted that young people are part of the solution to challenges in their communities. He spearheaded the IDB’s Sports for Development Initiative. This initiative uses the power of sports to help youth take advantage of social and economic advancement opportunities. The initiative has four areas of focus: youth development, health and wellness, social inclusion, and violence prevention. Through this initiative, partnerships have been established with governments, Coca-Cola, Fifa, NBA, NFL, Nike Foundation, UN, USAID, FC Barcelona, Gatorade, Real Madrid, among many others. In 2000, the IDB youth program received the United Nations World Youth Award for its achievement in implementing the UN world program of action for youth. In 1999, Fabian founded the Many Hats Institute (MHI). MHI is an international organization that is dedicated to improving the conditions for children worldwide. It is supported by a network of renowned professionals from diverse backgrounds, who raise funds and provide assistance to promote community development and engage young leaders to become resources for their communities. Initiatives have included a Placido Domingo concert to raise funds for the victims of an earthquake in El Salvador. MHI has teamed up with the World Wildlife Fund, Nature Conservancy, Harvard Business School, Mastercard and AOL among others to leverage the time, talent and resources of the “many hatters” from around the world. Fabian serves on various boards including Company E, Sports for Sharing, Medora Ventures and Reach Your Peak. He has spoken at numerous world economic forum events, Clinton global initiative annual meetings and a host of United Nations ministerial sessions. Fabian was born in Argentina and completed his BA in public affairs at the American University and a graduate certificate in public relations at New York University.

John Mulholland is a native of San Francisco. His degrees are a Bachelors in Management and a MA in Arab Studies at Georgetown Un. Mr Mulholland has resided in seven countries including over 20 years in the Arab World. He speaks five languages. He is married with four grown children. He makes his home in Alpharetta, Georgia, USA

José Neto is an Agronomist. Graduated at The São Paulo State University. Postgraduate at Fundação Getúlio Vargas. Current Advisor of the President of the São Paulo State Social Fund. Deputy Secretary of the Urban Development Secretariat of the City of São Paulo and General Coordinator of the Connect the Dots Project (2019/2020). Advisor of the President of the Metropolitan Planning Company (2016). Head of the Technical Advisory Office of the General Coordination of the Serra do Mar Project (IADB). Executive Director of Fundação Florestal.

Manuel Olivera currently is the Director for Latin America of C40 Cities, a network of 96 leading mega-cities in the fight against climate change. This NGO connects member mayors who constantly exchange their experiences, has 17 thematic networks in which officials from all cities participate, and with numerous programs promotes a post-Covid 19 just and green recovery agenda. In the 12 C40 Latin American cities, his regional team supported the preparation of climate action plans, the formulation of projects for their implementation, and the procurement of resources, all aimed at complying with the Paris Agreement. Since 1980 he has successfully performed in various public and private positions, has been a professor and participated numerous times as a lecturer in the country and abroad. Apart from his degree in biology from the Universidad de los Andes in Bogotá, he obtained a master's degree in resource evaluation at the University of East Anglia, Great Britain and in socio-economics of development at the School of High Studies in Social Sciences in Paris, in addition to having made specializations in project evaluation and urban financing. He has been an environmental consultant in numerous credit and cooperation projects with the World Bank, UNDP, UNEP and the IADB, apart from having played a leading role in environmental transformation in the Colombian private sector as the first Environmental Manager of the Andi and as Director of the environmental authority of Bogotá during the first Mayor Peñalosa´s administration. Among many achievements it´s worth mentioning the electric taxi pilot in Bogotá, replicated in cities such as Hong Kong, London, New York, Montevideo, the effect unleashed by the C40 and the Clinton Foundation through the hybrid and electric bus test program in Latin America -financed by the IADB- which helped to take off the market for zero emissions technologies in the region with already more than 2200 buses running in cities such as Santiago, Medellín, Guayaquil, Sao Paulo, Mendoza, Montevideo and Bogotá, the latter city with 1485 already procured.

David Pines has over 20 years of global executive consulting with Gap International, Inc. Prior to joining the private sector, David was an educator and the co-founder and Executive Director of both the Genesee Valley Outdoor Learning Center and the Foundation for the Future of Youth. He was a consultant to the executive branch of 3 U.S. administrations on youth policy, environment, and education. He was a Vice President of the International Development Conference in Washington DC. Mr. Pines has been accountable for Business Development, Government Relations, Technology Innovation, and Executive and Leader Development. He is recently retired as the Chief Operating Officer of CanopyLAB, a Danish Educational Technology company committed to provide quality lifelong learning experiences and opportunities for all people worldwide.

Natalia Restrepo graduated from Political Science and began to pursue her passion for education. She began teaching and did her post graduate studies in bilingual education focusing on teaching Social Studies and History for English as a Second Language Learners. After eleven years in the classroom she began pursuing an interest in technology and education and began developing projects that brought together the works done by NGOs, civil society and individual teachers. She currently works for CanopyLAB, a Danish Ed-tech company.

Linamara Rizzo Battistella is a Full Professor at the Department of Legal Medicine, Medical Ethics, Social and Labor Medicine, Faculty of Medicine, University of São Paulo (2005). She is a Specialist in Physical Medicine and Rehabilitation, and her areas of interest are Functional Assessment and Quality of Life-in particular, International Classification of Functioning, Disability and Health (ICF). President of the Board of Directors of the HCFMUSP Physical Medicine and Rehabilitation Institute and Lucy Montoro Rehabilitation Institute, and Co-Coordinator of the WHO/WHO Health-Related Rehabilitation Guidelines Development Group, since 2012. Coordinator of the Residency Program in Medicine Physics and Rehabilitation at FMUSP. She was Secretary of State for the Rights of Persons with Disabilities of the Government of the State of São Paulo, from 2008 to 2018.

JoAnn Rolle holds a PhD. in Economics from Howard University. Dr. Rolle has served as the Dean of the School of Business at Medgar Evers College, City University of New York (CUNY) for the past seven years. Dean Rolle is an accomplished leader with a consistent history of success who served in the U.S. Government and I.B.M. before her academic career. She served as C.E.O. of a university; seven years as C.A.O.; and ten years as a Business School Dean at two universities. During her career, she launched two entrepreneurial centers and many entrepreneurship programs. She has taught entrepreneurship and economic courses. She is a business consultant with board experience. Dr Rolle awards include two Citations Brooklyn, NY Borough President Eric Adams for Leadership & Community Service. She has been recognized as a Top 25 Influential African American Women in Business. She has delivered Keynote speeches and workshops to include the U.N. in N.Y.C. She is a Price-Babson Symposium for Entrepreneurship Educators fellow, Administrative Fellow, Harvard University, Member of the Economic Club of New York, Fellow of Centre for Business & Economic Research.

Fethi Sellaouti is a professor at the Faculty of Economics and Management of Tunis, University of Tunis El Manar. He holds a PhD in economics from the University of Paris I-Sorbonne and associate researcher at the PS2D laboratory.

Cees Smit Sibinga is a clinical hematologist and Transfusion Medicine Specialist. He is professor of International Development of Transfusion Medicine at the University of Groningen, The Netherlands. His special interest is in education, quality management and the organization of blood transfusion vein-to-vein. He created the Academic Institute for International Development of Transfusion Medicine at the University of Groningen and organized 28 International Symposia on Blood Transfusion in

Groningen, wrote and edited over 40 books and over 400 peer reviewed scientific publications. He has been involved with WHO as a Senior Adviser on Blood Transfusion since 1980. He has been active in numerous Transfusion Medicine development programs in Africa, Eastern Mediterranean, Southeast Asia, Central Asia and the Western Pacific focused on structuring blood systems, developing quality system management and clinical blood transfusion principles. He served AABB as a lead inspector and vice-president for Consulting Services.

Lilian Aparecida Treff is Manager of the Strategic Program and Project Nucleus of the Institute of Physical Medicine and Rehabilitation, Hospital das Clínicas, Faculty of Medicine, University of São Paulo – IMREA HC FMUSP. Specialist in the creation of Project Management Methodology and PMO implementation. Master in Business Administration in Business Management. Postgraduate, Lato-Sensu in Higher Education Didactics (Universidade Presbiteriana Mackenzie), Specialization in Project Management (Vanzolini Foundation – USP) and Knowledge Management, Corporate Ed. and Organizational Learning – FIA/USP. International Education Agile with Atlassian (United Kingdom, London) Jira and Certificate Introduction to Neuroeconomics: How the Brain Makes Decisions by National Research University Higher School of Economics – HSE (Moscow-Russia). Outstanding national and international experience of 15 years in leadership positions in the area of Project and Process Management, Change Management, Strategic Planning and People Management. Certified Personal & Professional Coaching; (SBC); Executive Coaching by Metaforum Internacional – Human Change Association. Awarded Professional "Comendador" of the Year - Brazil Excellence and Quality Award (June) 2017, in the "Training in Professional Development of Education & Citizenship" category by the Brazilian Leadership Association. Reviewer for In.Cube – Inova HC strengthening the support network program and further fostering the development of innovation in public health.

Poshan (Sam) Yu is a Lecturer in Accounting and Finance in the International Cooperative Education Program of Soochow University (China). He is also an External Professor of FinTech and Finance at SKEMA Business School (China), a Visiting Professor at Krirk University (Thailand) and a Visiting Researcher at the Australian Studies Centre of Shanghai University (China). Sam leads FasterCapital (Dubai, UAE) as a Regional Partner (China) and serves as a Startup Mentor for AIC RAISE (Coimbatore, India). His research interests include financial technology, regulatory technology, public-private partnerships, mergers and acquisitions, private equity, venture capital, start-ups, intellectual property, art finance, and China's "One Belt One Road" policy.

Yue Zhao is an independent researcher. His research interests include knowledge management and business analytics.

Index

A

B

C

D

E

F

G

H

I

K

L

M

N

O

P

R

S

T

U

V

W

Y

Z

www.ingramcontent.com/pod-product-compliance
Lightning Source LLC
LaVergne TN
LVHW062137300926
849161LV00010B/2553